Fourth Edition

Managing with Information

Jerome Kanter

Executive Director,
Center for Information Management Studies
Babson College

Prentice Hall
Englewood Cliffs, New Jersey 07632

Library of Congress Cataloging-in-Publication Data

Kanter, Jerome.
    Managing with information / Jerome Kanter.—4th ed.
        p.   cm.
    Rev. ed. of: Management information systems. 3rd ed. c1984.
    Includes bibliographical references (p.) and index.
    ISBN 0-13-561614-X
    1. Management information systems.
T58.6.K363   1992
658.4'038—dc20   91–34944
                                                          CIP

Acquisition editor: Valerie Ashton
Editorial assistant: Ann Marie Dunn
Editorial/production supervision and interior design: Fred Dahl, Inkwell
Cover design: Karen Salzbach
Prepress buyer: Trudy Pisciotti
Manufacturing buyer: Bob Anderson

Previously published as *Management-Oriented Management Information Systems,* 2nd ed. and *Management Information Systems*, 3rd ed.

 © 1992, 1984, 1977, 1972 by Prentice-Hall, Inc.
A Simon & Schuster Company
Englewood Cliffs, New Jersey 07632

Printed in the United States of America
10 9 8 7 6 5 4 3 2 1

ISBN 0-13-561614-X

Prentice-Hall International (UK) Limited, *London*
Prentice-Hall of Australia Pty. Limited, *Sydney*
Prentice-Hall Canada Inc., *Toronto*
Prentice-Hall Hispanoamericana, S.A., *Mexico*
Prentice-Hall of India Private Limited, *New Delhi*
Simon & Schuster Asia Pte. Ltd., *Singapore*
Editora Prentice-Hall do Brasil, Ltda., *Rio de Janerio*

To Susan, Henry, Peter, and Dorrie

Contents

v

CHAPTER 3

Business Models and Information Systems Architecture, 50

CHAPTER 4

The Mortar of IS: Data Base, 84

CHAPTER 5

Telecommunications and Distributed Systems, 119

CHAPTER 6

The Organizational Evolution of IS, 151

CHAPTER 7

The Application Development Cycle, 172

CHAPTER 11

The Impact of IS on Management: Managing with Information, 287

CHAPTER 12

New Information Technologies, 319

Case Studies

There are 26 cases in the book, one at the ends of Chapters 1 and 14, and two at the ends of the other twelve chapters. In addition, there are five appendices including two case studies (Appendices A and B). The cases are based on the author's consulting experience or are extracted from current publications.

Harris Manufacturing, 21

A company develops what they call interfunctional or integrated IS aimed at effecting the operating results of the business. The case reviews the functions automated and the economic returns.

Global Networking at Federal Express, 44

This case describes the COSMOS or packet tracking system developed by Federal Express. It is a classic case of a system that centers on the customer and can give a company competitive advantage.

Warburton Chemical, 46

The president of a company founded by him is facing a possible acquisition and is unhappy with his IS group after talking with a friend. He wants a plan for future IS direction.

Merk Industrial Products, 79

A company initiates a planning study by organizing a task team and the effort is kicked off by a letter to all concerned.

How Ford is Reinventing the Wheel on a Global Basis, 81

This is a classic example of the concept of re-engineering. The Ford company with the help of a worldwide telecommunications system changes the way products are designed.

Richard Abbott, Applications Development Director, 259

This case describes the impact on an IT department and its people of the popular trends of downsizing, outsourcing, and using CASE techniques.

Managing Application Development, 260

Using the concept of risk analysis described in Chapter 8, this case shows how that technique can be used to determine the kind of project management and attention needed for different types of projects.

Decision Support System at Frito-Lay, 282

A real world example of how one company, Frito-Lay, uses its Decision Support System (DSS) to keep track of 14 million snacks sold weekly through 400,000 sales calls. The case describes the kinds of reports and analyses available to management.

Ross Toggs Department Stores, 284

A classical example of a management science application applied to department store distribution.

John Preston, Director of Marketing Support, 315

A typical case where a Marketing Director questions his personal use of a computer posing the issue of whether a line manager can spend his time more productively by letting someone else use the PC.

Fact-Based Thinking, 316

This case describes how a CEO uses IT as part of his job, setting the standard for the use of executive support systems ranging from E-mail to market forecasting.

Fielding Electronics, 340

A "high tech" IS director introduces new hardware technology in a very short time to a company that is not ready to assimilate it. It doesn't work and the director loses his job.

Taking Stock of EDI, 341

Electronic Data Interchange (EDI) is one of the growing new uses of IS, tying together vendor and customer. This excerpt describes how several companies are employing EDI.

Ethics Quiz, 365

The question of computer ethics has become a serious one because IT has changed the definition of property and human rights. This excerpt presents a list of ethical questions faced by today's IT users.

Managing with Information

The title *Managing with Information*, seemingly a small distinction from the more popular term *management information systems* (MIS), connotes the focus and approach of this book. The term management information systems (MIS) implies a profession that is responsible for developing computer applications for the rest of the enterprise. But the information systems (IS) world has changed. IS is no longer a separate entity. Much, if not all, of what was done in the central IS department has been decentralized or distributed to the functional line departments. Decentralization or distributed systems have not only put the hardware and software on departmental desks, but have put the IS decision responsibility there as well. The continuing advances in case of use and user friendliness allow everyone in the corporation to become an information systems user.

A manager manages *with* information, and computer systems provide a breadth and depth of information that can boggle the imagination. The computer has become an embedded part of the environment, like the telephone or copier. Managers determine what they need to manage their responsibilities. Information enables a company or department to differentiate its products and services to gain competitive advantage. IS has become too important to delegate. The IS department is not the owner of company data, but the custodians. You don't call the IS specialist, you decide what information you need to make decisions and then employ the required systems. It is of no major concern whether the data are in your custody or in the custody of the IS department.

While it is true that managing with information is not a new concept, the advent of technology surrounding and supporting the computer provide new dimensions of information availability and use. Coming within a time window of 30 years, it can rightfully be called a revolutionary change—managing with information in the 1990s is a quantum leap over managing with information in the 1960s. It is just not the same ball game. Management now realizes that information is a resource equaling or exceeding the worth and power of the other more widely accepted resources—materials, product, personnel, facilities, and money.

There is still the need for a central IS group to manage the growing complexity of the enterprise-wide systems, and to maintain a unified systems and telecommunication architecture for use by other divisions of the company; but the number of people required for this work has leveled off and, in some cases, significantly diminished. Part of managing with information is to understand what functions central IS performs and how to utilize central IS resources in decision making. This book covers those issues. The need for business-oriented, but computer/information-literate young people will grow dramatically in the coming years. Computer/information literacy will be significant both for those who choose to support line departments by developing applications and for those who will be line department professionals and managers with no specific IS responsibility. The book covers these issues as well.

A distinction should be made between computer literacy and information literacy. The former implies a basic understanding of computer hardware and software. A person who is keyboard facile, knows how to use the basic software packages like word processing, spreadsheets, and some data base manipulation is computer literate, but may not be information literate. Information literacy implies a higher order of understanding, a perspective on the use of IS both to support and shape an enterprise. An information literate manager addresses such questions as, "What is the role of computer systems in terms of supporting and shaping my job function? What are the tradeoffs between investment and benefits, time expended, and time saved? How can information be used strategically?" The concentration is on why and what, not how.

This book is directed at imparting information literacy, not computer literacy. It assumes the latter has already been acquired. Though a course based on this book is appropriate for someone majoring in information systems, it is primarily directed at the business student or liberal arts student who will probably not seek a professional career within the central IS organization, but who will be, as the book title suggests, "managing with information."

This is not a technical book. It is written by a businessman who entered the information systems field from a line management position, that is, from the outside in. It remains a precept of the author that this is the proper perspective from which to view technology and information systems. The simple, but oft overlooked message, is that a thorough understanding of business needs must precede any relevant discussion of technology. It is still true that advanced computer technology can get you where you don't want to be faster than any devices heretofore available. With that warning let us continue our journey.

Background for the Revision

This is the fourth edition of this textbook. The first three were accomplished while I was in business. I was an IS practitioner at the Kroger Company and at Honeywell Information Systems. I am told that most MIS textbooks are the products of professors, so this places me in the exception category. I feel my writing the books while in the business environment added a practical and managerial perspective. Many of the readers and professors who used the book in their courses agreed with me. It should be stated that while in business, I taught graduate IS courses at Babson College and Northeastern University, and for the American Management Association.

In 1987, I joined Babson College to manage the Center for Information Management

Studies (CIMS). I also teach at Babson. The Center has 28 corporate sponsors who look to CIMS for workshops, conferences, working papers, and research to maintain their currency on IS matters. This continues to keep me in daily contact with IS and the business world.

In 1989, Babson inaugurated its eighth president, William F. Glavin. Soon thereafter, President Glavin, who has a broad business and academic background, launched a series of strategic committees to look to the future of business education and what niches Babson should fill. Information systems played a large role in these initiatives since Bill Glavin was vice chairman of a high-tech company, Xerox, and brought with him a belief in the vital importance of IS in the future business world. One of the committees on which I served was called "Management Education in the 21st Century." We concentrated on what the world would look like in 20 years or so, what business would be doing, how they would be doing it, and what the successful business people would have to know. I focused on the impact of IS, and this gave me an excellent base point on which to begin the research on this fourth edition.

Another major assist in developing the focus of the revision has been an IS curriculum advisory committee formed of senior IS executives of CIMS. This group has given us their views as to what should be taught in business schools and has reviewed our entire IS curriculum. They are telling us what they are looking for in future graduates, both for their central IS function and as business professionals and managers in the line departments of their companies. Their input has been fed into the faculty computer committee here at Babson.

Organization of the Book

The book has 14 chapters, each with an introduction and summary. In addition there are case studies and/or assignments at the end of each chapter, which pertain to material in the chapter. Each chapter has its own bibliography.

Chapters 1, 2, and 3 can be viewed as a unit. The role of management is stressed before discussing the impact of information and information systems, again the outside-in view. Viewing business as a system itself forms the introduction to information systems. The "essential" of integrating IS planning into business planning is stressed. Rather than focusing on hardware and software, these introductory chapters explore concepts such as the potential for using IS to shape or support a strategic thrust of a business. The first chapter builds on the basic Anthony triangle of strategy, management control, and operational control—still a valid concept and starting point for an exploration of IS. Chapter 2 emphasizes the importance of planning and reviews the major "constructs" of Porter's strategic model, Nolan's stages concept, Wiseman's strategic option generator, McFarlan's strategic positioning matrix and Rockart's critical success factors. Chapter 3 presents a top-down understanding of the business through business processes and the development of a data model. The essential ingredients for developing an overriding IS architecture that mirrors the business are presented. The first three chapters present a motivation for continuing the book and the reason why future business people, whether IS career oriented or, more likely, general management oriented, must understand the potential of IS. It is important to cover the management and planning aspects up front—to form the base point for proper assimilation of the remaining material.

Chapters 4 and 5 are the necessary underpinnings of IS, because no matter what you do with IS you have to consider the storage and maintenance of data, and the communication of the data for individual, departmental, or enterprise use. In these chapters and in those that follow, distinction is made among enterprise-wide, departmental, and individual foci. It is the thesis of the book that the future manager will be an individual user, but must also be aware of the scope and the operating characteristics of more complex departmental and enterprise-wide systems. The trend is definitely toward the distribution of IS, but, in all but a very few companies, there is an important function served by a central IS operation, and it is important for the line manager to understand the purpose and "fit" of these enterprise systems as well as the departmental ones.

Chapter 6, a pivotal chapter, builds on Chapter 5, examining the impact that technology, LANS, powerful desktop computers, workstations, and client servers are having on the distribution of IS functions. A strong case is made that decentralization or distribution of IS fits better with the evolving management style, that is, with allowing decisions to be made at the level closest to where the action is, usually at the customer level.

Chapters 7, 8, and 9 can also be viewed as a unit. These chapters cover the elements that are needed to develop systems—whether they be enterprise, departmental, or individual in scope. It is the thesis that the individual manager must have an understanding of the complexities and components of the central systems, as well as the systems that are more individual in nature. The systems life cycle, including the use of productivity tools (e.g., CASE) and the management of systems development, is covered in these chapters. Project management, security/backup, and application feasibility are some of the issues explored. Chapter 8 is devoted to the important subject of assessing the value and risk of systems development. Thus, this section of the book stresses the practical and essential factors necessary to make something happen.

Chapter 10 is a lead-in to Chapter 11. It is devoted to a discussion of management science or decision support systems. Though these types of approaches are usually developed by company specialists, because of their potentially significant impact on business decisions, it is felt that a general understanding is vital for the general manager. This chapter provides that understanding. With Chapter 10 under our belt, we broaden the impact of IS on management in Chapter 11, dissecting the manager's job and then showing how IS can abet the administrative functions as well as the decision making or innovative functions. Executive support systems are emphasized. This chapter hits hard at the major focus of the book, "managing with information."

Chapter 12 reviews the newer technologies and their potential value to business in the years ahead. Some of the most pervasive of these technologies are reviewed along with the impact they will bring to the business world. A case study of expert systems is presented.

Chapter 13 is entitled "Information Systems and Society," and presents a different but important perspective—that of the societal impact of computers and IS in our personal lives. Subjects such as invasion of privacy, the physical and psychological effects of automation, and the resistance to change are reviewed. This chapter also emphasizes the importance of education, both inside and outside schools, in providing the framework for the introduction of technology into our society.

Chapter 14 continues the look ahead by discussing the future business and management environment we will find in the twenty-first century. It builds on a study conducted by Babson College on management education in the twenty-first century. Two subjects conclude the book. The first is the impact of the global business environment and the development of the concept of a global information officer (GIO). The second is the potential impact of technology on education and learning. Though this may be possibly a bit far-fetched, the next edition of this textbook might well be an on-line version, accessed from an individual personal computer, utilizing case studies in a multimedia mode to personalize the material based on the personal objectives of the student.

Pedagogical Aids

The book includes pedagogical aids, but, again, the perspective is that of management— such that concepts and overall understanding are more important than rote knowledge of specifics relating to hardware and software. Thus, case studies are embedded in every chapter with several longer ones in the appendix. Practical, real-world news clips and personal experiences are included. The instructor's guide includes a course syllabus with chapter and outside reading assignments, exam questions, as well as a suggested paper or special project list, and practical projects to be performed in conjunction with businesses in the area. Each chapter has its own reference list.

ACKNOWLEDGMENTS

First, I would like to thank my assistant, Jill P. Stoff, whose skill and contributions were invaluable throughout the lengthy process. My daughter-in-law, Dorrie Kanter, assisted in the preparation and editing and her contribution and talents have been much appreciated. Patrice McCauley, a Babson student, has been particularly helpful to me not only in typing sections of the book, but in doing library searches and reference checks.

A second group of assistance has been rendered by members of the Babson Information Systems faculty. Steve Schiffman and Steve Gordon have provided their significant expertise in review of specific sections of the book while Edward Cale, director of IS curriculum, has been extremely valuable in discussing and reviewing much of the book's contents and using it in preliminary form for a graduate IS class. He has been my sounding board. David Kopcso, participated in the important launch stage of the book by helping define the scope, contents, and intended audience. All of the above people work for Babson division chairman, John C. Saber, and I owe John a debt of gratitude for both his direct and indirect support.

I am also grateful to my colleagues both from my business years and my academic years for coauthoring papers and articles that I use throughout the book. They give the book a more practical and meaningful direction. Included are articles with Jack Walsh, now at Digital Equipment Corporation, on project management; Joe Miserendino, now with the

Colonial Penn Insurance Company, on IS architecture; Dick Dooley, now head of his own firm, The Dooley Group, on management and organizational issues; David Kopcso, now with Babson College and Barbara Braden of Bull HN on expert systems; Paul Greene, now with Babson College on telecommunications; Steve Schiffman and Faye Horn, both from Babson, on customer driven applications; and Richard Kesner, now with Babson College, on the global information officer.

I have used constructs that were developed by some outstanding people in our profession. Not only have I read their writings on the subject, but I have had the opportunity to work with them and to hear and see first hand how their techniques are utilized. I have had the privilege of knowing Richard Nolan of Nolan, Norton & Co. and Harvard and using his Stages Theory for assessing IT status; Jack Rockart of MIT and the use of Critical Success Factors; Warren McFarlan, Jim Cash and Jim McKenney of Harvard and their Strategic Grid and Risk Assessment methodologies; and I benefitted greatly by working with Charles Wiseman of Theseus Institute on Strategic Information Systems. My thanks to all of these industry giants.

Jerome Kanter

Chapter 1

Information Systems—
Establishing the Framework

INTRODUCTION

In beginning the exploration of information systems and their role in a business enterprise, we must first build a framework to facilitate a meaningful discussion and understanding of the subject. The framework starts with the analysis of a business, its overall objectives and strategies, and the processes it needs to perform to remain competitive and to succeed. The initial framework employed is the classic management triangle, which breaks down a business into three process levels. From there we view the information systems that support these three process levels and the managers who are responsible for carrying out the processes.

Managing with information involves gathering the necessary data (raw material) and processing those data into meaningful information (finished goods). This chapter emphasizes the various dimensions of data and information and shows how an information system is the key to unlocking the power that resides in the data. As the elements of a system are developed, the realization is made that business itself is a system, the understanding of which is the cornerstone for effective information systems (IS). Finally, ten characteristics of successfully managing with information are presented. These form the framework for the remaining chapters and are the precepts on which the book is built.

CATEGORIZATION OF BUSINESS PROCESSES

Figure 1.1 indicates three levels of business activities or processes carried out in operating a company. These three levels, the classic management triangle, were first described by Robert B. Anthony in 1965 and are still valid in portraying the functioning of a business enterprise.

The first level, operational control, indicates processes performed to control the basic product or services produced by the company. In a manufacturing company, examples of operational control are the processes that move a product from one assembly point to the next and the actions that take place at each assembly point. In a bank, operational control includes the physical sorting, recording, and posting of checks. In a retailing or distribution operation, it involves the physical flow of merchandise through warehouses and retail stores.

The next level, management control, includes the functions that facilitate the management of those processes delegated to the operational control level. An example of a management control process is the production function where products are scheduled through the various fabrication and assembly points within a factory. The feedback from the production scheduling process enables management to control the operation. In a retail operation, the merchandise managers place orders for merchandise based on the movement of items in the store and the forecasted future demand.

The top level of the triangle represents strategic planning processes—the processes that determine which products to produce in the first place or, more broadly, which markets or businesses the company should be in currently or should plan to be in. These are brief examples that should help define the three levels; later sections build on this basic Anthony triangle. It represents a very useful classification schematic for establishing the proper perspective and providing a foundation for beginning the exploration of IS.

FIGURE 1.1. Levels of business activity

CLASSES OF INFORMATION SYSTEMS

With the understanding of the three kinds of processes that take place in a business, we can view the nature of the information systems that support these processes. The information systems that support the operational control processes are called transaction-processing systems. These systems are often termed the bread-and-butter applications—those that process incoming orders for a company's product and develop the information required to ship the items and then bill the customers for the cost of their orders. Another category of transaction-processing systems is the internal type, for example, those that manage the administration of company personnel including the processing of pay checks.

The management control information systems mainly center on providing managers with information to control operations and make decisions that optimize the delivery of products to customers. Production scheduling has been mentioned as an example and also inventory control systems, as well as financial control systems. As might be expected, systems with control in their titles usually fall into this category. These systems often employ decision rules and algorithms that help manage the processes. An example is a forecasting model that is used to project sales and demand for the company's product. The management control systems work directly with the operational control systems, but at a higher level, in that the goal is not to focus on individual transactions, but to manage the resources and facilities that control the total process.

The strategic planning information systems are more elusive than the other systems. This is because the process itself is not as structured as the other areas, and a certain degree of structure is a prerequisite for developing information systems. An example of a planning system is a mathematical planning model that can show the interaction of internal factors (past sales movement, relative product line acceptance) with external factors (inflation rates, unemployment statistics, and the like) to project the impact of different strategic directions.

LEVELS OF MANAGEMENT

Knowing who performs these processes within a business is very important to understanding the purpose and function of information systems. The people who perform the processes are the ones who manage with information. Figure 1.2 shows an organization chart of a manufacturing company.

There are several ways to describe the various management levels. Although lines of demarcation are not absolute, one can distinguish certain layers within the organization. For the most part, top management perform the strategic planning processes; middle management, the management control processes; and operating management, the operational control functions.

In attempting to distinguish the layers of management, we may find it difficult to stick to only three levels when most companies have an organizational hierarchy consisting of eight or more levels; that is, some managers are eight levels or more removed from the company president. One of the purported operational advantages enjoyed by Japanese companies is an organizational structure having as few as five levels separating the factory worker from the president.

FIGURE 1.2. Company organizational chart

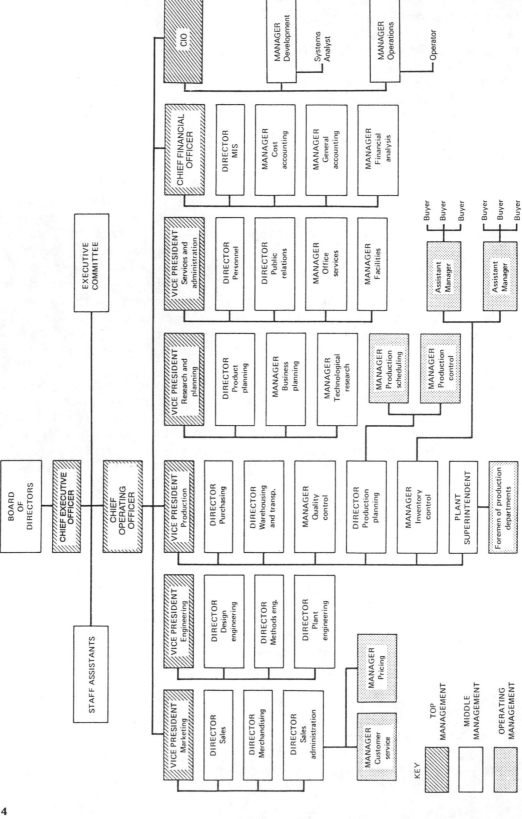

Figure 1.3 summarizes the interaction of the three levels. Top management establishes the policies, plans, and objectives of the company, as well as a general budget framework under which the various departments will operate. These factors are promulgated and passed down to middle management, where they are translated into specific revenue, cost, and profit goals, particularly if each department works under a cost or profit center concept. These are reviewed, analyzed, and modified in accordance with the overall plans and policies until agreement is reached. Middle management then issues the specific schedules and measurement yardsticks to operating management. The latter level has the job of producing the goods and services required to meet the revenue and profit goals, which in turn will enable the company to reach its overall plans and objectives.

The so-called flattened organization has been evolving for several decades. Leavitt, Whisler, and Drucker wrote about the elimination of the entire middle management level as computerized information systems enabled senior management to incorporate the role of middle management in its domain. This has not occurred as yet, but the trend is definitely in that direction.

THE INFORMATION SYSTEMS ORGANIZATION

The title of chief information officer (CIO) is indicated on the organization chart in Figure 1.2. The IS organization is discussed later in the book, but suffice it to state here that this title is being used to recognize the significance of information in managing a business. The

FIGURE 1.3. Interaction of business activity

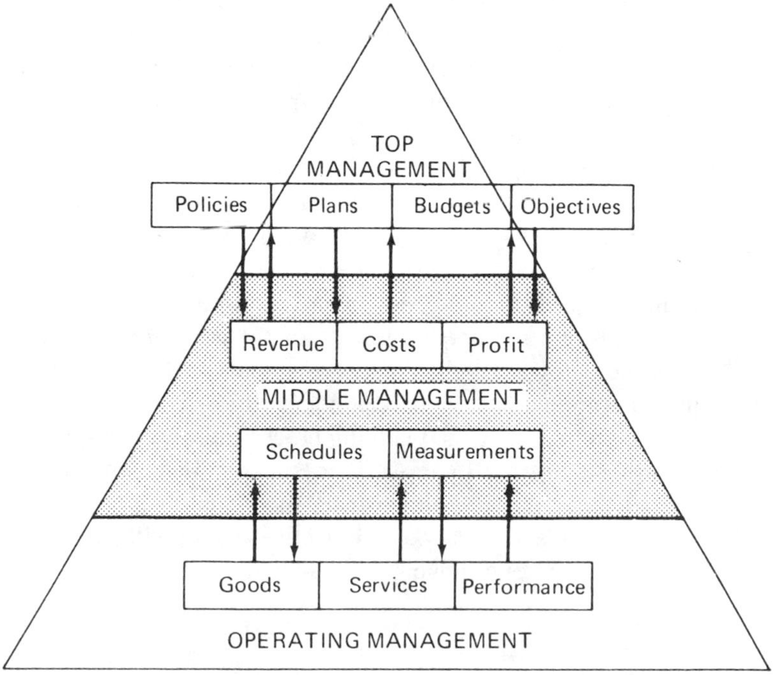

position is on the level of other senior managers reporting directly to the CEO. The chart indicates the two major functions of development and operations, but there are other important functions that report to the CIO, such as the telecommunications operation. The operation of the CIO has the same three levels of management as do the other major functions in the business. The managers reporting to the CIO would be middle managers, while the groups of systems analysts, programmers, and operators would have lead supervisors or managers representing the lower management level.

Though there are exceptions, the organization of IS is becoming more departmentalized or decentralized. It is one of the major trends that has been evolving for over a decade. In particular, any of the departments on the chart in Figure 1.2 could have its own systems development group and, because of the power of inexpensive personal computers and workstations, could have its own operations group. In many cases, the operators could be the managers themselves. However, in all but a few rare cases, there remains a need for the CIO and staff to set IS policy and to develop and manage systems that operate across the enterprise.

THE PLANNING PROCESS

Many companies have some form of long-range plan, typically for five years or longer, which acts as the master strategy and road map tying together the processes just mentioned. The plan promulgates the major business, market, and product strategies of the company for the next five years or longer, indicating the resources in the form of facilities, people, technology, and money necessary to accomplish the strategies. In addition to the strategies, the overall company goals are stated for the long-range plan period including performance indicators such as revenue, profit, return on investment, return on assets, market share, and the like. The goals are broken down by product line or operating division or both. The yearly operating plan of the company comes directly from the long-range plan, usually being identical for the first year or the first two years.

The long-range plans and the yearly operating plan are the basis for the formulation of individual objectives and goals, both of the numeric type and of the event type. An example of a numeric goal is a specified sales or shipment volume, while an event goal might be the delivery of a new product on a specific date or the completion of a new facility. The degree to which these objectives and goals cascade through an organization is a function of the planning process and the operating style of the company; however, the trend is continually to link more lower-level management goals to the company's long-range and operating plans. This approach obviously provides a more cohesive, direct, and motivated organization. The point of raising the planning process here is to emphasize that this should be the true starting point for IS. If IS is to support management, and management is goaled and measured by the long-range plan, then it is obvious that the contents of the plan are vital to the overall goals and objectives of the IS operation. Indeed, IS must itself be a part of the long-range plan—both influencing and being influenced by it.

DISTINCTION AMONG MANAGEMENT LEVELS

It is significant to compare the job content of the three levels of management. Though the reader is no doubt familiar with the various management roles, it is useful to mention them again to emphasize that the principal target and raison d'etre of information systems are management. Figure 1.4 contrasts the levels by reference to twelve characteristics. It brings out that top management is more involved with planning and a longer time horizon; deals with complex, fairly unstructured activities; and deals with fewer people but has a much broader scope than does lower-level management.

Lower-level managers place more emphasis on control than on planning; deal with more structured, measurable activities; and have less breadth and less complexity in their tasks; but they deal with many people on a day-to-day basis. It is important to think of these attributes when developing information systems to support the different levels of management.

TYPES OF MANAGEMENT INFORMATION

Information has come to be recognized as an increasingly valuable commodity required by management in order to plan and control business operations effectively. Data are the "stuff" of management systems just as material is the "stuff" of production systems. For purposes of definition, this analogy is shown in Figure 1.5. Data are defined as raw material and may enter the processing system from the keyboard of a personal computer, from optically

FIGURE 1.4. Job content of management levels

Characteristic	Top management	Middle management	Operating management
1. Focus on planning	Heavy	Moderate	Minimum
2. Focus on control	Moderate	Heavy	Heavy
3. Time frame	One to five years	Up to a year	Day to Day
4. Scope of activity	Extremely broad	Entire functional area	Single subfunction or subtask
5. Nature of activity	Relatively instructured	Moderately structured	Highly structured
6. Level of complexity	Very complex, many variables	Less complex, better defined variables	Straightforward
7. Job measurement	Difficult	Less difficult	Relatively easy
8. Result of activity	Plans, policies and strategies	Implementation schedules, performance yardsticks	End product
9. Type of information utilized	External	Internal, reasonable accuracy	Internal historical, high level of accuracy
10. Mental attributes	Creative, innovative	Responsible, persuasive, administrative	Efficient, effective
11. Number of people involved	Few	Moderate number	Many
12. Department/divisional interaction	Intra-division	Intra-department	Inter-department

FIGURE 1.5. Process flow

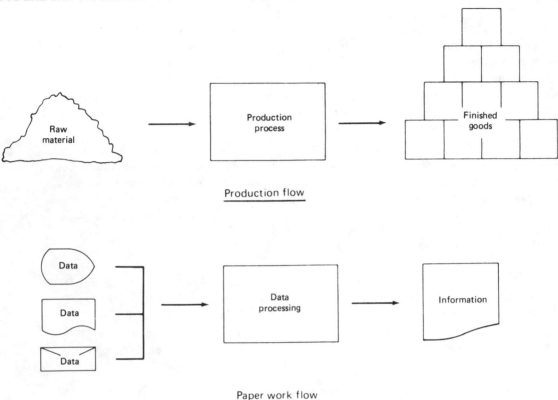

sensed documents, from writings on the back of envelopes, and so on. Processed data are called information, which is in a form to assist management and other users.

Information is now considered a resource on the level of money, material, facilities, and people. Indeed, some IS departments are called *information resource management.*

Business Dimension of Information

We have noted that different levels of management utilize different types of information. There are a variety of ways to classify information. Figure 1.6 represents the business dimension of information over a continuum with top management at one end and operating management at the other. Middle management, as always, falls in between, having elements of both.

The factors shown in the figure are obviously related. For example, it is difficult to write a computer program using information that is unstructured. Structured information tends to be rhythmic in that it follows a repetitive pattern that occurs at prescribed time periods. Thus the shop supervisor has the monthly production schedule for a particular product, which indicates that 50 units are scheduled for each of the next ten days. He or she will want to review on a day-to-day basis the information that indicates the material cost, labor cost, and expenses incurred to see whether the schedule is being met and whether it is

FIGURE 1.6. Business dimension of information

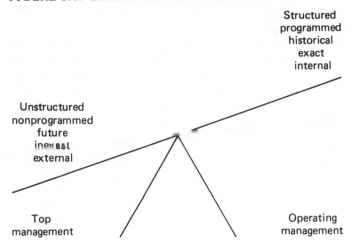

being met efficiently. Because the information is structured, it can be programmed. Rules and procedures can be established to develop schedules and measurements that will be most efficient for the known operating conditions. This is why more computerized information systems are programmed to assist operating management than to assist top management. The nature of top management's responsibilities revolves around strategic planning, where the nature of information is unstructured and therefore difficult to incorporate into a computer program. For example, it is difficult to determine with exactness the market share of a company's products or the particular penetration in a specific market segment.

Information for planning purposes stresses the future and thus is inexact when compared with information required at the operating level. This is not to say that top management is not interested in past history and in operating results. However, past results must be reviewed in light of external conditions and the marketplace in which the company competes. The focus of top management is on future plans and policies. The matrix shown in Figure 1.7 focuses on the difference between internal and external data/information.

Internal data are a by-product of the normal operations of a business. For example, a recording of inventory usage for the past week is typical internal data. Generally, internal data are historical or static in nature; they are after-the-fact data. This point is true at least in category A, data reported but not statistically processed. In the case of inventory usage, if the information is limited to prior history and no attempt is made to sample statistically or to draw meaningful correlations from it, it represents internally reported data. However,

FIGURE 1.7. Information matrix

	Reported	Processed
Internal	A	B
External	C	D

if inventory usage is statistically plotted to project future usage patterns, which are used to set optimum inventory levels, this information represents an example of category B—statistically processed internal information.

External data/information has its source outside the operations of the company. An example is population growth in the market served by a company, or the changes in ethnic makeup of the market. Category C reports the data but makes no attempt to analyze them statistically, and category D uses various mathematical techniques to analyze and correlate the data. A sales forecast that projects the future based on historical sales movement would be category B information; whereas a sales forecast that also includes external market statistics and trends would be a combination of B and D. The relative use of the various forms of data/information by a computer system is consistent with the alphabetic sequence; that is, A is found in a computer system more often than B, B is found more often than C, and C is found more often than D.

Technical Dimension of Information

The concept of a data base, which is so important to a management information system, is described in more detail in a later chapter. Simply stated, the data base is a unified collection of data that are utilized by various information systems. The form, capacity, and degree of integration of the data depend on the needs to which the data are put, plus cost considerations. The technical dimensions of the data base are such elements as access time, capacity, interrelationships of data elements, security, and validity. The cost considerations involve the summation of the following three costs:

1. Cost to acquire data

2. Cost to maintain data

3. Cost to access data

Figure 1.8 describes the data base concept, depicting three data bases or classes of

FIGURE 1.8. The data base concept

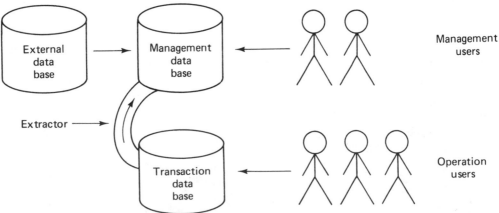

data. The transaction data base includes the detailed transactions that occur in the day-to-day operation of the business, such as individual sale of items or individual receipt of inventory. These transactions are recorded against the inventory and sales files. The data at this level are voluminous and detailed. Access to the data is gained by programmers or operators whose work is dedicated to this function. Access languages are optimized for this purpose.

On the other hand, management users require only summary and cumulative information, and usually not on a repetitive or instantaneous basis. Therefore the access languages are simple, easy to learn, and adaptable to intermittent use. Managers also require external data, as explained earlier, so that extractor programs are developed to move the external and transaction data into a data base accessible by management users.

WHAT IS A SYSTEM?

We have discussed management, business organization, and information. The all-encompassing framework that describes how these units interact is the system. There are many definitions, but Webster's Unabridged Dictionary comes fairly close to one that will suit our purposes. Webster defines system as "a set or arrangement of things so related or connected to form a unity or organization." Examples given are the solar system, an irrigation system, and a supply system. Indeed, this definition is so broad that many things with which we are familiar can be termed systems. An even broader definition is suggested alternately by Webster—that a system is a regular, orderly way of doing something. For purposes of its use in information systems, the systems module of Figure 1.9 is a useful method of describing the related things that are brought together to form a unity. The systems module has the four elements of input, processing, output, and feedback/control. Every system has these four elements in common. For example, the broadest view of a manufacturing company indicates that it is a system comprised of input in the form of raw material, piece parts, and subassemblies; processing in the form of manufacturing facilities; output in the form of finished goods; and feedback/control, either internal via quality control procedures or external via customer reaction.

The total economy has been viewed as an input/output matrix in a manner similar to the systems module. Educational and medical institutions can be viewed as systems modules with people as the prime input and output. On a more personal scale, most of us prepare our income tax returns on a systematic basis, gathering the input in the form of earnings records and deduction receipts, processing the information mathematically in accordance with preestablished rules and regulations, and producing as output the com-

FIGURE 1.9. Systems module

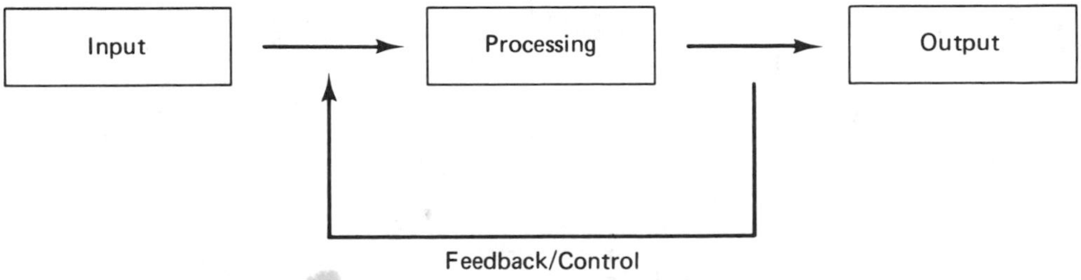

pleted tax return that is sent (sometimes electronically) to the Internal Revenue Service. The feedback/control comes in the form of a notice indicating either that the mathematical processing is wrong or that the interpretation of the IRS rules is in error.

Feedback/control is a very important element in system operation. Control can be automatic, so that the system is programmed to detect errors or potential errors and flag them to the operator. It is possible to correct some of the errors automatically based on the preprogrammed logic, but other errors require manual intervention; the latter constitute semiautomatic feedback loops. The program that doesn't encounter some foreseen or unforeseen problem during its lifetime has not yet been written. Effective system design requires careful attention to feedback/control; indeed, it can be considered a separate and distinct phase of system development. Feedback/control determines whether output measurements are outside of established tolerances or not and, if they are, what modifications of the input will bring the output back within tolerable limits.

DISTINCTION BETWEEN BUSINESS PROCESSES AND INFORMATION SYSTEMS

Although the distinction is difficult to make, it is important to understand the difference between a physical business system or process on one hand and an information system on the other. A physical system is the process itself and is concerned with the content, or *what* is going on. An information system, in the sense in which we use the term, is concerned with the form, or *how* something is being accomplished. The general schematic shown in Figure 1.10 is a physical system that exists in an automated bakery.

The dough, the principal input, enters the oven. Automatic controls continually monitor the temperature and humidity, actuating certain remedial functions if the elements fall above or below specific predetermined tolerances. This is an example of a process control system or a closed-loop industrial process. It is a physical system. For the most part, information systems try to achieve the same level of control over physical processes that are not as receptive to the closed-loop type of treatment. An example is a discrete manufacturing company as compared with a continuous-process manufacturer. In discrete manufacturing, there are a number of individual work stations where raw material is fabricated and assembled into various in-process stages until a prescribed finished-goods item is produced. This differs from the process type of manufacturing, as in cement plants, petroleum

FIGURE 1.10. Physical system or process

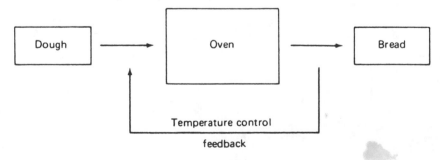

companies, or bakeries, where there is a continuous process of feeding raw material in one end and obtaining a finished item at the other.

An information system for a discrete manufacturer would be a production scheduling system that takes orders for particular items for a particular period of time and develops a work schedule to produce them. The information system is based on the physical facilities that are available. The primary job of systems analysts is not to initiate changes in organizational structure or the information requirements of management or to make changes in the physical systems or processes that exist within a company. However, as systems analysts become familiar with the existing processes, it is possible that they will discover ways to improve them. When properly reviewed with management, this can be most significant. This approach is called reengineering the process rather than merely automating the existing one. This can be a powerful and innovative contribution.

Managing with information encompasses both physical and information systems. An information system can be designed to enable management to obtain a clearer view of the company's use or misuse of its facilities. It can suggest alternatives and test the potential consequences of these alternatives to improve the use of facilities. The ramifications of adding a warehouse or increasing production capacity by an additional assembly line can be better ascertained through the use of a properly designed information system. The point is not that information systems and physical systems are unrelated activities that can or should be tackled separately; rather, a distinction is made between the role of management and that of the systems analyst.

The terms *physical system* and *process* have been used interchangeably. In developing an IS, the starting point is an understanding of the physical systems or processes that occur in a given company. Once these processes are understood and their interconnections ascertained, information systems can be developed to support the processes. The designation of the processes facilitates the breakdown of IS into information subsystems, which we can then implement one at a time, knowing they will fit together as the phasing proceeds. It is like starting a jigsaw puzzle by filling in the border: The overall size and structure can thus be determined. Starting with the internal pieces of a jigsaw puzzle may also get you there, but it will take a bit longer. The analogy fails at this point because starting with the pieces with IS will most likely leave you with some gaping holes and misaligned pieces.

BUSINESS PROCESSES

Figure 1.11 illustrates the business processes of a manufacturing company. It is a highly simplified schematic that suffices for our purposes here. The boldface arrows at the bottom of Figure 1.11 follow the physical flow of material through the factory. Raw material, piece parts, and supplies originate from a variety of vendors and flow into the factory. Within the factory, the materials are stocked in finished stores, semifinished stores, or raw material, depending on classification and physical storage facilities. Materials are then requisitioned from the inventory holding areas to the fabrication and assembly operations necessary to turn the materials into finished products. Inspection stations at selected points in the operation check for both quantity and quality of product. Finished goods are sorted in inventory areas within the main factory or in finished-goods warehouses at various locations

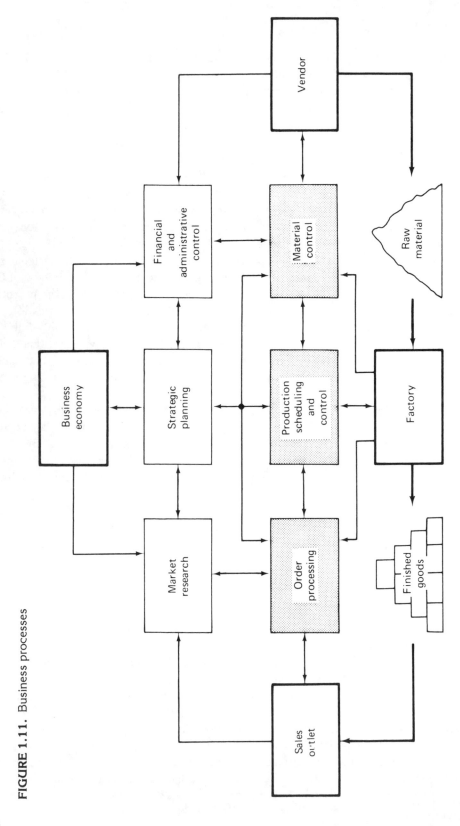

FIGURE 1.11. Business processes

throughout the country. As orders are received, the goods are released from the factory or warehouse and transported to the required sales outlet. Sales outlets range from large distributors to direct shipment to individual consumers.

The heavily outlined blocks (vendor, factory, sales outlet, and business economy) indicate physical entities in contrast to the other blocks, which represent processes to control the physical flow of goods from the vendor through the factory and into the hands of the consumer. The prime business objective of a manufacturer is to facilitate this material flow in the most economical manner while satisfying customer demand to the extent that the incoming sales cash stream exceeds the outgoing cash stream. The resultant profit must produce a return on investment that meets the business goals of the company.

Turning now to the business processes that control the physical flow, the order-processing process fits in at the front end. This process provides direct contact with the sales outlets, handles the flow of orders into the factory, expedites orders, and facilitates customer payment for goods shipped. Order processing is linked directly to the material control system. The job of materials control is to ensure that there is a balanced finished-goods inventory to satisfy customer demand in the required time frame. Materials control is also indirectly related to the production planning and control process. It establishes when production orders must be initiated to replenish stock levels. In addition to finished-goods inventory, the materials control process controls piece parts, assemblies, raw material, and other in-process inventories. Moreover, materials control is directly linked to the vendor. Items that are not manufactured must be requisitioned from outside suppliers; therefore the purchasing function is an important part of the materials control process.

Production scheduling and control is undoubtedly the most significant process at the operating level. It is here that orders and forecasts for orders, which together form the gross manufacturing requirements, are screened against available stock to determine net requirements (the amount that must be produced to satisfy customer demand). Scheduling the production of net requirements while making the most economical use of the manpower, machines, and material at the company's disposal is the job of production scheduling and control. The arrows in Figure 1.11 indicate a tie-in of production scheduling and control with the factory. This link is a most important one.

The market research process analyzes sales trends and provides both long- and short-range forecasts for the strategic planning system. The financial and administrative control process is responsible for the accounting statements of the company and plots cash positions for various time intervals. The administrative control process is responsible for the most efficient utilization of the company's personnel resources. The strategic planning process receives summary reports from the other systems, particularly market research and financial and administrative control; combines this information with that from outside sources, such as gross national product and political factors; and assists in making the top policy decisions for the company. These decisions include profit and budget planning, resource and capacity analysis, new product development, and general business objectives, both short and long range.

The crosshatched boxes of Figure 1.11 represent processes that are relevant to middle and operating management levels. The unshaded boxes represent processes that are significant to the strategic area of operations, or mainly to top management.

We have built a business model—not a mathematical model, but a process representation of what a company does. The concept of business as a system has been used to show that, like any system, it is comprised of subsystems or, in this case, business processes. It is a bit surprising that many IS efforts begin without a thorough understanding of the business model.

CHARACTERISTICS OF SUCCESSFULLY MANAGING WITH INFORMATION

It should be apparent that information systems are vital to company operation. It can be said that today few, if any, enterprises can operate without information systems. The first step in understanding their potential impact on the business operation is to break through the semantic barriers, as we do in this chapter. This section summarizes the pertinent character-istics of IS and the underlying guidelines of managing with information. These precepts serve as a framework throughout the book as we refer to and build on them.

1. Management Oriented/Directed

This is the most significant characteristic of managing with information. The system is designed from the top down. This does not mean that the system will be geared to providing information directly to top management; rather, it means that the system devel-opment starts from an appraisal of management needs and overall business objectives. It is possible that middle management or operating management is the focus of the system, so that their needs are the cornerstone on which the system is built.

A marketing information system is an example. Basic sales-order processing, the shipment of goods to customers, and the billing of the goods are fundamental operational control activities. However, if the system is designed properly, this transaction information can be tracked by salespeople, sales territory, size of order, geography, and product line. Furthermore, if designed with strategic management needs in mind, external competition, market, and economic data can be created to give a picture of how well the company's products are faring in their marketing environment and to serve as a basis for introducing new products or markets. The initial application can be geared to the operational and management control areas, but in such a way as not to preclude its integration into a strategic planning subsystem for upper management.

Because of the management orientation of IS, it is imperative that management actively direct the system development efforts. Involvement is not enough. In terms of the preceding examples, management must determine what sales information is necessary to improve its control of marketing operations.

It is rare to find an IS where managers themselves, or high-level representatives of their departments, are not spending a good deal of time in system design. It is not a one-time involvement, for continued review and participation are necessary to ensure that the implemented system meets the specifications of the system that is designed. Therefore, management is responsible for setting system specifications, and it must play a major role in the subsequent tradeoff decisions that inevitably occur in system development. An important element of effective system planning is the process for determining the priority of application development. A company without a formal application approval cycle and a management steering committee to determine priorities will never develop an effective IS.

2. Business Driven/Justified

A fundamental tenet of meaningful and successful IS is that it be driven by the business and not the other way around. The plans of IS must be linked to the overall business plans of the enterprise. The strategies of the corporation must set the IS priorities. For example, if a major thrust of the organization is to compress the time to introduce new products, this sets the IS priority; if the major thrust is to improve customer service, this sets the IS priority; if the major thrust is to reduce cost, this sets the IS priority. The justification will be to make a significant contribution to achieving these business priorities. Certainly an IS function can make a contribution in nonstrategic areas of the business, but the big payoffs and value will come when IS is aligned with and driven by the overriding objectives and strategies of the business.

3. Integrated

Integration of information subsystems provides more meaningful management information. For example, in order to develop an effective production scheduling system, we must balance such factors as: (1) setup costs, (2) work force, (3) overtime rates, (4) production capacity, (5) inventory levels, (6) capital requirements, and (7) customer service. A system that ignores one of these elements—inventory level, for example—is not providing management with an optimal schedule. The cost of carrying excess inventory may more than offset the other benefits of the system. Integration, in the sense intended here, means taking a comprehensive view or a complete-picture look at the interlocking subsystems that operate within a company. One can start an IS by attacking a specific subsystem, but unless its place in the total system is realized and properly reflected, serious shortcomings may result. Thus an integrated system that blends information from several operational areas is a necessary element of IS.

4. Common Data Flows

Because of the integration concept of IS, there is an opportunity to avoid duplication and redundancy in data gathering, storage, and dissemination. System designers are aware that a few key source documents account for much of the information flow and affect many functional areas. For example, customer orders are the basis for billing the customer for goods ordered, setting up the accounts receivable, initiating production activity, making sales analyses, forecasting sales, and so on. It is prudent to capture this data closest to the source where the event occurs and use it throughout the functional areas. It is also prudent to capture it once and thus avoid the duplicate entry of source data into several systems. This concept also holds in building and using master files and in providing reports. The common data flows concept supports several of the basic tenets of systems analysis—avoiding duplication, combining similar functions, and simplifying operations wherever possible.

The development of common data flows is an economically sound and logical concept, but it must be viewed in a practical and pragmatic light. Because of a company's method of operation and its internal procedures, it may be better to live with a little duplication in order to make the system acceptable and workable. IS and integration are more important for their ability to blend the relationship of several functional areas of a business and to produce more meaningful management information, than for producing that information more economically. In IS, effectiveness gets the nod over efficiency.

Given the track record and experience to date, one should look closely at the degree of integration of common data flows. Although benefits exist, the degree of difficulty is high, and many would-be implementors have failed because they underemphasized the complexity and amount of time involved or did not possess the necessary system design skills. What is being questioned is not the desirability of building the concept of common data flows into the system; rather, it is the degree to which the concept is used. Building a system that cannot operate unless all data springs from a common data path is usually an unwise design concept—as many companies have discovered to their detriment.

5. Heavy Planning Element

Complex, enterprise-wide information systems do not occur overnight; they take from three to five years to get fully established firmly with a company. Therefore, a heavy planning element must be present in IS development. Just as a civil engineer does not design a highway to handle today's traffic but to handle the traffic 10 to 20 years from now, so the IS designer must have the future objectives and needs of the company firmly in mind. The designer must avoid the possibility of system obsolescence before the system gets into operation; needless to say, sound system planning is an essential ingredient in successful IS.

A phasing plan is an essential ingredient to IS planning. While an enlightened management will see the future benefits from implementing systems in an integrated fashion around a data base, it can't tolerate a complete hiatus during the transition phase. Plans must include some enhancement of existing systems concurrent with the implementation of the new IS. The practical philosophy is that IS is a compass. While the final goal is never completely reached, IS provides a meaningful direction toward which one strives. A phasing plan with intermediate benefits accruing like time capsules is an appropriate way to proceed.

6. Subsystem Concept

In tackling a project as broad and complex in scope as an enterprise-wide information system, one must avoid losing sight of both the forest and the trees. Even though the system is viewed as a single entity, it must be broken down into digestible subsystems that can be implemented one at a time. The breakdown of IS into meaningful subsystems sets the stage for a prioritized implementation. Although the functional areas of sales-order processing, material control, and so on, as illustrated in Figure 1.11, have been referred to as systems, in reality they are subsystems that, in turn, can be broken down into additional subsystems. This subsystems analysis is essential for applying boundaries to the problem, thus enabling the designer to focus on manageable entities that can be assigned and computerized by selected systems and programming teams.

7. Flexibility and Ease of Use

Despite a careful analysis of future management information needs, it is impossible to predict what is desired three to five years hence. This is true in most industries, and especially in industries with rapid change patterns. It is naive to think that anyone possesses the omniscience to predict the future.

With this as a premise, the next best thing an IS developer can do is build in the flexibility to incorporate as many future nuances as possible. Even then, future happenings will sorely try the flexibility boundaries of the system. Building an IS on a solid data base foundation is a good starting point for flexibility. On the lighter, but realistic side, expect Murphy's law and Reilly's law both to occur. Murphy's law states that anything that can happen will, and Reilly's law states that Murphy is an optimist.

A feature that often goes with flexibility is ease of use. This means the incorporation of features that can make the system readily accessible to a wide range of users and easy to use once they are ready to try it. One of the major information systems trends is broadening the base of users, consistent with evolving end-user languages and IS access methods. The IS should be able to incorporate the best of the improving user windows into the IS data base.

8. Data Base

As explained earlier, the data base is the mortar that holds the functional systems together. Each system requires access to a master file of data covering inventory, personnel, vendors, customer, general ledger, work in process, and so on. If the data is stored efficiently and with common usage in mind, one master file can provide the data needed by any of the functional systems. It seems logical to gather data once, properly validate it, and place it on a central storage medium that can be accessed by any system. However, it is not unusual to find a company with multiple data files, one serving one functional system and another serving another system. This is obviously not the most efficient way to operate. Data base concepts are discussed thoroughly in a subsequent chapter. Although it is remotely possible to achieve the basic objectives of IS without a data base, thus paying the price of duplicate storage and duplicate file updating, more often than not the data base is the sine qua non of managing with information systems.

9. Distributed Systems

The majority of companies implementing IS have a geographic network of sales offices, distribution points, manufacturing plants, divisions, subdivisions, and so on. Some of these entities are operated in a completely independent fashion and therefore may not be a part of the integrated IS. More often than not, the remote sites do have a connection with each other and with a host operation. In order to create an effective IS without arbitrary geographic boundaries, some form of distributed systems (DS) is necessary. DS is covered in a later chapter, but for now it means that two or more information subsystems in different locations act in a cooperative fashion—they share data over a network. This is a simple definition for a concept that is vital to effective IS. DS can be thought of as the delivery system, placing information in the hands of those who need it when they need it. Teleprocessing, networking, or just plain communication systems are an important part of DS, and DS is an important part of IS.

10. Information as a Resource

The information resource management (IRM) concept is an overriding philosophy. Pervading the entire organization must be the concept that information is a valuable resource, particularly in the management control and strategic planning areas, and must be properly managed. This is a subtle but important change in thinking. It was common in the past to view data processing as an entity unto itself doing its own thing. The new outlook is that IS is more than a support for the business; in many instances it is inextricably bound up in the business itself. One of the manifestations of IRM is that IS will have a higher reporting relationship in the organization and will become more a part of the organization's executive committee.

Most every organization will have some form of centralized IS operation managed by a chief information officer (CIO) or equivalent. This group has among its responsibilities the establishment throughout the organization of the proper IS environment, which creates a proactive, competitive, and innovative spirit whether the functions be centralized or distributed. Following the ten guidelines described in the foregoing can be a principal step in that direction. The first two instill the proper business and management perspective into the organization. Characteristics 3, 4, and 8 ensure the proper integration and commonality for enterprise-wide applications. Characteristics 5 and 10 are principal tenets throughout the book, stressing the need to link IS planning with business planning and to view information as a valuable company resource or asset. Characteristics 6 and 7 stress systems concepts that are fundamental to success; that is, that break large applications into manageable subunits and make these units flexible and easy to use. Characteristic 9 stresses the importance of data sharing via a communications network that links supporting units across a geographical spectrum. Together, these ten characteristics form the underpinnings of an IS operation that can help a company obtain a competitive advantage.

SUMMARY

In order to put the concept of information systems into proper context, this chapter has presented an analytical framework from which to view the subject. Three levels of management were distinguished, and the salient job characteristics and responsibilities of top, middle, and operating management were contrasted. Information was viewed from the business dimension and the technical dimension. The types of information required by the three management levels were discussed.

A basic systems module introduced the discussion of different types of systems. A physical system or process was distinguished from an information system with the statement that the systems analyst is primarily responsible for the information system that supports an existing or newly engineered physical system. The development of a business entity comprised of processes was developed using a manufacturing company as a model. Ten basic characteristics of managing with information were presented. These form an important infrastructure for the remainder of the book.

The chapter established the viewpoint and perspective of IS, introducing and defining the elements that are explored in later chapters. Because of the heavy dependence of subsequent chapters on this one, the reader should have a good understanding of the analytical framework described here before proceeding.

Case Study

Harris Manufacturing

Harris Manufacturing, Inc., with four plants, sixteen assembly departments, about that many fabricating centers, and more than 200 machine centers, has installed what they call an interfunctional information system.

The operations are characterized by a nationwide distribution network. The product moves through 38 branch offices and 312 authorized distributors—all of which maintain some inventory. Authorized distributors generate 37 percent of the orders but account for only 24 percent of the sales. Most of the business is done through the branch offices.

The product line is large. Products are classified into 176 family groups, representing 12,000 finished goods (listed in the catalog), of which 3600 are carried in inventory and 8400 are made to order. Approximately 1500 new items enter the product line annually, and a similar number are discontinued.

These 12,000 finished goods require 25,000 component parts, of which 6600 are carried in inventory and 18,400 are made to order.

The interfunctional system already has paid off substantially, and refinements continue to increase the benefits. In the seventies, Harris was achieving a 90-percent customer service level (i.e. 90 percent of the orders were being delivered according to original customer requests with no delays or adjusting of dates). The sales/inventory ratio was a respectable 4.2. However, the production cost variance averaged 16.3 percent. Clerical expenses ran 3.6 percent of sales.

This was not good enough in a highly competitive business. Since the primary asset a company has (in addition to high-quality, reliable products) is customer service, an improvement in customer service was given top priority. The nature of the business and products makes it very difficult to meet a 90-percent on-time delivery target. It was felt that 95 percent would create a major competitive advantage.

Three areas of cost control also were given high priority:

1. Production costs must be controlled within tight tolerances. This is especially true in a business where prices are negotiable at field sales level.

2. Distribution costs, especially those associated with a nationwide disbursement of inventory, must be controlled within reasonable limits relative to needs for customer service.

3. Clerical costs in a growing business must be contained and, if possible, reduced.

An interfunctional integrated, information system was instituted, a system which integrated sales, inventory control, production, and administrative operations. Performance in the four areas of high priority was greatly improved.

1. *Customer service.* Fully 97 percent of orders were filled as requested, a substantial improvement.
2. *Inventory turnover.* The sales/inventory ratio was 6.2, a 50-percent increase over the previous performance. More improvement was expected.
3. *Production-cost variance.* This category had all but disappeared, being controlled within a 1-percent tolerance. This was possible because timely, accurate information now was available when needed.
4. *Clerical expense.* The ratio of clerical expenses had dropped to 2.8 percent, an unusual achievement in a rapidly growing business that had to face increasing rates of clerical labor.

STUDY QUESTIONS

1. Are you impressed with the improvements in customer service, inventory turnover, production cost variance, and clerical expense?
2. Do you think all these improvements can be related to the introduction of technology?
3. Will these gains give Harris a competitive advantage? How sustainable will it be?
4. Do you know of any situations where the results of IS were measured as in this situation?
5. Which activity areas were the focus of IS—operational control, management control, or strategic planning? Do you agree with the emphasis?
6. How would you go about evaluating the benefits of IS? Are there reliable and realistic measurement yardsticks?

SELECTED REFERENCES

Anthony, Robert M., *The Management Control Function.* Boston, MA.: The Harvard Business School Press, 1988.

Anthony, R. M., *Planning and Control Systems: A Framework for Analysis.* Cambridge, MA: Division of Research, Graduate School of Business Administration, Harvard University, 1965.

Churchill, N. C., J. H. Kempster and M. Uretsky, *Computer-Based Information Systems for Management—A Survey.* New York: National Association for Accountants, 1968.

Henderson, John C., "Building and Sustaining Partnership Between Line and I/S Managers." *Massachusetts Institute of Technology Working Paper*, September, 1989.

Rockart, John F., and James E. Short, "Information Technology and the New Organization: Towards More Effective Management of Interdependence." *Massachusetts Institute of Technology Working Paper*, September, 1988.

Planning for the Effective Use of Information Systems

INTRODUCTION

Chapters 2 and 3 are companion chapters. Chapter 2 deals with the fundamentals of planning, defining, and describing why and what one plans and how one plans. The evolution of planning is explored using the Nolan stages as a base point. The emphasis in Chapter 2 is on the why and what of planning; that is, the determination of what is the most effective use of IS, when should it be employed in an organization and for what applications. Chapter 3, on the other hand, reviews how to plan, how to establish the overall architecture or model that will ensure the necessary integration, and management of interdependence.

This chapter develops the concept of IS as a strategic resource or tool. This idea has come on strong in the eighties and remains a powerful concept in the nineties. Some feel that the role of IS as a strategic weapon has peaked and been neutralized since most companies have explored most of the possibilities. However, this is far from the truth, and the use of IS for competitive advantage is limited only by lack of vision and foresight of a company's management. Three popular and useful techniques are explained in this chapter. The first is the approach described by Michael Porter and Victor Millar (later more fully covered in several Porter books). This approach has been employed by many companies and remains a focus of popular seminars and conferences. The strategic grid, a construct enabling a company to ascertain its strategic IS positioning, is then presented. The second approach is that of Charles Wiseman who has written two books, as well as many articles, on the subject of strategic information systems. Wiseman builds on Porter's structures and adds a methodology for seeking out candidate application areas for strategic systems.

The last of the three frameworks is the very popular concept of critical success factors (CSF) as first expressed by John F. Rockart, director of MIT's Center for Information Systems Research, and then extended by a host of educators and practitioners who have conducted research on and written about the employment of CSFs in a number of different ways. CSFs are in a different category from the Porter or Wiseman frameworks, but they afford a higher-level umbrella of consensus about what is critical to a company's success and can help an organization determine just what are the key factors to reach their objectives and to succeed. This chapter, then, serves as a logical introduction to the next chapter. Together they provide the necessary strategic front-end thinking and planning that must precede any meaningful inroad into the use of IS.

IS STAGES ANALYSIS

Richard Nolan, the head of a successful consulting firm and a professor at the Harvard Business School, has developed a staging theory to explain how a company's IS function has evolved over the years. The premise is that companies progress through six stages of growth, each stage being characterized by unique elements. Adapted over the years, the stages analysis now provides a framework that works surprisingly well for most companies. The stages approach is useful in analyzing where a company is in its IS evolution, where it appears to be headed, and the management practices required to make the evolution most effective. It also points out mistakes made in previous stages that should be avoided in future stages.

Figure 2.1 illustrates the stages concept. The curved line represents the IS budget over the six stages. The slope of the curve is double S-shaped, with budgets rising rapidly during stages 1 and 2, leveling off in stage 3, rising steeply again in stage 4, and beginning to level again in stages 5 and 6.

Stage 1 begins with a company's purchase of a computer system. Since most medium to large companies already have computer systems, this stage is history as far as the majority are concerned. A company may, however, start a new division or purchase a new company that does not have a computerized information system. If the lessons learned from the stages discussion are not heeded, it is possible to go through the entire painful cycle again; indeed, reinventing the wheel remains a popular pastime with many.

Stage 2, contagion, involves a rapid proliferation of applications without a growth plan or a controlled framework. Most companies proceeded through this stage in the late fifties or early sixties, when unbridled technical excitement and management laxity permitted proliferation of computers and applications, only some of which were directed at areas of real payoff.

Stage 3 usually begins with management's awareness that the company's computer systems are out of control, that computer budgets are growing at a rate of 30 to 40 percent a year and more, and that the return on investment is in serious question. A period of free-wheeling or what Nolan calls "management slack" is replaced by a period of strict control, often so strict that it is damaging to future growth. Somehow, out of stage 3 the

FIGURE 2.1. IS stages analysis

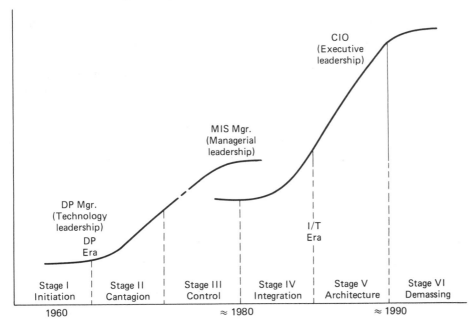

Source: Nolan, Norton, and Co., Lexington, Ma.

realization emerges that applications have not been aimed at the management levels and that those aimed at the operational control areas lack the required responsiveness and flexibility.

Stage 4 initiates a retooling and a redesign of applications to the on-line responsive mode, built around an integrated data base; thus this stage is called integration. Stage 4 establishes the IS foundation and leads to the architecture stage (stage 5), where a major change occurs in the role of IS. The realization that an overall IS blueprint or road map must be put in place (IS architecture) in order to share company-wide data and have intra- and intercompany communication.

Stage 6, called demassing, is placing control for IS into the hands of line management. Subsequent chapters elaborate on this important phenomenon. With the overall architecture and telecommunications network in place, managers have the flexibility to obtain the data they need to operate—to "manage with information."

Dick Nolan's stages analysis presents a useful perspective by which to synthesize the changes that have been and are taking place in IS. Some professional IS observers see the stages a company goes through, not as six, but as two alternating cycles of growth and control or ingestion and digestion. In whatever way the cycle is viewed, it is generally agreed that those companies employing the style and practices of the later stages will have the more effective IS operation. A key lesson to follow is to incorporate a greater degree of planning and control during periods of rapid growth so that integration and repositioning can evolve more naturally and effectively. The greater the fragmentation, the more difficult it will be to achieve control and integration—elements that are necessary prerequisites to information resource management.

IS PLANNING

Planning a job or a project before launching it is logical and practical. While individuals and companies realize the worth of planning specific tasks and projects, the application planning of a major and complex function of a business is not as readily seen. Projects usually have a one- or two-year time horizon, while planning for a major department or function such as IS requires a longer time horizon, usually in the three- to five-year range. Examples of effective, comprehensive five-year IS plans are not as prevalent as they should be.

Planning has gone through a stage evolution consistent with the stages theory concept of information system growth within most companies. It is not just an IS issue but a corporate one as well. Managers have always been leery of planning. Planning is hard work, not much fun, ill-defined, not immediately rewarding, and can detract from time devoted to the day-to-day operations of the business. Also the classic profile of the type A executive indicates a natural block to the planning function. Type A executives are action oriented, aggressive leaders with short attention spans who are impatient with activities that don't promise concrete and immediate payoffs. Planning does not fit the natural mind set for the type A manager. As a result, during the late fifties and early sixties, there was a negative corporate environment for planning. Since any IS planning methodology must match and fit the company culture, it was obviously not a good time to do much serious thinking about developing an IS long-range plan.

The late sixties and most of the seventies might be characterized as a complacency era, with corporate leaders exhibiting a laissez-faire attitude toward planning. Executives realized that planning was necessary, but they really didn't know how to do it: Whatever was required, it certainly didn't demand much of their personal attention—so they conjectured. During this period, managers gave lip service to planning, perfunctorily nodding whenever the subject came up. A sharp dichotomy between planning and doing was drawn, with planners assigned full time to the task but in an ivory-tower environment where they would work separately and not interfere with the nonplanners (the workers). Massive documents were produced and put on the shelf, where they gathered dust except when withdrawn to display to visiting consultants, auditors, college professors, or planners from other companies. These thick tomes were quite impressive but did not really direct the strategies and actions of the company. They gave management a warm feeling and assuaged a planning guilt complex, but did little more.

The eighties initiated a firm belief in a new concept—*pragmatic planning*—planning that is jointly conducted by executives and planners, that addresses the key business directions of the company and is followed and modified as market changes dictate. The plan is the basis for action, not a book that's put on the shelf for review by the intelligentsia.

What prompted this new and serious look at planning is a bit obscure. It may have been the inflationary economy and its impact on future growth; it may have been the political changes in regulation, taxes, and budgetary direction; it may have been the emergence of foreign competition, particularly the Japanese model of doing business based on a long-term planning foundation; or it could have been just an awakening by executives to the importance of looking out further and the realization that they had to be involved in the process. Whatever the cause or causes, it became evident that a manager's job and the success of the enterprise depended on a dual responsibility: to perform to meet the current year's goals and to plan to meet future years' goals. This establishes a corporate environment that is healthier and more receptive to IS planning.

Planning in the nineties recognizes that IS is a resource and of immense value in gaining competitive advantage and in competing in one's industry. The concepts of strategic information systems and IS architecture are the sine qua nons of staying in business.

Evolution of IS Planning

In the early stages of IS, applications were initiated and implemented as separate entities without much attention to integration. The aim was to get a specific application up and running to satisfy a particular user's need. The first emergence of planning was project planning, for it was found that many of the earlier applications did not really satisfy user needs once the implementation was completed. Users would say, "That isn't what I told you" or "You should have done what I meant, not what I said." Projects typically were behind schedule and took more resources than were contemplated—and by an order of magnitude or worse. It soon became clear that identifying the project milestones, gaining user sign-off on specifications, and scheduling management reviews throughout the cycle produces better products.

The proliferation of applications during the contagion stage resulted in heavy demands for computer time. This initiated the second kind of IS planning—capacity planning. Though capacity planning remains to this day more art than science, IS managers had to find a way to project future computer hardware requirements in an era of growing application backlogs. Capacity planning permits the modeling of the current workload in order to project future volume levels and the need and time frame for added capacity.

With the increase in computer resources, management became alarmed over the sharply rising cost of IS services. This led to a third type of planning—resource or budgetary planning. IS managers began developing annual operational plans, which necessitated looking ahead at least a year to project what hardware, software, people, and facilities were required to run the operation and handle the growing portfolio of computer applications.

As IS matured, an assessment of management needs showed a requirement for integrated data files and architecture in order to provide meaningful management information to run the business. This finally ushered in long-range planning—the need to formulate the direction and strategy of the IS function to support the business in the next three- to five-year period or longer.

Long-Range IS Planning

In considering an IS long-range plan, we need to keep several precepts in mind.

Planning is a verb, not a noun. Planning is not a once-a-year function that produces a report and gets management's blessing. Rather, it is a continuous process that takes place throughout the year. The report is reviewed and updated continually; it is a living document. Most planners and executives would agree that the effectiveness of planning is in the process rather than in a particular document that becomes the final output.

The IS plan must be consistent with the corporate business plan. The IS plan must dovetail with the corporate plan. Since the IS plan supports the future business, the future business direction of the company must be known before any meaningful IS plan can be developed. This usually means that the planning cycle of the IS plan is in sequence with the corporate planning cycle. A set of corporate strategic guidelines will kick off the planning cycle for the year. The IS cycle should commence at that point and coincide with the key management review points of the corporate schedule.

Management involvement and commitment are essential. Involvement and commitment go hand in hand in that commitment without involvement is usually lip service, rather than something that arises from understanding and participation in the review process. In order to achieve this participation, an information steering committee is usually required. Since each manager is involved in his or her own department plan, conservative and sensitive use of managers' time is important. Meetings should be well structured and focused on broad strategic issues rather than short-term tactical ones. The makeup and operation of the management review board or steering committee is extremely important. The plan's content obviously is crucial, but its perception by management can be equally crucial.

Planning is everybody's job. Though a specific individual or department is responsible for developing the IS plan, such persons are the catalysts or agents, chartered to select a planning methodology and to ensure that the planning process takes place according to the methodology and is consistent with corporate guidelines. They can contribute to the plan's content but are not responsible for it. The key department managers and the IS executive bear the responsibility for providing the strategic directional content. Planning is not a function to be delegated.

Organizational behaviorists point out that it is difficult for a manager to successfully implement a plan that was dictated from the top without his or her involvement or commitment. Grass-roots planning, where the people responsible for implementing the plan are also involved in the planning process, has proven more workable than ivory-tower planning.

It takes several cycles to institutionalize a planning process. It was noted earlier that planning is not an easy task and runs against the grain of the action-oriented, hard-driving manager. Therefore, no matter how sound the methodology chosen or how efficient the techniques for developing the plan, it will take more than one iteration to establish the process firmly within a company. Planners instituting the process should not be discouraged the first time around. Often the first year's plan is not completely understood by either the IS people implementing it or the IS users supported by it. An assessment should be made at the completion of the first planning cycle in order to improve the process during the next cycle. Modifications may include items such as an off-site, half-day workshop to review the final version, a different composition of the steering committee, or a change in the scheduling of various milestones. Remember that planning is a verb; it is a continuous process.

An additional and important point is that with more of the responsibility for IS placed in the hands of line managers, there is a need for two concurrent IS plans: the overall IS architecture that drives the necessary information integration, and the individual department or functional line plans that support the departments but are consistent with the overall company plans.

Contents of a Long-Range Plan

Figure 2.2 segments the contents of an IS long-range plan into fifteen categories. The contents answer six basic questions:

1. Where are we?
2. Where do we want to go?
3. How do we get there?
4. When will it be done?
5. Who will do it?
6. How much will it cost?

While the contents will vary for different companies, depending on their planning evolution, Figure 2.2 presents a good starting point. Some sections will be emphasized one year and deemphasized in another. For example, at a particular development stage, the establishment of IS management control techniques may be of principal significance, but be downplayed in subsequent years. This is true also for other areas such as policies or transition strategies. Often planners feel that, if a plan doesn't change dramatically each year, it is not a good one or they are not doing their jobs. This is not the case, because if a good solid vision of the future is established and if meaningful, well-founded strategies are put in place, they may hold for several years to come with but minor fine tuning. An extremely useful technique is to develop a difference document that summarizes the key changes of this year's plan from that of the preceding year. Management is particularly interested in this focus.

The fifteen sections of the plan include the following:

1. Corporate guidelines
   (a) Strategic—markets/products
   (b) Volume indicators
   (c) Functional/organizational changes
2. Environment
   (a) Industry trends
   (b) Technology scan
   (c) Government regulations
   (d) Work force composition
   (e) Customer/supplier relational changes

FIGURE 2.2. Content of an IS plan

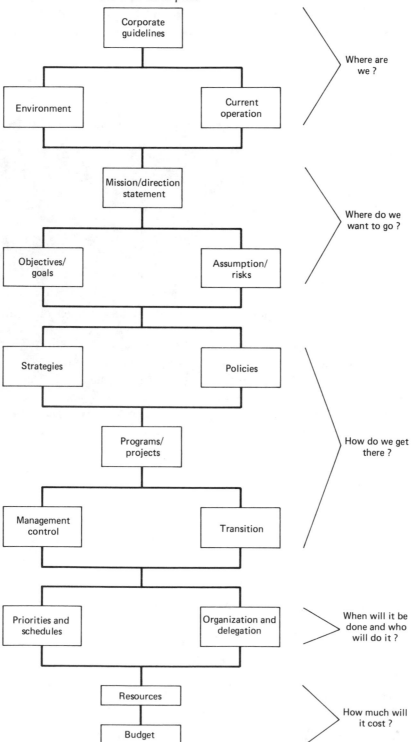

3. Current operations
   (a) Budget/organization
   (b) Strengths/weaknesses
   (c) Strategy/products
4. Mission/direction statement
   (a) Purpose or reason for IS
   (b) Main business of IS
   (c) Objectives of IS
   (d) Scope of users
5. Objectives/goals
   (a) Targets and time factors
   (b) Results expected
   (c) Qualitative and quantitative goals
6. Assumptions/risks
   (a) Internal and external constraints
   (b) Assumptions and potential consequences
   (c) Major risks
7. Strategies
   (a) Major strategies to reach objectives
   (b) Timing of strategies
8. Policies
   (a) Major current policies (internal and external to IS)
   (b) Projected policy changes required and time frame
9. Programs/projects
   (a) Current program-projects in process
   (b) New ones required
10. Management control tools
    (a) New procedures/methods needed
    (b) Timing and approach to develop new control techniques
11. Transition plans
    (a) Old environment
    (b) New environment
    (c) Plan to go from old to new
    (d) Necessary user and operational conditioning
12. Priorities and schedules
    (a) Ranking and prioritization of programs and projects

(b) Timing and schedule of programs/projects

13. Organization and delegation

(a) Organization to manage IS

(b) Delegation of authority and responsibility

14. Resource projections

(a) Equipment projections

(b) Software projections

(c) Facilities projections

(d) Personnel requirements (hiring, maintaining, training, developing)

15. Operating budget

(a) Incremental budget by new program/project or zero based

(b) New budget projected for each of planned years.

INFORMATION SYSTEMS AND COMPETITIVE ADVANTAGE

Michael Porter has developed several constructs that are quite useful for explaining competitive advantage systems and illustrating potential applications thereof. Figure 2.3 shows the first of the Porter constructs, the value chain.

The construct breaks down the things a company does to conduct business into functions called *value activities*. These activities start with inbound logistics through operations, then involve outbound logistics, and finish with sales and service. The price that customers are willing to pay for a product or service represents the "value" that the company creates. To the extent that the value is greater than the cost to produce the product or service, the company is profitable.

FIGURE 2.3. The value chain

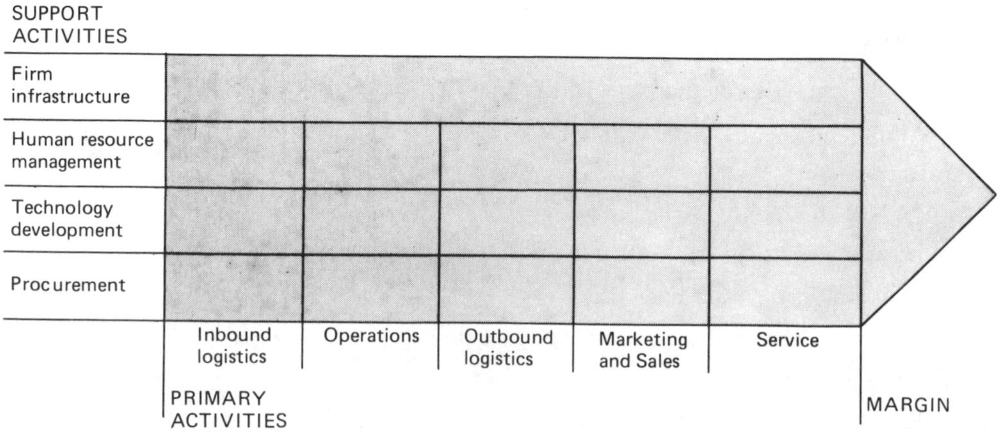

SUPPORT
ACTIVITIES

| Firm infrastructure |
| Human resource management |
| Technology development |
| Procurement |

Inbound logistics | Operations | Outbound logistics | Marketing and Sales | Service

PRIMARY ACTIVITIES   MARGIN

The value chain helps develop "leverage points" where costs can be contained or customer value can be developed.

The primary activities are familiar to business people: They start from supplies and materials coming into the company from outside vendors and suppliers (inbound logistics) and flow through operations, outbound logistics (the reverse of inbound) and include the marketing sales and the service to the customer, both presale and postsale.

The support activities that cut across all the primary activities include procurement; various technologies such as factory/warehouse automation and information technology; and human resource management, a function common to all enterprises. The infrastructure support includes general management, legal, accounting, and finance—which have jurisdiction over the entire chain.

It is important to realize that these value activities do not operate independently— there are important linkages between activities and this can prove a fruitful area for IS to add value. For example, self-diagnosis devices are designed into the product so that the product emits appropriate signals when the condition for potential breakdown is present. Likewise, just-in-time deliveries from suppliers can reduce inventory costs and reduce economical lot sizes so that the organization can be more responsive to customers. Global linkages are and will be playing a more significant role in competitive advantage. For example, if a company has installed PCs as direct ordering devices for their products, this may be extended to the European Economic Community (EEC) by providing foreign language ordering interfaces.

The important point is that information technology has become a vital factor affecting all points of the value chain, including the linkages between points as discussed in the foregoing. And the diversity and innovation found in new hardware and software, plus the rapidly improving performance to price ratio, are continually opening up new possibilities. This is not to mention products that will have technology built right into them, like logistics and maintenance computers in the dashboard of automobiles.

GENERIC COMPANY STRATEGIES

Another Porter construct states that a company gains competitive advantage over its competitors by:

Performing these value activities at lower cost,

Differentiating its product or service by the value activities, or

Filling the needs of a specialized market by the value activities.

These are termed the three *generic strategies* that give a customer a competitive edge. Each value activity can be influenced by information technology.

Let's now turn to possible approaches of using information technology within each of the three generic competitive strategy areas and emphasize the specific impact on benefits and cost.

The low cost strategy. If a company follows the low-cost-producer strategy, applications that take cost out of the product or service are considered strategic information systems. Tangible benefits are relatively easy to find in this situation. An example is automating a manual input process so that what is being done by 15 clerks will be accomplished by 5. Another tangible example is an inventory control system that reduces average inventory carried by $1 million. The carrying costs of that inventory—say at a rate of 20 percent—creates an annual saving of $200,000.

The aim of General Motors Corporation's Saturn plant in Tennessee was to produce a new line of small automobiles to compete with foreign cars. Manufacturing savings from computer-aided design and computer-aided manufacturing systems are projected by comparing new production processes with existing GM fabrication and assembly plants. The objective is to gain market share by being able to offer the lowest price.

Several companies are marketing IBM personal computer clones. These are personal computers that duplicate the logic and circuitry of the IBM personal computer. They differ from the IBM compatibles, which, although able to execute the software that runs on the IBM machines, are not identical in hardware structure. They are hardware, rather than software, compatible. Therefore, many IBM compatibles have functionality that goes beyond the IBM model; however, the clones do only what their IBM equivalent can do.

As one might imagine, the clones rely solely on a low cost strategy—that's their only competitive edge. Therefore, they must assemble the cheapest combination of components they can provide—memory chips, boards, power supplies, disk controllers, disks, printer boards, printers, keyboards, etc. An information system that can abet this low cost strategy is vital to success; for example, a data base of component items with associated costs and supplies, so that when there is a change in costs, they can immediately shift vendors or combinations of components. A simulation model can project the best combination of parts and components to produce the lowest cost, and historically show what cost savings can be attributed to the information model.

Differentiated product of service strategy. There are many examples of cases where IS has been the basis for a company's ability to differentiate its product or service. For example, putting terminals in key customer offices supports a differentiated product service, as it makes it easier for customers to buy from that supplier than from its competitor. In so doing, it locks in the customer and also increases sales. This is the strategy that was employed by American Hospital Supply.

A classic example is that of Coleco Industries, Inc., which differentiated its Cabbage Patch doll by giving each doll a name and providing adoption papers to each owner upon completion of an adoption form. Thereafter, Coleco sent a birthday card on the anniversary of the purchase of the doll. Obviously an information system was required to keep a data base on the millions of dolls that were sold each year along with their owners and their addresses. There was no question that this feature was attractive to the young market audience and added to the product's sales. Coleco is no longer in business because it couldn't produce another blockbuster product like the Cabbage Patch doll.

Specialized Market Strategy. The Chrysler Corporation, with its Jeep line, has a specific market niche, selling to what might be called the luxury summer home population or camping market. This four-wheel-drive market is vital to Chrysler, and an information system that abets this strategy is in the competitive-edge category. Chrysler sends letters to Jeep Wagoneer owners, offering them a VIP identification card and special service plans emphasizing that the owner has acquired a special car and will be treated accordingly. The VIP support system seeks to establish brand loyalty and also to encourage Jeep owners to act as references to prospective buyers. A computer system that facilitates this process is important to Chrysler.

Fidelity Investment Inc., like many investment and banking institutions, is going after an emerging market segment, the home computer market. Fidelity has extended a service to the home whereby a customer can gain access to investment information (broad economic trends and statistics, as well as individual company product and financial data). In addition, home investors have access to real-time stock quotes and can place buy and sell orders via their home computers, which are tied to Dow Jones Information Services and Fidelity computer systems. This is a good example of focus on a special market segment; indeed Fidelity, according to industry statistics, has captured about half the on-line brokerage business originating from the home.

Porter's three generic strategies are a good starting point for viewing the way IS can abet or even be the principle source of a strategic advantage. We now turn to another Porter model, keeping in mind that they are all related.

COMPETITIVE FORCE MODEL

Another Porter construct is the competitive force model, see Figure 2.4. This shows four forces that determine the competitive structure and profitability of an industry. This model has proven an excellent vehicle for discussing the competitive position of companies and particularly how IS can influence each of the five elements, thus reshaping the competitive positioning. A company wants to position itself so that it reduces the bargaining power of both its suppliers and buyers (customers). On the buyer side, we have already discussed putting PCs into the offices of key customers, and if we allow them to tap our data base to find the latest pricing, quantities, and delivery times available, this will make them even more dependent on us. A comprehensive vendor listing and qualification model can provide alternate sources of supplies, thus removing the dependency on several large suppliers who could raise prices at inopportune times.

The high cost and expertise involved in developing sophisticated information systems can be a deterrent to new entrants to an industry. For example, the cost and complexity of an airline reservation system can discourage new competitors, while the advanced cash management systems that some financial institutions have developed can prove to be a similar deterrent for would-be competitors. On the other hand, flexible computer-aided manufacturing methods can turn out new products for entry into specialized niche markets, thus allowing a company quickly to enter specific new areas of opportunity.

A good example of a substitute product is fax communication in lieu of mail. The postal system, though in the public sector, is affected by fax as are companies, such as Federal Express, that handle written messages. It is conceivable that fax could cause a serious dent in or completely destroy the overnight mail portion of Federal Express

FIGURE 2.4. Competitive force model

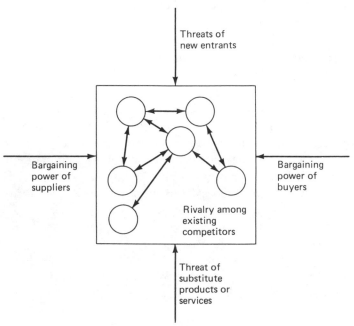

business. Another example of a substitute product created by information technology is the use of multimedia transmission and videoconferencing as a substitute for conferences and business meetings. This technology would have a dramatic impact on the travel and hotel business if electronic meetings became a viable substitute for face-to-face interaction.

Porter's constructs are valuable lenses through which to view the potential use of IS for strategic competitive advantage. Some say that this concept peaked in the eighties and that the strategic uses of IS have saturated the business world to the extent that—to use a poker phrase quoted from Max Hopper of American Airlines—"they were needed as openers but are no longer the trump cards." This caused a mild form of rebellion on the part of prominent spokespersons for strategic IS. Warren McFarlan of the Harvard Business School, Jim Wetherbe of the University of Minnesota, and other prominent practitioners and consultants don't feel that strategic systems are yet ready for the graveyard.

STRATEGIC IMPACT OF AN APPLICATIONS PORTFOLIO—
THE STRATEGIC GRID

Another construct that is a useful analytical tool is that developed by Cash, McFarlan, and McKenney of the Harvard Business School. Depending on the industry and the competitive environment of a company, there is more or less opportunity for IS to be a strategic commodity. It is important to know this because it has a major impact on the type of IS practices that are relevant.

The first step in assessing the strategic content of an applications portfolio is to develop a listing or inventory of major applications. It is important to maintain the proper detail level so that only the major information systems subsets are included—not every minor program. The listing should normally consist of no more than 40 to 50 systems. These applications should be plotted against the strategic grid (see Figure 2.5).

Batch billing or financial monitoring systems are examples of applications in the support quadrant. These systems normally do not have an impact on the key strategies of the business as they center on transaction processing at the operational level.

An on-line airline reservation system is an example of an application in the factory quadrant. This system is most definitely a strategic tool for an airline, and, since it is on-line, any downtime or interruption can be catastrophic. The factory quadrant implies that the system is mature and no major new developments or enhancements are planned, and that it operates as a factory to a manufacturer, turning out the product of the enterprise.

An application portfolio with development emphasis in the turnaround quadrant indicates that the company is moving toward a strategic focus of its IS function. Although current applications are not strategic in nature, future or planned applications most assuredly are.

Figure 2.6 indicates the activities or procedures that have proven effective for IS application portfolios in the support or strategic mode. Normally those applications falling in the factory quadrant of the strategic grid would benefit from the procedures listed in the support quadrant provided these applications are not subject to change—a major provision. In this capacity, driven by an industrial engineering focus, the objective is to improve efficiency (in response time, cost control, handling of increasing volumes, etc.) rather than to concentrate on effectiveness. Turnaround mode can normally benefit from a support focus for existing applications and a strategic focus for the major new applications.

In a review of an applications portfolio, anomalies often come to light. For example, it has been found that companies in support mode application areas often have high-level steering committees and high levels of user interaction. While a modicum of user involvement is useful, management is not overly concerned with support applications, which they feel can properly be the province of the IS staff with limited management review. The

FIGURE 2.5. The strategic grid

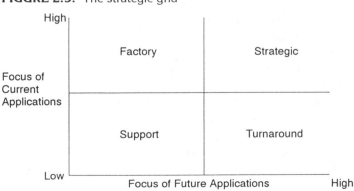

FIGURE 2.6. Activity procedure matrix

Activity or Procedure	Support	Strategic
Steering Committee	Low	High (Senior Management)
Planning	Low → Medium	High (Link to Corporate)
Risk Profile	Low → Medium	Medium → High
IS Reporting Level	Low	High
User Involvement	Low → Medium	High
Technical Involvement	Low	High
Expense Control Emphasis	High	Low → Medium
IS Director's Managerial Focus	Low → Medium	High
Business Skills Emphasis	Low → Medium	High

specifications are clear and new strategic ground is not being broken. Mis-matches of procedures for applications in different quadrants of the strategic grid can be quite counterproductive. Correcting these mis-matches can prove most beneficial.

FRAMEWORK FOR IDENTIFYING STRATEGIC OPPORTUNITIES

A good deal of discussion has focused on the issue of how strategic or competitive systems came to be. One camp feels they just happened and the classic systems talked about are the products of circumstances or serendipity; that is, they were not methodically planned. Another view is that they are the by-products or outgrowth of other main line systems developed by companies. For example, companies have customer billing systems, and it was a logical extension for customers to enter orders directly into the system via PCs in their offices to expedite the process. This was really the start of electronic data interchange (EDI), which presents a multitude of opportunities for strategic systems—the point made is that it just evolved kind of naturally.

There are others who believe that strategic systems can be discovered and planned by a concerted management awareness and a process that can link that awareness to selection and implementation. Charles Wiseman has written about such a process in his book on strategic information systems, a book which, by the way, has sold seven times the number of copies in Japan as in the United States. The Japanese must feel that strategic systems are still important and that there is a process whereby they can be discovered. Wiseman builds (extends) on the Porter construct by providing what he calls the framework for identifying strategic information systems (SIS) opportunities (see Figure 2.7).

Along the y axis are the strategic thrusts including Porter's differentiation and cost, but three new thrusts are added; innovation, growth, and alliance. Innovation allows the introduction of a product or service that completely transforms the way business is conducted in a particular industry. Growth means achieving competitive advantage either by volume or by geographical expansion. This is a particularly pertinent area with the increased emphasis on the global nature of business. Alliance is an extremely important part of the strategic equation—mergers and acquisitions, not the conglomerate kind, but the synergistic kind where there is a natural fit of product or service or marketing channel that can present strategic opportunities.

FIGURE 2.7. Framework for identifying strategic opportunities

Strategic Target

	Supplier	Customer	Competitor
Differentiation			
Cost			
Innovation			
Growth			
Alliance			

Strategic Thrust

The structure becomes a matrix that is quite useful by adding the x axis or, as Wiseman calls it, the strategic targets, which are the supplier, customer, or competitor (these have already been defined in Porter's model). With this model in mind, a company went about the process of uncovering strategic opportunities. Figure 2.8 describes the actual process. Following a tutorial on the subject of SIS, the group participating in the discovery process analyzed a set of actual SIS microcases that were drawn from a variety of industries. These were discussed in relation to the matrix (Figure 2.7). After a review of the company's competitive position, subgroups were formed to generate SIS possibilities and then to discuss them with the total group to eliminate duplication and consolidate ideas. The groups were assigned to brainstorm on different parts of the matrix. The remaining SIS ideas were then evaluated based on selection criteria, and so-called blockbuster ideas were chosen for further analysis.

Figure 2.9 shows the evaluation criteria, bringing in the elements of cost, technology and resources required, and the risk of the project failing or not meeting original specifications. It is interesting that, in the case discussed, each of three brainstorming sessions generated over 100 SIS ideas; there was no scarcity of creative juices. There was a weeding out process while looking for blockbuster ideas (defined as those with potential to give the company strategic dominance) and near-blockbuster ideas (those with very high potential but not quite blockbuster scope). In this particular situation, the company rated the top eleven proposals; six were termed blockbusters, and five were classified as very high potential. The company thought the project most useful and has since scheduled additional SIS sessions. The company has made this process a required preliminary to the regular, long-range planning process and has implemented some of the ideas generated. The total

FIGURE 2.8. SIS idea-generation steps

Step	Activity	Purpose
1	PRESENT TUTORIAL ON COMPETITIVE STRATEGY AND SIS	Introduce the concepts of strategic thrusts, strategic targets, and competitive strategy
2	APPLY SIS CONCEPTS TO ACTUAL CASES	Raise consciousness about SIS possibilities and their strategic thrusts and targets
3	REVIEW COMPANY'S COMPETITIVE POSITION	Understand competitive position of the business and its strategies
4	BRAINSTORM FOR SIS OPPORTUNITIES	Generate SIS ideas in small groups
5	DISCUSS SIS OPPORTUNITIES	Eliminate duplication and condense SIS ideas
6	EVALUATE SIS OPPORTUNITIES	Evaluate competitive significance of SIS ideas
7	DETAIL SIS BLOCKBUSTERS	Detail each SIS blockbuster idea, its competitive advantage, and key implementation issues

FIGURE 2.9. SIS evaluation criteria

• Degree of competitive advantage

• Cost to develop and install

• Feasibility (technology and resources)

• Risk

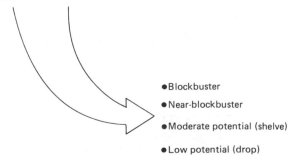

• Blockbuster

• Near-blockbuster

• Moderate potential (shelve)

• Low potential (drop)

the few attempts to systematically analyze and look for opportunities to use IS as a strategic weapon.

CRITICAL SUCCESS FACTORS

Another technique that has proven quite helpful for developing a management view of what is important is employment of critical success factors (CSF) analysis. CSFs, as defined by Dr. John F. Rockart, Director of the Center for Information Management Research at MIT, are the few key areas where things must go right if the business is to flourish. For any business there exists a limited number of areas in which results, if they are satisfactory, will ensure competitive performance for the organization. CSFs do not comprise a list of 15 to 20 items; the key is that there are only 5 to 8, and the secret is to be able to cull the list down to those crucial items. Once agreed on, these few CSFs can guide the actions of management and the company. Priorities are set and the executive's time and attention must be on these five to eight critical matters. CSFs are a focusing and concentration force.

Objectives are distinguished from CSFs, as the former represent goals or endpoints, and CSFs are the driving forces or means to achieve the endpoints. Several examples bring this out. In one of the earlier examples, Dr. Rockart interviewed the dean of the Sloan School of Management at MIT. Starting with a list of 25 or so, it was eventually culled to the following three:

Quality students

Quality faculty

Reputation

The goals were outstanding education and outstanding research; these were objectives. It soon became apparent that the keys to obtaining these objectives were to have the best possible student body and the best possible faculty; the education and research would follow. Also important was maintaining the reputation of a top management school. An example occurred just after the list was compiled: One of the school's economic professors did a television ad for a trucking company. The dean immediately told the professor this was not helping the image of the Sloan School, and the ad was canceled. This was a top priority item and action had to be taken quickly as a CSF was involved. It is apparent that finance, fundraising, and the like are not on the list. While this may be critical for other schools, it was not for MIT—the thinking being that with the best students, faculty, and image, the funds would follow.

Another example of CSFs is a grocery supermarket chain. The objectives are straightforward, involving the meeting of profit and return on assets goals. Assuming the proper store location, since this is obviously a very important overriding success factor, it has been found that there are five CSFs:

Product mix

Balanced inventory

Service

Sales promotion

Price

Product mix is very important—that is, having the items that people demand and will not accept a substitute for, such as certain spaghetti products in an Italian community or other offerings desired by specific ethnic groups. Because most of the assets of a supermarket are tied up in inventory, having just the right amount is very important—not being short of items, but also not having surplus stock. Service is also crucial, such as automatic checkout lanes that operate efficiently, and help and advice on meat and deli items. Sales promotion that attracts customers to the store and using the media that are seen most by customers represent another CSF. Price is obviously an important CSF, particularly in poorer neighborhoods.

In a study of the senate of a large state, a study that included intensive interviews as well as a questionnaire to each of the 38 senators, the following senate objectives and CSF list were developed. It was found quite helpful in guiding subsequent systems development.

Goals:

    Favorable constituency perception

    Sponsorship and enactment of pertinent legislation

    Participation in positive programs

CSFs:

    Develop experienced, competent, and loyal office staff

    Have timely access to relevant information

    Ensure judicious prioritization and usage of time

    Maintain positive communications with constituents

    Command respect and support of peers

    Manage to CSFs of associates

CSFs within a company are hierarchical and are determined by a number of factors (see Figure 2.10). Companies operate in a society or environment and within an industry. That society is becoming more diverse and global while competition within an industry has intensified. A look at the general CSFs of competing in tomorrow's business environment and competing with companies in a specific industry is a starting point for analyzing one's company, department, and individual CSFs. A company has an overall set of CSFs that should guide every department and individual in the company, but beneath these are specific CSFs oriented to the objectives of the department and the objectives of the individual.

Another important concept is that there will always be what are termed *temporal factors* (Figure 2.10). These are distinguished from overall longer-range CSFs because they arise from a current condition that may have to be faced and resolved while still maintaining a focus on long-term CSFs. In some cases, they may be called *short-termed crises*. An example could be a cash flow problem caused by the government's slowdown in paying

FIGURE 2.10. Critical success factors

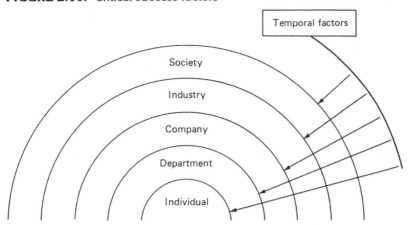

bills. Cash flow becomes a temporal CSF that must be faced but not at the expense of maintaining emphasis on the derived CSF list. It is a case of balancing short and long term, a situation that has been true since the first business enterprise.

Figure 2.11 shows how the CSF process can be a guide to long-range planning. A well thought-out series of interviews and meetings can transform individual CSFs into a departmental and overall organization set. This forms an umbrella for determining what data are necessary to measure and support these CSFs and what systems development efforts are needed to produce this information. The data may come as a by-product of the internal

FIGURE 2.11. CSF procedure for IS planning

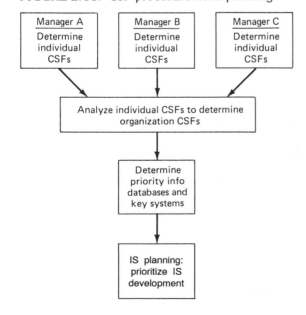

transaction systems already in place, from outside sources of data, or from entirely new applications that may have to be built. The question must continually be raised: If what I am working on is not somehow tied to a departmental or company-wide CSF, how important is it that I continue to expend my energy on it?

SUMMARY

The theme of this chapter has been planning and the foundation thinking that underscores a planning effort. The change model as developed in the Nolan stages was reviewed as a starting point—the stage a company is in may dictate the planning process employed. General principles of good planning were reviewed. Planning is not an academic, esoteric exercise. It should be viewed as a basis for action. Humorous views of planning have emerged over the years, among them being the dictums, "Ready, Fire, Aim" and "Losing Sight of the Forest and the Trees." The first implies a shotgun, short-term, reactive approach, while the latter suggests planning can become so long-range and visionary that reality is lost. Effective planning falls somewhere between these two extremes.

The concept of IS as a strategic force was emphasized. Several constructs that have proven useful were reviewed. The Porter models were described featuring the value chain, which helps to view how systems can be used for competitive advantage. The Wiseman construct presents a technique for actively seeking out opportunities for focusing systems on what he terms *blockbuster ideas.* Finally the critical success factor concept was viewed as a way to consolidate management thinking into a set of selected high-priority CSFs, those few activities one needs to do well in order to succeed. CSFs present an easily understood approach that can be used in concert, or in some cases, in lieu of the other planning concepts discussed in this chapter. We now turn to ways to build an information model or architecture that forms the structure for carrying out one's long-range plans.

Case Study

Global Networking at Federal Express

Almost overnight, Federal Express Corporation created the marketplace that it continues to dominate. Prior to inception of Federal Express in 1973, there was no overnight delivery service—certainly not on the scale envisioned by Federal Express president and CEO Fred Smith. Smith's novel idea, by now, is well known and well understood: a hub and spoke logistics network that enables a package originating in one location to end up, by 10:30 the

From *Stage by Stage,* William R. Synnott, Nolan, Norton, and Co., Lexington, MA, 1991.

next morning, at another location *anywhere* in the United States. Thus was born a new paradigm for the physical movement of materials through the country.

INFRASTRUCTURE OF THE EARLY YEARS

The founder of Federal Express understood that the physical transport of packages from one location to another was only half the business battle. Gathering, maintaining, and tracking information—about the packages, about the senders, receivers, drivers, and couriers—was the other half. Any package that was important enough to warrant sending via overnight delivery was assumed to be so important that people would want information about its whereabouts at any time between the moment it left their hands and the moment it arrived in the hands of the recipient.

Within several years of Federal Express' first flights into the night skies over Memphis they had implemented the COSMOS information systems. COSMOS was a customer history data base that any customer service operator in the company could access to provide information about a package. COSMOS has grown into a customer information system that enables Federal Express to track a package every time it changes hands or direction. A customer inquiring about the whereabouts of a package can be told not just that it was picked up at 6 P.M., but that the package is, at that moment, in this or that location, on this or that leg of its journey. Not only has COSMOS helped Federal Express maintain an on-time delivery rate in excess of 99 percent, but it has enabled the company to include detailed information about deliveries and recipients on more than 99 percent of its customer invoices. For Federal Express, this capacity translates directly into revenues, for customers receiving invoices without recipient and time of delivery information can ask Federal Express for a refund.

DEVELOPING THE NETWORK

The phenomenal amount of information captured maintained in the COSMOS data base is largely a function of the implementation of barcode scanning technology at all stages of the logistics network. Couriers and drivers scan packages as they are picked up; the information is relayed from the truck to the local Federal Express office via mobile digital radio (where possible), where it is sent, via a domestic network backbone consisting of 59 T1 trunk lines, to the main COSMOS processing center in Memphis. Within five minutes of pickup, Memphis knows where that package is and where it is going.

As the package moves towards its destination, other barcode scanners record its passage: through the originating hub, through the clearing hub, through the receiving hub, through the doors of the delivery truck. Within five minutes of the arrival of the package, the COSMOS data base in Memphis has been updated with the information of the arrival.

For customers, the COSMOS capabilities ensure the timely delivery of information about their packages; for Federal Express, the COSMOS capabilities go much further. Not only does the company know where a single package is at all times, they also have all the information about all the packages moving through a given hub and all the packages on a given plane, and this information has enabled Federal Express to alter the way it does business.

Federal Express has been able to use its information technology and its information network to bypass the Memphis superhub in some cases. No longer do packages originating in New York, for instance, need to pass through Memphis on their way to Boston. The information in the network enables Federal Express to implement local routing practices that move these packages more efficiently than ever. As a result, Federal Express has been able to increase its carrying capacity, which had been defined by Memphis International Airport's capacity to accommodate Federal Express' fleet of planes.

The information in the network is also used on the local level to increase the efficiency of pickup and delivery. Because the trucks and drivers are connected to the network via radio the drivers can be told, while en route, that they should modify their routing plans to pick up several more packages. But the system does not stop there: information fed to the drivers includes the optimal driving route, the location of the pickup on the street or in the building, the name of the contact person, and, finally, a new optimized pick up schedule. In short, the network brings real-time optimization to the business of picking up packages.

STUDY QUESTIONS

1. What is the biggest advantage of COSMOS? What is the real payoff?
2. How does COSMOS change the type of people Federal Express needs for package delivery?
3. Do you think Federal Express imagined the add-ons to the basic system that occurred in subsequent years?
4. Is this an example of a strategic system that gives a company a competitive edge?

Case Study

Warburton Chemical

Paul Buchanan, Director of IS at Warburton Chemical, had called a meeting with his staff as a first step in developing a new IS strategy. Sam Warburton, the chairman and CEO, thought his company could be getting more from their information system investment and directed Buchanan to present him a plan of how to do it. The triggering event was a discussion Warburton had with a respected fellow executive. Though his firm was only a fraction of the size of Warburton Chemical, the executive had described the meaningful reports that he personally received from IS and how information technology had given them a leg up on their competition. Sam Warburton was deeply concerned as he thought of IS performance in his company.

Warburton Chemical had been a Sam Warburton creation since its founding some 25 years earlier. It had grown rapidly under the owner's entrepreneurial reins and now had sales in excess of $500 million. There were strong rumors that Warburton was considering an acquisition offer from a large oil company.

Buchanan opened the meeting by indicating that their systems must be more user oriented. They had emphasized the operational, lower-level applications and had spent an inordinate amount of time and money fine-tuning, rewriting, and upgrading the old programs when there were far more important management applications. The rest of the meeting was spent on a review of the Warburton organization, the various departments, and the individual department managers. It was obvious that Sam Warburton ran the company with his unique personal style and that the organization had developed in an unorthodox way. For example, though planning was not a strong function with the company, the planning director reported to the vice president of engineering, who was one of the most influential executives. It was also an anomaly that Finance had responsibility for purchasing and inventory control—two functions normally in the bailiwick of manufacturing. All this surprised the IS group, because it was the first time they had really thought about it. Also they wondered what its relevance was to them anyway, and why an entire meeting was spent reviewing people and their organizations. Each person present had a huge backlog of work, and this type of meeting wasn't helping them get at it. Buchanan knew that the talk of the possible acquisition had reached all of them, and he concluded the meeting by asking what impact such a move would have on their systems efforts and particularly their future direction. The consensus was that this was for the higher echelons to worry about; their job was to continue with their current applications and to make them run as efficiently as possible.

Buchanan mulled over the meeting in his mind and pondered his next step. His background had been technical; an engineer by education with a sharp computer bent, he had joined Warburton five years earlier and had always impressed the executives with his grasp of the job and his quick answers to technical questions. Now he wondered whether it was a new ball game and whether he had the skills or background called for in this new arena.

He was uneasy, too, about his staff's reaction to the meeting. Though they were conscientious and attentive, he sensed a real concern on their part. Planning, strategy, and organization were all new terms to them. He didn't want to stretch them too much, because he considered them one of the best technical groups in the industry, a group that knew how to build applications and how to get something up and running on a computer. Turnover in his group had been low—in a market where good system analysts and programmers were in great demand.

STUDY QUESTIONS

1. Is this a good time for Buchanan to introduce his new idea?
2. What is the significance of Warburton's organization to the IS group?

3. Is there a danger in developing systems aimed at particular individuals rather than at specific business processes? What happens when changes occur in organizations?

4. What do you think of the attitude of Buchanan's staff? Do you think it is a normal one? A desirable one?

5. What is it going to take to satisfy Sam Warburton? What should be Buchanan's reply to his comment about getting more from IS?

6. What should be Buchanan's long-range strategy for IS? How should he go about developing it?

SELECTED REFERENCES

Administration of Information Resources, Report 187545 (Sept. 1980). New York: The Diebold Research Program.

Alloway, Robert M., *Defining Success For Data Processing*, WP1112-80. Cambridge, MA: Center for Information Systems Research, Sloan (MIT), March 1980.

Bullen, Christine V. and John F. Rockart, *A Primer on Critical Success Factors,* Cambridge, MA: Center for Information Systems Research, June 1981.

Couger, Daniel J., "Low Social Need Strengths (SNS) of Computer Professionals and the Impact on Curriculum Design," *Proceedings of the First International Conference on Information Systems* (December, 8-10, 1980), Philadelphia, Penn.

Diebold, J., "Information Resource Management—The New Challenge," *Infosystems* (1979), pp. 50-53.

Hammer, Michael, "Reengineering Work: Don't Automate, Obliterate." *Harvard Business Review*, July-August 1990 Number 4, p. 104.

Hopper, Max D., "Rattling SABRE—New Ways to Compete on Information," *Harvard Business Review*, No. 3, (May-June 1990), p. 118.

Kanter, Jerome, "MIS Long Range Planning," *Infosystems,* Hitchcock Publishing Co., June 1982.

Matlin, Gerald L. "IBM: How Will Top Management React?" *Infosystems* (Oct. 1980), pp. 40-48.

McFarlan, F. W., "Management Audit of the EDP Department," *Harvard Business Review* (1973), pp. 131-142.

McKenney, James L. and Warren F. McFarlan, "The Information Archipelago—Maps and Bridges," *Harvard Business Review* (September-October 1982), pp.109-119.

McLean, E., and J. Soder, *Strategic Planning for MIS*. New York: Wiley-Interscience, 1977.

MIS Planning for 1981-1983. The Diebold Research Program Working Session 80-2 (1980).

Nolan, R.L., "Business Needs a New Breed of EDP Manager," *Harvard Business Review* (1976), pp. 283-293.

Nolan, R.L., "Managing the Computer Resource: A Stage Hypothesis," *Comm. ACM 16,7* (1973), pp. 283-293

Nolan, R.L., "Managing the Crisis in Data Processing," *Harvard Business Review* (1979), pp. 115-126.

Nolan, R.L., "Managing Information Systems by Committee," *Harvard Business Review* (1982), pp. 72-79.

Porter, Michael, *Competitive Strategy: Techniques for Analyzing Industries and Competitors.* New York: Free Press, 1980.

Porter, Michael, *Competitive Advantage: Creating and Sustaining Superior Performance.* New York: Free Press, 1985.

Porter, Michael E., "How Information Gives You Competitive Advantage," *Harvard Business Review*, (July-August 1985), pp. 149-160.

Rackoff, Nick, Charles Wiseman, and Walter A. Ullrich, "Information Systems for Competitive Advantage: Implementation of a Planning Process." *MIS Quarterly* (December 1985).

Rockart, J.F., "Chief Executives Define Their Own Data Needs," *Harvard Business Review* (1979), pp. 81-93.

Wiseman, Charles, *Strategic Information Systems* Homewood, Ill.: Richard D. Irwin, 1988.

Withington, F.G., "Coping with Computer Proliferation," *Harvard Business Review* (1980), pp. 152-164.

Chapter **3**

Business Models and Information Systems Architecture

INTRODUCTION

The contents of this chapter fit between the IS long-range plan and the design phase of the application development cycle. The methodology of building a business model and understanding the business are essential prerequisites to establishing application priorities and then implementing them.

This chapter explores in more detail the business processes first described in Chapter 1. Figure 1.11 depicted the basic processes that are the building blocks of an information system. We will now delve deeper into these processes, illustrating how they can be identified, classified, and placed in proper perspective to one another.

The way to approach IS development is to look first at the broad road map and then break it down into progressively finer and finer detail until individual milestones are established. In actual practice, the development involves working at the problem from both ends. It is similar to establishing an annual plan for a business operation. Theoretically, the best approach is to work from the top down, with top management expressing the basic strategies and goals of the organization and then passing them down to lower levels of management for use as guidelines in establishing lower-level plans. In reality, time pressures and feedback requirements necessitate simultaneous work plans. These plans, worked both from the top down and the bottom up, are correlated at various stages in the planning cycle. Thus, while the general flow is top down, there are a series of interactive feedback loops before finalization of the plan. This is true with information systems.

A series of matrices are described that analyze the interrelationships of four entities: the organization, business processes, information systems, and data base. These views stress the interdependence of these elements in building an information architecture that can support the business, currently and into the future. While some systems operate across the entire organization, others are departmental or individually focused and can operate as separate entities. Frameworks employed in this chapter assist one in making the distinctions.

A discussion of IS architecture concludes the chapter. The metaphor is a city architect who cannot design a city or a highway system without knowing existing electrical systems, environmental factors, communication systems, and a host of other elements. So the information systems architect must consider geography, people and culture, hardware and software platforms, and communication networks. The successful architect must properly balance these factors.

BUILDING THE BUSINESS MODEL

The approach to IS is first to develop a business model comprised of the business processes or activities that are the essence of the business. This is not a mathematical model, but the portrayal of a business as one large system showing the interconnection and sequence of the business subsystems or processes that comprise it. The procedure to accomplish this is described in Figure 3.1. The arrows denote that the planning is accomplished from the top down while the implementation is from the bottom up. Based on business strategy and objectives (the long-range plan), a business model comprised of business processes is developed. These processes are managed and controlled by various individuals in various organizations. The IS is developed to provide the required information to the organization to manage the processes that are part of the business model. The data base is the source of information and drives the IS.

As we have seen, business can be viewed as a system itself, pumping products or services through its operation while deploying money, people, facilities, and material as its resources. Information is not listed as a resource, as this is the area on which we will concentrate in building an IS. It will be added as we go. Figure 3.2 shows the concept of business as a system.

The easiest way to understand the processes that underlie a management information system is to use an example. The example we use here is a typical company in the food-distribution business. We could equally well have chosen a distributor of any type of product or group of products, a manufacturer, an insurance company, a bank, an educational or government operation, a hospital, or a service company. The type of company is relatively unimportant; the general principles of business-process analysis and classification and the methodology of looking at a company's information system to support a series of interlocking subsystems, are applicable and pertinent across industry lines. We now build a business model of a distributor.

Our business-process model begins with the sales activity or sales process. It has been often stated that "nothing begins until something is sold." This point is certainly valid, and

FIGURE 3.1. Building an MIS

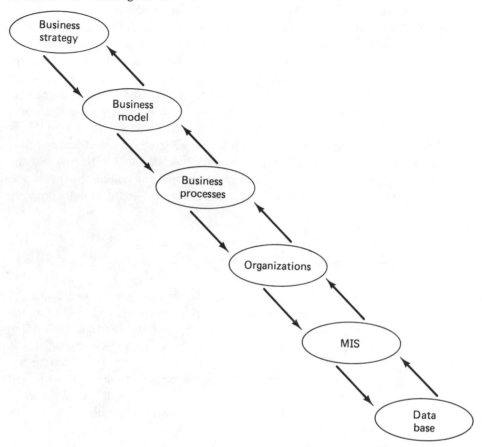

FIGURE 3.2. Business as a system

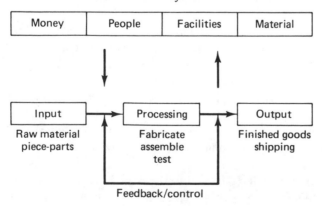

we will see that sales-order processing is a primary process interconnected to other processes that comprise our model. Figure 3.3 is the starting point of the business model.

It is obviously important to satisfy customer demand, for doing so is the principal reason for being in business. Management should continually strive to give the customer the best product at the best price, and at the same time should realize a profit in line with the product being offered. The basic cycle starts here, because what goes out of the stores must be replaced. As the shelves in the store are depleted, certain store-order operations are put into play that result in the reorder of goods to replenish the shelves. The store will reorder goods on the basis of turnover and the lead time required to replenish the item. The store order is one of the basic source documents that initiates a long series of activities throughout many departments. This document enters the first of the processes—that of order processing. This process screens the orders for errors in omission as well as commission, and ensures that the order is valid before it proceeds further into other processes. The connecting arrow to accounting processing indicates that the order is the basis for setting up accounts receivable and eventually reconciling the cash payment for the goods.

Another source document is the record of sales or the movement of items from the store. This source document will eventually produce meaningful sales statistics and analyses as output from the accounting and marketing processes.

FIGURE 3.3. The order-processing, stores-control, and account processes

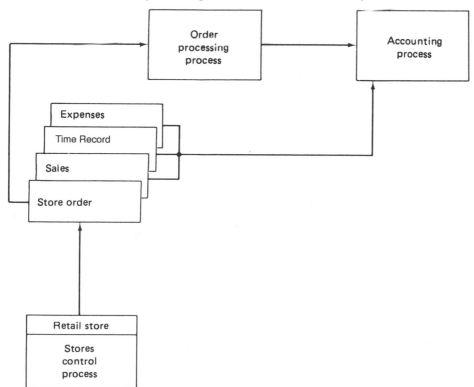

In addition to the store and the record of sales, it takes people to run a store, and they must be paid according to services rendered. A time record represents the medium for recording hours worked; in Figure 3.3 it is shown entering the accounting subsystem. Similarly, the expenses of store operation (heat, light, and maintenance) are recorded and entered into the accounting process. This would be the case only if the company controlled its own stores (as in a chain operation).

The stores-control process is now seeing the impact of automated information systems. Checkout-counter devices can optically read imprinted prices and item numbers on products, automatically producing the customer sales total and recording as a by-product the item and quantity sold as input into the order-processing subsystem. Another activity within the stores-control process is the scheduling of checkout personnel based on a simulation of activity through the store as a reflection of historical sales patterns and known conditions. For example, a study can indicate the requirement for a Thursday and Friday when Saturday is a holiday; also it is known that about 70 percent of the business for the week is done on Friday, Saturday, and Sunday. These factors can be reflected in a queuing model to assist in the scheduling of personnel.

Figure 3.4 adds the inventory control subsystem as well as the materials control and transportation processes. After the store order has been validated by the order-processing process, it moves to the inventory control process, where it must be screened against the

FIGURE 3.4. Addition of inventory-control, materials-control, and transportation processes

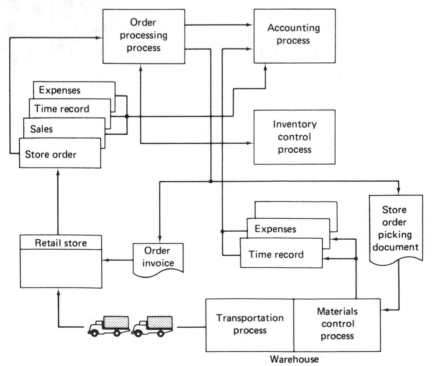

current inventory in the warehouse. This process is indicated by the two-way arrow connecting the order-processing and inventory control processes. If there is sufficient inventory on hand, order-processing produces a store-order picking document for the warehouse and an order invoice for the retail store. Since employee labor and operating expenses were recorded at the store level, they must be recorded at the warehouse level. These items can be seen entering the accounting process in Figure 3.4. The blank record is explained in Figure 3.5.

The materials control and transportation processes are excellent examples of how integrated processes operate. For example, the basic information on orders and movement from the warehouse can be used to lay out warehouse space more efficiently. Similarly, the information on each order, such as the cubic content and weight of items comprising the order, can be used to load and route trucks. These valuable by-products can often be real payoff applications. Thus, the same basic raw data is processed in a little different way to help in handling another functional activity.

Figure 3.5 adds another process to the overall integrated model—the purchasing process. This process depends on the strength of the inventory control process. A well-conceived inventory control process provides for automatic ordering based on such considerations as customer service, economic order quantity, and lead time. Orders were screened against inventory records in Figure 3.4. When the inventory of particular items reaches a predetermined reorder point, the inventory control process directs the purchasing process to write a purchase order. The purchase order is made out and sent to the respective vendor or manufacturer. The vendor in turn fills the order, ships the product to the warehouse, and submits an invoice for entry into the accounting process. This process initiates accounts payable activity and the eventual reconciliation of cash payments. The arrow indicates the

FIGURE 3.5. Adding the purchasing process

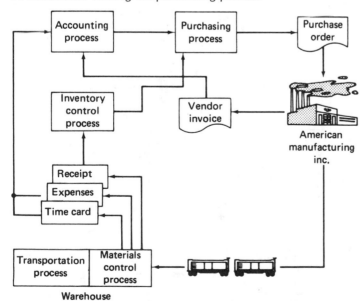

connection of the accounting and purchasing processes. It is significant to realize that most, if not all, of this could be accomplished by electronic data interchange (EDI).

The blank record of Figure 3.4 can now be identified as a receipt record. This record enters the inventory control process to update pertinent inventory records; it is also passed through to the accounting process to form the basis for vendor payment.

Figure 3.6 brings together the processes that have been mentioned up to this point. Two additional arrows have been added to the illustration. The first connects the inventory control and accounting processes. This step is necessary because inventory data are a requirement of accounting reports. The second arrow shows the important output of the accounting process. Accounting acts as the scorekeeper for all the processing mentioned thus far. It accumulates such data as store orders, cash sales, expenses, receipts, and vendor invoices, and from this basic source information produces a host of meaningful management reports. Three of these reports are noted in Figure 3.6—profit and loss statement (profitability by region, by store, or by department) or sales by salesperson or item grouping. The reports might also indicate inventory turnover or return on inventory investment.

The processes discussed thus far are basic ones common to most businesses. They

FIGURE 3.6. Basic processes

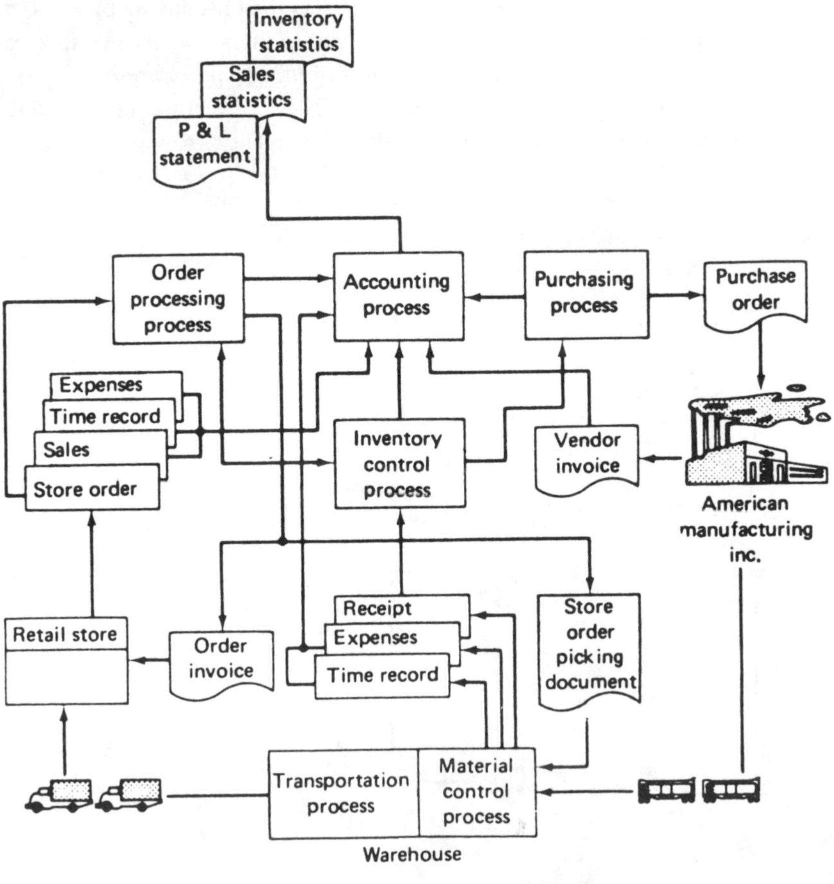

Warehouse

cover the operational control and management control activities discussed in Chapter 1. Figure 3.7 shows more advanced processes that can build on the basic ones already described.

Marketing and strategic planning are the processes that produce the real payoffs for a company. As a by-product of the basic processes, the marketing process uses the basic source data that have been collected and filed. However, the data are processed in different ways to answer specific management questions—questions such as the effect of promotion on sales; the effect of pricing changes and product mix; the comparative advantages of a limited, as compared with a full product line; the significance of store layout and shelf allocation on profit, and the desirability of introducing new items or product lines.

Another key output of the marketing process is the sales forecast. The forecast is based on historical sales movement (information coming from the accounting process) as well as on projected external events (buying trends, economic factors, and so on). The sales forecast is significant to all aspects of the business. It is shown in Figure 3.6 entering the inventory control process as a basis for establishing inventory policy, and entering the strategic planning process as a basis for influencing total company goals and objectives.

The strategic planning process is the core of the business model. It is here that the major company decisions are made. Reports produced by the accounting subsystems are digested, reviewed, and analyzed; overall company policies are determined and promulgated. In addition to the historical or internal data, the strategic planning process uses external data gathered from outside sources. On one side are the basic economic factors, such as trends in gross national product, political factors, and population growth; on the

FIGURE 3.7. Addition of marketing and strategic planning

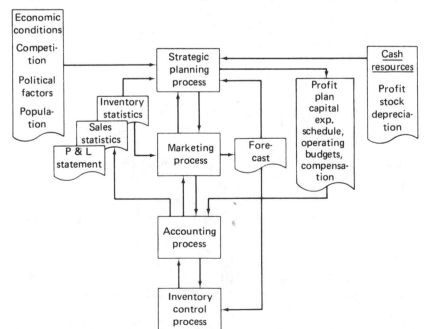

other side are the available cash resources, such as profit plow-back, new stock issues, and depreciation. The results of the strategic planning process are marketing policies as well as the profit, capital expenditure schedule, and operating budget. These figures enter the accounting process to form the basis of measuring actual operation. They form the yardstick for measurement. The cycle is thus completed. Figure 3.8 presents the complete integrated business model that we have been building in stages.

Figure 3.8 shows nine processes that comprise a business model. These nine are major processes, each of which can be further subdivided. For example, the financial and accounting process includes subprocesses for accounts receivable, accounts payable, general ledger, payroll, cost accounting, and the like. A significant point to bear in mind in planning an IS is to lay out the overall road map or model first. It is true that the initial focus may, for

FIGURE 3.8. Business model for a distribution company

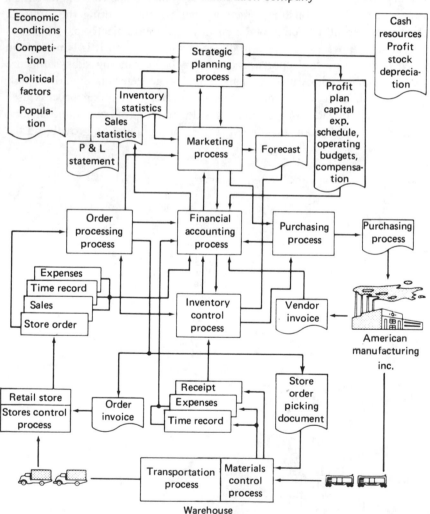

example, be on improving sales-order processing; however, this should be undertaken in light of where that particular process fits into the whole.

Middle and top management can understand a framework similar to that illustrated in Figure 3.8. Too often the first thing they are shown is a detailed flow chart of the order-processing cycle. This is discouraging to them, for they are unaware of where order processing fits into the overall process network and what part it will play in a management information system. Although interested and vitally concerned with improving the order cycle, thereby improving inventory turnover and reducing capital requirements, they would like to get a "feel" for how the by-product data from this application can help them pinpoint unfavorable sales trends by product line and store location, as well as suggest action to improve the situation. Developing a business model for your company in your industry is an important first step in developing and gaining the benefits of IS.

INTEGRATION AND INTERRELATIONSHIP OF PROCESSES

At the beginning of the Industrial Revolution, business was run by individual entrepreneurs who did the planning, selling, producing, accounting, and other necessary jobs. The basic data and information needed to carry out these duties were filed in the entrepreneur's head. The data processing system was integrated, because there was a central source of information from which sprung all policies, plans, and decisions. However, the tasks began to grow more complex until the entrepreneur could no longer handle all of them unaided. It became necessary to hire people to help, and to set up functional responsibilities, such as accounting, production, and engineering, and to assign people to these various functions. Functional specialization would be a later development. But as business evolved, the entrepreneur could not train people him- or herself. Colleges and universities offered to assist in the task. As university curricula were developed, fences began to appear that were to become the functional boundaries within a business—the accounting profession was formed, the advertising profession, and so on.

This is not to say that these functional boundaries were logical in nature; it just happened to be the way they were recognized within a business organization. With the entrepreneur we had a natural integrated system, but the growth of functional boundaries determines the kind of data utilized by the various groups and tends to limit the scope of problems and the vision of individuals tackling these problems. This explains, to a great extent, why early information systems emphasized accounting applications. The computer was under the control of the finance department, and the functional boundaries of accounting perpetuate applications like payroll, accounts receivable, and accounts payable.

This situation suggests a real challenge for management. The top executive must somehow get the various functional heads to coordinate their activities—to achieve the same effectiveness as the single entrepreneur. The integrated model is a prime vehicle for accomplishing this step, emphasizing that although the whole is made up of parts, the parts must not be so specialized and unique that their function as part of the whole is forgotten.

Obviously management cannot play a passive role in the design and development of an integrated system. Since the system crosses all functional boundaries, only top management can ensure that the computer will best serve the overall needs of the company and not be used for parochial interests.

Figure 3.8 enables the systems analyst or business manager to see the inter-relationships of processes. The tracing and interaction of key source data illustrate the necessity and practical implications of designing systems that avoid redundancy and take advantage of common data flows. The sales forecast is a prime example. The forecast is a key strategic tool in the operation of any company. First of all, a sales forecast is crucial to the planning process. It is the basis for determining whether a new item should be introduced or an entirely new product line developed. It forms the rationale for establishing plant capacity and long-range facility needs. It is a key determinant for budget preparation and profitability projection. In the operational and control area, the sales forecast determines purchasing policies (how much to order, when to order), manufacturing policies, work levels, hiring, training, quota setting, machine loading, inventory levels, and the like.

It would appear prudent to recognize the commonality and significance of the sales forecast and to take these elements into account in designing an information system. It is common to have a variety of forecasting systems, some of which are mutually inconsistent, in use within a single enterprise. Thus, the manufacturing manager may be formulating a production schedule on forecast A while the materials control manager, who is responsible for supplying raw materials to enable forecast A to be met, may be ordering on the basis of forecast B. This seems a strange way to operate, but some companies do operate this way. It is a classic example of a lack of system integration.

The preceding discussion does not imply that the same forecast should be used in every instance. Indeed, there may be logical reasons for using different forecasts. For example, it may be wise from an inventory standpoint to use a higher or more optimistic forecast, thus risking a chance of overstocking at a time when particular products are hard to procure. On the other hand, it may be logical to use a lower or more realistic forecast in setting sales and quota goals for salespeople lest their motivation and performance be adversely affected. The important point is that the concept of integration should be recognized: There should be a single function dedicated to sales forecasting. Forecasting should be accomplished by the group having access to the most current and meaningful data and having the ability to process best those data. All forecasts should emanate from the same quantitative data. If adjustments are desired to reflect various probabilities and risks, these adjustments should be made by the same group. Thus, a forecast could consist of a most likely, most optimistic, and most pessimistic outlook. The various departments could then select the forecast that represented the level of risk and management judgment that they thought best under the circumstances. However, in no case should the situation arise where the manufacturing manager and the materials manager use different forecasts—one second-guessing the other. In this case, they should get together, jointly agree on a forecast, and proceed to provide the necessary resources to meet it.

It is surprising, when reviewing a business model, to discover that almost all the information needed to drive it emanates from a rather small number of common source documents. It is also surprising to see the interconnection of processes that were thought to be entities in themselves but that are really connected by a common flow of data. A prime example is a purchase requisition. This document initiates a long series of activities, starting with the writing of a purchase order by the accounting department, and including the physical receipt of the goods, the quality control check, the updating of inventory records, the establishment of accounts payable, and eventual vendor payment. Thus, the purchase requisition affects the accounting, financial, quality control, receiving, purchasing, and inventory control functions. An integrated system approach recognizes, rather than ignores, these interrelationships. The system may begin with the automation of a specific function, but only after the total picture is studied. Then subsystems can be added after, with minimum effort and duplication.

ENTERPRISE VS. DEPARTMENT SYSTEMS

In building the IS model, the distinction is made between systems that are interdependent and those that can operate as an entity in themselves. Examples of the former have been presented. There are also many examples of the independent variety. A marketing or sales office can maintain a data file of its customers and prospects. If customer billing is done locally, there may be no reason why the sales office cannot maintain its own independent system. A distributor of a large manufacturer may be able to operate its own shipment and reordering system without reference to any central system. Because of the naturally decentralized way managers operate, it seems positive, whenever possible, to decentralize systems development and operation. The rule should be that wherever there is no major connection of one system to the other, systems should operate independently.

Later chapters show the positive reasons for distributed or decentralized operation. Technology has developed very positive decentralized economies where the processing power and data storage capacity are cheaper in small units. Economies of scale have been overturned. Also, software has been introduced that is powerful, yet easy to learn and operate. It is optimized for the unsophisticated or intermittent user of information. But more important than the hardware and software, it is a more natural and effective way to manage—that is to have direct control over the data and information that is pertinent to you. The decentralized mode holds even if some redundancy is necessary. For example, even if customer billing and accounts receivable is a centralized operation, it may be prudent to maintain duplicate customer files at the corporate office and in the marketing/sales office or department. Then the local office does not have to connect to corporate to obtain information on their customers; they have the information locally, under their own control. A good rule is that when there is any possibility of going one way or the other, it is always preferable to decentralize or distribute a function.

MANUFACTURING BUSINESS MODEL

Figure 3.9 adds six processes to the distribution model to produce a manufacturing model. Since most manufacturers perform, in some manner, the distribution function, the major difference between the two operations is that the distributor orders all manufactured items from a vendor while the manufacturer produces the items and orders only raw materials, assemblies, and piece parts. The physical facilities now include a factory as well as a warehouse.

The manufacturing model adds the engineering and research process (E&R), which

FIGURE 3.9. Business model for a manufacturing company

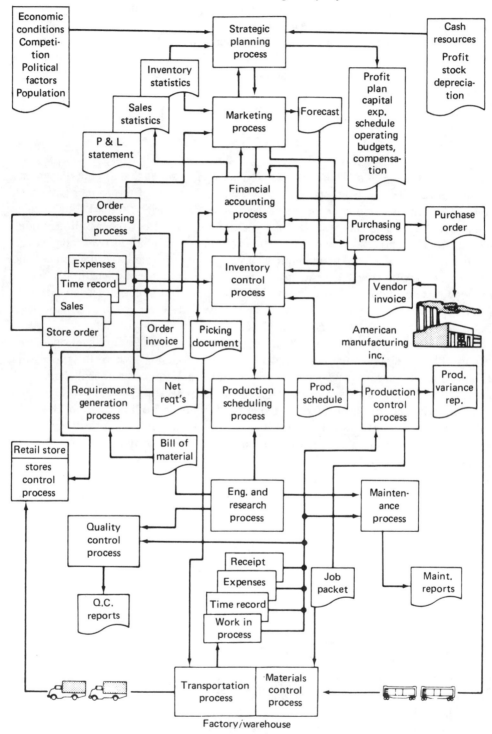

is a vital one to a manufacturing operation. The engineers design the products the company produces and develop bill-of-material and routing-sheet information. Basically, the bill of material indicates the components and assemblies (and quantities of each) required to build an end item, whereas the routing sheet indicates the type and sequence of production operations necessary to transform the raw materials and components into finished goods. The E&R process is also responsible for establishing requirements and standards for quality control and machine maintenance.

Figure 3.9 indicates the interrelationship of the E&R process with quality control, maintenance, production scheduling, and requirements generation. Let us see how these subsystems are tied together with the distribution processes described earlier.

The requirements-generation process takes finished-goods requirements (sales forecast plus sales orders minus finished-goods inventory) from the inventory control subsystem and, utilizing the bill-of-material information from the E&R process, determines the requirements for subassemblies, piece parts, and raw materials by multiplying the number of finished-goods items by the components that constitute each end item. The total for each subunit is then measured against inventory records to produce net requirements.

This netting process is direct input into the production scheduling process. The routing data, also supplied by the E&R process, is combined with net requirements to produce a production schedule. The production control process deals with the day-to-day implementation of the production plan by issuing job packets to the factory (telling them what jobs to work on, the sequence, the scheduled completion dates), accepting feedback (including labor, materials, expense, and work-in-process data), and producing a variety of quality control and maintenance reports and analyses. The result of these six manufacturing processes is to maintain an availability of finished-goods items in the warehouse to satisfy customer demand and interface to the distribution process (order processing, inventory control, accounting, and transportation), which has been described previously.

These types of models can be developed for other industries to form the basis for an information architecture and a comprehensive understanding of the business. Figure 3.10 is an insurance company model.

BUSINESS PROCESSES

Now that the business processes have been described and their interconnection illustrated, let us categorize or classify them. Doing so helps the IS designer determine where to start, what resources are necessary, what capabilities are required, the degree of difficulty to be expected, and the potential benefit to various levels of management. Figure 3.11 further classifies the fifteen processes illustrated in the manufacturing information model. The three major categories are supportive, mainstream, and administrative. The supportive category includes marketing, strategic planning, and engineering and research. The supportive processes differ from the mainstream processes in that the latter control the physical line operation of the business, the flow of raw materials through the plant into the hands of the ultimate consumer.

The supportive processes are obviously most significant in establishing the plans, budgets, and facilities, as well as the basic decision rules embedded in the mainstream processes; however, they differ from the line or mainstream functions. The administrative

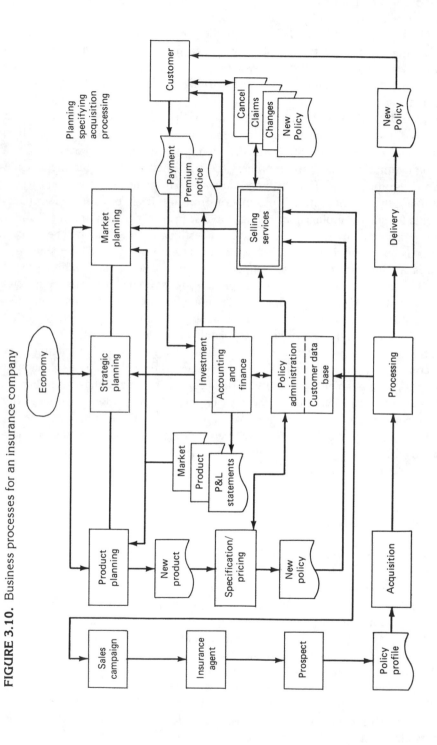

FIGURE 3.10. Business processes for an insurance company

FIGURE 3.11. Business-process classification

SUPPORTIVE

Marketing
Sales analysis
Sales forecasting
Advertising
Sales administration

Strategic Planning
Econometric models
Market models
Simulation
Decision theory
Investment analysis
Facilities planning

Engineering and Research
Design automation
Project control
Numerical control
Configuration management
Industrial engineering
Bill of material generation

MAINSTREAM

Sales Order Processing
Customer billing
Order filling
Transportation

Inventory Reporting and Control
Stock status reporting
Statistical replenishment.

Requirements Generation
Gross requirements generation
Net requirements generation

Production Scheduling
Fabrication and assembly scheduling
Shop loading
Issuance of job packets

Production Control
Performance vs plan analysis
Variance reporting

Purchasing
Receiving
Quality Control
Maintenance

ADMINISTRATIVE

Financial
Accounts receivable
Accounts payable
General ledger
Cost accounting
Fixed asset accounting
Budgeting
Financial models
Key rated analysis
Profit and loss statements

Personnel
Payroll
Payroll reports
Wage and compensation
analysis
Performance appraisals

Legal

processes involve the accounting for facilities and people necessary to run the business. These processes satisfy the external requirements of a business placed upon it by various government and regulatory agencies. Thus, taxes must be paid, profitability reported to the Securities and Exchange Commission, and the business operated within the framework of proper licenses and contracts.

Figures 3.12, 3.13, and 3.14 further characterize the processes on the basis of twelve criteria. An example will explain how to read the charts. The sales-analysis process is marketing supportive and aimed at operating and middle management. Sales-analysis reports are usually produced on a weekly basis; the decision rules required by the process are well understood, straightforward, and highly structured; and the complexity level of mathematics or computer processing required is low. The principal data base elements from which the necessary information is extracted are the customer and sales files. This type of data is internal to the company's operation (sales history) in contrast to external data (economic trends, buyer profiles), and the time demand is medium—that is, the information must be timely, but normally it can be produced on a scheduled basis. The transaction volume is heavy because the analysis is built from customer orders. Because the sales analysis can be scheduled and because it requires a compilation of data, the mode of operation is batch, though it could be on-line to improve responsiveness. The historical frequency of implementing this process is high, and because of the composite of characteristics, the degree of difficulty in implementing is low.

Additional study of the characteristics chart can help establish a priority analysis of processes based on the relative weights placed on the various criteria. Thus it may be wise to start with processes that are easy to implement; conversely, if the systems capability is present, the company may choose to tackle processes that are aimed at higher levels of management, thereby going after the bigger payoff and benefit.

SUPPORT ELEMENTS FOR THE BUSINESS MODEL

Referring back to Figure 3.1, we see that once the business model and business processes are identified, an IS is built to support the organization that performs these processes. A typical organization was reviewed in Chapter 1. Figure 3.1 also indicates that a data base underlines the IS. Data base is the subject of Chapter 4. The next step in understanding IS is to go through the following type of analysis.

A series of matrices is produced to show the connection and relationship of organizational entity, specific information system, and data base in relation to business processes. A series of four matrices or cross-comparisons are developed as indicated by the numbers 1 to 4. The four matrices are: (1) business process by organization, (2) business process by information system, (3) organization by data base, and (4) information system by data base.

1. Business Process by Organization

Figure 3.15 lists organization entities across the top and business processes down the side. An asterisk indicates that the particular organization has major responsibilities for the business process, while a solid dot indicates involvement in the process. In implementing

FIGURE 3.12. Supportive-process characteristics

Process	Type of function	Major management focus	Cycle	Form of processing	Processing complexity	Data base	Type of data	Time demand	Transaction volume	Typical mode of operation	Frequency of implementation	Difficulty of implementation
Sales analysis	Mktg. supp.	Opert'g & middle	Weekly	Structured	Low	Customer & sales files	Internal	Medium	Heavy	Batch	High	Low
Sales forecasting	Mktg. supp.	Middle	Monthly	Structured	High	Sales history	Internal	Low	Heavy	Batch	Med.	Med.
Advertising	Mktg. supp.	Middle	Monthly	Unstructured	High	Sales history	Internal external	Low	Light	Batch	Low	High
Sales administration	Mktg. supp.	Opert'g & middle	Daily	Highly struc.	Med.	Customer & inventory	Internal	Med. to high	Heavy	Direct & Batch	High	Low
Econometric models	Plan'g supp.	Middle & top	Monthly	Structured	High	Gen. Ledger accounting	Internal	Low	Light	Batch	Low	Med.
Market models	Plan'g supp.	Middle & top	Monthly	Unstructured	High	Sales history	Internal external	Low	Med.	Batch	Low	High
Decision theory	Plan'g supp.	Middle & top	Weekly	Unstructured	High	---	Internal external	Med.	Low	Batch	Med.	High
Investment analysis	Plan'g supp.	Middle & top	Monthly	Sturctured	Med.	Gen. Ledger accounting	Internal	Low	Low	Batch	Low	Med.
Facilities planning	Plan'g supp.	Middle & top	Monthly	Structured	Low	Gen. Ledger accounting	Internal	Low	Low	Batch	Low	Med.
Design automation	Engr'g supp.	Opert'g & middle	Daily	Structured	High	Product file	Internal	High	Med.	On line	Low	High
Project control	Engr'g supp.	All levels	Weekly	Structured	Low	---	Internal	High	Med.	On line	Med.	Med.
Numerical control	Engr'g supp.	Operating	Weekly	Structured	High	Product file	Internal	High	Med.	On line	Low	High
Configuration management	Engr'g supp.	Opert'g & middle	Weekly	Structured	Low	Product file	Internal	Low	Med.	Batch	Low	Med.
Industrial Engineering	Engr'g supp.	Opert'g & middle	Daily	Structured	Med.	Personnel file	Internal	Med.	Med.	Batch	Low	Med.
Bill of Mat'l generation	Engr'g supp.	Operating	Daily	Highly struc.	Med.	Product file	Internal	Med.	Heavy	Direct & batch	Med.	Med.

FIGURE 3.13. Mainstream-process characteristics

Process	Type of function	Major management focus	Cycle	Form of processing	Processing complexity	Data base	Type of data	Time demand	Transaction volume	Typical mode of operation	Frequency of implementation	Difficulty of implementation
Customer billing	Main-stream	Operating	Daily	Highly struc.	Low	Customer file	Internal	High	Heavy	On line	High	Low
Order filling	Main-stream	Operating	Daily	Highly struc.	Low	Customer file	Internal	High	Heavy	On line	High	Low
Transportation	Main-stream	Operating	Daily	Highly struc.	Med.	Cust.& vehicle	Internal	High	Heavy	On line	Med.	Low
Stock status reporting	Main-stream	Opert'g & middle	Daily	Highly struc.	Low	Inventory file	Internal	Med.	Heavy	On line	High	Low
Statistical replenishment	Main-stream	Operating	Daily	Structured	High	Inventory file	Internal	Med.	Heavy	On line	Med.	Med.
Gross Requirements gen.	Main-stream	Operating	Daily	Highly struc.	Med.	Inv. & product file	Internal	Med.	Med.	Batch	Med.	Med.
Net requirements generation	Main-stream	Operating	Daily	Highly struc.	Med.	Inv. & Prod file	Internal	Med.	Med.	Batch	Med.	Med.
Fabrication & Ass'y scheduling	Main-stream	Operating	Daily	Structured	High	Inv.Prod.& facil.file	Internal	Med.	Med.	Batch	Low	High
Shop loading	Main-stream	Operating	Daily	Structured	High	Inv.prod.& facil.file	Internal	High	Med.	On line	Low	High
Issuance of job packets	Main-stream	Operating	Daily	Structured	Med.	Inv,prod.& facil.file	Internal	High	Med.	Online	Med.	Med.
Performance vs plan analysis	Main-stream	Opert'g & middle	Weekly	Structured	Med.	Inv.work in process	Internal	Med.	Low	On line	Med.	Med.
Variance reporting	Main-stream	Opert'g & middle	Weekly	Structured	Med.	Inv.work in process	Internal	Med.	Low	On line	Med.	Med.
Purchasing	Main-stream	Operating	Daily	Highly struc.	Med.	Vendor file	Internal	Med.	Med.	On line	Med.	Med.
Receiving	Main-stream	Operating	Daily	Highly struc.	Low	Inventory file	Internal	High	Med.	On line	Med.	Low
Quality control	Main-stream	Opert'g & middle	Weekly	Structured	Med.	Product & facilities	Internal	Med.	Med.	On line	Low	Med.
Maintenance	Main-stream	Operat'g & middle	Weekly	Structured	Med.	Prod. & facil.file	Internal	Med.	Med.	On line	Low	Med.

FIGURE 3.14. Administrative-process characteristics

Process	Type of function	Major management focus	Cycle	Form of processing	Processing complexity	Data base	Type of data	Time demand	Transaction volume	Typical mode of operation	Frequency of implementation	Difficulty of implementation
Accounts receivable	Admin. finan.	Operating	Daily	Highly struc.	Low	Customer	Internal	Med.	Heavy	Batch	High	Low
Accounts payable	Admin. finan.	Operating	Daily	Highly struc.	Low	Vendor	Internal	Med.	Med.	Batch	High	Low
General ledger	Admin. finan.	Operating	Weekly	Highly struc.	Low	Acct'g	Internal	Low	Low	Batch	Low	Low
Cost accounting	Admin. finan.	Opert'g & middle	Weekly	Structured	Med.	Inv. & gen.ledger	Internal	Med.	Low	Batch	Med.	Med.
Fixed asset accounting	Admin. finan.	Opert'g & middle	Weekly	Highly struc.	Low	General ledger	Internal	Med.	Low	Batch	High	Low
Budgeting	Admin. finan.	All levels	Monthly	Structured	Med.	General ledger	Internal external	Med.	Low	Batch	Med.	Med.
Financial models	Admin. finan.	Middle & top	Monthly	Structured	High	General ledger	Internal external	Low	Low	Batch	Low	High
Key ratio analysis	Admin. finan.	Middle & top	Monthly	Structured	Med.	General ledger	Internal	Low	Low	Batch	Low	High
Profit and loss statements	Admin finan.	Middle & top	Monthly	Structured	Low	General ledger	Internal	Low	Low	Batch	Med.	Med.
Payroll	Admin. pers'l	Operating	Weekly	Highly struc.	Low	Personnel file	Internal	Med.	Med.	Batch	High	Low
Payroll reports	Admin. per's1	Operating	Weekly	Highly struc.	Low	Personnel file	Internal	Med.	Med.	Batch	High	Low
Skills inventory	Admin. pers'1	Opert'g & middle	Weekly	Structured	Low	Personnel file	Internal	Low	Med.	Batch	Low	Med.
Wage and compensation analysis	Admin. pers'1	Opert'g & middle	Weekly	Structured	Low	Personnel file	Internal	Low	Med.	Batch	Low	Med.
Performance appraisals	Admin. pers'1	Opert'g & middle	Weekly	Structured	Low	Personnel file	Internal	Low	Med.	Batch	Low	Med.
Legal	Admin. legal	Middle & top	Weekly	Structured	Low	Specially prepared	Internal external	Low	Med.	Batch	Low	Med.

FIGURE 3.15. Business process by organization

Organization / Business process	Controller			Marketing			Production					
	Cost accounting	Accounts receivable	Accounts payable	Sales administration	Sales	Sales planning	Inventory control	Production scheduling	Transportation			
Order processing												
Order entry		●		*	●							
Order processing		●		*	●	●		●				
Billing		*		*	●							
Shipping		●		●	●	●						
Inventory control												
Inventory accounting	*			●			*	●	*			
Inventory control	*						*	●	*			
Costing	*						●					
Product build												
Production scheduling	●			●			●	*				
Material req's							*	*				
Shop control							●	*				

an IS, people who are responsible for the process are the principal recipients of the IS support. We do not start with the people, since people and organizations show a great deal more volatility than do processes. Since we want to build our IS on a long-term basis, we want to ensure first that the processes are supported before we look at the departments and individuals responsible for carrying them out. This chart identifies the key departments from which we can find out more about the processes and the information needs. It also points out potential overlap (several departments having a major responsibility) for a specific process. In establishing interdepartment IS priorities or in gaining specification sign-off for a particular application, we would certainly want to use this chart.

2. Business Process by Information System

Organizations developing information systems usually are not starting from scratch; they have existing systems in place that are supporting business processes to some degree. Figure 3.16 indicates by a cross (x) where current information systems (the horizontal axis) are supporting business processes (the vertical axis). This brings out the current coverage of systems and indicates areas that are not supported. For example, the market research process

FIGURE 3.16. Business process by information system

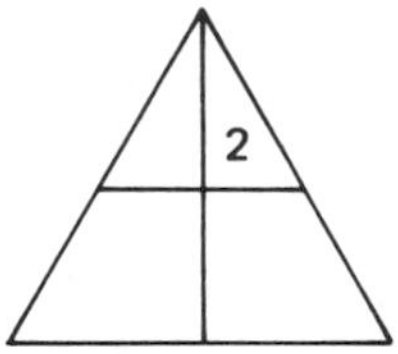

Business process	Order processing	Order billing	Accounts receivable	Inventory control	Purchasing	Production scheduling	Bill of material	Shop floor control				
Order entry	X											
Order processing	X											
Billing	X	X	X									
Shipping	X	X	X									
Inventory accounting	X			X		X	X	X				
Inventory control	X			X		X	X	X				
Costing				X								
Production scheduling	X			X		X	X					
Material req's				X		X	X					
Shop control				X		X	X	X				
Market research												

is not supported by an information system. This is not surprising because this process relies heavily on external data that is difficult to capture in electronic form. This schematic also shows potential overlap and redundancy. For example, the inventory accounting and inventory control processes are each supported by five information systems. Further analysis is needed to ascertain whether there is duplication (file redundancy and the like). The redundancies, voids, and gaps are leading indications of future IS plans and implementation.

3. Organization by Data Base

Figure 3.17 shows the data base mapped against the organization. We have already stated that data are a valuable resource. This chart shows which organizations rely on information that comes from the data base indicated. In this instance there is no data base for sales history or competitive sales. Creation of the data base may assume a high priority status, as these areas usually are critical to the marketing department. This analysis brings out the reliance of information users on common data files, emphasizing the importance of organizing and creating a data base that is easy to access from a multiplicity of vantage points.

4. Information System by Data Base

As we have noted and we examine in greater detail in Chapter 4, the data base is the crucial reservoir for providing information for IS and for the organization.

This matrix (Figure 3.18) and the previous one relate data to these entities. Figure 3.18 places a cross where the data base provides information to support a particular information subsystem. In this instance we see two voids, in that a data base does not exist for the product planning or market research systems. This is not unusual, but it may pinpoint an area of future development if management gives it a high priority and there are resources to implement. This matrix also shows that certain data base files (e.g., product) have broad across-the-board utilization in many information systems. The need for unity and integration is apparent in these situations. This analysis adds another important insight into the future development of IS.

These four matrices are key analytical tools for beginning the development of IS to support the business and the business model developed earlier in the chapter. The role and influence of management is crucial in determining the ultimate requirements and in establishing the priorities for development. The business model and matrices provide an excellent framework for gaining the necessary management involvement in the process.

DEVELOPING AN INFORMATION SYSTEMS ARCHITECTURE

The previous analysis of business processes and models has formed an information systems architecture. There are other factors to consider in building the architecture.

Increasingly, members of senior management are beginning to worry about their company's IS resource and its ability to respond to a combination of increasing technological options; and changing business conditions brought about by globalization, deregulation,

FIGURE 3.17. Organization by data base

Organization 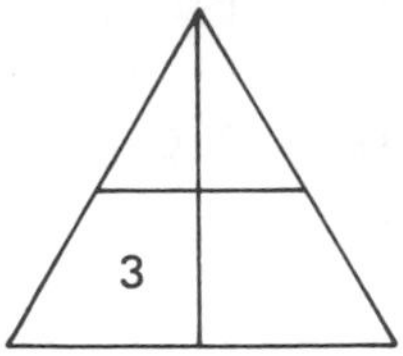 △ 3 Data base	Controller			Marketing			Production				
	Cost accounting	Accounts receivable	Accounts payable	Sales administration	Sales	Sales planning	Inventory control	Production scheduling	Transportation		
Customer		X		X	X			X	X		
Product	X			X	X		X	X			
Vendor			X				X				
Employee					X			X			
Price				X	X						
Parts							X	X			
Sales history											
Competitive sales											

acquisitions and mergers, increased competition, and changing economic, political, and social conditions. Both IS people and user/managers are beginning to realize that they need information systems that are flexible and adaptable to these massive changes. A flexible information systems architecture can provide a foundation for the required IS adaptability.

Cornelius H. Sullivan, Jr. defined architecture as "an effort to achieve fit or harmony between form and context." The architect designs a street, a building, a city (the form) that meets the requirements of the people (the context). The context includes the financial

FIGURE 3.18. Information system by data base

Information system 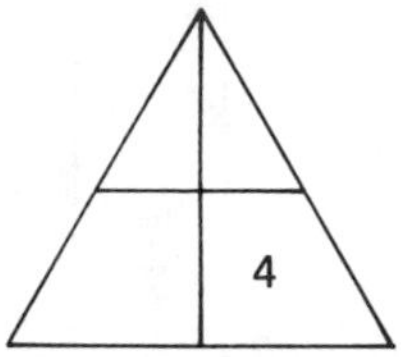 / Data base	Order processing	Order billing	Accounts receivable	Inventory control	Purchasing	Production scheduling	Bill of material	Shop floor control	Product planning	Market research		
Customer	X	X	X									
Product	X	X		X	X	X	X	X				
Vendor					X							
Employee												
Facilities						X						
Price	X	X	X									
Parts						X	X	X				

resources, building and health codes, and environmental constraints. The success of the architecture is measured by the fit of form and context. There is, of course, a time dimension involved: The architect must take a look at population trends and traffic growth so that his or her architecture adapts to a future context as well as a current one.

The analogy holds for the information systems architect. The form differs as does the context, but the objective remains the same—to find a meaningful fit between the two. The information systems architect, like the building architect, faces the challenge of the past.

Information systems, like buildings and streets, just grew. Pressures of time and cost favored alterations, add-ons, extensions, patches, and the like. The conflict arises when the context becomes so demanding and volatile that the form finally does not possess the flexibility to respond at all.

This is what is referred to as "biting-the-bullet time." Let's consider an example. Several years ago traffic on Boston's Southeast Expressway had increased to a point where refurbishment was mandatory (patches would no longer do and more lanes were needed). The form no longer fit the context. Boston commuters had to spend more time or take another route while a new architecture was being developed. As with a building, we don't like to break down an outside wall. But if we run out of temporary inside walls to modify, there's no other choice. A well-thought-out IS architecture minimizes the demolition of outside walls.

Developing an information systems architecture that matches form and context is becoming top priority for IS executives and is gaining the attention of senior management as well. An architecture that can handle the complexities of today's business, yet provide the built-in flexibility and expandability to incorporate tomorrow's growth and new requirements, is necessary; its development is no mean task.

GEOGRAPHIC INTEGRATION

An additional factor that must be coupled in IS architecture is geography. In addition to knowing *what* information is needed, we must know *where* it is needed.

Geography is a vital integration element and obviously must be carefully considered as a contextual factor in the architecture. The intracompany dimension pertains to relationships within the enterprise as opposed to relationships with outside enterprises. Companies have remote sales offices, corporate facilities, manufacturing operations, and service units. Their roles and responsibilities must be analyzed as to their fit in the organization—that is, whether they are part of the functional activity, the business unit activity, or both. Geography may mean across the parking lot, across the city, across the country, or across the world. Geographic integration obviously is a very volatile factor, changing as the organization changes.

Intercompany integration is the linkage with institutions or agencies that are not under the direct control of the company. A trend in information systems is to use information systems technology to develop intercorporate connections. For example, an electrical distributor might have terminals in the purchasing offices of its key customers. The terminals communicate directly to the host company's data base, producing inventory status, ship dates, prices, and the like. In addition, the distributor may have terminals that link to its major vendor's data base, providing similar information.

Architecture must also take into account requirements imposed by outside agencies whether they be the Internal Revenue Service, the Office of Safety and Health, or the variety of regulatory agencies. Usually these requirements would be met with by-products of existing data bases or applications, rather than separate system entities.

Another example of inter company integration is on-line access to the thousands of external data bases. The type of data ranges from financial information and investment statistics to market and planning data. The objective is to integrate the data from outside sources with pertinent internal data to develop strategic investment or marketing strategies.

POLITICAL AND CULTURAL CONSIDERATIONS

In addition to geographic issues of the type discussed, political and cultural factors within a company are extremely important. People are the ultimate contextual element.

The people constituting the organization motivate it. They provide the political and cultural energies that we might identify as "driving" forces. One driving force may be an *efficiency motivation*—information systems budgets have grown so big and so fast that the prime motivation is to contain the costs. A company may feel that it is spending too much for what it is receiving.

Or the driving force may be a *control motivation*—management feels that the technology has taken over, micros and workstations are showing up all over the place, everyone has his or her own data files, and no system communicates with any other. It's an environment of technological clutter.

On the other hand, the company climate may foster an *effectiveness or transformation motivation*—a realization that information systems technology can play an increasingly significant role in the business and indeed can be the dominant force enabling a company to remain competitive. In this mode, IS is considered a future investment similar to an investment in plant, building, and research and development. It's a longer-term view of information as a critical resource.

Lastly, the driving force may be *decentralized motivation*—based on the view that the information systems function has always been a fortress unto itself with the moats being huge backlogs and inordinately poor response times. Managers are tired of waiting and want to act; they want responsibility for satisfying their own information needs, establishing priorities, assigning resources, and deciding how much they will pay for information services.

Of course, it is vitally important to determine the driving forces within the company. You may not agree with them but you'd best be aware of them before tackling the architecture issue.

HARDWARE/SOFTWARE PROCESSING PLATFORMS

To this point, we have not mentioned hardware and software. It is obvious that they do come into play, but only after the other factors mentioned in this chapter have been thoroughly reviewed.

Not too many years ago, hardware/software processing platforms were the elements that came to mind most frequently when architecture was mentioned. This is not the case anymore. Now, the application and information/data precede the computer system in architectural priorities, but it is also true that the three are related: Both the application packages and data base software influence the selection of computer hardware.

The hardware platform(s) are the engines that support the architecture and provide the processing power. The selection involves careful calibration and forecasting of the processing capability required and its best physical deployment. This is where the centralized/decentralized concept comes into play, determining whether the "processing boxes" should be placed close to the point of transaction (departmental function) or at some intermediate or central point. The decision must be tempered by a host of cost and efficiency tradeoffs, such as communication costs versus processing costs and use of micro versus mini versus mainframe.

Similarly, the selection of systems software is an integral part of the processing platform. Included are operating systems, transaction processing software, data base management software (tied very closely to the data dimension), and communication software. Systems software, the layer upon which application systems are built, obviously must be selected with a great deal of understanding of its fit within the overall architecture.

COMMUNICATIONS/NETWORK

Communications, covered in Chapter 5, provide the delivery service linking the other elements. Architecture involves the development of a communications network that accepts transaction data and management requests for information, and delivers responses to the many systems users at each remote physical business entity. The decisions here include selection of communications channels, carriers, standards, protocols, capacity, response time, and so on. The options are many, whether one is looking at interbuilding communications involving some sort of local area network, intercity communications using a wide area network, or a global network.

Communications considerations normally involve linking computer use at three levels of the organization. The first is the *personal level* where an individual utilizes information processing to satisfy such personal needs as calendars and schedules, word processing, or spreadsheet analysis. The second is the *departmental level*, where individuals share common peripherals and data bases to communicate among themselves in performing departmental business. The third is the *enterprise level* where individuals and departments link to corporate information or communicate to carry out a task for the total organization. Communications architecture provides for the current and projected needs at these three levels. Since it also must provide for any intercompany communications, the design of the communications network requires a high level of technical expertise and experience.

The concept of architecture has been based on the definition of architecture as a fit between context and form. The elements of context and form have been described, with the warning that both are in a state of rapid change. Information systems design itself is far from a mature discipline. Thus, the challenge is to carve out an architecture in an environment where the essential elements are in flux. Following are some ground rules to consider:

Focus on a future vision. An architecture cannot be built on the linear extrapolation of the past. Instead, a shared vision of the future must serve as a target. The information systems architecture must be based on the kind of business operation that is envisioned and the prevailing strategies, future directions, and growth patterns. It should depict where you want to be, not where you are. Only after you know where you want to be, can you develop strategies addressing how to get there from here.

Consider architecture as the top-priority job. Though most challenging and difficult, developing an architecture is the most important single task for an information systems function. Because it has proven so illusive, IS groups have voted to proceed a piece at a time, without an overall design. While this method satisfies the short-term requirements, a serious price is paid in the long run. Patches can be put in place to keep a system in operation, but they are only temporary expedients. Sooner or later, an "outside wall" must be knocked down.

Maintain a high degree of flexibility. Despite a serious effort to project a shared vision of the future, it is still difficult to be exact because of the aforementioned conditions. Thus, the architecture must provide considerable systems flexibility to build an open-ended architecture that can accommodate as many options as possible. This is particularly true in areas such as telecommunications, where standards and common protocols are still evolving.

Don't introduce constraints prematurely. It is also important that the initial design be logical rather than physical. The architecture, like a city planning design, implies the general specifications for the types of materials to be used but rarely specifies brand names or exact composition. The benefits are twofold. First, the conceptual design is not limited by the constraints inherent in a particular hardware architecture, data base management system, etc. Second, the design is open-ended and provides leeway for the implementers to use the most cost-effective materials and to take advantage of improvements and advancements in the physical technology.

Architecture has been defined as a fit between form and context. A framework was developed for looking first at context and then at form, in the quest to integrate the two. This is not an easy job; in fact, the difficulty of establishing a meaningful systems architecture is exactly why more companies have not tackled it. The task takes time and resources, the right people, and a long-term senior management commitment. However, having an architecture is essential because information technology can now provide major strategic advantages for companies. With so much at stake, management must not only understand the concept of information systems architecture but also demand an architecture that can grow and expand with the enterprise.

SUMMARY

This chapter has emphasized that a thorough and comprehensive understanding of the business processes precedes the planning and implementation of IS. The sequence of IS development emanates from the building of a business model. The business model in turn is comprised of a group of interlinking or integrated processes. A distribution-company model was developed to illustrate the concept followed by the addition of processes pertinent to a manufacturing company. The resultant processes were then analyzed via a series of characteristics that will assist in the selection and priority setting of IS implementation.

The business model methodology was then expanded as a basis for looking at the underlying organization, existing information systems, and data base requirements. Four matrices were developed to help comprehend the interaction of these elements with the business processes and provide the information necessary to run a competitive business and meet the operational goals of the enterprise. Architecture was defined and additional discussion centered on the geography of IS, political and cultural issues, selecting hardware/software platforms, and the communications network element.

Throughout the chapter the word *management* appears; the repetition has the purpose of providing the desired degree of emphasis. This theme is carried throughout the book. We next turn to a discussion of data base, the integrating element undergirding the IS model developed in this chapter.

Case Study

Merk Industrial Products

The corporate planning vice president and IS vice president of Merk Industrial Products agreed that a major planning effort was required to plot the future direction of the company's IS efforts. Their only questions were the way to go about it and the time to allow for its completion. After a month's study of various planning methodologies, including a review of what consultants offered as well as computer vendors, they decided on a technique called Process 1. This would take a concerted three-month effort by a team of eight people, some working full time and others part time. The Process 1 team would be headed by the president's hand-picked staff assistant, a bright, energetic MBA who had built an excellent reputation in his six months with the company. The team was comprised of a mixture of non-IS managers, an individual from corporate planning, and several key people from the IS department. A letter from the corporate planning vice president explained the project:

```
From:   R. L. Preston, Corporate Planning
        B. J. Harrison, IS Division
To:     Management Distribution List
Subject: PROCESS 1 PLANNING STUDY
cc:     J.P. Wharton, President
```

I am sure all of you are aware of the dynamic nature of our business. Our success in the future will depend greatly on how we plan and react to the business environment. I am pleased to inform you that we are initiating a major effort to analyze our current and future information needs. I have authorized a study group that will conduct an in-depth study on how we use information and its relation to our business, and to recommend a systems architecture which will guide us in the development of the information systems we will need to manage Merk Industrial in the future. Our goal is to complete this project in three months.

A steering committee comprised of the department heads of Engineering, Manufacturing, Finance, Marketing, and Field Operations will be responsible for reviewing progress and approving direction.

A study team will be directed by John Parks, Assistant to the President, with our divisional personnel involved on both a full-time and part-time basis.

We will be using a methodology called Process 1, which has been helpful to other companies in evaluating and planning for their information requirements.

Process 1 involves a thorough review of our business and the business processes that are performed. This is followed by a formal analysis of current and future data needs and how our information systems meet these needs; gaps and voids will be pointed out. A full report with recommendations for action will be presented to each of you at the conclusion of the study. Please give your full cooperation in the conduct of this important planning effort.

_____   _____

R. L. Preston   B. J. Harrison

STUDY QUESTIONS

1. What do you think of Merk's approach to IS planning? Are they going about it the right way?

2. What are the major obstacles to carrying out the study?

3. Do you think eight people working three months is too much to ask? Do you think Preston and Harrison can gain the cooperation and endorsement of the key department managers and the assignment of their key people to the study?

4. Do you think the letter will serve its intended purpose? Is that the way to launch the program? Are there other approaches, or should the letter perhaps be supplemented by other actions?

5. What are the benefits of undertaking this planning effort?

Case Study

How Ford is Reinventing the Wheel on a Global Basis

The building of an automobile has been one of the most complex manufacturing challenges of the twentieth century. For each new model, designers and engineers must meticulously sketch out thousands of parts. Factories must be retooled to machine and assemble them. Coordinating the work of designers, engineers, and manufacturing people is a gargantuan task as changes in one stage ripple through the rest of the process.

Pressure from Japanese competitors to cut time and costs out of the design-to-development process grows every year. And that's why Ford Motor Company has embarked on an ambitious journey to redefine the way it produces cars for the global market.

As Ford evolved as an international powerhouse over the century, it found that cars the Germans liked were different from the cars the British liked, which were different from the American versions. Building cars to meet local tastes required hiring designers who were close to those markets, then supporting them with engineers and manufacturing plants as sales volumes (or country trade requirements) warranted.

The design-to-engineering-to-manufacturing process requires daily and close coordination between these professionals. Having them thousands of miles away was unwieldy. They had to be close geographically. The decision on locating the various phases of design to the manufacturing process, therefore, was not based on economics but rather on the logistical problems of coordinating work across great distances.

The result: unique cars demanding their own designs, engineers, and manufacturing facilities. For example, in Europe alone, Ford has eight factories that are fed by another 25 plants producing components. The U.S. has an even larger infrastructure in place. One design, one engineering and one manufacturing organization could not serve the world.

Of course, that was before information technology changed the rules of how work could be accomplished. Today, computers linked via vast telecommunications networks enable a designer in Detroit to gaze at the same blueprints that an engineer in Brussels and a manufacturing professional in Spain are examining. People no longer have to be together to work together.

That leads us to the next logical argument: If information technology allows us to disperse functions like R&D, design, engineering, and manufacturing professionals clustered around every product?

The answer is no. While those parts of the business closest to the customer (notably sales, marketing, and research and development) should remain local, the other parts of the "value chain" (engineering and manufacturing, in Ford's case) away from the customer can

From CSC Index Publication *CSC Insights,* "Engineering the New Global Corporation," Summer 1990.

be located anywhere. Rather than the next office or town, they should reside where the best talent exists, anywhere on the globe.

Essentially, this is Ford's vision for building the "world car"—a car to be marketed and produced globally. Former Chairman Doanld Petersen envisioned the production of a small car (called Tempo and Topaz in the U.S., and Sierra in Europe) that would use identical parts save for some exterior differences. The job of designing, engineering, and building the car would be parceled out around the world to "centers of responsibility." In other words, one design team, one engineering team, one set of parts. Overhead would be greatly reduced.

The "glue" holding together functions that are oceans away would be a computer and communications technology. Videoconferencing would let designers in Detroit hold intensive discussions with engineers in England. Computer-aided design systems electronically connected on both sides of the Atlantic would allow car designers in Europe to update their plans and notify engineers in the U.S. instantly.

A major step in that direction is a computer system that makes changes on parts specifications immediately available to manufacturing personnel, so they can rapidly adjust their tools and techniques. In the auto business, the delays and snafus from last-second parts changes are a major factor in the long development time of new car models.

"Through on-line access, the systems provides the necessary data on new parts to everyone throughout the company who needs to know," says S.I. Gilman, executive director of information systems and Ford's top information technology executive. "In a company the size of Ford, disseminating those parts specifications could take weeks. On a computer system, nearly instantaneously."

All together, some 12,000 engineers and manufacturing personnel can tap into the data base, which operates on a mainframe computer at Ford Headquarters. If a part doesn't fit a new model, the designers can change it, and the change is communicated to Ford operations throughout the world.

Known as the "worldwide engineering release system," because it releases elaborate engineering documentation from the parts designers to people who will manufacture the parts, the computer application was an enormous undertaking. The biggest difficulty was getting design engineers from around the world to standardize their business practices, such as who has the authority to change a part and how to do it.

The system is part of a larger effort at Ford to push common design in cars and parts, while still allowing for regional and local differences. It has turned out to be a challenging though rewarding step toward a global auto industry.

STUDY QUESTIONS

1. Would engineers have a tendency to resist global engineering approaches? What are the pros and cons from their view?

2. Is the Ford approach applicable to other products and markets? Which ones come to mind?

3. Is this approach a return to centralized IS? Is it bucking a trend that may prove difficult to counter?

4. The case mentions communication technologies like videoconferencing. Are these needed for this type of approach? What other technologies abet this type of operation?

5. How can this system compress the design cycle for a new car? Does it replace or enhance creativity?

SELECTED REFERENCES

Burk, Cornelius F., and Forest W. Horton, InfoMap: *A Complete Guide to Discovering Corporate Information Resources.* Englewood Cliffs, NJ: Prentice Hall, 1988.

Honeywell Consulting Services, *A Planning Method, Instructional Guide*, 1982.

IBM, "Business Systems Planning: Information Systems Planning Guide," Doc. GE20-0527-2, Technical Publications, White Plains, NY: IBM Corp., 1978.

IBM, "Business Systems Planning: Information Systems Planning Guide (Application Manual), 2nd ed., Doc. GE20-0527-2, Technical Publications, Dept. 824, White Plains, NY: IBM Cor., 1978.

"Integrated Environments: Open Windows or Closed Doors?: *Datamation*, May 1, 1989, p.21.

Kaufman, Roger, *Strategic Planning Plus—An Organizational Guide.* New York, NY: Scott Foresman Professional Books, 1991.

"Micro Mainframe Links," *Data Management,* November 1987, p.17.

McWilliams, Gary, "Integrated Computing Environments," *Datamation*, May 1, 1989, p. 19.

QED Information Sciences, Inc., *Information Systems Planning for Competitive Advantage.* Wellesley, MA, 1989.

Sankar, Yassin, *Management of Technical Change.* New York, NY: John Wiley & Sons, 1991.

Schwartz, Peter, *The Art of the Longview—Planning for the Future in an Uncertain World.* Bantam Doubleday Dell Publishing Group, Inc., 1991.

Chapter 4

The Mortar of IS: Data Base

INTRODUCTION

The preceding chapter made it obvious that data is the key element that drives information systems. *Data* was defined in the very first chapter as the raw material of IS. The objective of IS is to transform that data into meaningful management information, which is defined as the finished goods in the process. The business processes are supported by information that emanates from a data base; the business model is built on a data base foundation: It is the glue or mortar of IS. An important lesson from the previous chapter is that data often must be integrated or linked in order to provide the requisite information to the many classes of IS users.

This chapter looks at data base from the outside in—from the user viewpoint. The importance of data to an organization is stressed, showing how data, both from within the organization and outside of it, are used to develop strategy and make decisions. Then the various user views of data that are made possible by current hardware and software are explored. It is important to look at data base development, as with any business application, with these views in mind. The ultimate worth of a data base system is to be able to extract data without weeks of training and preparation. Management is interested in determining the marketplace for the company's products, the competitive forces, and how to make products more marketable—not in learning obscure data retrieval languages.

After a thorough treatment of user views, the fundamentals of data base software are reviewed, including data dictionary, data structures and "schemas," and ways to index and cross-index data for retrieval. The major categories of data base are described, including hierarchical, network, relational, distributed, and individual PC-based systems. Finally the organizational and management considerations for successful employment of a data base are studied. Data represent the vast resource of knowledge upon which an institution operates. The institutions that organize and maintain this knowledge base in a meaningful and effective way will have a significant competitive advantage.

THE USE OF DATA THROUGHOUT THE ORGANIZATION

A simple definition of data base is given by James Martin, a leading authority: "A data base is a collection of data that is shared and used for multiple purposes." Data are organized around files arranged so that duplication and redundancy are avoided. Information concerning ongoing activities is captured once, validated, and entered into the proper location in the data base. The key element in a data base concept is that each subsystem utilizes the same data base in satisfying its information needs.

In the development of systems, companies typically implemented applications on a one-by-one basis, giving little or no thought to the integration of data files. This is the root of the problem in the development of on-line, integrated, data-oriented applications. The perception of need for a data base usually follows the realization that as much as 70 percent of the system development dollars are spent in maintaining old applications as opposed to the development of new applications. Fragmented development results in each application having its own independent data file. Even minor changes to either the file or the application have serious rippling effects on the operation. With this burden, application backlogs grow and users become disillusioned, seeking information help outside the channels of their internal IS operation.

Another development has been the demand for and shift to applications that support management control and strategic planning as opposed to operational control. In order to serve middle and upper management levels, data must be accessible in both a vertical and horizontal mode. The vertical mode permits access to an individual data file, where the desired information emanating from the file is summary, cumulative, or selective. Thus, a sales manager wants a report showing sales by region by salesperson, sequenced in descending order by the salesperson's performance to quota. The horizontal mode allows information to be derived across file boundaries. An example is a banking application where data are captured and stored for various customer files, for example, a file for each demand deposit account, savings account, loan, trust, and so on. A manager wants to know the names and balances of customers who have three or more individual accounts with the bank. This involves the horizontal linking across boundaries usually indexed by customer name or account number. Fragmented data storage facilities do not permit this type of operation; both vertical and horizontal file access are extremely limited and cumbersome at best.

Figure 4.1 superimposes a data base alongside the activity triangle introduced in Chapter 1. The data required for operational control activities are built around transactions. Thus, in a distribution environment, orders are the principal transaction, with order-process-

FIGURE 4.1. Data base support of applications

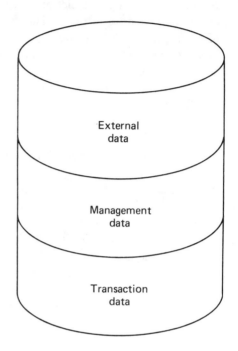

ing systems managing individual orders against a customer and inventory file. In banks, a basic operational control application is demand-deposit accounting, where customer accounts are maintained, updated by checks either debited or credited to the individual account. The checks represent transaction data and the magnetic coding of checks has enabled this process to be carried out automatically.

The data files of these applications, however, with their origin in the fragmented development era, have not permitted the timely and meaningful extraction of data that, when combined with other data, such as performance criteria, enables the information system to support management needs. Strategic planning requires the combination of external data— for example, competitive trends, inflationary pressures, productivity figures—with transaction and management data to support upper levels of management.

USER VIEW OF DATA BASE

Before discussing the workings of a data base, it is appropriate to review the variety of data base users, since this is the real end product and the reason for its being. Figure 4.2 depicts the gamut of end users ranging from the IS specialist on the right-hand side to the management generalist on the left. The chart is split in two with IS users on the left and IS providers on the right. It is obvious that the middle and top management users on the left have a completely different perspective and view of the data base than the systems analysts and programmer/operators on the right. Not only are their needs different, but the methods of access to the data base are of an opposing nature.

FIGURE 4.2. Data base users

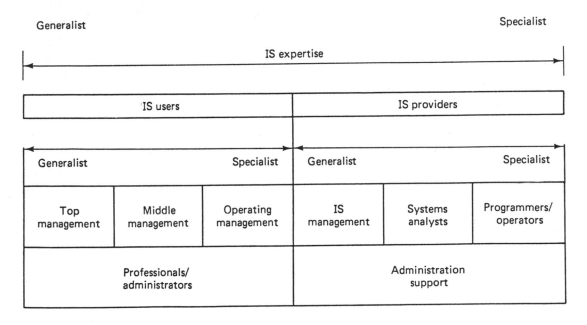

A key difference between the users on the left and right is that of ad hoc usage versus dedicated or productive usage. The systems analysts spend full time developing production programs and applications that will be used on a repetitive basis. Therefore, their objectives are more oriented to efficiency. They are able to learn a language or interface technique that produces acceptable response time and turnaround time for the ultimate users. Since they are spending full time with the language, they can sacrifice ease of use for more efficient operation, and it is true that one does add resource overhead and execution time, as one gets further from the native mode instruction set of the computer.

On the other hand, ad hoc or nondedicated users' principal need is to have a language that is easy to learn and simple to use. Since the information is a support function for accomplishing their jobs (jobs that are not to produce information), they do not want to spend an inordinate amount of time learning new skills. These users have short attention spans when it comes to writing out instructions to access a computer data base.

The comparison of these two classes of usage, ad hoc and dedicated/repetitive, brings up the classic tradeoff of effectiveness versus efficiency. Management users are more interested in effectiveness—that is, the end product rather than the degree of efficiency with which it is produced. Within reason of course, they don't care how many translation instructions are executed when they give an inquiry to a data base—they don't spend that much time at it—but when they do need the information, it is vital that they get it. Today's trend, with the reduction in hardware cost and the increase in personnel cost, is that the tradeoff, even at the systems analyst/programmer level, is shifting toward effectiveness.

End-User Windows

Figure 4.3 depicts the variety of end-user languages or data windows through which information is obtained. Several examples of user languages are illustrated. With the range and number of data base users expected to expand in the years ahead, end-user languages are most significant. The IS tools are to the right of the figure, representing the software translators or interfaces and the data storage media for the data base. The first level of software translation is the interpretation of the user window being employed. This software layer translates the logical view of the data into the physical view necessary to access the data or whatever data storage device is used. The data base management systems residing on the top of the operating systems enable the transaction to occur. The physical data storage can be hard disks or personal computers, minicomputers or mainframes. Compact disks, read only memory (CDROM), and optical disks are also being used more and more for both on-line storage and backup. In the case of optical disks, so called optical juke boxes, storage up to 200 gigabytes of data can be employed. Multiple units can create additional data storage if required.

FIGURE 4.3. End user data windows

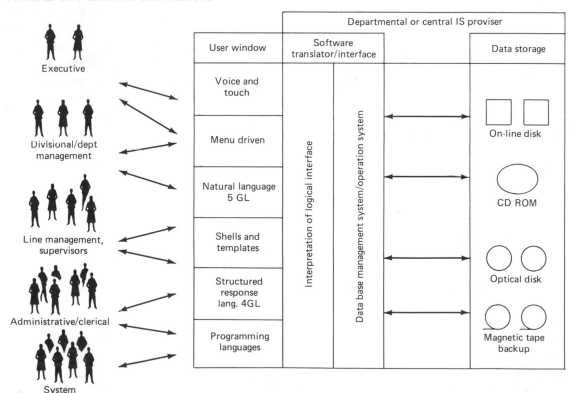

Voice and Touch

At the top of the user language list is the instrument most used by executives to gain management information: the voice. Ultimately, it represents a goal of future data base systems—the ability of the system to recognize directly the verbal commands of an executive and to deliver the required information. Currently, there are voice recognition systems that can comprehend a limited vocabulary, but it will be some time before executives can use a machine the same way they can use an administrative assistant—and even with the machine, an individual's particular management style may still favor the assistant. Touch screens exist, primarily as executive workstations, where the executive can point to a button or a figure on the screen to access specific information. The finger or stylus breaks an *x/y* light plane permitting the system to know which part of the screen was activated.

Menu-Driven

The next level of user window is the popular menu, probably the most common interface device in use today. The menu may display the same type of choices as the touch screen, but this time, the user either moves the cursor to the desired button or uses a mouse to point to the button and then clicks to activate. The menu has proven to be a most desirable interface, particularly for intermittent users. It simulates the logic that individuals follow and is quite self-instructive. One doesn't have to remember or look up esoteric codes to seek data; the system, through a series of menu choices takes the individual to where he or she wants to go. Most data base management systems facilitate the comprehensive use of menus.

Natural Language

English-language query systems are available where commands can be given in complete sentences or in sentence fragments to manipulate a data base and to format meaningful reports. Numeric data can be counted, summed, divided, multiplied, correlated, averaged, selected based on minimum and maximum ranges, and so on, while alphabetic data, along with the arithmetic data, can be produced in a variety of report formats.

The following is an example of how such a system is used. This is a simple data base request, but the reader should be able to see the power of the tool and its possible extensions for management use.

Natural Language Example

System. In a few moments you will be conversing with the system. The file for this demonstration consists of an employee file. Feel free to ask any questions phrased in any way you wish about this data. The system will try to answer your questions.

System. You will first be asked for your name and company affiliation. This information will be maintained on log files. You may begin asking questions when the system prompts you.

System. I'm ready to answer your questions pertaining to: The employee file. Please type in your name and affiliation.

User. John Doe, Acme, Mfg.

System. State request.

User. What's in the files?

Answer. Fields of the employee file

Field Name	Searchable	Sortable	Format	Length
Name	Yes	Yes	Alphabetic	20
City	Yes	Yes	Alphabetic	15
State	Yes	Yes	Alphabetic	2
Job	Yes	Yes	Alphabetic	20
Phone	Yes	Yes	Alphabetic	8
Salary	Yes	Yes	Alphabetic	6
Sex	Yes	Yes	Alphabetic	1
Age	Yes	Yes	Numeric	2
Family Status	Yes	Yes	Alphabetic	10

System. Next request.

User. Print a report of salaries broken down by city within state.

System. Continue or define further.

User. For the New Hampshire and Connecticut people earning over 4000 and show names.

System. Print a report of state, city, salary, and name sorted by state and city of employee with salary over 4000 and state = New Hampshire or Connecticut.

Answer. The number of records to retrieve is 5.

System. How many records do you want listed?

User. All.

Answer.

State	City	Salary	Name
Connecticut	Stamford	$48,000	Van Duyn
		$ 6,000	Morrison
Connecticut	Stamford	$54,000	
Connecticut	Total	$54,000	
New Hampshire	Hanover	$24,000	Samuelson
		$ 4,200	Russel
		$ 5,500	Schriber
New Hampshire	Hanover	$33,700	
New Hampshire	Total	$33,700	
Grand Total		$87,700	

Shells/templates

Another way to access and use data bases is via a shell or template. Shells or templates are overlays that do a good deal of the setup work for the eventual uses. They act as bridges between the user and the underlying complexity. They shield the user from the detailed operation of the system. The basic and best-understood shell is the spreadsheet. It allows the accountant or analyst to see a computer system through a familiar metaphor, the rows and columns that comprise a spreadsheet. It is an extension of his/her natural way of attacking a problem. A spreadsheet by itself is a shell, but it could also have a template overlay that makes it even easier to use. Suppose a business analyst wants to project profit for the next five years based on rising material cost and changing consumer demand. The model of the company's profit and loss statement can be calculated using the spreadsheet so that the analyst only has to input the various cost and demand percentage changes to project the impact on profit and loss.

Data base retrieval can be established along the same lines. A library of commonly used reports can be developed such that the user can select the desired shell or template and have the data base system search and find the missing data and plug it into the report. This is somewhat similar to the menu but can be even simpler for the class of user that only requires data for a well-defined set of reports. Thus, there are degrees of interface languages available to suit the different classes of user depicted on the left of Figure 4.3. The key is to find the best fit.

Structured Query/Response and Structured Language

Structured query/response is quite similar to the natural language explained in the foregoing, but it is a far more structured language for obtaining simple ad hoc reports. Line managers and supervisors require more repetitive access to specific data files and are able to learn a more structured form of interface. This language falls somewhere between natural language and relational tables. For example, the notation used would be "List all employees with salary > 8000 with code I through 8 and dependents < 4." Thus the language is a shorthand form, more congenial to middle or lower levels of management than to those at higher levels.

The structured language is similar to the foregoing but is used for repetitive reports and routines rather than for short ad hoc requests. Thus, it results in the development of a procedure that can be repeated over time. Because it is repeated, the language is richer and a bit harder to learn, but it results in more efficient use and is more conservative of system resources. Structured procedural languages are being used more by systems analysts and programmers. They lie somewhere between the easier ad hoc languages and the more cumbersome programmer languages such as the C language and COBOL. As mentioned, the declining cost of hardware in relation to salaries makes this an increasingly attractive approach.

Programming Languages

Up to this point, we have been emphasizing the use of data base management systems by department users, people with no heavy specialized training or professional programming background. We have also been emphasizing the accessing of data from the data base in the form of reports and analysis. When we think of developing, maintaining, and updating the data dictionary and in developing enterprise-wide application systems, we must consider another user interface, that of programming. Complex applications can be developed using structured programming languages like Structured Query Language (SQL) which will be covered shortly, but it may still be prudent to write the application program using the C or C++ language or Common Business Oriented Language (COBOL). The closer the language is to the native instruction set of the computer, the fewer cycles the program will take and the more efficiently it will run, using the minimum computer resources. Of course, with hardware costs going down and processing speed rising so dramatically, the tradeoff continually favors using less experienced programmers, employing higher-level languages, and using more machine cycles. However, there remains a place for programming.

SPECIFICITY VERSUS TIME TO DEVELOP

Figure 4.4 applies some perspective to this matter and shows a series of application development tools on a two-grid matrix of specificity versus time to develop. Specificity means the degree of tailoring of the solution to fit a specific problem. Some jobs, because of efficiency demands or job uniqueness, require such specificity. These applications usually take longer to develop and require experienced programmers. They are shown in the upper right. On the lower left are applications requiring low specificity, applications that can usually be provided by generators, utilizing package subroutines to accomplish the desired functions. In the middle are the interfaces we have been discussing; the voice/menu and natural languages fall more to the lower left of the matrix and the structured languages fall

FIGURE 4.4. Application development tools

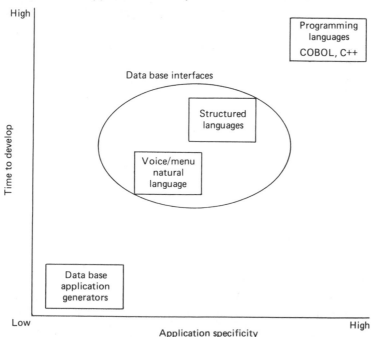

more to the upper right. As in most situations, the tool used depends on the job to be done, the time demands, and the skill mix of the personnel.

Armed with a description of the data base languages, we now turn inward to the workings of the data base itself and the employment of data base software systems.

DATA BASE SOFTWARE

The information resource management (IRM) concept emphasizes the significance of the information resource on a par with money, facilities, and personnel. It asserts that the same disciplines applied to the more traditional resources should be applied to the information resource. The elements applicable to managing a valuable resource are: control, organize, plan, safeguard, measure, and protect. Data base software, usually called *data base management systems (DBMS)*, represents a key tool to managing this important resource.

The move to on-line applications and management's burgeoning appetite for information pose problems for conventional data processing techniques. Demands for short-lead-time, one-time, or irregularly required reports; requests for data from several files; and the need for predicting future management needs all pose quite a challenge, for few managers can look ahead and predict with any degree of certainty what they will need in the way of information. It is difficult enough to get a clear picture of what information management wants today. Moreover, different managers on the same level often require quite different reports. This uncertainty is often discovered by a system analyst—after having developed a system and produced a report thought to be the one the manager said was needed, only to find it is not what the manager wanted at all. The only way the systems analyst can improve the situation is to follow the precept, "Don't give managers what they *say* they want but what they *mean* they want." Needless to say, this situation presents a real problem for IS designers.

Conventional methods of file design and acquisition have not been responsive (turn-around time for requests for data has been days or hours when it should have been seconds), have not been flexible enough to cope with the inevitable business changes that affect information systems, and have placed too great a burden on the system analyst's time. Old systems were built around a file structure that is embedded in each and every program written to process or access that file. This means that each time the file changes, the programs utilizing that file must also be changed. For example, the Social Security Administration had to modify hundreds of existing programs when a change in social security benefits affected the file structure of recipients. The result cost hundreds of thousands of dollars. This situation could have been avoided had the file structure not been embedded in each program using the file. The interweaving of file structure and programs has been a major contributor to high reprogramming costs and inflexibility to changing conditions. Data base software solves this problem by utilizing a common file-description interface between the program and the data file, as shown in Figure 4.5.

An example illustrates how the separation of files and programs facilitates change. A change occurs in the data file; for example, a company's product line may expand to the point that a five-digit item number is needed where a four-digit number previously sufficed. If there is no common file description serving as the link between the data themselves and

FIGURE 4.5. File descriptor interface

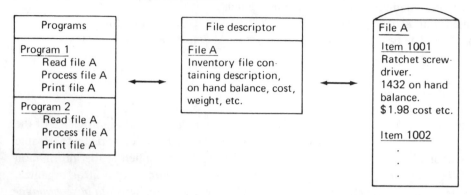

the many programs that utilize them, each and every reference to that file within each program must be altered. Because of the magnitude of the change, and to ensure that all data references are flagged, program retesting and checkout are required. With the file description, only the description itself is changed to indicate that the full size of the item number is now five digits. The data file, of course, must be updated to change the item numbers from four digits to five.

Data base software is crucial to IS designers because its purpose is to resolve the problems described. It attacks the problem with three major techniques: (a) data dictionaries to classify and define the various elements that become part of the data base; (b) file structures to increase the usefulness, flexibility, responsiveness to change, and accessibility of data; and (c) data base languages to facilitate ease of access to the data base for managers, system analysts, clerical workers, and programmers.

Figure 4.6 lists the functions that must be performed on data to create an effective DBMS. The first two functions are handled by the data dictionary. The next three fall under

FIGURE 4.6. Data base functions

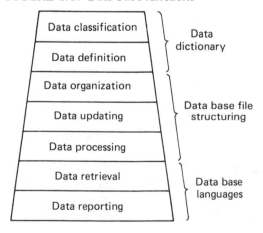

the file-structuring portion of the DBMS, while the latter two are covered by the data base languages associated with the DBMS.

DATA DICTIONARY

The heart or hub of a data base management system is the *data dictionary*. A multimillion-book library is useless without an index; the encyclopedias of the world are inert storehouses of knowledge without a guide to their organization and use; the largest collection of legal briefs and precedents lies fallow without access keys—and so it is with a data base system without a data dictionary.

The files of data previously mentioned are broken down into *data fields* or *elements*. The key to a data dictionary is to define and tag each element so that it can be accessed for a specific use. People call the same thing by different names, and, conversely, the same name may refer to several things. A data dictionary avoids this confusion and redundancy, or at least plans for the redundancy, by defining each data element and giving it a name or identifier. A data dictionary is similar to a bill of material in a manufacturing operation. The bill of material indicates for each end product the parts and assemblies that came together to form the finished item and the sequence and order (relationship) in which they were used. A part and assembly may be used in several end products, and this must be known by the bill of material. As the bill of material is the heart of production scheduling and control, so the data dictionary is the heart of information scheduling and control.

The dictionary aids users by letting them know which data are available and how they can be obtained. A management user or an application programmer would consult the data dictionary to determine whether the data required were already captured and, if so, to assess how to identify and access them; thus they avoid developing a program to collect data that are already collected, labeled, stored, and ready to use. Users write programs that refer to data structures that in turn contain the data elements. The data dictionary maintains all these relationships.

Development of a comprehensive data dictionary can help clear up organizational irregularities with regard to data. Some departments or persons may be taking an ownership role with regard to certain data files within their purview. They may regard the data as their proprietary possession, when in reality they may have significant value for other functions and departments within the company. A customer file, for example, may be viewed by the marketing department as their sole possession, although the file can be of extreme value to various product and strategic planning activities. For the most part, data should be viewed as a resource of the total company; particular departments should be given custodial responsibility for specific files but not control over who has access to it. This is a different decision level. The development of a data base around a data dictionary brings to the surface these organizational data irregularities.

The dictionary also provides a much-needed standardization mechanism. Data are continually changed, updated, modified, processed, combined, collated, sorted, and so on. Standardization, as provided by the data dictionary, abets the proper functioning of these transactions. The data dictionary can be viewed as the corporate glossary of the ever-growing information resource.

DATA INDEPENDENCE AND SCHEMAS

In the pre–data base era, each application often had its own data base associated with it. Application A would use data base X, while application B used data base X and Y. Then along came application C, which used parts of X and Y and also a bit of its own data base. Serious problems arose when a change occurred in an application program or a change in the data base structure. For example, a change in data base X would necessitate changes in all three applications (sometimes quite extensive). A change in any of the applications might affect its ability to access the various data bases.

This spawned the concept of data independence, which is a requisite of integrated data base systems. Data is structured to be independent of the applications that use it. The technique that accomplishes this is called *maintaining logical and physical data independence.* The logical view of data is that of the application programmer, whose concern should not be where the data physically resides but only what content is necessary to feed the application. To accomplish this, a data base organization is established—built around a software data base management system and administered by a data base administrator— which provides what might be thought of as a data mapper, linking the logical view of data with the physical view in such a way that neither view must be known by the other. The translation takes place every time an application program accesses a piece of data, but it is transparent to the person writing the program.

Of course, the purpose of all this is to enable programs to be changed simply and efficiently without worrying about the data and vice versa. This is no trivial advantage, as a large IS department can spend several million dollars each year to maintain existing programs.

Another set of terms used in data base parlance is *schemas* and *subschemas.* The overall global view of a data base, similar to the view used by the aforementioned mapper, is called a *schema.* The application programmer's view is referred to as a *subschema,* or sometimes the local view as compared with global view. Figure 4.7 illustrates the concept of data independence and schemas. Application programmers, referring to data in the local, logical, or subschema form, interface to the global view or schema, which provides the mapping and conversion to the physical data stored in on-line disk files.

FILE STRUCTURE

The purpose of the file structure element of data base software is to facilitate the functions of data organization, updating, processing, and retrieval. A key characteristic is to allow cross-indexing or the chaining of related items so that they can be retrieved in a manner consistent with application and user needs. In simple sequential file structures, the information concerning a particular inventory item is stored on an inventory file, while the information concerning a particular customer is stored on a customer file. An additional open-order file will list the detail of each customer order that has not been delivered. This file combines information (actually duplicates it) from both the customer file and the inventory file. Although perhaps tolerable under batch sequential approaches, this method is not feasible, either economically or in terms of time demand on systems utilizing

FIGURE 4.7. Data independence

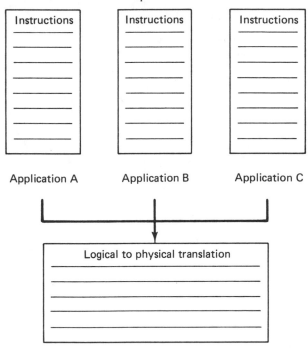

Application A   Application B   Application C

Global data base logical organization

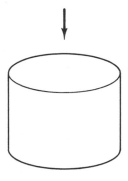

Physical data base

direct-access storage. Features of data base software allow data to be stored once on a direct-access file with the appropriate elements linked or chained for rapid access. Storage duplication is thus avoided. For example, Figure 4.8 indicates two files of nonredundant data, one an inventory file indexed by item number and the second a customer file indexed by customer number.

The purpose of this example is to give the reader some feeling for the complexity of file design—the need to access information by different keys and indexes and the need to

FIGURE 4.8. Example of file linkage

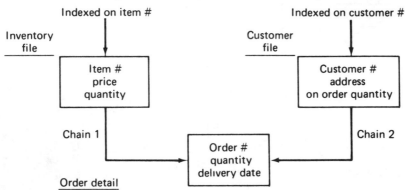

link together files and information. The subject of data base management is a far-reaching one that deserves in-depth study and analysis on its own. This section serves only to point out the degree of difficulty and attention that must be paid to maintain, update, and retrieve information from a data base.

The data base system establishes a chain that provides a link to all the orders for a particular item while at the same time linking that same order data to the relevant customer record. By utilizing these chaining techniques, the file can be reorganized, alternate chains can be developed, and updates can be made with minimum effort and program reworking. In addition, the system provides the ability to express associations between different files without redundant data storage.

File retrieval is aided by a technique of multiple indexing that allows data access by any of several keys. Figure 4.9 is an example of a payroll file for which multiple indexing is desired. The requirement is to set up an employee information file in such a way that data can be retrieved by employee number or by employee with particular job codes or with specified length of service. The illustration shows a sample file with four employees indexed by employee number, job code, and length of service.

The indexes consist of key values that occur in the file, together with record addresses of records containing the values. It is apparent that retrieval by any of the three keys—employee number, job code, or years of experience—is equally efficient. In addition, this file structure can handle multiple-condition retrievals very efficiently. An inquiry requesting all employees who have two years experience at job code 12 can be handled by comparing the lists of addresses for job code 12 and two years experience and finding equalities; in this case, the record at address 30 is the only one that meets both conditions.

A more pertinent example would be a banking customer file for which it is desirable to link savings, loan, and deposit accounts by individual; to be able to access the information by one of several keys, including customer account number or name; and to retrieve data such as savings accounts with over $1000 or accounts with no activity for 60 days or longer. The file-structuring element of data base software enables the system designer to accomplish these requirements in an efficient and economical manner.

FIGURE 4.9. Sample payroll file

Employee #	Index
100	10
126	20
133	30
141	40

Job code	Index
10	40
12	20 30
14	10

Length of service	Index
1	40
2	10 30
4	20

Address	Data
10	100
	ABC
	2
	14
	2
20	126
	DEF
	1
	12
	4
30	133
	GHI
	3
	12
	2
40	141
	LMN
	3
	10
	1

Record format

Employee number
Name
Salary code
Job code
No. years experience

CLASSES OF DATA BASE SYSTEMS

This section mentions the various classes of data base systems, devoting more space to the relational model, as it appears to be the prevailing standard in IS use. Though many companies implemented hierarchical and network data bases and still maintain them, the trend is definitely relational. Companies using hierarchical or network approaches spent large amounts of time and money and have many crucial transaction-oriented applications that depend on these data bases. It is a mammoth effort to convert to the relational model, and these companies recognize the resources and risks involved in so doing. Therefore, hierarchical and network approaches will exist into the next century, but the new ones will be relational. The general classes of data base systems are:

- hierarchical
- network
- relational
- micro-based and client server

Hierarchical Model

Both the hierarchical and network models are designed to handle large transaction-based applications. The early computer applications were sales-order processing, check processing, inventory updating, patient billing, insurance file maintenance/premium billing, and the like. The characteristics of these applications are a large, well-defined master file of information and a huge number of well-structured transactions that are processed repeatedly against the file. Early data bases were optimized around this process.

It is not important for the IS generalist to fully understand the underlying design structure of these types of data bases; rather they are mentioned to note their existence and to show data base evolution. Hierarchical and network models are the province of the central IS staff as it takes experienced systems analysts and programmers to develop, maintain, and use them. On the other hand, relational data bases can be effectively used by departmental people who are not IS specialists.

The hierarchical model follows an organization similar to that of a structured institution; that is, there is a pyramid or tree structure. Figure 4.10 illustrates a hierarchical model.

The root refers to the particular file, in this case the salesperson. The file is broken into regions, called level 1 nodes, and salesperson within each region, Level 2 node (also called parent/child). The data elements or key values for each salesperson are included for each level 2 node. All key values are arranged with a pointer to link each value to a specific node or data record. Hierarchical data bases have a one-to-many relationship, compared with the many-to-many relationships of the network model. The hierarchical model is highly structured and requires a controlled, finite, rule-based approach. The benefits are that there is a high level of control, backup, and security built into the system. Change control, the ability to change data formats or to enter transaction data, is strictly governed. Both the hierarchical and network models optimize computer cycles; that is, the approach is geared more to the internal data base structure and less to the need to provide flexibility and range of use by the variety of people who may have need to access the data base. The relational model has just the opposite orientation. The hierarchical model is characterized by IBM's Information Management System (IMS) released in 1968 which has dominated the marketplace for the last two decades.

FIGURE 4.10. Hierarchical model

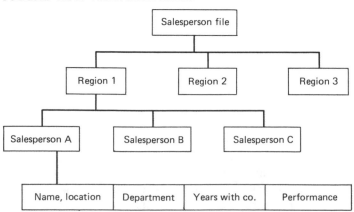

Network Model

The network model is the oldest of the data base management systems, characterized by the development of Integrated Data Store (IDS) developed at General Electric in the mid-sixties under the leadership of Charles Bachman. IDS grew to be the standard of the CODASYL group, an organization of major hardware and software vendors—the same group that developed the standard programming language, COBOL. The major computer vendors, IBM, DEC, UNISYS, Hewlett-Packard, Prime, and others all came out with network data base systems, as did independent software companies like Cullinet (now Computer Associates) and Cincom.

Network data bases feature a many-to-many relationship; each "child" can have more than one "parent." For example, a salesperson record may also include sales by specific product category. Management may want to compile sales by the major heading of product rather than by sales region. Data in the same field can be captured both by region and product as the following illustration shows:

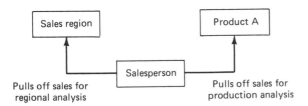

While both the hierarchical and network models are workhouses for volume transaction applications, they cannot easily handle ad hoc requests in a format that is user friendly to departmental people. The request format must be structured and organized and the user must know something about file structure and file layout. The relational model, to which we now turn, provides ad hoc request flexibility.

Relational Data Base

The relational model was developed with the user in mind, and the user in mind is not the programmer, as was the case with the hierarchical and network models. On the surface the model is simple and deals with a data file the way a basic spreadsheet does. It has rows and columns, the rows representing individual records and the columns representing attributes of each record. The key is the separation of the logical and physical levels. The user does not have to know anything about the physical storage of the data—doesn't need to express complex data structures. The user deals with the logical view of the file, and that view is the familiar two-dimensional table.

The surface simplicity is a bit deceptive because, underneath, the relational model is based on sophisticated mathematical algorithms and notation. However, this is all transparent to the targeted user, who is a department person or a middle-level manager. This is not to say that IS professionals cannot use the fourth generation language that is used to access data and to generate programs and applications that are based on the data. Indeed they do use relational models to build elaborate enterprise-wide systems. The professionals need not be trained to the degree of those writing programs for hierarchical and network models and they can become productive considerably faster. The principal drawback, as has been mentioned, is that the code generated from 4GLs is not as efficient as COBOL or C code. However, the reduction in hardware costs and chip speed are making this a desirable tradeoff.

The relational model was proposed by Dr. E. F. Codd in 1970. IBM gave credibility to the concept by their development of DB2. In its initial form, DB2 was a mainframe product but there are now many miniplatform products, popular ones being Ingress, Oracle, and Informix. There are also a variety of microplatform products including dBaseIV and Rbase. The mini and micro relational systems have the advantage of running on several vendors' hardware, which gives them a wider appeal.

Figure 4.11 illustrates the way data are represented by the relational model. The upper table represents a variety of data elements on each of a company's sales regions, while the lower table presents data about each of the company's salespeople. Note that this table is linked to the other table by the last column, which includes the region of each salesperson.

Structured Query Language (SQL)

We now look into the language used by relational models. Professionals usually design and construct the data files, for this requires a good amount of expertise and experience. Therefore the attention here is to the language rather than the development tools and procedures.

Structured Query Language (SQL) is the language that is used in most relational data base systems. It has achieved popularity in the user community and is the standard adhered to by major data base providers. It is the basis for the American National Standards Institute (ANSI) and is available for data base software systems like IBM's DB2, Ingress, Oracle, dBase IV, and Rbase. SQL is fairly easy to learn and can be used by nonprogrammers. There is still a question as to whether it is appropriate for all classes of users, particularly those who access the data base intermittently. SQL is called a structured language, and indeed there are a rigorous set of rules and procedures that one must follow. However, it is termed

FIGURE 4.11. Relational model

Region No.	Location	No. salesperson	Budgeted sales	Actual sales
1				
2				
3				
4				

Salesperson	Years with company	Last year's sales	This year's budget	This year's actual	Region no.

a fourth generation language to distinguish it from programming languages like COBOL or PASCAL or C. Compared with them, it is a major leap forward.

A few examples will give the reader some idea of how the system works and how one can obtain information from a data base that has already been compiled. The fundamental SQL instruction or command used to retrieve data is the SELECT command. The basic format of this command is three subcommands or clauses as follows:

SELECT: This subcommand designates the particular data items to be accessed.

FROM: This subcommand designates the particular table storing the data item(s).

WHERE: This specifies the particular search parameters defining the data items to be selected.

Several examples should clarify how the language operates. Let's assume we have created a salesperson file with the following data items:

Salesperson	City	State	Sale(s)	Goal Achievement (%)
Clarence Barrow	Pittsfield	MA	50,000	10
Roger Smith	Montpelier	VT	25,000	10
George Hall	Boston	MA	225,000	40
Amy Brown	Hartford	CT	242,500	55
William McIntyre	Keen	NH	185,000	20
Bradford Dorley	Providence	RI	142,000	25
Harry Parsons	Bangor	ME	214,000	60
Elizabeth Jones	Burlington	VT	140,000	35
Tom Winnegar	Boston	MA	275,000	60
Robert Villesy	Springfield	MA	242,000	70

Example: A company has several hundred salespeople scattered throughout the United States. A marketing vice president wants to know how many salespeople in region 3 have sold $200,000 or greater thus far in the year. This is the command the VP (or assistant) would use to obtain the information:

SELECT name, city, state, sales, goal achievement
FROM salesperson
WHERE sales >=$200,000

This will produce a report that appears as follows:

Salesperson	City	State	Sale(s)	Achievement (%)
George Hall	Boston	MA	225,000	40
Amy Brown	Hartford	CT	242,500	55
Harry Parsons	Bangor	ME	214,000	60
Tom Winnegar	Boston	MA	275,000	60
Robert Villesy	Springfield	MA	242,000	70

It should be added that the WHERE command is quite versatile. A set of logical or boolean qualifiers is employed to set up conditions for including particular data items. In this instance we have qualified our instruction to select only those salespeople who have sold $200,000 or more. Other logical qualifiers are as follows:

= equal to	≠ not equal to
< less than	> greater than
<= less than or equal to	>= greater than or equal to

In addition to the foregoing qualifiers, compound selections can be made where two or more conditions must be met before the row is retrieved. We use the logical expressions AND or OR. The use of the connector AND means that both conditions must be met, whereas the use of OR means the row is displayed if either condition is met. Examples of the foregoing in the salesperson table are as follows:

SELECT name, city, state, sales, goal achievement

FROM salesperson

WHERE sales >=$200,000 and goal achievement >=50%

This instruction would select four records and include Amy Brown, Harry Parsons, Tom Winnegar, and Robert Villesy.

In a similar manner, the result of the following instruction should be apparent:

SELECT name, city, state, sales, goal achievement

FROM salesperson

WHERE sales >=$200,000 or goal achievement >=50%

This instruction would select five records, George Hall, Amy Brown, Harry Parsons, Tom Winnegar, and Robert Villesy.

Other SQL functions include the ability to sort output by use of the "order by clause." Thus, in the foregoing example we could sequence salespeople by their dollars and sales by adding the clause: ORDER by sale(s). We can also perform the group functions of averaging, summing, determining the minimum or maximum value, and counting the numbers in a column. It all appears quite easy, and indeed it is if only simple operations are required. But there is a lot to SQL beyond the simple commands illustrated in this analysis and it is well to heed the statement of a prominent data base expert, George Schussel, who said, "SQL is like playing chess. You can learn all the basic moves in half an hour, but it takes practice the rest of your life to become any good." For most of us, it is probably enough to know the basic moves.

Micro-Based and Client Server Systems

With the increased power and storage capacities of personal computers, the development of powerful micro-based data management systems presents an inviting possibility; versatile DBMS like dBase IV, Rbase, and Paradox, to name a few. These systems are inviting and can be developed by individual departments without the oversight or awareness of the IS professional staff. While this is seductive, caution must be exercised because many of the same design considerations are present in departmental micro-based systems as there are in the larger ones. The elements of backup, security, data dictionary, flexibility, and modularity are most significant. A data base can start as a small effort and grow to be a competitive force in running the business. The risk is that the necessary controls and safeguards have not been built in. Volume production and added complexity can overload the system and cause serious interruption. Because the system is not well-documented (in some cases not documented at all) the alterations and corrections are quite difficult. Another caveat is that many of the micro data base systems are really not that at all, but are basic file managers. This can be quite misleading as the users' needs very frequently exceed the capabilities of the software employed.

Data base development can be from the top down or from the bottom up. It is important to scope the size of the application before deciding on the DBMS to employ. No one desires to bridle the enthusiasm and innovation of departments who have the real perspective on how to serve their customers better. However, one must have experience to recognize future size and scope to avoid disappointment and a reduction in service to those same customers the system was designed to help. It is usually prudent to consult with either internal or external consultants before embarking on an application involving data base.

Client servers is an architecture that employes data base systems in ways that assign the complex data base tasks to a mini- or micro-based server while permitting the flexibility of clients to format and derive reports and screen formats to support their functional activity. Client servers are growing in popularity and may represent the best compromise of all the data base models previously described in this section. Chapter 6 develops the client server model and discusses the tradeoffs of letting the IS central staff professionals do it, versus letting the department personnel do it. It is a most important issue facing IS.

DISTRIBUTED DATA BASES

It should be noted that distributed data bases are concerned with where the data records are located; they can employ hierarchical, networking, or relational models. A distributed data base coordinates data that are stored at multiple facilities throughout the geographic territory in which a company conducts business. For example, each sales region may order products from its own warehouse. The product file for the warehouse is maintained locally. But suppose that a sales region can order similar products from other regional warehouses when inventory is depleted at the local warehouse. Also, customers in one region may place orders in another region. In this type of situation, it may be wise to have a distributed data base approach. Thus, an order placed on a warehouse in region A will automatically access the inventory file of other regional warehouses in order of their proximity if the local warehouse is out of stock. There is a linkage between the various data bases.

This adds a complexity to the data management job as the various data bases must be designed as an entity and must be linked via some type of communication network. A key to success for distributed systems is user transparency, meaning that a user seeking data for handling a transaction, producing a report, or answering an inquiry, has access to local data bases and remote data bases without realizing there is a distinction. Of course the user may be made aware, for example, of from where the order is being shipped—but there are no processing complications.

Determining where the data base is located involves an analysis of frequency of access, communication efficiency, and cost. For example, if 90 percent of the information needed by management for a particular region comes from the local activity, then it may make sense to avoid communication costs and potential delay by storing the major data base locally. The 10 percent would be accessed from the central data base over a telecom network. However, if the figure is closer to 50 percent, the tradeoff may favor a central data base accessed by all regions. The introduction of distributed data bases raises another degree of complexity. Data dictionaries must record and account for geographic location of data, while message traffic becomes an added factor in the analysis and design of the system. In some cases, it may be better to replicate the data at night by transmitting updated files to remote locations rather than have people at remote sites access the central file. These factors may be the reason why distributed data bases have evolved slowly and are not as widely used as the other data base models.

ORGANIZING FOR DATA BASE

Many IS organizations have a data base administrator reporting directly to the IS director. This position, filled by a properly qualified individual, is one of the more important facets of successful data base implementation. This individual must have, not only technical expertise, but also a business and management orientation, since he or she is responsible for administering a resource vital to the needs of all management levels. The data base administrator (DBA) is the keeper of the data dictionary and provides guidance and direction for new application development. It is often the DBA who makes the tradeoff decision on shared data or controlled redundancy to serve a specific and important user need.

Another important function to the DBA is to ensure that proper training courses are available and utilized by the various levels in the organization. A data base consciousness must pervade the organization, and properly directed courses are a principal tool in accomplishing this.

Finally, in order to succeed, a top-level and company-wide commitment to the data base concept is necessary. Management must understand and realize the significance of the information resource management concept. This must be more than a perfunctory nodding or a broad-scale blessing; it must involve a participative role—attending a data base class, acting on an information steering committee, or taking part in an information system project that has immediate impact on a manager's specific job function.

COST OF DATA BASE DEVELOPMENT

It should be apparent at this point that the cost of developing a data base is not inconsiderable. When one considers the benefits, one should also consider the cost side. First, there is the people cost of the data base administrator and any associates who are needed initially to set up the files. Second, there is the cost of establishing the files. This procedure usually involves both transforming manual data into electronic media and converting existing electronic media into the new format. Also involved is the cost of converting, modifying, or rewriting existing programs, which may use the old file formats.

Not to be overlooked are the costs of hardware and software additions necessary to implement an integrated data base. At a minimum, additional data storage devices are required, and if there is an increase in processor and peripheral activity, it may necessitate equipment upgrade or addition. Also, the cost of data base software must be taken into account. A major switch to a data base–oriented approach is a far-reaching decision and should be viewed as a long-term company investment. A careful design and phase-in plan must be employed, and the total project should be considered a multiyear effort.

DATA BASE: PERTINENT QUESTIONS AND ANSWERS

To summarize and complete the discussion of data base, I would like to refer to an excellent manual written by Westinghouse Tele-computer System Corporation and described by William E. Bender of Westinghouse Electric Corporation in *Management Informatics,* Vol. 3, No. 2. The manual, in question-and-answer form, is aimed at "providing a clear understanding necessary to realistically evaluate benefits of the data base approach." I think it succeeds. I have excerpted questions that I think are appropriate for the level of discussion aimed at in this book.

1. The Problem of Definition

Q. What does data base management really mean?

A. Ambiguity surrounding its definition, together with misunderstanding of its purpose, have helped surround data base management with mystery.

The use and description of data base management systems have covered both ends of the spectrum: Some describe them as the panacea for all data processing problems; others consider them little more than present-day file maintenance systems.

In its simplest form, a data base is a collection of data from which a company would like to establish and maintain certain relationships. A data base management system structures and maintains these relationships. Complex structures and relationships are not necessary, and all corporate data need not be included in one data base. Through use of data base management systems, a company's data are now structured and related and therefore obtainable in a more orderly and logical fashion.

Q. Does a data base management system encompass all corporate data?

A. It is impossible to state in all cases which data may be processed through a data base management system, but two key points can help answer this question. First, the user must define what the system is to provide (a subset of what it can provide); and, second, the user must define relationships among data according to the way he or she views the operating environment of this company.

For certain applications with their associated files of data, data base management techniques may be too sophisticated and cannot be beneficially applied; however, many other applications, which may appear quite complex by conventional standards, can be simplified through data base techniques. Each situation is unique and requires an individual analysis and approach.

2. The Technical Aspects of Data Base Management

Q. What does a data base management system do?

A. A data base management system performs the following functions:

1. *Organizes data.* Data are organized or structured according to the specifications of the data definition language. These specifications are introduced by the data base administrator at the time the data base is established, and may be reintroduced as the data base configuration changes. Data are organized in the manner most suitable to each application.

2. *Integrates data.* Data are interrelated or linked together at the element (named field of data) level and can, therefore, be assembled in many combinations during execution of a particular application program. The data base management system is the vehicle used to collect, combine, and return a portion of the available data to the user.

3. *Separates data.* A data base management system serves as a filter between application programs and their associated data. It separates application logic from the input/output logic needed to calculate addresses, follow chains or links, block/unblock data, locate records, and select data elements. In addition, it separates the logical description and relationships of data from the way in which the data are physically stored. The data base remains secure and intact even though it is processed by different programs that describe the data in different ways and that may be written in different programming languages.

4. *Controls data.* A data base management system appears to an application programmer to be an extension of the operating system software. As it receives data storage requests from host programs, it controls how and where data are physically stored. On data retrievals, it locates and returns requested elements of data to the programs.

5. *Retrieves data.* A record of data can be obtained via a data base management system: (1) serially (in its physically stored sequence), (2) sequentially, according to the value of a user-specified key, (3) randomly by key, (4) randomly by address, and (5) by structural link. All or any portion of the data record can be returned to the user.

6. *Protects data.* A data base management system protects and secures both the content of a data base and the relationships of data elements. Data are protected against access by unauthorized users, physical damage, operating system failure, simultaneous updating, and certain interruptions initiated by a host program.

Q. How does a data base management system work?

A. A data base management system is generally composed of three subsystems, which operate as follows:

1. *Data base definition.* In this subsystem, the schema (complete description of the data

base) is specified through use of a special language known as the data description language (DDL). It is generally not necessary to specify a complete description of the data base at one time, especially when the data base is subdivided into named areas of addressable storage (files). In this case, the data base can be defined or redefined one file at a time for maximum flexibility. For each file, a specified organization technique governs the file's mode of processing. Many data records, data elements, and linkages with other files can be defined within a file structure.

2. *Data base communication.* Once the data base has been defined, elements of data can be stored and subsequently retrieved and/or updated through a data manipulation language (DML). In a host language data base management system, the DML is a set of CALL statements or CALL macros contained in application programs and processed by the communication subsystem. Through this communication subsystem, each application program can receive the particular elements of data it needs (the subschema) in a variety of sequences.

3. *Data base support.* The support subsystem performs data base utility or service functions, which generally include change file capacities, list files, alter file passwords, print file statistics, change record lengths and blocking factors, dump and restore files, and unlock files.

3. The Data Base Environment

Q. How can I guarantee the integrity of my data base?

A. A data base is susceptible to five phenomena, each of which can destroy its integrity. Each is described below, together with the appropriate corrective action:

1. *Access by unauthorized personnel.* One of the four techniques or combinations of them can be used to isolate classified or proprietary data from unauthorized personnel:

   a. Password security. For any user to read or update a file, he or she must know the password for the file.

   b. Access by element name. To retrieve or update an element of data, the user must know the name of the element.

   c. Data break-out. Highly sensitive data can be broken out into a separate file that can be stored off-line.

   d. Access list. A list of program names with authority to retrieve and maintain elements of data can be stored by the data base management system, and accesses can be checked against the list.

2. *Simultaneous update.* In a multiprogramming environment, it is possible for two users to update the same file concurrently. Whenever dependent updates are made by more than one program at the same time, unpredictable results may occur. These simultaneous updates can be prevented by locking out other maintenance transactions to the files while one transaction is being processed.

3. *Host program interrupt.* An abnormal end (ABEND) processing module can be provided to trap user interrupts, write current buffers to their respective files, and close the files.

Changes to the data base can be written to a log file and this log can be applied to the data base, at the user's discretion, to return the data base to the exact form it had prior to the run of the application program. These two features permit the user to continue execution from the point of the error or to restore the data base and rerun the entire job.

4. *System error.* The ABEND processing module cannot trap system errors; therefore, a data base must be restored to the exact form it had prior to the current run of the application program. When such errors occur, the data base can be recovered by applying the transaction log or by rebuilding the individual files of the data base using a sequential backup copy of them.

5. *Physical damage.* If information cannot be retrieved from a file because of a defective track or physical damage to a disk pack, the file should be rebuilt from the latest backup. Utility programs supplied by the hardware manufacturer may be applied to recover from these errors.

Q. Who should design a data base system?

A. The design of a data base system requires commitments from both user management and data processing management. Because the design of a data base system specifies how information will originate, who will use it, and how it will be used, functional users should participate in its design. Without functional user participation, there is no real assurance that the logic of the system and its output will be of value to the users.

Equally important, however, is the assistance and advice on technical matters from IS. Again, without their technical guidance, there is no assurance that the system is technically feasible.

The key in designing a data base management system is to have the right people assessing the right problems. Let the functional user assess the economic and functional problems, and let data processing assess the technical problems.

Q. What are the management implications to be considered when installing a data base management system?

A. Initially, organization politics may cause resistance to the installation of a data base management system because its installation may cross organization lines. Data files that are the responsibility of one functional area may become accessible to other functional areas. Files may become part of a larger unit (a data base) where data are shared. While this is usually advantageous because it reduces data redundancy, it may cause functional departments to feel that their ability to control data is restricted.

Q. How will a data base management system affect the role of the functional user?

A. Since the value of any system and data processing application is measured by its benefit to the functional user, the possibility of greatly increased capability in the data base systems environment brings a strong focus on the role of the functional user.

The principles of good systems design are equally applicable within the data base systems environment. The joint effort of users, systems analysts, and programmers to achieve optimum systems design is still a valid approach.

In addition to the traditional participation in the design and operation of a data processing application, a new perspective for the functional manager emerges. To fully benefit from the increased capabilities offered, the user must be prepared to participate in the selecting of facilities and in designing a system that satisfies his or her requirements. Identifying the tradeoffs and justifying the cost of implementation require a user to assess accurately the relative merits of the different possibilities. User acceptance and support during implementation are vital to ensure that transitional problems are minimized and adjustments to user interfaces are made as required. Without user support, an excellent system can fail; with total user commitment, even a mediocre system can at least partially succeed.

4. Assessing the Benefits and Risks of Data Base Management

Q. What can a data base environment provide that a company cannot obtain now?

A. A company will reap two significant benefits by moving into a data base environment: (1) maximizing the information the company collects and uses about products and customers, and (2) tailoring the IS department to meet more adequately the needs of the company.

Until the advent of the data base environment, there had never been an easy way for business management to structure and relate corporate data in order to obtain the maximum amount of information. Each time management wanted to see data related in a different way, new programs had to be written, files tailored, and special computer runs made. The result was often a disillusioned management, unable to understand why an expensive computer and a talented professional and technical staff could not relate data.

In the final analysis, a data base environment will provide centralized management of a company's most valuable resource—the data used in day-to-day operation. This centralized management provides convenient expansion and integration of applications with minimal data redundancy; reduced data and program maintenance; and smaller, more manageable programs.

This leads directly to the second most important benefit—the ability of the data processing department to respond more effectively to the unique reporting demands that most businesses require. Data processing can work more closely with functional users and more closely tailor its needs to the overall needs of the business. The result is a data processing department able to respond to unique requirements without sacrificing service to individual functional users.

Q. What are some of the important aspects to be considered in assessing the potential usage of a data base management system?

A. One of the most important aspects is a thorough understanding and analysis of the information flow among the functional departments. This understanding of information flow is vital to the construction of a data base and implementation of data base management system, since it forms the basis for the data relationships. A lack of knowledge in any area can result in an inadequately structured data base.

It is also important to know exactly what the data base approach is to accomplish and to define measurable objectives. Too often the objectives are as general as "to improve information for decision making" or "to provide more timely information." Each of these objectives is fine as far as it goes, but neither is specific enough to be achieved practically. The key is to have very precise objectives that are supported by a detailed and thorough plan.

Q. What are some of the benefits of a data base management system?

A. There are many benefits to be derived from installing a data base management system. Some of the more tangible ones are:

1. Reduced programming costs. Because many of the input/output (file definition and file maintenance) routines normally coded by the programmers are now handled through the data base management system, the amount of time and money spent writing an application program is reduced.

2. Reduced development and implementation time. Because programmers spend less time writing applications, the amount of time required to implement new applications is reduced.

3. Reduced program and file maintenance costs. Nearly 60 percent of the programming dollar is spent on maintenance. Data base management systems reduce this expenditure by performing file maintenance in a more convenient and more efficient manner. Program maintenance is also reduced because the volatile areas of programs, input/output, and file descriptions are handled via the data base management system.

4. Reduced data redundancy. Redundant data items cost money in storage space, programmer time, and data maintenance. With a data base management system, data items need be recorded only once and are available for everyone to use. Programmers do not spend time coding file descriptions that contain the same data elements found in other files, since each element of data is maintained by a single source.

5. Increased flexibility. Data base management systems make the data processing organization more flexible and enable it to respond more quickly to the expanding needs of the business. Unique reporting requirements are more adequately met, because special files do not have to be created or redesigned, and programming changes are minimized.

Q. How can I minimize the risks in introducing a data base environment?

A. One sure way to minimize any risk is through careful and intelligent planning.

A second way is to start small. Don't try to create a totally integrated data base in the first go-round. A step-by-step approach is best.

A third way is to deal with a company whose product has a good reputation, whose financial status is good, and who will be around in the future when support is needed.

A fourth way is to select good people to staff the data base administration and planning functions.

The fifth and probably the most underestimated way is to educate the individuals who must function within the data base environment. If they do not understand data base concepts and do not believe in the data base management software product, problems are likely to occur.

Q. How do I evaluate data base management software?

A. Five areas must be considered:

1. Hardware considerations. Another important point is the impact of the data base management system on the current hardware configuration. The system should be independent of the unique characteristics of the direct-access storage devices on which it operates. It should support processing during a transition period when files of data are

being converted from one device to another. Also, memory requirements must be considered. Despite the introduction of virtual memory and substantial reductions in the price per kilobyte, memory continues to be a relatively expensive commodity. If the installation of a data base management system results in the rental or purchase of additional memory, then this cost must be considered as part of the price of the product. Equally important is the length of time the memory is tied up. For users of small machines, it should be possible to roll the product in and out of memory so that it is resident only when needed.

2. Protection of data. Data base management software should also be evaluated on its ability to protect data from misuse and destruction. Data must be protected from unauthorized personnel, computer operation errors, and even from errors in the data base management system itself.

3. Ease of program conversion and product use. A data base management system must be as applicable to existing application programs as it is to newly designed systems. It should be possible to apply data base techniques to a single file of data and later expand to an integrated data network with minimal conversion programming. The data base management product should be easy to use and understand. It should require minimal training of personnel and minimal "fine tuning" and reorganization of files of data.

4. Product price. How much for how long? The obvious question to consider when evaluating the price of a product is: Do the benefits derived from the use of the product offset its price? The price of a maintenance contract and the price of future enhancements must be factored into the analysis. Certain software suppliers who lease their products on an indefinite basis (i.e., the product is never owned by the user) may make the price justification impossible. Also, it may be convenient to have a contract with the supplier that enables you to apply all or a portion of the monthly rental payments toward a future purchase.

5. Supplier's stability and level of support. The supplier of a data base management system should keep the product operational with each new release of the operating system. Also the supplier should be continually enhancing the product to the current level of technology, should be readily available whenever an error in the product is detected, and should be willing to provide, perhaps on a fee basis, extra assistance whenever needed.

Q. What is the most important factor in implementing a data base management system?

A. The most important factor to consider in the installation of a data base management system is *education.* Personnel must be trained in the data base area, the software product, and the application techniques. Training must include top-management-level presentations to ensure that the company's business plan is consistent with the information systems plan, thereby committing management to the data base approach. Functional management must understand the applicability of the new techniques to their departments the role they must play in working with the data base administrator to define specification requirements. Finally, the programmer/analyst must feel comfortable working with the software, knowing in general how it operates, how to use it, and when and how to back up the files of data. If education is emphasized and a company considers data base management as an evolutionary process that follows realistic schedules, then the system will have a very positive influence on the business.

SUMMARY

We call data the mortar of IS; rather it is the mortar of business and the key to competing in the increasingly global economy. Power and success go to those who can manage the increasing deluge of data; it goes to those who can interpret and act on the data rather than drown in it. With the universal product code (UPC) and optical scanning we can collect sales information by item, by the hour of the day and store it, process it, and make real-time merchandising decisions; we can share data on an intercompany basis as do American Airlines and CitiBank (where air mileage from American's frequent flyer program is awarded to CitiBank's credit card users—one mile for every dollar spent using the credit card), and we can access outside on-line data bases. An exciting example is Dow Jones: With a Thinking Machines, Inc. massively parallel 65K microprocessor system working in concert, we can access five years of *The Wall Street Journal* for specific word or subject reference in half a second. To my way of thinking, that is real power!

Management's appetite for information has reached a stage where the fragmented data bases of the earlier developments do not suffice. Data must be organized in such a way as to permit management browsing across heretofore self-contained and bounded data files. This is the perspective of the chapter. The user's view of data was described, running the gamut from the top executive to lower management levels to IS systems analysts. This outside-in approach facilitated an understanding of *what* was required in the way of information before the *how* of data base use was discussed. A variety of access methods or user languages were reviewed, emphasizing the concept of user-friendly systems. Data bases can lead the horse to water, but easy-to-use data base languages are what make him drink.

Data base software was then reviewed, and a description was given of the techniques of the data base dictionary and file structure that are the essential underpinnings of the software. Despite the improvements in software, practical tradeoffs must be made to satisfy the variety of company needs. In this regard, the subjects of geographically shared data bases and controlled redundancy were introduced. The four classes of data base management systems were introduced, with emphasis on the relational model. The need for developing a strong data base administration function led by a data base administrator reporting to the IS director was then mentioned.

Data base is the mortar of IS, but, because of historical application evolution, the development of a data base management system may require significant retooling and reconstruction. It may be possible to bridge from your current system to an integrated data base approach, or it may be necessary to start from scratch; in either case it is going to take time and resources. The strategy and conversion plan are vital considerations. Management cannot and will not countenance a plan where additional applications must be postponed for a matter of years. At the same time, continued building on a shaky foundation can prove very dangerous. The answer rests with business-oriented tradeoffs—the development of a staging plan that arrives at an integrated or unified data base, but is phased such that a moratorium on new development is not necessary. The best minds of the company should be put to bear on this data base implementation plan. If the concept of information as a vital company resource is valid, there is no other way.

Case Study

Midwest Bank

Midwest Bank decided to launch a comprehensive review of their IS operations. An eight-person team spent ten weeks, full time, to review the basic business processes, organization, information users, information systems, data classes, and data processing organization. The information was then synthesized into a report to management, recommending an overall systems architecture and strategy and application development based on user priority assessment. The effort at Midwest had top management commitment; the resultant document was well received and, in essence, was accepted as the statement of the IS direction of Midwest Bank for the next five years.

It was apparent to Midwest that they had developed applications in a fragmentary way, lacked an integrated data base, didn't know in what direction they should be headed, and were facing increasing demands on the part of their users. This scenario was typical of many operations the size of Midwest.

An initial recommendation was to evaluate and select a data base system that would enable Midwest to integrate its data files, so that operating management could derive the management information they said was imperative. A Data-Base Selection Committee was formed, selection criteria quickly agreed upon, and the following letter sent to three leading vendors of data-base management systems.

Dear Vendor:

I am pleased to announce the approval of the Data-Base Management System Selection Project for Midwest Corporation. This project will select the Data-Base Management System software that will become the basis for data-base development within Midwest. Your Data Management system has been selected as one of the three products that will be evaluated by this project.

Enclosed you will find a copy of the project plan document, which describes the project tasks, the methodologies to be used, and the project participants. There are several formal vendor interface points such as:

—Review and respond to the Criteria Document.
—Supply detailed technical information to be used to evaluate your project.

—Supply product-User names for us to contact in our data gathering.
—Review and comment on the findings document.

Your prompt response at these interface points will be necessary for us to meet the project schedule. However, your contributions throughout the project are invited, and we will be happy to consider any pertinent input at any time.

Sincerely,

STUDY QUESTIONS

1. Do you think Midwest was wise in conducting the comprehensive IS review? Do you think the study team size and time frame excessive?

2. Would you anticipate that data fragmentation would be a finding in a study conducted by a bank?

3. How would you evaluate the way Midwest is going about selecting a data base system?

4. Are they too restrictive in limiting the study to three vendors?

5. What should be the criteria for bid invitations in view of the fact there are more than 50 competent data-base systems on the market?

6. What do you think some of the key decision factors should be in Midwest's selection of a data-base system?

7. Should they be more definitive, that is, relational or distributed?

Case Study

National Telephone

National Telephone, a leading independent carrier, has developed over the past six years a large data base that they called NMDB (National Marketing Data Base). This 30-billion-character file is the basis for a diversified number of marketing analyses and reports used by sales managers, product managers, administrators, forecasters, and planners. The reports range from a simple request for sales by particular customers to complex modeling, projecting a full P&L statement for a proposed new product line. Users of the data base range from clerical personnel to department vice presidents.

Input to NMBD emanates from the billing file, which records individual sales transactions. The billing file is organized by customer, since billing is its principal application. The billing system was the first to be computerized by National Telephone. Over the years it has evolved from a batch/tape to an on-line system; however, the original system design has been carried forward through the series of conversions that have taken place. While the billing data base satisfied the order processing and accounts receivable functions quite well, the marketing and planning departments have found it progressively more difficult to reformat the data base into NMDB. One major reason is that the company's strategy is placing more emphasis on product line performance. Therefore, sales by product and product line are essential. NMDB is oriented to product but can also produce analyses keyed by customer. Current billing procedures result in a considerable time lag between the time a transaction occurs and the time it can be transferred to NMDB by the required product categories. For years the systems analysts of NMDB have been trying to have the billing system analysts rectify the situation, but without success. They know that maintaining two huge and somewhat redundant files is an expensive proposition, but somehow they have been unable to reach a solution.

The problem would soon surface anew, because the new vice president of product marketing, Ralph Lesser, was preparing a presentation for the president of National that would indicate it was becoming impossible to manage a product line without current and accurate product line results. Lesser knew this was going to irritate the vice president of IS, Bob Frank, but he felt also that Frank's people had not been able to resolve the problem and hadn't given it the priority he knew it warranted.

STUDY QUESTIONS

1. How did this problem come about? Do you think it could have been avoided?
2. Could Bob Frank have recognized the problem and put a plan in place to rectify it before Lesser brought the issue to the president?
3. Should the billing file have been constructed with the flexibility to effectively handle product information or any information required by management?
4. Do you think Lesser is acting in a responsible manner?
5. What should Frank do to resolve the problem? Is a redesign necessary, a new data base structure, faster data base reporting, or what?

SELECTED REFERENCES

Date, C., *An Introduction to Database Systems*. Reading, Mass.: Addison-Wesley, 1975.

Diehr, George, *Database Management*. Glenview, Ill.: Scott, Foresman Company, 1989.

Hawryszkiewycz, I.T., *Database Analysis and Design,* 2nd ed. New York: Macmillan Publishing Co., 1991.

Hawryszkiewycz, Igor T., *Relational Database Design*. New York: Prentice Hall, 1990.

Kreitzer, Lawrence W., "Data Dictionaries—the Heart of IBM," *Infosystems* (February, 1981), 64-66.

Martin, J. *Computer Database Organization,* 2nd ed. Englewood Cliffs, N.J.: Prentice-Hall, 1977.

Martin, J., *An End User's Guide to Database*. Englewood Cliffs, N.J.: Prentice-Hall, Inc., 1981.

Martin, J., *Strategic Data-Planning Methodologies*. Englewood Cliffs, N.J.: Prentice-Hall, Inc., 1982.

McFadden, Fred R., and Jeffrey A. Hoffer, *Database Management,* 3rd. ed. Redwood City, CA: The Benjamin/Cummings Publishing Company, Inc., 1991.

Mittra, Sitansus, *Principles of Relational Database Systems*. Englewood Cliffs, NJ: Prentice Hall, 1991.

Nolan, R. L., "Computer Data Bases: The Future Is Now," *Harvard Business Review* (1973), pp. 98-114.

Pratt, Philip J., *A Guide to SQL*. Boston, Mass.: Boyd & Fraser Publishing Co., 1990.

Ricardo, Catherine M., *Database Systems: Principles, Design, and Implementation*. New Rochelle, N.Y.: MacMillan Publishing Co., 1990.

Synott, William R. and William H. Gruber, *Information Resource Management*. New York: John Wiley & Sons, 1981.

Ullman, J., *Principles of Database Systems*. Woodland Hills, Cal.: Computer Science Press, 1980

Chapter 5

Telecommunications and Distributed Systems

INTRODUCTION

The vice president of Sales arrives at 8:30 A.M. and immediately checks his electronic mail messages. He notes that the corporate office will announce at the close of the day the intended acquisition of a prominent competitor. One message gives details of the bid offer and the reasons for the acquisition. The V.P. wants to inform his national account managers of this move so that their key customers will know before the information hits the street tomorrow. The company has a policy of informing its customers of new products or organizational developments. This has increased customer loyalty. He sends a confidential electronic message to his 50 national account managers advising them to schedule meetings with their account contacts tomorrow morning. At 8:45 A.M. the vice president of Sales leaves his office for his morning staff meeting.

A major package deliverer implements a nationwide packet tracking system. When a package is picked up, the shipping document is scanned by a hand-held reader. When the driver gets to his car, he transmits the information to the home office computer system. When he arrives at the distribution hub, the package is scanned again. The scanning and transmission to the home office continues on the delivery side, such that an inquiry to the home office as to the whereabouts of a packet can be answered immediately. In all, the package is scanned six times from pickup to destination.

These are two scenarios that are being repeated in other settings throughout the world. They have in common the use of telecommunications to give a company major business and strategic advantages by compressing the information delivery cycle, and, in a growing number of cases, providing a company with a new service or product that affords real competitive advantage.

Michael Hammer and Glenn Mangurian writing in the *Sloan Management Review* point out many examples of the combination of telecommunications and information processing that allow companies to attain critical business and strategic goals. In his book *Competing in Time,* Peter Keen clearly illustrates that the new telecommunications systems provide much more than compressing the time of information delivery, but are "strategic resources that are changing the face of business."

The previous chapter discussed data base and its importance to IS. Other major ingredients are telecommunications (communications), networking, and distributed systems (DS). Communications provides the transmission (the wires, cable, etc.) for IS and the data base. The network is the assemblage of equipment (both hardware and software) by which connections are made between workstations. Workstations are then considered "on the network." DS provides a structure for allowing some or all of the processing, data storage, or control functions to be situated in different locations and connected by telecommunications.

Companies have gone through cycles of IS architecture, the first being the use of small computers in multiple geographic sites. Then the trend was toward centralization and the more-bang-per-buck syndrome—based on the principle that the larger computer systems were the most economical on the basis of processing power or storage capacity per dollar of expenditure. The mini and micro revolution has reversed that trend, offering an economical way to disperse resources; therefore, the trend today is definitely toward decentralization and a distributed IS environment. Another name for describing the dispersion of resources is *downsizing,* the term connoting that, with the increase in power, lowering of cost, and reduction in size, what had to be accomplished on mainframes can now be accomplished on minis or micros in a departmental setting.

Communication is defined as the transmitting of data from one site to another, formerly via telephone lines, but now including cable, microwave, optical fiber, and satellite facilities. The personal computer has become as ubiquitous as the telephone. The personal computer has produced new demands for the communication of data inside a facility, within a company, and globally. In this chapter, we will discuss how voice, data, image, and graphics are transmitted from one location to another. After reviewing telecommunications and the basic elements that comprise it, we will analyze the concept of distributed systems, give examples of its use, and discuss the benefits and downside risks.

TYPES OF LONG-RANGE COMMUNICATION

Communication is defined in the *American College Dictionary* as "the imparting or interchange of thoughts, opinions or information by speech, writing or signs." Without the ability to transmit knowledge and ideas, there is no civilization. What we are concerned with here is how information in the form of "speech, writing or signs" can be communicated through time and space. This is the objective of computer-based teleprocessing systems—to send and receive information from one location to another (space) so that the activity can be carried out quickly (time).

The techniques of transmitting messages (see Figure 5.1) from one location to another can be seen as a key element in a civilization. Primitive societies developed long distance communications using drums and smoke signals. We can begin to see trade-offs that must be considered in evaluating teleprocessing systems. A smoke signal has a much longer range than a drum but is ineffective where dense forests, mountains, or overcast skies obscure vision. Every means of transmitting messages—runners, men on horseback, automobiles, and airplanes—has strengths and weaknesses.

Telegraphy

The era of electronic communications began in 1844 with the invention of the telegraph. In October 1832, sailing home from Europe, Samuel F. B. Morse discussed with other passengers a recent publication by Michael Faraday on electromagnetism. Morse planned to make a telegraph recording instrument and devised a dot-dash code based on the absence or presence of electrical pulses.

In March 1838, after a successful demonstration before President Martin Van Buren and his cabinet, Congress appropriated funds for a practical test of the telegraph. Morse's

FIGURE 5.1. Methods of communication

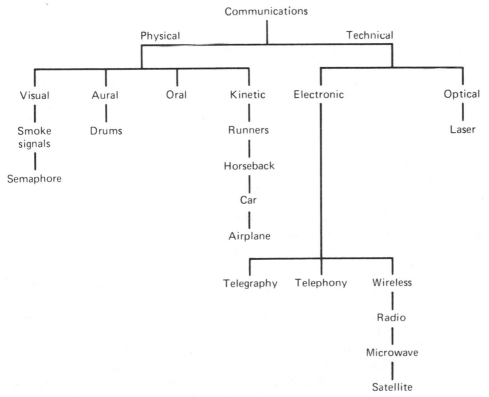

transmission in 1844 of "what hath God wrought" from the Supreme Court chamber in Washington to his partner in Baltimore over a 40-mile line was a landmark in communications.

A company was organized to extend the line to Philadelphia and New York City. By 1851, 50 companies using Morse patents were operating in the United States; a decade later, Morse systems were operating in Europe.

The majority of the messages in the early days concerned train dispatching. The telegraph line shared the right-of-way with the rail line, while telegraphy and railroads supported each other's growth.

Automatic telegraphy, defined broadly to mean those systems where signals are transmitted by machine and recorded automatically, was the next major development. This development replaced the telegraph key and the dot-dash Morse code with the teleprinter and the five-pulse Baudot code. With this code, it is possible to represent 32 different combinations: 26 for the alphabet and six for special functions. It is much more efficient than the dot-dash code. The pulses are delivered by a keyboard device to the telegraph line; at the receiving end they activate a teleprinter to print the message. Automated telegraphy introduced transmission and reception of messages punched on paper tape. These automatic methods were the forerunner of today's teleprocessing systems.

Telegraphy still provides low-cost data transmission where low speed is not a drawback, but its use has declined with the advances in telephony and microwave communication.

Telephony

Another major development took place in Boston on June 2, 1875, when Alexander Graham Bell heard the twang of a steel spring over an electric wire. Earlier, Bell had described an apparatus that could transmit speech. It consisted of a strip of iron attached to a membrane. When activated by a voice, the membrane vibrated before an electromagnet, inducing an electric current. Bell filed an application for a patent, and in March 1876 transmitted the first complete sentence. It was not quite as grand as Morse's message. He called to his assistant at the other end of the line, "Mr. Watson, come here; I want you."

The first commercial telephone was put into operation in May 1877, and by 1879 there were more than 50,000 telephones within the United States. Today many households have multiple phones—the total approximating 200 million.

Advanced technology has made it possible to conduct many conversations simultaneously over a single pair of wires. Coaxial cables and relays permit sharing hundreds of conversations. The first commercial manual telephone switchboard allowed the alternate switching of telegraph and voice communication over the same line. Dial systems were in use by 1892. More recent innovations include automatic switching systems and direct distance dialing.

Telephony advanced voice communication and provided the vital technology breakthrough for (nonverbal) data transmission. Telephone facilities carry data between computers and remote terminals, and between computers, in volumes that increase astronomically each year. Estimates are that in the future more than half the volume will be digital data going to and from computers, but, in retrospect, prognosticators were saying that 20 years ago. Like many technologies, the seers overestimated the penetration. Suffice it to say, however, that communication of nonverbal data is an exciting growth area.

Wireless Communications

The ability to communicate long distances without wires came in 1895 when Guglielmo Marconi developed the first wireless telegraph. Reginald Fessenden, an American physicist, demonstrated the first radio transmission of voices in 1900. Until then radio messages had been sent using the Morse's dot-dash code. In 1901 Marconi transmitted a radio message across the Atlantic. Commercial broadcasting began in the United States in 1920.

Television transmitting is similar in principle to radio but it is modified to handle the very wide frequency bands required for the video signal.

Microwave is a short radio wave. Microwaves came to notice during World War II with their use in radar. Microwave networks can carry thousands of conversations simultaneously. Since microwaves travel in straight lines, relay towers must be constructed in the line of sight. Because of the curvature of the earth, towers are usually no more than 30 miles apart.

Recently, communication satellites have assisted the communication of data within the United States and between continents. They serve as microwave relay stations. A satellite must be in a line-of-sight position from both relay points on the earth.

Cellular radio permits the transmission of voice and data from a car, boat, or plane. This allows companies like Federal Express to know that a particular package is in a truck going from company A to Federal Express terminal station 1 enroute to company B. In the same vein, companies now employ wireless transmission inside a building such that instead of laying wire or cable, they use radio waves to pass data between computer workstations. The affords maximum flexibility when remodeling or reorganizing an office or facility.

Fiber Optics

Probably the most important advance in wired communication service is that of fiber optics. *Fiber optics* is a process utilizing silicon rather than copper as the base element for communication lines. Silicon, a nonmetallic chemical element, is more prevalent than any other element except oxygen, and one of the benefits of fiber optics is lower cost per signal transmitted. Light-emitting diodes are employed to send signals via these fiber lines, which are no thicker than violin strings. Thus this medium offers the potential of lower cost, higher speed, and greater capacity. There is no question that fiber optics is playing an increasingly important role in future communication systems.

ELEMENTS OF A COMMUNICATIONS SYSTEM

The best way to explain a communications system is to describe a simple configuration and the elements that comprise it.

A schematic of a typical communications module is shown in Figure 5.2. The

FIGURE 5.2.

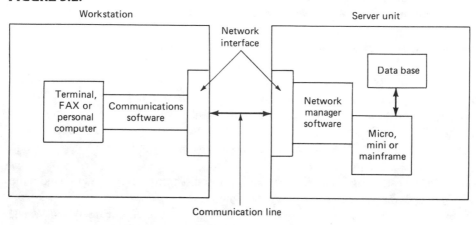

workstation is the sender and receiver of requested data. A combination of hardware and software is used to connect the workstation to the communication line. The network interface converts the keyed-in characters to electronic pulses for transmission over the communication line. At the receiving end, another network interface unscrambles the pulses from the different workstations. The communicated message is sent to a server unit which accesses the data base and accomplishes the necessary processing before returning the data to the workstation. A network manager supervises the messages coming in from multiple stations. The network manager is an extended piece of software that monitors and coordinates the network traffic.

When the entire message—for example, an inventory file inquiry—is delivered, the server has been instructed to seek out the appropriate inventory record from the data base, determine whether the requested quantity can be filled, and send back an appropriate message.

The schematic of a typical communications system in Figure 5.2 has six elements:

1. Workstation
2. Communications software
3. Network interface
4. Communication line
5. Network manager
6. Server unit

1. Workstation

The growth of the workstation segment of the information processing industry (primarily personal computers) in a word has been extraordinary. The overall trend of computer "extensibility," with the provision of computer power first to diverse locations within a building, then to remote locations in outlying plants and offices within the United

States and finally on a global scale, has accounted for this amazing growth. The proliferation of PCs, along with the incorporation of low-cost, microprocessor-based intelligence, represents a propelling force in the industry.

In many applications it is necessary to display graphic material in the form of charts, pictograms, design models, and the like, and some terminals are geared to handling just that type of application. There are two general types of graphic terminals—business graphics and design graphics. The latter are used primarily by design engineers and model builders to design automobiles, buildings, printed circuit-board layouts, and the like. Business graphics become important to management users of information systems who want to see business results and projections in chart and graphic form (pie charts, bar charts, or regression curves). A color capability also becomes important in graphic terminals.

We should note that special function terminals such as graphic, optical, or voice need not be treated as separate units, since these functions can often be provided as options to personal computers.

Optical readers can sense numbers, letters, and special symbols and can send this data to the computer. This eliminates the need for an operator to manually key the data. Effective applications include utility bills, insurance premium invoices, documents using the Universal Product Code (UPC) or other turnaround documents produced by a computer.

While still developing, voice recognition devices can translate the human voice into computer input. An individual voice print is established to allow for the idiosyncrasies of speech patterns. The individual is thus identified and is permitted to input commands and data to the system. On the output side, a voice synthesizer facilitates verbal commands and data as system output.

2. Communications Software

Added to a personal computer in communications mode is a software module that is activated when the workstation is ready to send or receive data. Each workstation on the network has its hardware/software module. It accomplishes functions such as error checking, data validation, message formatting, and ensures proper timing and sequence of communication. The software must be compatible with the network manager of the particular server unit. The software of the workstation is simple in scope when compared to the network manager software.

3. Network Interface

The network interface, usually a circuit board, ensures that the signal coming from the workstation is consistent with the signal utilized by the communication line. If the signals are different, it converts the workstation signal to that of the line. The network interface at the server end does the same. A common network interface is a modem. The name *modem* stands for modulator/demodulator. On the transmission end, the modulator converts the computer codes to tone signals for transmission over a telephone line. (Data signals are transmitted as tones.) On the receiving end, the demodulator converts the tone signals back to computer code.

The ordinary telephone lines can handle only analog signals while most computers can handle only digital signals. Analog signals capture voice and enable the transmission across the line. The analog signal is in the form of waves of different frequencies. The digital signal is a series of digital ones and zeros as illustrated below:

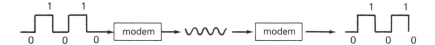

There are communication systems that work exclusively in digital mode and thus do not require modems. Both voice and data flow across the communication line in digital (binary) form. The Integrated Services Digital Network (ISDN), sponsored by AT&T, uses technology that can send voice and data over a single ordinary telephone line. This has advantages or application and cost in a growing number of operating environments.

4. Communication Line

The job of selecting the proper balance of communication lines is very difficult. This section will merely describe some of the selection criteria. The key criteria are set in boldface type.

Bandwidth determines the maximum transmission speed possible. Which bandwidth should be used depends on the volume and peak loads of the particular application. Narrowband transmission permits speeds of 300 to 1200 bits per second (BPS) while broadband transmission depends on wireless types of transmission (such as microwaves) or special television-quality coaxial cable and operates at speeds from 192 BPS to millions of BPS. Baseband employs only a single channel while broadband employs multiple channels. Their use is determined by cost/performance tradeoffs.

Data communications techniques tend to distort signals in a variety of ways that can cause loss of transmission or loss of the message. A process called **conditioning** adjusts the frequency and response elements in order to remove these distortions. Conditioning amounts to tuning a specific communication line for peak performance. Various conditioning services are available to ensure higher validity of data transmission and fewer line losses.

Another consideration in selecting communication lines is whether you require **simplex, half duplex, or full duplex capability.** Simplex mode allows communication only in one direction; that is, a terminal may receive data but it cannot transmit (or vice versa). Half duplex allows communications in both directions, but only one direction at a time. Full duplex allows simultaneous communication in both directions over the line.

Two classes of timing schemes are used in transmitting data, **asynchronous** and **synchronous.** In the asynchronous mode, special timing signals called start/stop bits are transmitted with each character. In the synchronous scheme, timing signals are sent much less frequently—for example, once per hundred characters transmitted.

The asynchronous scheme is used most often with low-speed terminals (2400 bits per second) operating over voice-grade lines. The synchronous scheme is used with more sophisticated terminals on higher-speed lines (above 2400 bits per second). The higher-quality line requires less timing information to keep it in step, permitting more message information to be transmitted per unit of time.

Whether an application should employ a **dial-up (switched) network** or **a private (leased) network** is a function both of the volume of communications and of the traffic patterns of the communication network. Most large companies find they require a combination of dial-up and private lines. AT&T offers WATS (Wide Area Telephone Service), a flat rate service for long distance calls, and TWX (Teletypewriter Exchange Service) for teleprinters and low-speed messages. AT&T also provides T1 and T3 service for those companies with large volumes who can take advantage of high-capacity, high-speed private lines. Data Speed is offered for higher-speed transmission requirements. Western Union provides TELEX (similar to TWX) for low-speed communications and Broadband Exchange Service for higher speeds and more flexible service.

Another service is that of VANS or Valued Added Networks. Companies such as GTE Telenet and Tymnet in addition to AT&T have established services for communicating digital data that provide data processing services such as message store and forward, forms creation, and data storage in conjunction with communication handling.

The two most significant **transmission codes** commonly in use are the Epsidic code, the ad hoc standard as initiated by IBM, and the American Standard Code for Information Interchange (ASCII) seven-level code. The selection of a code depends upon requirements such as compatibility, speed, error checking, validity, the software being used, and the terminal being used. There exists today a plethora of standards, the closest to emerging common ones being those designated by the international standards organization.

These same companies offer packet switching where the message is broken into pieces or packets and sent to the destination in subdivided form over different routes to optimize speed and capacity of transmission. The user of the service does not notice this process but assumes the entire message is sent as an entity.

5. Network Manager

Between the incoming data and the server is a rather intricate software system called a *network manager.* It is the vital part of a communications system providing the necessary intelligence to coordinate the entire network. It receives and sends messages to the server. It does a pre-edit—formatting and arranging the messages—before passing them along to the server for processing. It manages the speed imbalance between the communication line and the processing unit. The network manager sequences messages based on a preconceived priority scheme. Its specialty is in the preparation, editing, error checking, and formatting of messages prior to their being sent or received. Network management software can either reside on a dedicated server or on the same server that accesses the data base.

Network managers are normally developed by software or hardware vendors, not by the in-house technical staff. Evaluating and selecting a network manager is one of the most important elements in a successful telecommunication system. With the proliferation of workstations, servers and data bases, all prime elements in the system, the selection of a network manager that can handle a variety of diverse units is made all the more important and difficult because the industry still lacks accepted communication standards.

6. Server

The server unit is the nerve center of the entire communication network. It has the computing power and software programs to process the messages, access the data base and process the data before sending it back to the workstation.

Servers were exclusively the domain of the mainframe until about ten years ago. The mainframe was the only device that possessed the necessary processing power, high bandwidth to input/output devices, high capacity channels for accessing large data bases, and the memory capacity to store the necessary operating software systems.

Now the situation has reversed itself, and most servers are mini or micro computers. This is because the size and cost of circuitry has dropped so dramatically that the power and capacity previously found only in mainframes is now available in minis and micros at a fraction of the cost. Another precipitating factor is the availability of large data files that can be accessed by minis and micros. CDROMS (compact disk, read only memory) and optical disks present high volume, low-cost data base storage for minis and micros. The client/server architectural model that is becoming increasingly prevalent will be discussed more fully in the next chapter. For our purposes here, the mini or micro based server is a key element in telecommunication networks.

The foregoing six elements comprise the basics of a telecommunications system. Though the configurations may differ widely, every system must consider and be built from these six elements. We now take a look at how companies are using internal PBXs and local area networks (LANs) to implement communication systems within their organizations.

INTERNAL OR LOCAL COMMUNICATIONS

The PBX Approach

Significant changes are occurring in the internal communications world. Private PBXs offer a way to handle the connecting and switching of messages within an organization. They perform the role of the network manager. PBXs (private branch exchanges) can utilize either existing telephone wiring (twisted pair) or new *data highways* consisting of coaxial cable, which (like cable TV) demands a fairly radical new installation. Optical fiber is growing as a vehicle for local as well as long distance communication. The more prevalent communication handler, however is the local area network (LAN). The PBX has evolved from the voice or analog world while the LAN's origin is handling data.

The PBX, which can be supplied by AT&T or companies such as NEC or Northern Telecom, is actually a computer that can not only switch messages like an existing switchboard but also store messages, collect, sort, forward, switch, optimally route, retrieve, and so on. The PBX, because it is a computer and can be programmed, can also perform other functions such as heat and air conditioning control, lighting utilization, and other office-related activities. Also the PBX is a digital switch, which means that both voice and data are carried by the same signals, thus eliminating the modems that were needed in our external communications model to condition digital data for transmission across voice lines.

There are cost tradeoffs in using a PBX rather than conventional message switching. The data highway or coaxial cable is more costly to install, but it does offer more capacity and higher-speed transmission, which may be demanded by a particular internal communications system. The concept—and the trend—is to provide a single digital communications network in which voice messages and data messages are transmitted over the same line without buffering or modulating devices. This affords far more options, flexibility, and eventually lower costs—or at least costs that are less sensitive to volume increases.

Figure 5.3 depicts an internal PBX communications system. The first floor houses the host computer, which communicates to both the internal and external worlds. The second floor depicts an office environment, which has batteries of facsimile machines, word processors, copiers, office terminals, and phones all linked to the host via the PBX. This configuration is host based, but there also could be secondary LANs to allow access to a local data base that stores the data unique to the particular office floor, such as personal letters, personal phone messages, and personal data files. The devices mentioned are also linked via the PBX to the host computer on the first floor and to other computer systems in the outside world.

The company's executive offices are on the third floor, which, like the second floor, has its phones and word processors. There are also graphic terminals for supplying executives with charts and graphs of business activity, and personal computers for developing reports and processing data from an executive's own personal file. This personal computing can be accomplished independently of the host computer on the first floor. Conversely, the executive can tap the host data base if it is required. Teleconferencing and videoconferencing are other capabilities controlled by the PBX to the outside world (employing satellite transmission because of the high data/voice volume) and connected to the PBX's of the linked facility. There are predictions that, with the rising global nature of business and high cost of travel, from 25 to 50 percent of current business travel will be replaced by tele- and videoconferencing.

The potential uses of an internal/external communications system are quite exciting. For example, an executive committee of a company might be contemplating the introduction of a new product line into a new marketplace. Calling on the host data base on the first floor, they view a presentation of historical movement of product lines with similar characteristics on the graphic terminal. External market data from a linked market research company's data base are also obtained. The internal and external data are then modeled and optimal bottom lines are produced based on a variety of interacting variables. A risk assessment is also produced. Finally, a videoconference is held with members of the executive committee of the division who are to be responsible for financing and marketing the new products. This approach can be a very effective operation in companies, depending on their size and operating culture. However, the dominant trend is the use of an integrated set of LANS to accomplish the same type of applications.

FIGURE 5.3. Internal communications system

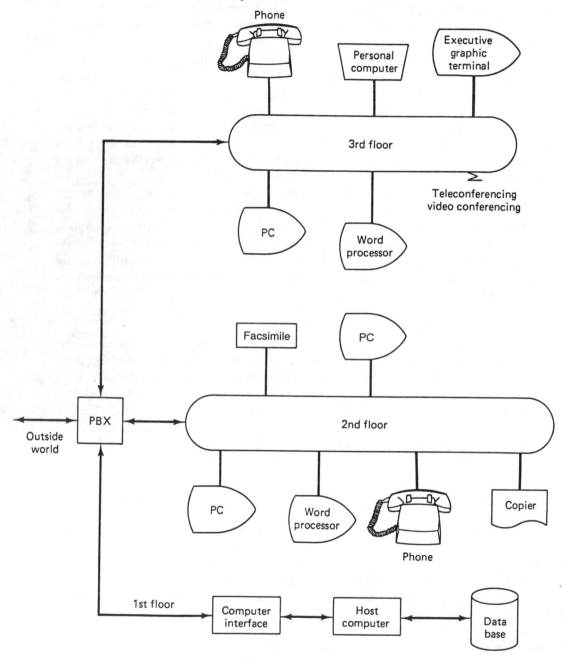

LOCAL AREA NETWORKS (LANS)

A local area network is a logical extension of the personal computer era. It has become the more prevalent alternative to the PBX, acting as the network manager or it can be used in conjunction with a PBX. It enables PC users to share resources and to communicate with each other. The physical connection can either be a regular telephone line, a cable, or a fiber optic cable. Also, wireless systems are available where data is transmitted using radio waves. The simplest way to understand the concept is to show how a single PC can be linked to a series of LANS each time extending its scope and capability. I consulted extensively with a State Senate and will use this an an example of an evolution into LAN usage. This particular Senate had a very advanced vision of how a network could make them more effective, and proceeded to implement that vision.

At the beginning of the the senate study, many senate offices had free-standing PCs doing mostly word processing, and in some offices desktop publishing, producing and distributing newsletters to their constituencies. There were several very rudimentary LANS, where laser printers were shared. The study showed the benefits of a setup similar to Figure 5.4, and today most offices have some version of this approach. A senate office, and there are 38 of them, consists of from six to eight people who communicate to the senator's constituents, do research on upcoming bills, and manage the business matters of the office. Personal computers are connected and not only share a laser printer, but have a client server that provides data to the senate office staff. The office maintains a constituency data base which it uses for sending out information and for answering inquiries. This has improved responsiveness—which is of obvious importance to a senator who eventually will be seeking reelection. Since there is no connection outside the office, data from other offices must be entered into the system either by exchanging diskettes or by manually entering it. This leads to the logical next stage of the process.

Figure 5.5 shows two senate offices linked to a Senate backbone LAN. Once connected to this LAN, new horizons appear. Senate offices can communicate with other senate offices including the party caucus, which is a separate office that conducts research and studies on behalf of the particular party. There is a Republican party and a Democratic party caucus. Another important linkage is to the senate floor. Currently senators have PCs at their desks in the senate chamber where they can connect to the office, to the party caucus office, or to their counterparts in the house. This is very useful when particular unscheduled bills are put on the agenda and the senator wants background information on the specific bill. Other connections on the backbone LAN include the House of Representatives, the senate

FIGURE 5.4. Senate office LAN

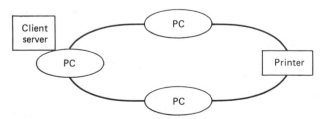

FIGURE 5.5. Senate backbone LAN

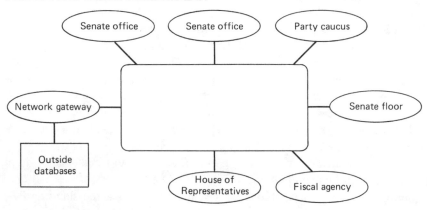

fiscal agency, which provides the budgetary and financial data on bills and programs, and through a network gateway, to a range of outside data bases including the libraries of the major state universities. One can begin to assess the power of information that this brings to a senator and a senator's office.

NETWORK GATEWAYS AND BRIDGES

The senate example describes individual senate office LANs that connect to other LANs within the senate, to other agencies within the state administration, and to agencies outside the state administration. A *network* is defined as an assemblage of hardware and software through which connections are made between workstations.

Thus a LAN is a network. Each LAN has its own network manager. Often, for a variety of reasons, it is desirable that LANs that were developed individually be linked to each other in the network. Since the network managers may not have the same protocols and linkages, additional hardware/software modules must be introduced to provide the connection.

These connections, called *gateways* or *bridges,* enable LANs to communicate with other LANs. They use different techniques to facilitate the connection. A gateway utilizes circuitry to convert protocols of one LAN to another while the bridge employs a higher set of protocols whereby the disparate LAN's protocol becomes a subset. The gateway or bridge provides different techniques to accomplish the same objective—facilitating the connectivity to allow a person on one LAN to communicate with a person on another LAN. In the case of the senate, the backbone LAN has the necessary gateway circuitry to act as a kind of LAN switch or interconnect vehicle.

PBXs and LANs, though they can provide networks beyond a specific complex of company buildings within a city, must connect to wide area networks (WANs) to communicate to other facilities, other cities, other countries, as well as intercompany [companies connected to their suppliers and customers via electronic data interchange (EDI)]. These connections require the use of value-added network providers, long distance carriers like

AT&T and MCI, satellite services, or private long distance systems mentioned earlier. Thus gateways and bridges are needed to connect with LANs and PBXs throughout the world via wide area networks.

Topology Choices

Having explained the workings and connectivity of LANs, mention should be made of the various topologies of LANs. There are three fundamental types of topologies: the bus, the ring, and the star. The selection of a topology depends on factors such as user needs, ease of use, ability to handle different loads and speeds, future growth plans, cost, ability to operate during a failure of one or more of the units tied to the LAN, and the compatibility with other LANs and operating units on the system.

Figure 5.6 illustrates the three topologies. A *star network* ties all the units to a central hub computer, which can be part of a larger hierarchical network where hubs are connected upward eventually linking to a central mainframe or large computer in the corporate office. If the central node of any of the hubs is inoperable, the total system is inoperable. This is not true of the *bus,* which is a peer-to-peer network. In a *ring* topology, the stations are arranged along a ring and a specific signal is transmitted through each of the stations. This type of approach was originally considered low on the reliability scale since, if one station was down, the entire system was down. Now bypass circuitry and component redundancies play a major role in reducing this risk. It has become practical to mix topologies within a network, and indeed most companies utilize the mixed approach. Hardware and software advances have facilitated this approach.

FIGURE 5.6. LAN typologies

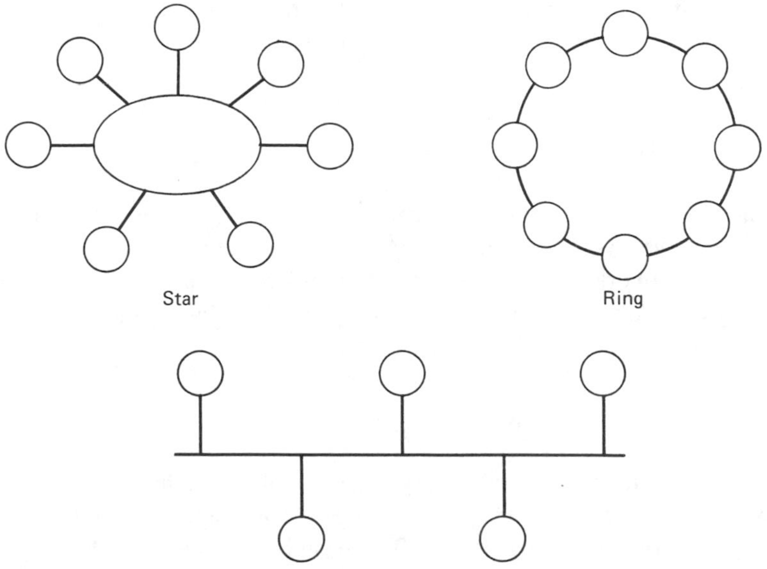

Star

Ring

Bus

TELECOMMUNICATIONS NETWORK PLANNING

The ultimate in telecommunications systems is to enable the user to make information inquiries, send information, or conduct business using information in a way that is natural, efficient, and effective. This requires comprehensive network planning and the development of a flexible yet standard network architecture. Such an architecture must be able to change and expand as the business changes and expands. It must be able to operate if mergers or acquisitions occur. The architecture must be able to communicate with a whole host of third parties including customers, vendors, competitors, and outside data base sources—and to do all this on a global basis. This is a tall order to say the least. It requires a dedication to sound principles of network planning. Some of the considerations in the planning process follow.

Consistent with Overall Company Strategies

Like the overall IS plan, the communications portion must fit with future company directions. It may be a concerted company strategy to expand into the global arena by acquisition of sales outlets or manufacturing units or they may envision establishing alliances with companies already operating in the countries. If that is a likelihood, the communications network must be designed with this possibility in mind.

Reliability and Security

Recent illegal intrusions into so-called "secure" information systems have brought attention to the need for security precautions. This becomes a mandatory requirement for most systems. In addition, back-up is necessary where down time would be costly or damaging to an operation. An on-line ordering system would fall into this category. The growing frequency of viruses also make programs to prevent this type of intrusion a mandatory systems requirement.

Ability to Handle Multimedia

Early telecommunication systems were optimized, sometimes exclusively dedicated to handling textual data. However with the attractiveness of multiple forms of data, graphs, moving pictures, and voice, networks must provide the flexibility to transmit multimedia when the occasion dictates it. This has an impact on the type of hardware and software employed and the selection of communication media.

Architecture

Many issues must be considered in establishing a communications architecture (as discussed in Chapter 3). Earlier in the chapter the three types of topologies were reviewed as well as the different components of a network. These and other elements must be considered in an architecture.

The availability of private satellite communications and value-added networks, as described earlier, warrants the establishment of communication protocols that enable a company to take advantage of these services. An integrated network calls for the capability to transmit messages and data streams across communication lines via microwaves or satellites between terminal substations and server computers. Sometimes the network is hierarchical, where branches report to regions and so on, or it may be a ring structure where branch offices communicate to each other as well as to higher-order offices. Architecture provides the framework for future growth and expansion.

People Skills and Capabilities

This subject will be discussed in the following chapter. The telecommunications function has a heavy technical element in it and the necessary people skills must be available. Because the technology is changing so rapidly, the focus must be continually on the new technologies and how feasible it is to incorporate them into the architecture. For example, LAN capability is changing rapidly (e.g., wireless LANs), and there are literally hundreds of vendors in the field. This requires a combination of knowledge and perspective to make the right decisions. Another factor to consider is whether to hire and train one's own telecommunication people or to use one of the rising number of service companies (outsourcing) to provide the necessary expertise.

Interoperability

It is necessary to design the system such that customer and vendors who must be linked to the network can be added without major changes in hardware and software. This may involve the move to the standard or open systems model. It is also important for the company itself to take advantage of new communication products without major software changes. Interoperability is becoming a vital element in systems planning.

Establishing Standards

Because of the emphasis on globalization caused by the changing nature of business, the standards as promulgated by the International Standards Organization (ISO) become very important, despite the fact that ISO standards and others are in a continued state of refinement. This organization comprises around 90 members and was founded in 1947. Each nation's principal standardization body is a member of ISO. In the case of the U.S. the American National Standards Institute is the representative.

The ISO has defined a seven-layer protocol (see Figure 5.7), starting with a basic standard for physical interconnect, level 1, proceeding to the seventh level, the application connection. The first level implies only the physical recognition of data being exchanged; it may be in an incompatible format for its intended use. The ultimate is that the communicated data can tie directly to the designated application, the seventh layer. The influence of this protocol continues to expand and solidify, and although it will always be an evolutionary process, ISO offers the best hope, and appears to be outdistancing the variety of ad hoc standards that have emerged.

FIGURE 5.7. ISO open systems interconnection reference model

Description

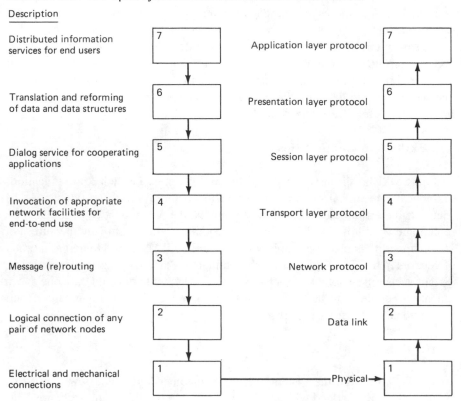

DISTRIBUTED SYSTEMS

Communications allow the access of data and processing power from remote sites. Communication costs have not dropped as much as computer costs. However, fiber optics and other developments auger well for lower communication costs. Options for centralizing data processing and decentralizing (distributing) both exist, but the trend is towards the distributed model.

Distributed systems (DS) are built around an approach that distributes the data base and processing capability to remote sites based on the type, number, and variety of work stations, their data processing requirements, the degree of control desired, the type of business organization, and overall economic considerations.

The term "distributed" is a bit of a misnomer because, while functions and resources are distributed, there is still a central discipline or control over the remote processing units. The key to DS is that the host computer and distributed processing nodes are cooperative; that is, they are designed to be able to communicate with each other for those applications that require it.

As mentioned, mini and micro developments have made it economically feasible to have local processing capability; thus the trend is to distribute processing to remote subunits while maintaining the ability to talk to the host computer system and to other subunits via an established network protocol. The transfer of processing power and data storage to mini and micro computers at the department level is commonly called *downsizing*. Two examples follow to give an overview of how distributed systems function. The first example is a highly centralized integrated network while the second falls in the category of highly distributed or loosely coupled. The highly centralized example is an IS operation in a large international bank; the loosely coupled example is a U.S. company in the distribution business.

International Bank

International Bank, a fictitious name for a real bank, is one of the largest in Europe. It is organized such that each branch renders total banking services to a specific geographical territory. A group of branches in turn is directed by an area general manager. Each area has an average of 200 employees under its management; as business and areas grow, the company has a policy that a new division is formed when the number of employees exceeds 200 people. The current number of areas is 250, with 350 expected in the next five years as the bank continues its rapid expansion. International Bank believes in a decentralized mode of operation, leaving major decision authority in the hands of the area general manager, each area functioning as a cost and profit center.

International Bank evolved to a totally centralized system in the late seventies and early eighties; they started with their current distributed approach in the late eighties. The rationale for switching was (1) the ability to better serve the company's needs while being consistent with the prevailing decentralized mode of operation, (2) improved performance geared to higher throughput and turnaround time, and (3) improved system availability translated into higher up-time and ability to serve the growing number of users. The existing work load is divided into 250 areas currently serving 2000 branches with a total of 7000 terminals. It is expected that in five or ten years there will be 350 areas with 2500 branches and 10,000 terminals.

The distributed system envisioned by International Bank is illustrated in Figure 5.8. There are four levels of distribution in the network. The first level is the home office, which has the master central data base, maintaining the names, identification, key subtotals, and summary information of every account within the network. A backup processor is present in case of failure of the first processor. The second level is the area office, which communicates to the central system via a miniprocessor tied into a communications front-end processor of the host system. Each area processor has a data base of the accounts within its geographical territory. The third level is the branch, which utilizes concentrators to collect, edit, and prepare for transmitting the data required for second-level processing. The fourth level is the terminal work stations. These work stations are a combination of personal computers, automatic teller machines (ATMs), bank teller units, printers, and the like, depending on the specific activity performed by the branch. Thus you can see the networking effect of home office mainframe processors and a data base communicating to area offices, which in turn communicate to concentrators at the branch, which control the variety

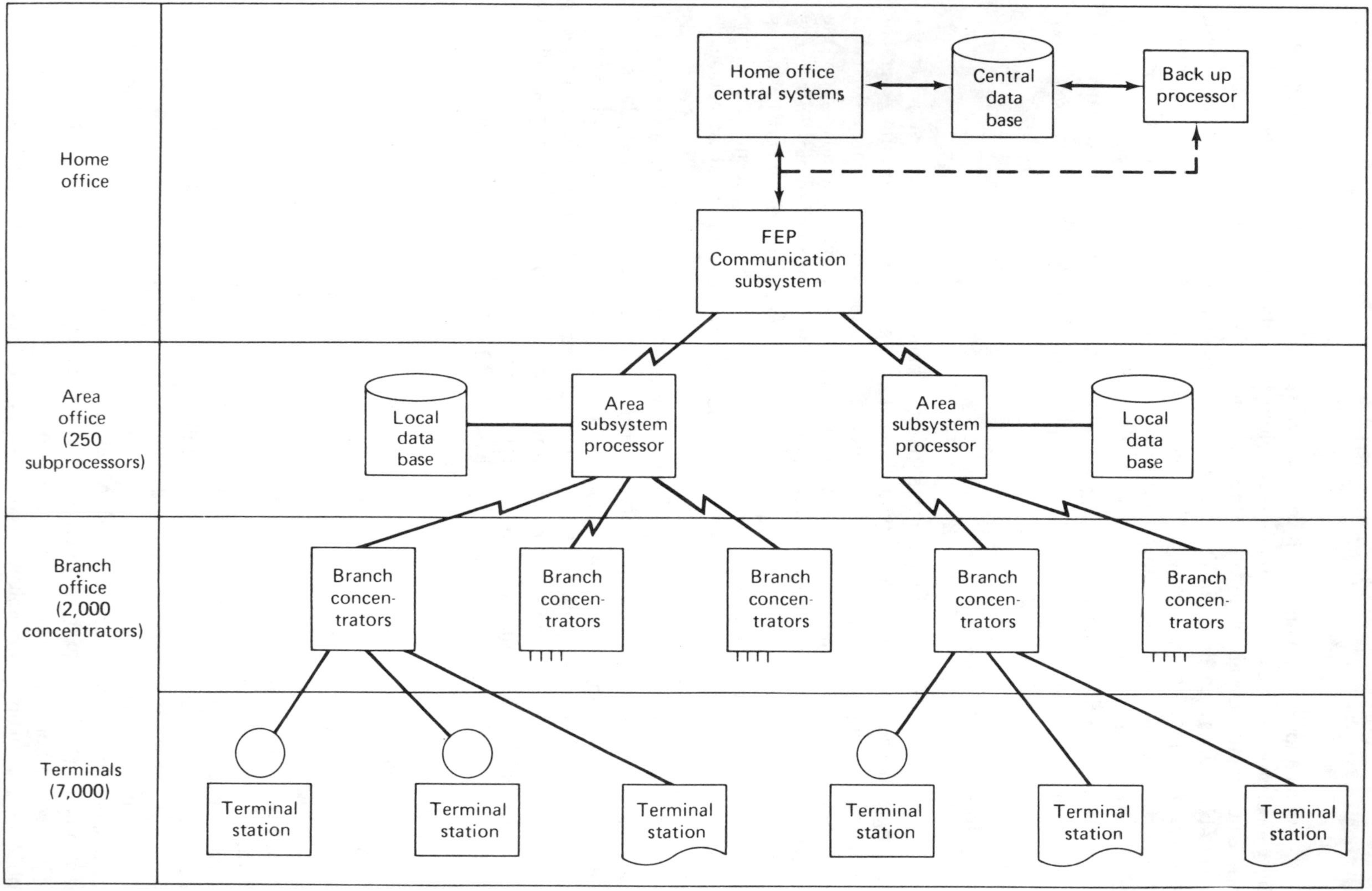

FIGURE 5.8. Distributed processing network of International Bank

of terminals in various locations within the branch. There are a limited number of LANs in the areas and branches, but a good deal of the communication takes place between the units over leased long distance telephone lines. The variety of value added and private services is minimal compared to that in the United States.

The estimated total cost of this system is the approximately $125 million purchase price of the hardware and software complement plus about $20 million per year to operate. The latter costs include personnel, facilities rental, communication lines, power, hardware maintenance, supplies, operators, and so on. The bank feels the cost is about equal to that of their previous system; the benefits result from improved customer service by virtue of greater system availability, capacity, and response time. It is interesting that while the bank believes in organizational decentralization, its approach to IS, while distributed, follows a historical centralized model.

National Distributors

National Distributors distributes three lines of products, which are not related to each other—electronic products, plumbing and building supply products, and automotive parts. The management strongly believes in a decentralized organization and in giving maximum authority to divisional managers. They also feel the same about their IS organization, and in the late eighties they embarked on a program of distributed systems. So strong is their belief in decentralization that they prefer redundancy rather than telling a division manager that he has to do something a certain way.

The corporate office has a single computer system (see Figure 5.9) that provides information services to its electronic products division and also takes care of the corporate applications, which mainly involve the consolidation of financial reports from the three operating divisions. The computer facility is operated as a service facility. There is complete independence of application development: one group works for the corporate controller and is responsible for corporate applications; another works for the general manager of the electronic products division. The reason for the single computer center is that the electronic products division operates only in the three states contiguous to the corporate office.

The plumbing and building supply division has two regions. While each region has complete autonomy in its operations, the East and West warehouses do cooperate in filling orders of customers when one warehouse does not have the inventory of a particular item. Thus, the building and supply central IS group maintains an inventory data base, which is updated each night by the East and West IS groups. The central group defines the common item identifiers and data-base organization, but has no authority over the IS operations of either of the two regions.

The auto parts division operates without a central inventory data base; each of the three regions maintains its own inventory and its own inventory records and fills orders only from its own stocks. If the East division is out of an item and the Central division has an overstock of the same item, this information is not known by either of them. On occasion a phone call is made from one region to the other to see if inventory of a particular item is available. Each region has its own autonomous IS group, the only connection to the corporate office being the communication of summary operating data for consolidating financial reports.

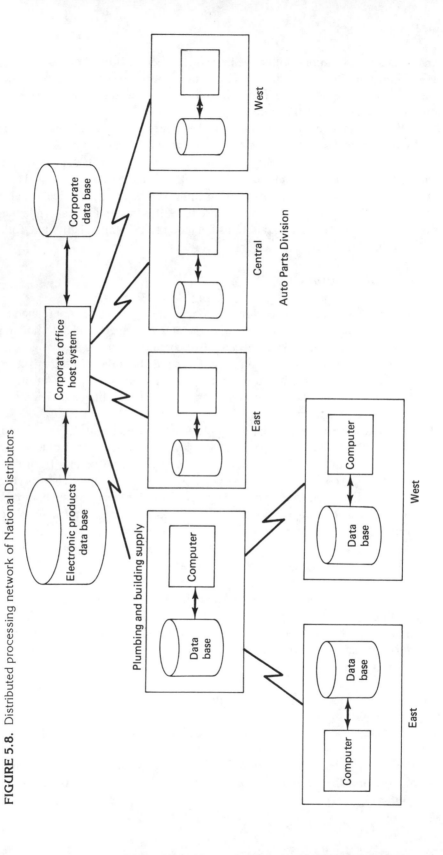

FIGURE 5.8. Distributed processing network of National Distributors

National Distributors is illustrative of a loosely coupled DS operation. The three divisions have independent IS groups; the only connection is via the communication of financial data. There is no data base sharing or centralized inventory control. The plumbing and building supply division does maintain a central inventory file, but the regions of the auto parts division maintain their own data base. It is most definitely an example of a loosely coupled operation, in contrast to the strictly controlled, hierarchical operation of International Bank.

As mentioned, downsizing goes hand in hand with the distributed approach, the trend being that more and more of the hardware and software as well as the design and development of applications is delegated to the department level. This delegation has potential for both positive and negative outcomes.

BENEFITS OF DISTRIBUTING/DOWNSIZING APPLICATIONS

There are significant benefits from distributing or downsizing the IS function. User satisfaction is normally much improved as ownership is passed to the user, and one is usually easier on oneself than when the option exists to blame another. If implemented correctly, distributed systems can be more flexible and responsive to change, an important attribute in the acquisition/merger/reorganize style that characterizes business today. A very important benefit is the increased productivity and responsiveness that a well designed departmental system can provide. The tools are in the office—not upstairs or in another building or another city. Condensing the decision cycle and the response to customers can mean real payoffs. The following are benefits of distributing or downsizing the IS function.

Simpler User Interface

User interfaces have improved far greater on desktop systems than on mainframes or minis. The pull-down menus and object-oriented icons are prime examples. Even with taking on the responsibility of computer operation and direct interface, it is often simpler than providing the information request to the central systems group. They are constrained by user interfaces that have been designed for dedicated and technical users, not the intermittent use that is characteristic of departmental deployment.

Shortened Development Cycle

Another benefit for those departments that design and implement their own systems is that often they can be completed faster. The problem with enterprise systems is that they involve groups of systems designers and programmers with the need for coordination and interaction. The theory of "divide and conquer" applies to departmental systems where many projects involve only one or two persons. An additional benefit is that often people close to the problems can assess the merit of application packages that can materially shorten the systems development cycle.

The information center concept, which figured so prominently in the middle 1980s, was an intermediate position between centralization and distributed. A skilled group of information technicians, trainers, and consultants was established to assist departmental users in doing their own computing. This was a transition step to true departmental operation. With the advent of "easier-to-use" software and more powerful hardware, there are fewer information centers today. But the information center serves to bring home a valid consideration—the need to establish the necessary training and transition plans to ensure the proper employment of full distribution.

Ability to Utilize Talents of Future Graduates

Future graduates from secondary schools and colleges will be more computer literate than previous generations. While they may not be IS specialists knowing how to program and manage networks, they will be comfortable with advanced PC operation, have a perspective on communication networks and data bases, and be able to specify and develop their own applications. The distributed approach allows the organization to parlay these skills and to gain IS innovation from people designing their own systems that are closest to the action.

Less Risk of System Breakdown

In central systems, a power outage, act of God (flood, hurricane), act of sabotage, or strike can shut down the entire network. In a distributed processing system, the local operations can continue without major service interruption. While increased reliability of hardware and software and fully redundant systems can reduce the chances of failure, the possibilities still exist.

Economy of Operation

DS enthusiasts claim there is economy of operation. They base their opinion on the more balanced approach and the use of low-cost mini- and microprocessors throughout the network. Communication unit costs have not dropped at the same rate as processing costs. Therefore the cost tradeoff favors processing over communication and thus favors distributed systems. Of concern, however, are the rising costs of departmental systems personnel, as remote sites develop their own staffs, often redundant to the host staff.

Flexibility to Fit Organizational Philosophy

To my way of thinking, this may be the most important rationale for distributed processing. In National Distributors, the information files and operational control are vested at the division level where the cost and profit center responsibility resides. This can be quite important in gaining management support and involvement in the system—vital factors that can often scuttle an otherwise well-conceived approach. Also, by having each division responsible for the data and files under its control, alternate ways to use the data can be discovered and often innovative business pursuits are the result.

POTENTIAL RISKS OF DISTRIBUTED/DOWNSIZING

The benefits of departmental or desktop computing are fairly well documented; the downside risks and problems are not as well depicted. Some major ones are as follows:

Documentation and Control

One of the major risks in departmental application development is that an initiative can grow from a simple spreadsheet program developed by a single individual to a major company application affecting sales, salespeople, and inventories. But often the necessary controls and checks have not been instituted, and the application is not designed for volume and the strain that the institutionalization of the application brings. Furthermore, some of the formulas may not have been checked for accuracy and validity, with the effect that the application may not be doing what you think it is. Lacking is the professionalism of IS career personnel who are knowledgeable and experienced in the elements of the systems life cycle. Other issues revolve around documentation and back up of data and interim results.

System Contagion

One cannot help but recall the Nolan stage theory (Chapter 2) when one looks at the decentralization issue. Nolan saw companies going through inevitable stages of (1) initiation, and (2) contagion, prior to developing the necessary (3) control to move to (4) integration, and on to stages 5 and 6.

The theory is that, after the introduction of a new technology or technological concept such as powerful desktop computers, contagion occurs where acquisition and use get a bit out of control, as more and more people want to get on the bandwagon and give the new device at least a test spin. As with mainframes and minis, proliferation can be an expensive and time-consuming exercise. While there is something to be said about a free market and the ability to improvise (with innovation often the result), the time quickly approaches when it becomes sheer contagion without the positive tradeoffs. The business of most functional departments is not running computer systems. Installing more and more powerful desktop systems can detract from the main strategic and tactical responsibilities of a successful department.

Cost

This was listed as a potential benefit but it is a two-edged sword. While there is considerably more MIP power per dollar on a desktop PC, to save money you have to use the MIPS on the right jobs. Also you have to reduce your central IS investment. Often one or both of these elements is lacking. It is reassuring to see the huge central IS budget dropping, but it may be a case of spreading the dollars to where they are still there, but spread so thin and evenly that they are difficult to count. Also, it is usually true that a company spends more (ranging from a factor of two to three) for people, documentation, training, software, and the like (soft costs) than for hardware (hard costs). The soft costs take on more of an illusive nature in a distributed operation.

Measurement of Benefits

The measurement of benefits can also be more difficult in a distributed environment. In high-volume, transaction-oriented central shops, the cost per transaction is a significant measurement. Similar measurements are more difficult when computing is dispersed throughout the organization. There are more intangible benefits as compared to tangible. Even rudimentary tools to calculate a "ball park" return on investment may be lacking or thought unnecessary. While over zealousness in this area can be counterproductive, some way of establishing development priorities is usually desirable.

There are ways to soften the downside risks of distributing/downsizing, and senior IS managers can help in this regard. The IS executive should establish a personal computing policy including a preferred vendor software and hardware list. The policy should gently guide the users around the shoals that the central IS department went through in the mainframe and minicomputer eras. A key is to build in the controls and other system life cycle procedures that will avoid the junking of applications as they grow and expand. In other words, to concurrently progress through Nolan's second and third stages.

WHAT FUNCTIONS TO DISTRIBUTE

The Boston Systems Group in Boston, Massachusetts, developed the factor list shown in Figure 5.10 to consider the degree of distribution (high point scores favor centralization while low point scores favor distributed). Obviously, these questions and scores are only guidelines, and the ultimate analysis that is used by a specific company must be carefully reviewed and discussed by the people affected. Cost is not included in this analysis. Careful thought must be given to a decision of this magnitude and impact. However, determination of the decision criteria and the relative position of a company rated against these criteria can prove quite positive. Such a process begins to bring out the significant factors underlying a move in one direction or another, and can serve as a good base for communication and joint agreement on the path to follow.

SUMMARY

This chapter covered the principles of communications, describing its history and evolution, along with the elements that comprise a communication system. External communication involves the linking of geographically dispersed facilities via telephone lines, microwaves, satellites, or fiber optics. Internal communications were also covered, where PBXs and LANS transmit voice and data within a building or buildings in close proximity. Advances in telecommunications and the advent of distributed systems are creating the need for added emphasis on these areas within the IS organization. A separate teleprocessing group is often the result, taking over voice as well as digital transmission. Heretofore some IS executives may have considered telephones beneath their dignity—for, after all, how could telephone directories, switchboard operators, or call buttons possess enough high technological con-

FIGURE 5.10. Distribution/centralization analysis

	Assigned weight	Score 1	Score 2	Score 3
1. Uniqueness	10	One user		Multiple user
2. Functionality	15	Simple		Complex
3. Inaccessibility impact	10	Minimal		Significant
4. Inoperability impact	15	Minimal		Significant
5. Mission criticality	20	Minimal		Significant
6. "Back-office" orientation	10	No		Yes
7. Interface complexity	15	Slight		Substancial
8. Degree of change	20	High		Low
9. Support aspect	10	Operational		Strategic
10. Data/department overlap	5	Little		Large
11. Competitive advantage	20	Small		Large
12. System lifetime	5	Short		Long
13. Governmental regulation	5	None		Substancial
14. Degree of justification	5	Minimal		Significant

tent to be relevant? The broadening scope of communication and the development of total digital communication places voice communications squarely in the IS domain.

The remainder of the chapter centered on distributed or downsized systems, defining and categorizing the different manifestations. Examples contrasted a centralized form of DS with a more decentralized type. The benefits and downside risks of DS were reviewed as well as a matrix for analyzing what elements of IS can be distributed or can remain central.

Chapters 4 and 5 represent the essence of IS. The data base holds the relevant data that drives the transactions of the business and also provides the meaningful management data that abets the planning and control of the business. Telecommunications is the delivery system for the data. Data base and telecommunications are both integral to IS. They must be combined in an information architecture, consistent with IS standards, that both supports and shapes the business. They are building blocks for survival. Chapter 6 will discuss more of the organizational ramifications brought on by the advent of new technology and new management styles.

Case Study

General Auto, Inc.

A TIME-SHARING APPLICATION TO AUTOMOTIVE MAINTENANCE PROBLEMS

System Background

About 1850 General Auto dealerships have access to United System's (US)Tack III Information Services Network. The primary function of the system is to trace the status of new car orders. A dealer can locate a car that is on order or learn delivery times instantly. A secondary function of the system is to process replacement parts orders.

It is the third application of the General Auto system with which this case will deal. The telecom application programs have been expanded to deal with a group of new and particularly difficult maintenance problems.

General Auto's automatic temperature-control systems and cruising-speed controls have become increasingly complex, to the point that mechanics are not really capable of fixing them without specialized help. Vehicle vibrations, a problem whose cause is usually complex, added to the need for outside help.

Working with General Auto headquarters' maintenance people and system analysts, US people flowcharted these diagnostic and maintenance systems. Programs were developed that worked through each system in a step-by-step fashion to identify each problem for the mechanic.

When a vehicle had a problem in one of these areas, the serviceperson accesses a local phone number from the terminal in the dealership. When connected to the network, he or she types in the user number, a password, the vehicle identification number of the car being worked on, and the area with the problem.

The terminal prints the diagnostic equipment needed and asks some progressively detailed questions isolating the malfunction. Once the specific location of the problem is found, the serviceperson goes back and makes the repair.

Economic Justification

With this system, economic justification is simple. The terminal, telephone modem, and initial communication expense are considered sunk costs, as they were incurred for the previous new car tracing and parts reorder applications. The cost for the new application includes the remote processor time and the time required for each connection. The initial investment was the systems and programming costs to accomplish the required application

To justify the system, these costs are weighed against the savings in mechanic time and parts. First, as these repairs were most frequently done on cars under warranty, the mechanic's time was charged to General Auto. If the car was not under warranty, time for the repair was charged on the basis of standard "book time" normally required by the mechanic to repair the car. For example, if the book time for repairing a cruise control was one-half hour, that was what the customer was charged, even if the mechanic actually took ten minutes or four hours. This system should have substantially reduced the number of jobs that required more time than the customer could be billed for.

Before development of the time-sharing application, the mechanic often found it easier to rip the entire troubled system out, send it back to General Auto, and install a new system. This resulted in a higher warranty charge to General Auto. On many of these occasions, General Auto found that a $400 warranty charge was made when the mechanic could have fixed the system in 15 minutes with a 10-cent resistor—if he had known the nature of the problem. In some rare instances involving unsolvable vibration problems (for preferred customers) dealers returned entire cars to General Auto for replacement.

The "rip out rather than repair" procedure also existed in other systems that were slated to be added to the maintenance program. If, for example, a car under warranty had a carburetor problem, a new carburetor would be installed. Both of these parts can be repaired cheaper, quicker, and at substantially less cost to General Auto than they can be replaced.

The dollar costs for each of these kinds of repairs obviously varies, but when balanced against the computer cost, the remote maintenance approach represents significant savings. During the first six months of use, the average cost per program use was about $2.10. At $60 an hour for service, plus the cost of unnecessarily replaced parts, the savings represented by the system are significant.

The Tack III Telecommunications Network

United System's Tack III network is composed of more than 2000 interconnected computers. It is tied to users in eighteen time zones by 500,000 miles of communication lines, including transoceanic cables and communication satellites. As the communications part of the system is owned or leased by United Systems, a customer can access the system with a local telephone call. Each General Auto dealer had at least one terminal in his dealership, usually in the parts office, where its heaviest use, parts reorder, occurs. A few large dealerships also have a terminal in the new car sales area for ordering and tracing new cars.

The maintenance application is written in a fourth generation language, which easily handles the comparatively simple maintenance programs. Output parameters have been carefully designed to be simple for the service people. Graphical user interfaces are used.

STUDY QUESTIONS

1. Is this an example of adding an application that utilizes an existing telecommunications network? How can companies ensure that this happens more?

2. What do you think of the way the maintenance application was justified? Are there any benefits that were overlooked?

3. How would the customer view rip out vs. repair decision? What about customer satisfaction?

4. How important is ease of use in this application? How important is response time?

Case Study

Natural Container Industries

Typical of the differing opinions concerning distributed IS are those expressed by Arthur Connelly, manager of systems at National's Turbine Division, and Arthur Seymour, president of the computer division for the last ten years.

Five years ago, concerned both by the rapid proliferation of computer expenditures and staff in the company, and some virtual disasters in systems design development effort, the president had directed that a centralized computing center be established in St. Louis and organized as a separate division within the corporate structure. At the same time the decision was made to locate all systems programming and computing power in the central computing facility while virtually all applications systems and programming would be done in the divisions. This pattern had been maintained, essentially unchanged, until the present.

Arthur Seymour, president of the computing division, noted in discussing his company's mission: "Our basic competitive advantage is our ability to produce reliable, cheap computing power for our sister divisions. If we fail in this dimension, we have, in fact, no reason for our existence." He noted the increased pressure his department had been under in the past two years and commented at some length on what he perceived as a growing incursion of microcomputer power. Deeply distressed at this development, he observed that it was his job to hold the line on these devices. He noted that the users and the software companies they hired had little understanding of internal control systems, operations documentation, and other elements of good data processing hygiene. He further noted that his company, in the short term, had few investment dollars and that the acquisition of microcomputers by sister divisions was clearly increasing the corporation's negative cash flows. The only sensible way to manage microcomputers, he said, was to have them all approved and evaluated by the computing division organization. Otherwise, a whole series of apparently individual correct decisions could add to one large mistake. He cited that

Excerpted from a Harvard Business School case.

twenty microcomputers acquired in the Turbine Division in the last year as evidence of this type of myopia.

Arthur Connelly, manager of the systems and programming group of the Turbine Division, had a very different perspective. He noted that four times in the past year there had been major problems with the operating system on the central computing activity and that during the month-end and quarter-end closes, there had been such severe capacity crunches as to sharply delay his receipt of vital management reports.

He noted that these twenty micros had bought him independence from the reliability problems of the central data processing activity and given him the flexibility to develop new and improved systems with better service to the Turbine Division. "The best control for microcomputers, at this stage, is no control. Later on, when we get more experience in these issues, we can then begin to be more rigorous on a corporate basis."

The conflict between these two executives eventually reached the chief executive officer's ears, and, looking at the growth trend in both data processing costs and the number of computers, he decided that the subject warranted a serious investigation. Accordingly, he established a computer priorities committee, composed of the presidents of each of the three major divisions and of two of the small divisions. As their first assignment he charged them with evaluating this particular subject and developing a recommendation.

STUDY QUESTIONS

1. What do you think of Seymour's attitude toward microcomputers?

2. Is Connelly justified in his perspective?

3. How can this issue be resolved? If both parties persist, what can be done and by whom? Did the president act properly?

4. Do you think this is a typical situation in many companies?

5. Is it conceivable that some companies would be better off in operating their IS on a centralized basis? Or is distributed processing the inevitable trend for everyone?

SELECTED REFERENCES

Black, Uyless, *Data Networks Concepts, Theory, and Practice*. Englewood Cliffs, N.J.: Prentice Hall, 1989.

Booth, Grayce M., *The Distributed Systems Environment*. New York: McGraw-Hill, 1981.

Bradsher, Keith, "Can Cellular Phone Companies Agree on a New Standard for Transmission?" *The New York Times*, September 16, 1990, p. 9.

Buchanan, J. R. and R. G. Linowes, "Understanding Distributed Data Processing." *Harvard Business Review* (1980), 143-153.

Butler Cox Foundation, "New Telecommunication Services." *Management Summary*, Report 78, December 1990.

"The Changing Value of Communication Technology," *Sloan Management Review*, Winter 1987.

Cook, William J., "Battle of the Network Stars," *US News & World Report*, May 21, 1990, pp. 49-50.

"Distributed Systems Architecture," no. CY 28 (1982). "ISDN—Integrated Services Digital Network," *IDC White Paper*. IDC Framingham, Mass., 1990.

Kanter, Jerome and Richard S. Wells, "Teleprocessing Systems Perspectives," *Journal of Systems Management* (March 1975), 10-15.

Keen, Peter G.W., *Competing in Time—Using Telecommunications for Competitive Advantage*. Cambridge, Mass.: Ballinger Publishing Company, 1988.

Lewis, Peter H., "NCR Introduces Its Version of a Network Without Wires," *The New York Times*, September 23, 1990, p. 8.

Mangurain, Glenn E., *Making the Business Case for Networking*, Index Group, Cambridge, Mass., 1987.

Martin, James, *Design and Strategy of Distributed Data Processing*. Englewood Cliffs, N.J.: Prentice-Hall, Inc., 1981.

Martin, James, *Telematic Society: A Challenge for Tomorrow*. Englewood Cliffs, N.J.: Prentice-Hall, Inc., 1982.

Martin, James, with Joe Leben, The Arben Group, Inc., *Principles of Data Communication*. Englewood Cliffs, N.J.: Prentice Hall, 1988.

Mertes, Louis H., "Doing Your Office Over—Electronically," *Harvard Business Review* (1981), pp. 127-135.

"OSI: The Global Network Architecture," *IDC White Paper*. IDC, Framingham, Mass., 1990.

Perry, George M., "An Information Systems Approach to Telecommunications," *MIS Quarterly* (September 1980), pp. 17-29.

Silver, Gerald A., and Myrna L. Silver, *Data Communications for Buisness*, 2nd ed. Boston, Mass.: Boyd & Fraser Publishing Company, 1991.

Stallings, William, *Business Data Communication*. New York: Macmillan Publishing Company, 1990.

Tanenbaum, A. S., *Computer Networks*. Englewood Cliffs, N.J.: Prentice-Hall, Inc., 1981.

Thurber, K., "Tutorial: A Pragmatic View of Distributed Processing Systems," Los Alemedos, CA: EEE Comput. Soc., 1980.

Walford, Robert B., *Information Systems and Business Dynamics*. Addison-Wesley Publishing Company, Inc., 1990.

Chapter 6

The Organizational Evolution of IS

INTRODUCTION

In this chapter we explore the impact of data bases (Chapter 4) and telecommunications (Chapter 5) on the organization of IS within a company. Several elements are responsible for the evolution of IS organizationally. The first element, and in my view the driving force, is the change that has occurred because management has discovered that people are motivated better and work better when they have a strong influence in what they do. Large bureaucratic organizations have not allowed this to occur. The other element is the technological change that we have been discussing. This chapter focuses on the evolution of the client server model, a model that is powered by the developments in data base and telecommunications.

After a discussion of the organizational and technical factors, the evolution of the organization of IS in companies is traced, from the small electronic data processing (EDP) department to the concept of chief information officer (CIO) and the distributed organization. The characteristics of the CIO and those of the telecommunications manager are covered. The latter discussion of the telecommunications manager and the training requirements for the position are the basis for implementing the distributed approach described in the last chapter; an approach that drives the new organizational thinking.

THE ORGANIZATIONAL ENVIRONMENT

The business world has experienced a long period of information systems decentralization/distribution that has continued since the mainframe/centralization era of the 1960s. There have been perturbations on the curve including a mild return of some companies to more centralization during the last several years, but the trend line has been constant. Many say the cause of decentralization is more powerful desktop computers; however, the major determinant is the preferred and proven successful management and organizational approach of delegating decisions to the lowest possible organizational level. People prefer to operate in this mode and seek to control the tools needed to accomplish their work. The technology is the enabler, not the cause.

Observers of organizational behavior see several process changes occurring and have written extensively about them. The traditional hierarchical organization is becoming more flattened; the historical pyramid is becoming truncated. More and more, important decisions of the company are coming from lower-level groups or individuals who are closer to the "action," closer to the point where products and customers meet.

Fortune 1000 companies have seen the smaller, faster-moving entrepreneurial startups become serious competitors. The entrepreneurs are able to turn corners more quickly, cut down the long product gestation period, and respond to customer demand. The metaphor is the highly maneuverable PT boat as opposed to the battleship. Successful enterprises will be those that provide an environment that encourages free thinking, entrepreneurship, and innovation. These companies will incorporate a decentralized, delegated style of operation.

The merits of organizational decentralization have been argued for the last two decades. MIT's "Management in the 1990s" project points out in several reports that innovation comes from the people who work with the product and with the company's customers, and from the customers themselves. Staff planning groups and corporate strategists are just too far away from the action. The studies point out case after case where innovative systems were conceived and developed, not by staff people or the central information systems folk, but by salespeople, production line supervisors, customer service supervisors, architects, or doctors. Story after story illustrate that innovation and attention to one's customers comes from the line, not from the staff.

ORGANIZATIONAL CONSIDERATIONS IN IS

It is extremely important to consider organizational issues in designing an information system architecture. In many instances, too much attention is paid to the technology of IS, while grossly neglecting the nontechnical elements.

In general there are three considerations of information system feasibility: technical, economic, and organizational. The technical aspects have received the most attention from systems designers. Organizational aspects have received the least. More emphasis must be given to the organizational dimension of feasibility if advanced distributed systems are to be installed successfully by more companies.

A particular application may be both technically and economically feasible and still fail to produce the predicted benefits because a company is unable to make it work. A perplexed management cannot understand why a well-conceived and well-designed system is not successful in the operating departments. Some reasons for such failure are motivational and psychological. These often can be resolved by proper training and indoctrination. Other reasons, however, are serious enough to warrant placing a lower priority on a particular application area until the problem is resolved.

Such a situation might occur, for example, when a sales administration function performed by local sales branches becomes part of a distributed system that processes orders and bills customers. The new system is designed and installed with little or no local participation at the sales branches. The branches try to circumvent the system, because they fear that account control is being removed from them. The new system develops a billing backlog, customers become irate, management becomes disillusioned, and the whole system eventually fails.

Before an application is instituted, it is necessary to assess management and organizational considerations. A company's organizational philosophy may be extreme centralization, extreme decentralization, or something in between. When a company is centralized, well-defined policies and procedures are developed at the headquarters level. Local offices and plants follow these regulations to the letter; any deviations must be approved by headquarters. This type of operation usually is effective in a highly structured marketplace, and where products have long production runs and fairly stable life cycles.

The decentralized philosophy places maximum leverage and decision-making responsibility in the hands of local offices or plants. This aims to heighten an individual's motivation to succeed and develop an entrepreneurial style of operation. This approach is effective where markets and products differ according to the local environment and where quick decisions and flexibility are required.

In most cases a company's organizational philosophy falls between these extremes. Also, an organization may change over time, moving from a centralized to a decentralized mode, and then possibly back toward more centralization. The changes result from normal organizational maturation, from different management styles, as well as from changes in a company's marketplace and products.

The design of systems must take into account the organizational mode of a company. Although theoretically a centralized system can be effective in a decentralized company, in practice a system has less chance of success if it runs counter to the existing organizational philosophy. Furthermore, a system must be amenable to change as the company moves from one stage of organizational development to another. Flexibility and modularity are important criteria in the design of systems.

Timing is another consideration when a new system is planned. For example, if a company is planning to move to a more decentralized organizational structure, but hasn't yet done so, it might be wise to begin with a more centralized approach that has the flexibility to move toward a decentralized mode later on. Key systems tradeoffs must be considered during the design of any system. These should not be based strictly on technological and economical considerations. Should a completely centralized data base be developed, for example, or should subsets of the central file be maintained locally? From technological and economic viewpoints, the centralized data base might appear to be the way to go. On the other hand, operational considerations may dictate that some redundancy in file storage is necessary for the system to work.

THE TECHNOLOGICAL ENVIRONMENT

There are prevailing technological developments that have accentuated the way organizations conduct their business. While there were time-sharing and on-line terminals in the sixties and seventies, the personal computer provided the real impetus in the early eighties. It was the beginning of the empowerment of the individual. The last half of the eighties served to strengthen this empowerment as the personal computer became a force to be reckoned with. More processing power, more memory, more storage, more software, more connectivity, and greater ease of use were placed on the desk. A desktop MIP (millions of instructions per second) became cheaper than a mainframe MIP by a factor of 20 or so. It made more sense to do it on the desk.

Now in the nineties, PC power continues to proliferate. The advent of LANs and other local and wide area connectivity, discussed in the previous chapter, are providing another power push toward the desktop. Abetted by the new wave of software built around the groupware concept, groups are able to communicate in local or dispersed locations, and departmental computing centers have become a reality.

Departments can now develop their own data bases on powerful client servers as well as have access to outside data bases and to their own corporate data bases. The latter is made easier by the increasing improvement and use of distributed data bases. But the important thing is that while there is still dependence on the central data base, software and connectivity developments have shifted the locus of power in many instances away from the central IS organization to the desktops within individual departments. This is a form or an extension of the distributed system approach described in the previous chapter.

EVOLUTION OF THE NEW ARCHITECTURE: THE CLIENT SERVER

Client server computing is a way of downsizing by putting a data base on a separate departmental PC (the server) while allowing departmental users to access the server from their PC (the client). It really is a revolutionary change from the manner in which IS has traditionally conducted its business. It changes the entire way IS is viewed: Instead of looking at things from the inside out (the central IS viewpoint), the client server looks at things from the outside in (the user viewpoint). It is a key driving force to supporting organizational decentralization.

As mentioned in the previous chapter, earlier architectures revolved around large mainframes that were the host computers for all the major applications of the company (see Figure 6.1). The central data base stored all the files that were needed to run the major transaction-processing applications such as customer, inventory, supplier, employee, and so on. The mainframe with its attendant data base was the center, the hub of everything. Accounting and human resource applications including payroll were processed on the same mainframe as the company's transaction processing systems.

Time-sharing allowed individual users to access the central data files for information; however, most of the remote telecommunications were from people involved in providing input or using output from the major transaction-processing systems. The optimization point

FIGURE 6.1. Mainframe architecture

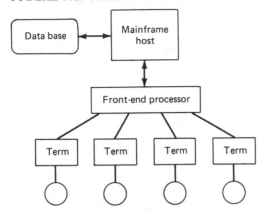

was "production"; cranking transactions through the system. Systems effectiveness was measured by transactions processed per minute. All user views of data transmitted to end user screens were formatted on the mainframe host. Ease of use and tailoring the system to the needs of local users were secondary considerations. The user was considered to be an IS professional, not a departmental person. The data base inquiry and processing languages were out of reach, that is, far too complex for the average departmental worker.

A separate processor, the front-end processor or FEP, was employed to prepare communication input and output before sending it to the host. The host maintained all information about the data base and would seek the files from the data base needed by the transactions, which could be handled either on-line or batch. Bandwidth was wide between the CPU and the data base and between the CPU and the FEP. Since most of the terminals were not PCs and had sparse, if any, processing power, the bandwidth between user and the terminal was narrow. Most of the action was accomplished at the central site, and the system was optimized to that end. The role of the user was to feed the mainframe, not the other way around.

HOW CLIENT SERVER ARCHITECTURE OPERATES

The client server architecture enters the picture and changes the focus (see Figure 6.2). Data bases are segmented by subject and assigned to servers. The assignments are made on the basis of which departments use which data bases. The user views and the formatting of data are made on the PC, not the server. The server is the data base engine as well as the communications processor. It is now focused on the data base job and is not involved in the multitude of applications performed on the mainframe. The client server is a specialist as opposed to the mainframe generalist.

The significant performance characteristic of the server is no longer millions of instructions per second (MIPS), but what may be called networks instructions per second, or how fast the server can move huge blocks of data through the system. The software that facilitates this process is the new relational and distributed data base systems. These systems

FIGURE 6.2. Client server architecture

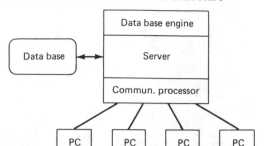

dramatically change the ways applications are developed. The data base software handles the tasks relating to data base management, data dictionary, data security, additions and deletions to the file, processing of user queries, and, in summary, all the tasks that translate a request to use the data base into the format prescribed by the various users. The user defines the screen formats and report layouts in a language that is easy to learn and easy to use. The system is now optimized around the user, and as such is much more responsive and flexible.

A simple way to envision the client server architecture is to think of an electronic mail application. The server maintains the data base, which in this case is the mailbox of everyone using the system. The server also maintains the passwords and mailing lists of the users. The client prepares the message he/she wants to send, and indicates the addressee(s). That's all the client does. The server handles the communications linkages and the necessary data base (mailbox) accesses, and completes the transaction.

The client can connect to more than one server to integrate data from another data base if this is necessary. In the case of electronic mail, this would be a connection to another institution's mailbox data base in another part of the city or world. Distributed data bases facilitate this interserver connectivity.

Client server architecture is a major change in the way IS is performed, and—because there was heavy investment in the past in hardware and software and, most importantly, in peopleware—full-scale utilization is just coming into being. Those manufacturers who have a big stake in the mainframe business do not want to see client servers replace their centrally based architecture overnight. The commercial beneficiaries of the client server market are the mini and micro vendors, as well as the telecommunication suppliers, particularly local area networks (LANs). The software players expected to profit are the relational and distributed data base vendors.

Within the corporation, the central IS professionals have grown up on a mainframe architecture they understand and believe in. The major proponents of the client server architecture are the clients (users), because they think it makes sense to control IS applications that affect their department and they like the ease of use provided by off-loading or downsizing the applications to departmental systems. However, to do this requires a major reengineering or transformation of a large number of mainframe applications that have been running for 20 years or so in the central environment. This situation calls for countering resistance to change, and a significant up-front investment. However, a major claim of client server systems is that they are far less costly to use and operate, once they are up and running.

The client server is the culmination of distributed processing. It empowers departmental users and gives them the ability to design and develop their own applications. The client server, combining the power and flexibility of data base and telecommunications architecture, is a driving force in accelerating organizational decentralization. It permits managers to manage with information, the essence of this book.

IS ORGANIZATIONAL MODELS

The effectiveness of IS within an organization depends on many things, among them senior management's leadership and commitment, the technical and business skills of the IS management and staff, the selection and use of technologies, and the planning and implementation processes employed. Another important factor is the organization of IS and its fit within the business structure. There have been a number of organizational models over the years that illustrate the changes in thinking about IS. A review of these models serves to establish the foundation for a discussion of centralized and decentralized/distributed organizations.

Figure 6.3 shows the evolution of three models of IS organization. Model A, which existed from the sixties into the early seventies, took for its title "electronic data processing," which was an apt name. Systems of that era, for the most part, analyzed the data flow and proceeded to convert and process the data electronically via computers. Model B existed from the seventies into the mid-eighties. During that time, both the function and title of the manager were elevated to the more sophisticated management information systems (MIS). This was to connote that systems were not just processing company transactions electronically, but were also developing useful by-product information to aid management in carrying out its functions. Model C, starting in the mid-eighties and carrying over into this decade, recognized the even higher impact of IS, and the IS head is now a company vice president or, in some cases, the chief information officer (CIO). The subject matter becomes

FIGURE 6.3. Changing functions and titles

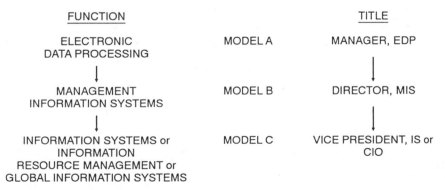

more generic, indicating that IS assists both management and workers throughout an organization such that the function and title emphasize the word *information.*

Figure 6.4 shows the early form of IS organization, model A, where the EDP manager reported to the company controller. The position was at least a rung below the other functional positions of marketing, engineering, and production, and was also considered below the ranking of the staff support groups such as human resources, legal, finance, and public relations. It was considered a technical position that had most impact on the accounting functions; therefore its positioning below the controller. The organization under the EDP manager was simple and usually consisted only of an application development manager and a manager who ran operations. Telecommunications was still in its infancy, and anything to do with telecom was usually accomplished by the operations manager. Planning for the introduction of new technologies or the use of IS in strategic ways was the responsibility of the EDP manager—if these things were considered at all.

Figure 6.5 shows model B where the MIS director now reports to the top financial executive or to an administrative vice president, but rarely directly to the CEO. The accounting image is gone to a certain extent as the role of IS broadens, a fact symbolized by the inclusion of the word management in the title and function. New groups are formed under the MIS Director including a data and technical operations group that begins to develop the IS architecture—principally the central data base concept that is used throughout the enterprise. Also, a separate telecom group is established, as well as an end user support group. The latter, sometimes called the information center, assists end-users in understanding how to employ the centralized systems, as well as in developing and operating their own systems. This is the beginning of the distributed movement. A department, usually one person, becomes responsible for the IS planning function.

Figure 6.6 is model C, the one we most commonly see in use today. The IS head now

FIGURE 6.4. Model A IS organization

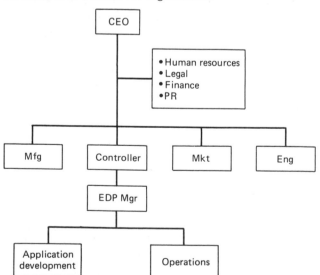

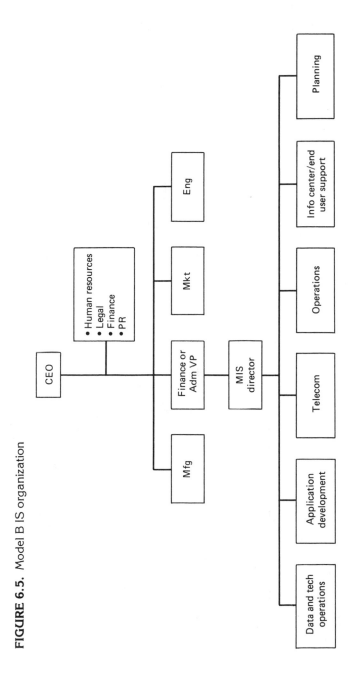

FIGURE 6.5. Model B IS organization

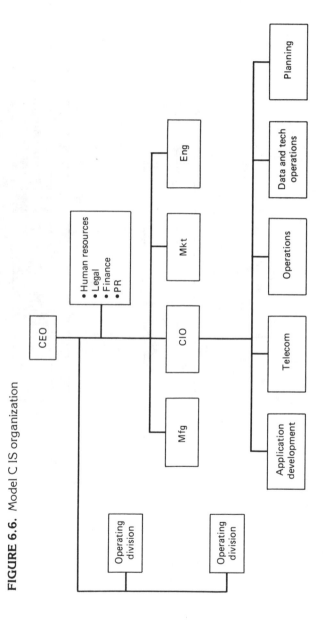

FIGURE 6.6. Model C IS organization

has vice president status and reports directly to the CEO. In about half the cases, he or she has the title of CIO. The information center group is no longer shown; departments have expertise to design their own applications and run them. Companies themselves are more decentralized and organized more along the line of strategic business units or decentralized operating divisions. In many cases, each division has its own application development group and sometimes does its own operational tasks as well. This is also true of the major functional areas in the corporate group such as marketing, engineering, and manufacturing. Also, as business becomes more global, some of these operating divisions become foreign based, and the work of the corporate staff is to optimize decisions across international boundaries. This is true of the IS function and the CIO has become, in global companies, a global information officer (GIO). The final chapter discusses global issues and the evolution of the GIO.

While the departments under the CIO do not decrease, the number of people in this group is markedly reduced with the advent of distributed systems. There is application development, but this is usually limited to support applications such as personnel and payroll or applications that consolidate financial summaries of the major operating divisions. The major transaction and informational applications are the responsibility of the operating divisions. The operation group runs the limited set of corporate applications, and there remains a data and technical operation group but their work is diminished as a result of the client server architectural model. The user support group has disappeared because the expertise exists in the departments. The users are solving their own problems. Planning and telecommunications increase in importance as they are the two functions that build the IS infrastructure that is needed to connect the internal distributed system with other external nodes as well as to other locations throughout the world.

THE CHIEF INFORMATION OFFICER

As indicated, the changes in organizational theory and structure, and the technological trends powered by the personal computer and telecommunications have forever changed the nature of the traditional IS operation. A survey of IS chiefs conducted by *Information Week* in 1990, reports an increase of 20 to 40 percent in total corporate spending for IS outside the IS budget, and 55 percent of the IS chiefs surveyed see the figure increasing significantly in the coming years. The Diebold Research Group in their annual surveys confirms this increasing spending rate outside IS. An additional trend is toward "outsourcing," the most dramatic instance being the shift of the operation of Kodak datacenters, telecom operations, and PC networks to outside vendors. The concomitant shift of dollars to end users and outsourcing has the effect of reducing dramatically the dollars directly controlled by the IS executive.

But does this make the function less significant, less crucial to business success? The paradox is that it does not. The job is changing dramatically, but most senior business people feel the function is more important to business success than it ever was. This is why people have been trying to come up with a title that captures the essence of this important new role. Though there is a bit of a backlash on the term *chief information officer* or *CIO*, it does serve to differentiate a new and important set of responsibilities.

A multibillion-dollar company with multiple operating units recently was searching for its first CIO. The executive vice president to whom the CIO would report explained that the company's organizational policy was a lean corporate staff, numbering under fifty—which is infinitesimal compared with other companies. Their view was to accomplish the "major work" within the business units and departments. They have instituted the practice of what they call "resource centers," that is, delegating cross-functional duties to one of the business units or functional groups. This responsibility would be outside the domain of the particular entity, but the manager would be measured by how well he or she employed the resource center and how well the functional unit did.

The executive VP saw the CIO as having only a handful of people, yet assuming the "resource center" responsibility for establishing the proper IS architecture to ensure company compatibility for things like electronic mail, data sharing and executive reporting. But the VP emphasized that the major IS strategy and company organizational strategy was most definitely decentralization. The CIO would have what has been not so fondly called "responsibility without authority." But the executive VP feels it is workable in the company's culture, and is the only way to proceed. The company sees that decentralization gives them the flexibility and customer awareness needed to remain competitive in their industry, and a lean corporate staff was the sine qua non of this strategy.

Here are some basic things the new breed of IS leader must be able to accomplish:

Build and maintain senior management credibility, as this becomes the real source of power and influence.

Develop and maintain currency-of-technology guidelines (a better term than *policy*) that logically lead to the ability to optimize system connectivity and to protect valuable data and other technology resources.

Recognize that the company or business focus is primary and must be supported and shaped by the technology; be comfortable dealing with senior management.

Realize that politics is an essential element in any systems architecture (while personally maintaining political neutrality).

Have design and implementation experience in the six architectural areas (i.e., telecommunications, networking, data base management, end-user computing, application development, and hardware/software platforms).

Balance long-term direction with short-term interruptions, while maintaining the confidence of senior management and peers.

Have a vision of what the company wants to be and do, and how a systems architecture can support that vision.

Be a technological "metering agent" for the company, able to balance what *could* be introduced with what *should* be introduced.

Possess enough business sense to know that budgetary considerations are important when introducing technology and building an information architecture.

Exhibit strong conceptual skills in order to understand a systems architecture that can expand as technology improves and where complex pieces can work together.

Have an innovative spirit that can discern those technologies that will emerge in practical form early enough to give the company a competitive edge. This means going beyond the "technology gatekeeper" role.

ADJUSTING TO THE NEW IS ROLE

It is fairly easy to develop the prescription for the successful IS executive and for those working in corporate IS in the new decentralized style of operation. There is no question that senior management credibility and rapport are absolute essentials. There is no question that the new IS executive must adapt to the role of consultant, advisor, director, and guider to the new IS decentralized structure. It is no longer a case of exercising power through direct budget and people control. To many who have grown up in the hierarchical business environment of the seventies and eighties, this is completely antithetical to their style and way of managing. The key question is How does one change? or, more directly, Is it possible for one to change?

Successful adaptation comes from an almost complete role reversal. The key is the statement that forms the title of a book by Babson College's, Allan R. Cohen and Stanford University's David L. Bradford entitled Influence Without Authority. They write of concepts that emanate from social psychology, such as mutual benefit, reciprocity, exchange, and currency. The concept of mutual benefit is that both participants must gain from a specific event or transaction. It would be hoped that even in hierarchical organizations, this would be recognized as the way to make things happen. However, in hierarchical setups, there is always "the boss's inherent power" to serve as a tie breaker. In the flattened organization, this power doesn't exist. It is absolutely necessary for people to build the concept of mutual benefit.

The authors point out that mutual benefit is based on a solid foundation of trust, but also the concepts of reciprocity and exchange must be considered. Reciprocity is highly explicit. The authors refer to debts and phrases such as "you owe me one" and "accumulating chits." You also must know in what currency the other person trades in. Currency can be recognition, reputation, visibility to higher ups, ownership/involvement, or money. The important thing is to know the currency in order to make the proper trades to gain the agreement and action you are seeking.

This is a difficult process for some managers to adapt to, but this is the new world of the CIO. He or she no longer has budget or organizational control. It has become a world of mutual respect and "influence without authority," and successful decentralization depends on adapting this new management style.

THE EMERGENCE OF THE TELECOMMUNICATIONS MANAGER

Chapter 5 emphasized the importance of telecommunications and distributed systems to the evolving role of IS. We now turn to the important matter of who manages the telecom function, where the function fits in the organization, what the qualifications of the telecom manager are, and where and how he or she is trained.

We have reviewed the three general organizational models that marked the evolution of the IS function since the early sixties. In the first organizational model the head of the information systems function was the EDP manager. Voice communications was separate from EDP while the the low volume of data transmission did not justify a telecom manager. Systems analysts within EDP handled what data communications there was as an offshoot of the application programs. In the second model, IS became highly centralized, and, while voice communications was still outside IS, there was a technical person who handled data communications, but he or she worked for a technical support manager who reported to the director of IS. With the decentralization of many IS functions to line departments and the centralization of a corporate architecture and policy/standards responsibility under a chief information officer (CIO), the title of telecommunications manager developed. This person reports directly to the CIO and handles both voice and data as well as image and text communication.

John Donovan wrote in the *Harvard Business Review* of the importance of the CIO as network manager. The valid definition of the CIO's job is to provide the architectural framework to allow the effective functioning of those applications and systems that cross departmental lines. Telecommunications, by definition, is a prime example of one of those systems. Certainly the CIO must be responsible for the data and voice telecommunications infrastructure. Donovan states that "the CIO must become personally and deeply involved in communications decisions, perhaps to the point of spending several hours a day on the design, maintenance and expansion of the physical network."

There is no question that the stakes are too high for not concluding that the telecommunications function belongs in IS, and that it should include voice as well as data. Communicating data is integrally tied to the processing of the data. This is true for data alone and is becoming more valid as technology facilitates the combination of voice, graphics, image, and data for transmission purposes. The advent of electronic data interchange (EDI) and related forms of interoperational systems is another compelling reason for the union. Quite a few years ago, Marshall MacLuhan spoke of a global village powered by a new wave of telecommunications technology. Few people today would take issue with his prophecy. If there is agreement on the organizational positioning of the telecom function, the remaining issues are the qualifications of telecom managers and how they are trained and developed.

QUALIFICATIONS OF TELECOMMUNICATIONS MANAGERS

We have reviewed the future telecom technology and how these developments will have a global and competitive impact on corporations and on society. There are more acronyms and numerical/alphabetic shorthand per square inch in the telecom world than in any other discipline. What is alarming is that there are, few, if any, articles on how to manage all of these new products and services. How does one plan, design, and implement systems based on this technology? Who and where are the leaders that possess the necessary vision and knowledge to lead such efforts?

The job of the telecom manager requires a combination of skills that is difficult to find in the same person. This role has evolved in the same way the CIO role has evolved. From a technical base point, the job has grown in scope to the point where management/business skills appear to be the more important attributes for the job. The function has grown from a closed environment with few telecom clients to an open one where everyone in the company is a client and there are additional clients outside the company. Many telecom managers have come through the technical route; that is, either they had been responsible for voice communications and datacom was added to their responsibilities, or they had been in the technical IS world and took over telecom as it became embedded within IS. In a smaller number of cases, the telecom manager had been manager of another function and possessed enough technical perspective to be placed in the telecom role.

What are the attributes required of modern telecom managers? This new role, the techno-business manager, combines the best skills of the technologists and the business-oriented manager. If the individual did not migrate from a data processing background environment, a broad understanding of information systems is necessary in order to relate to the potential integration of data and voice throughout the network. The cultivation of how the telecommunications mission is part of the totally orchestrated business mission is a must.

Managers inherently must have minds that are turned on by the evolving technology so that this inquisitiveness can be translated into sound business decisions. Such individuals must understand and move toward an overall networking architecture, be able to specify meaningful standards and protocols to allow interconnectibility and integration, and have the capacity to scan the emerging technologies for incorporation into their organizations in the proper time frame. A detailed knowledge of how the telecommunications system may be extended, how its diagnostics function, how the network recovery operates, how components are substituted in the system, and other basic control operations are central to total support of the business. Broad relationships must be cultivated with competitive vendors that could potentially support the mission. Currently, telecommunication vendors are the single largest source of knowledge for assisting a company in developing a telecommunications strategy.

Technology in and of itself is of little value without the ability to create strategic and tactical plans that support the corporate mission. The telecommunications system must appear to the corporation as a mandatory support system that enhances its competitive edge, rather than as a large overhead that receives the first budgetary axe. The heart of most major telecommunications systems is an integrated network control system that includes products supplied by a variety of hardware and software vendors.

Finding all the desired characteristics in one individual is difficult, since conflicting aptitudes are required. Compromises will have to be made, but reviewing the foregoing list of job aptitudes can facilitate the task. It should be remembered that the telecom manager's job is managerial and technical, not one or the other; the key is to maintain the proper balance, to know when to be one and when to be the other, and to be able to handle the duality. The new telecom manager is a special kind of person, with the special talents to work both within the IS and telecom domains and outside of them. Telecom technology has become so important to a company's competitive performance that the effort must be made to encourage the balanced role and to find the right person for the position.

The problem today is that many telecom managers are in their roles by default. This is not to belittle the current incumbents because in most cases they have done yeoman work, but it has been an uphill battle. The people responsible for filling these positions either are not aware of the significant role telecommunications can play in an organization or do not realize the nature of the job of telecom manager. The result is that there are inadequate job descriptions and scant guidance on how to measure job performance. The job is normally measured on an exception basis, noticed only if a telephone is not working, a voice messaging system is down, a customer can't get an order into the system, or network performance does not meet the needs of the organization.

TRAINING AND DEVELOPING THE TELECOMMUNICATIONS MANAGER

Merrill Lynch relies heavily on telecommunications to conduct its business, a business that is almost totally dependent on the ability to access and exchange data in a timely manner. The company's Executive Vice President of Operations/Systems and Telecommunications, after a lengthy search selected an outside vendor, MCI to take over the entire management and operation of the company's voice and data network. The company's annual telecom budget is $400 million. The Executive VP thought that MCI could bring an economy of scale and a deeper skill base than Merrill Lynch could hire. "Good telecommunications people," he said "are harder to find now because the job is more complex." A year later Merrill Lynch severed the MCI contract because they felt MCI lacked the people skills as well.

This story aptly describes the dilemma facing companies that are becoming increasingly dependent on telecommunications to run their business. Where do you get the expertise to manage an activity that is getting more complicated by the day? How do you stay ahead of the curve? Do you have to go outside or can you find and develop your own in-house talent?

The first consideration is that the IS function may be facing a severe managerial and technical shortage in the next decade. UCLA has been surveying incoming freshman in colleges throughout the country for the last twenty years. Results (Cale et al.) show that the number of students indicating interest in an information systems career has been declining. Most colleges are well aware that class sizes in IS courses are shrinking. At the same time Bureau of Labor statistics show that one of the fastest growing job fields will be in the information systems area. When coupled with the "baby bust" figures and the secondary school drop-out rates, it appears obvious that a serious shortage of both management and technical talent for managing the telecommunications area is inevitable.

However, the picture is not all dismal. Undergraduate and graduate schools across the country are gearing up to meet industry needs. There are currently over 20 schools offering degrees in telecommunications and the number is increasing. In addition, there are continuing education programs that stress the technical and managerial aspects of running the telecom function.

In addition to the increased interest in our schools, there are a growing number of training programs offered by equipment and service vendors, by training firms, and by trade and consulting organizations. These programs offer a far greater number of technical than management courses. This will have to change if business and institutions are to obtain the required telecom leadership. There is no question that a good deal of the management preparation in the telecom field will have to come from on-the-job training. This is a given in a discipline that is changing so rapidly. However, educational institutions can improve the establishment of the right educational foundation for follow-on training.

A major force in reducing the number of students majoring in IS or telecommunications is the image projected by these disciplines. In a freshman management class at Babson College, 40 students were asked to list the things that came to mind when they contemplated a career in information systems. A sampling of the replies included "boring, high tech, no fun, difficult, annoying, repetitive, sits at a desk and pushes buttons, structured, requires constant learning, restrictive," etc. This image agrees with other studies made of incoming freshmen and could be a major factor in declining enrollments. If these are misconceptions, and in most cases they are, it is up to educators to change the image and to change the curriculum to conform to the actual environment of IS jobs as they exist in the business world. This will involve blending in much more of the management and people role in course curricula.

However, there still should be a place for the true technicians, those that like to delve deeply into the technology. IS managers must establish an environment that attracts and maintains these types of talents. The true technician is not motivated by the same things that motivate others in the organization. They don't aspire to manage people and prefer working by themselves or in small groups. They are not interested in blending in with the infrastructure of the company. The "dual ladder" concept is quite important, that is, measuring and rewarding technicians by their output and accomplishment and not by the number of people they supervise or the size of the budget they control. This is a key element in attracting and maintaining the necessary talent in a market that is becoming increasingly competitive.

SUMMARY

For the most part, technology works best when it is an enabler, facilitating the implementation of the way organizations and people have found it best to manage and act. Decentralized decision making exploits expertise and knowledge at the lowest possible level in an organization. One of the revolutionary technological developments of the 1980s was the development of the powerful, inexpensive personal computer. Now we have the super-powerful desktop workstation. More important, through the developments in data bases and telecommunications, the client server architecture has been facilitated. Together, the new management style (the real driving force) and the continued technological advancements (the enabler) are changing the way companies operate. This combination has changed forever the management world. The new concepts have given enormous power to the individual and to the group. It may be called "power to the masses." These forces have also changed the IS organization. Three organizational models were presented, with the current model being highly distributed, but with a strong organization-wide role being filled by the CIO. Within this context, the role of the telecommunications manager was reviewed.

Managing with information involves active participation in the three levels of IS use. At the personal level, the manager should possess the computer literacy necessary to employ information to assist his/her personal efficiency and effectiveness. At the departmental level, the manager must know the functional demands of the job and have the perspective to see how information can help consolidate and motivate people to achieve departmental objectives. In addition, the manager must have the information literacy to recognize in specific instances how centralized systems, both supportive and strategic, can be employed enterprise-wide. Furthermore, the manager must understand the role he/she should play in helping to implement and to effectively use these systems. This is a tall order, but it is what is meant by *managing with information.*

Case Study

Downsizing: A Company's Experience

At John Hancock Insurance Co., which recently built a complex, microcomputer LAN-based systems for utilization review, central MIS and the Managed Health Care department agreed that a downsized application was in order—and managed to stay clear of politics.

The utilization review system, which tracks medical costs, was originally slated to become part of a massive nationwide claims payment system running on mainframes and accessed by terminals.

Charles Mahoney, senior consultant for Managed Health care, said it became clear that the systems programmers had a development backlog that would prevent them from meeting his department's needs anytime soon.

Also, the mainframe system, featuring complex screens, offered a six-second response time. The utilization review systems, used by nurses making telephone calls, required much quicker response.

Central IS agreed the need for timely development and fast response time indicated a micro-based solution was necessary. Also, MIS resources were already stretched because a complete rewrite of the claims payment system was under way, Mahoney said.

Mahoney said these factors helped eliminate any political concerns that might have arisen between the department requiring the system and MIS. He said MIS "felt fairly comfortable this was not a renegade project."

Mahoney noted since neither central MIS nor a decentralized IS unit had strong micro development expertise, a consultancy—the Boston Systems Group—was hired. MIS, interested in gaining micro experience at a time of stretched resources, proposed "partnering" with the department and contributed a full-time programmer to work on the consultants'

From *MIS Week,* September 11, 1989.

project team. The programmer will now lead two other programmers in maintaining and enhancing the system.

Mahoney said while originally the project was planned as "classic LAN file server and PCs," the system needed to meet actual requirements was quite sophisticated, featuring "a tremendous amount of integration." More than 100 Compaq 386 machines running a DOS application are connected nationwide. The system uses Ethernet, a Microvax running VMS as file server, and a Sybase RDBMS; the system is also tied to MVS mainframes.

The project ultimately turned out to be "one of the most complex developed outside of IS," and took about twice as long as the simple project first envisioned, Mahoney said.

STUDY QUESTIONS

1. This case illustrates both the positive and negative side of downsizing. Discuss both.
2. Why do you think this project turned out to take twice the time predicted for it?
3. Typically central IS has a large backlog, Is this a good reason for downsizing?
4. What do you think of the "partnering" concept and the introduction of a consultant?

Case Study

Brown and Gordon Auto Parts

Brown and Gordon Auto Parts (B&G) is the third largest auto parts manufacturer in the world. It is an autonomously run division of a large conglomerate, RST, Inc. Their headquarters and principal manufacturing facilities are in Cleveland, Ohio, but they operate plants in East Chicago, Illinois, Indianapolis, Indiana, Columbus and Cincinnati, Ohio, and South Bend, Indiana. Total annual revenues are close to $2 billion, but profits were reduced dramatically in 1989 and 1990 because of the recession and particularly because of the decline in automobile sales. Plant capacity has dropped to 60 percent, with a slight pickup in the fourth quarter of this year. (RST, Inc. has turned in record profits in the same two years, with all divisions save B&G performing beyond plan.)

Most of B&G's management team are old-line managers who have proven themselves in operational jobs and have worked their way up the hierarchy. They don't believe in frills or fancy procedures; rather it is to get the job done as quickly and simply as possible. It's a tough, no-nonsense management style. Because of the highly competitive nature of the business, accentuated by the recent business downturn, management has adopted a cost-cutting mode. Almost all investments or expenditures must be justified by tangible cost savings, and this usually means people savings. This is particularly true within IS, where expenditures are not approved until the number of job eliminations is verified.

IS ORGANIZATION

The IS Division is headed by R. L. (Buck) Steubens, MIS Vice President, who reports to W. W. Johnson, V.P. of Finance, who reports to the President of B&G, T. J. Baker.

It is generally accepted that Johnson delegates the IS responsibility totally to Steubens and is not himself a factor in decision making on IS matters. The two key IS directors are Tom Mansfield and Harry Crowley. Mansfield is in charge of the application development for all operations. Development personnel located in outlying plants develop applications for these plants but report to Mansfield. Operations reports to Harry Crowley. The outlying plants have their own operators, who report to local line management. IS operations are highly centralized, however, such that processing is done not locally, but via a telecommunications network to Cleveland's central systems.

Buck Steubens was concerned about the way his IS group was organized and was reviewing the following report, which was sent to him by a consulting firm he had asked to look into the matter.

Consultant Review of
Brown and Gordon Information Systems Function

Organization

B&G has a rather unique organization with two directors managing the entire information systems function. Missing is a third or coordinating element found in most organizations. This third element is responsible for integrating services that span the IS division—services such as standards, planning, education, project management, and often data-base administration. While where is nothing that says the B&G organization cannot work, interviews suggest that major application developments have been implemented without complete awareness of their fit with existing or future subsystems. Also there is a lack of emphasis on planning and education, two functions that are vital to future progress.

To make this dual-directorship concept work, standards and protocols must be better established to facilitate proper communications and integration at the working levels. It is conceivable that the CFO can be the integrating force, but this is too high a level in the organization, particularly in light of the expanding duties of the office. The integration must occur at lower levels.

The stated management organizational style at B&G is heavily people oriented. Thus, the primary criterion for assigning a job is the track record of the individual in getting jobs accomplished rather than an assessment of where the function best fits into the organization or where there is the necessary expertise. The design of complex integrated applications is a difficult task, and while the ability to get a job done is probably the number one attribute, it is not the only one.

Another expressed organizational style is adversary management, the theory being that pitting two competent managers against each other will result in a competitive drive to get the work accomplished. The question raised here is: does this approach work in a functional area of the business that needs integration and communication so desperately?

STUDY QUESTIONS

1. What is the company culture at B&G? What are the pros and cons of this culture?

2. What does the consultant report tell Buck Steubens? What action should he take?

3. Do you think the cost-cutting mode is a "given" for IS? Is it wise to justify IS expenditures on the number of job eliminations?

4. Do you link the organizational issues with the consultant's statement that there appears to be a lack of systems integration at B&G?

SELECTED REFERENCES

Cale, Edward G. Jr., Charles H. Mawhinngy, and David R. Callaghan, "The Implications of Declining Enrollments in Undergraduate CIS Programs in the United States," *Journal of Management Information Systems*/Summer 1991, pp. 167-181.

Dale, Richard, "Client-Server Database: Architecture of the Future," *Database Programming & Design*, August 1990, pp. 28-37.

The Dooley Group, *Developing the World Class Information Systems Organization* vol. 3. Wellesley, Mass.: QED Information Sciences, Inc., 1990.

Forrester Research Inc., "The Attraction Is Price," *Datamation*. March 15, 1990, pp. 49-51.

Forrester Research, Inc., "Is Client/Server Cheaper?" *The Professional Systems Report*. August, 1990, Vol. 7, No. 10.

Forrester Research Inc., "Minis as Servers," *The Professional Systems Report*. January, 1991, Vol. 8, No. 3.

Greene, Paul F., and Jerry Kanter, "New Kid on the Block," *Computerworld*. September 4, 1989.

Klein, Theodore, *Downsizing Corporate Systems: Coping with Decentralized Computing*. Boston Systems Group, Inc. 1990.

Lewis, Peter H., "Networld: The Talk Is of Strategic Partnerships," *The New York Times*. February 17, 1991.

Chapter **7**

The Application Development Cycle

INTRODUCTION

It is true that, no matter how good the planning and architectural design, nothing happens until someone implements an application. We now turn to the important subject of development. The process of development will differ depending on the size and scope of the project. Projects can be huge blockbusters requiring multiple person-years approaching in some case person-centuries, or they can be simple department-level applications that may require a few weeks. However, the latter are often underestimated and turn out to take two to three times their original projection. Regardless of the size of the project, certain rules of development should be followed to maximize the chances of success.

We proceed from the large to the small by starting with the traditional application development life cycle. The major areas of analysis, synthesis, and implementation are reviewed. This basic framework is relevant for all types and sizes of applications, omitting in the smaller projects some of the formality and detail. Each of the stages and substages is covered. The importance of economic justification and risk assessment is covered in the next chapter as part of the larger task of justifying the entire IS organization. Structured design methods are also reviewed as they remain on the scene as an approach to implementation.

An objective method of analyzing alternate use of outside resources is presented. The specific example used is the acquisition of an application package, but the technique can be used for the acquisition of other resources as well. An important part of the chapter is the explanation of computer-aided software engineering (CASE) tools to facilitate the development process. This is one of the most promising areas, and much is going on, with new tools and approaches appearing weekly. Finally, some thoughts on departmental application development are presented. As a manager, one has to use information coming both from the central IS function and also from one's own department. It is desirable to be familiar with developments in both arenas.

APPLICATION DEVELOPMENT CYCLE

Chapter 3 covered the modeling of the business as a starting point for system development—the top-down approach. Once the business and information models are developed, the subsystems identified, and the implementation priority determined, each application must be thoroughly planned, documented, programmed, tested, and put into productive computer operation.

Figure 7.1 illustrates the application development cycle. The hub of the wheel indicates that there are three general phases in this process: (1) analysis, (2) synthesis, and (3) implementation. Analysis is defined as the separation of anything into its constituent parts or elements. Synthesis, the opposite of analysis, begins to combine and build the parts or elements into a whole. The *analysis phase* dissects business operations to show up weaknesses and areas where information analysis can improve the planning and control of operations. The *synthesis phase* combines these elements in such a way as to improve the original operation.

The *implementation phase* is the proof of the pudding. Here the synthesis (or improved solution) is actually designed, programmed, and put into operation. An important part of this phase is the postoperational audit of the system to ascertain whether objectives of cost and performance were met. The concluding activity is the maintenance and modification of operational applications to ensure that they remain free of errors and discrepancies.

A further breakdown of the development cycle indicates that the analysis phase consists of two subphases: feasibility study and systems study. The *feasibility study* begins with the establishment of objectives, including the time and cost of the study, selection of the people who will conduct it, and the general manner in which it will be conducted. The feasibility study asks: Does this application offer sufficient benefits to a company to warrant further investigation? An effective *systems study* requires a considerable investment in time and money; it should be undertaken only if a preliminary study indicates that the proposed application presents a feasible solution to the problem. Further study may indicate that the application is not justified, but a company should be reasonably sure that the application is justified before embarking on a comprehensive systems study.

The systems study begins with an analysis of overall business objectives and focuses on the major benefits and objectives of the application. It also assesses the application's fit with other related applications. The systems objectives establish goals focused on the response time, user languages, system security, and the like. The total information system will be broken down into progressively smaller and smaller units of study until the focus is

FIGURE 7.1. Application development cycle

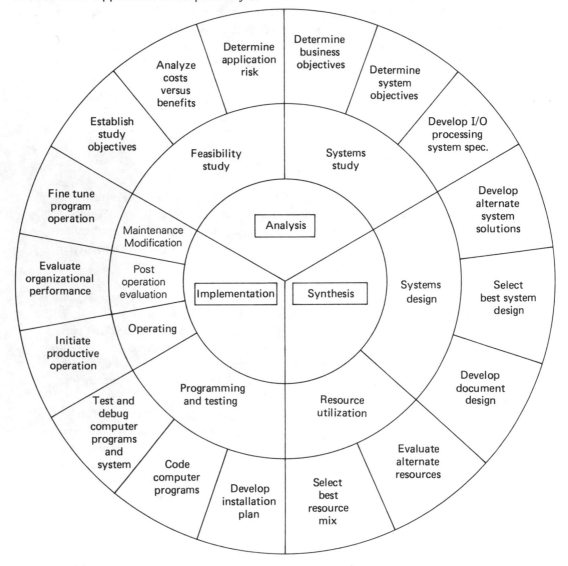

on meaningful and manageable subsystems. The input, output, and processing steps of these subsystems will be carefully analyzed to form the foundation for the synthesis phase of the application development cycle.

The synthesis phase consists of the system design and resource utilization subphases. The *systems study* answers the question *What is* being done? and compares that with what should be done. *Systems design is* concerned with *how* it is being done and compares that with how it should be done. In systems design, the detail produced during the systems study is used to develop alternate solutions that would better achieve the defined business and system objectives.

The *resource utilization* subphase explores various alternatives for providing the resources necessary to accomplish the job. These alternatives range from using a company's own system and programming personnel and its current computer, if there is available capacity; to employing outside assistance in the form of systems help, software help, computer time, or complete outsourcing of development.

The implementation phase includes developing the *installation plan,* which outlines the resources necessary to prepare for running the application. The installation plan and schedule determine the specific availability dates of the necessary resources. The implementation phase includes the *programming, operating, post operation evaluation,* and *maintenance and modification* subphases. The implementation staff, after selection and training, transforms the systems design specification into progressively greater and greater detail, thus preparing the system for computer processing. The resultant programs are tested both individually and as an information system and are finally put into productive operation.

The implementation phase does not end at this point but includes the important postoperation evaluation (Did the system do what it was supposed to do?) and maintenance/modification subphase. Postoperational review assesses the productive programs to determine whether they meet the system objectives and, therefore, the business objectives. The resultant system improvements and benefits are measured against those that were projected. The overall operational performance must be evaluated as a preliminary step to fine-tuning the running applications. It is inevitable that operational errors and program discrepancies will occur with time; a plan must be instituted for their resolution and correction. With the fine-tuning accomplished, both short- and long-range plans for future growth are refined.

In reality, the phases of analysis, synthesis, and implementation are never-ending cycles. As soon as initial computer applications are put into productive operation, additional ones are tackled. The operational applications must be periodically reviewed and updated to run more efficiently and to adapt to changing business conditions and needs.

APPLICATION BUSINESS PLAN

A growing number of companies that have a mature and comprehensive planning process are using the concept of a product business plan. For each major product or project undertaken, a planning guide is utilized to ensure that all the elements needed for the success of the program are included and properly reflected. I feel that this concept can and should be carried over to the planning of major application subsystems within IS and, indeed, to the entire IS development process. All too often the planning approach to IS is a fragmented one. Different individuals and different groups get together and frequently accomplish effective work, but their efforts are not coordinated and their overall plan is not set down and documented officially. This is the purpose of an application business plan—to provide a vehicle for stating the pertinent agreements and rationale under which the activity must proceed. The application business plan must be a live document that is continually updated and modified. If a new systems analyst or operating manager enters the project, the application business plan is the first document he or she should read in order to gain pertinent background.

Figure 7.2 presents an outline of the contents of an application business plan. The first section covers the rationale of the particular program—the purpose, objectives, goals, and similar factors—and the connection with the other portions of the management information system. The second section covers the definition and characteristics of the application. An individual not familiar with the application can obtain a concise but definitive explanation by reading this section. The next section covers the feasibility of the application. Whatever feasibility criteria a company employs, whether cost/benefit analysis or return on investment, the criteria and financial data are recorded in this section.

The remaining sections cover more detailed information about the application, the design and specification, the schedule and implementation plan, and, finally, the implementation status and review section. Thus the application business plan is an on-going document that covers the life cycle of the application from feasibility, justification, and design to implementation, schedule, and productive operation. A company must insist that no major program be authorized without a business plan.

An additional point is the possibility of dovetailing the application business plan

FIGURE 7.2. Application business plan

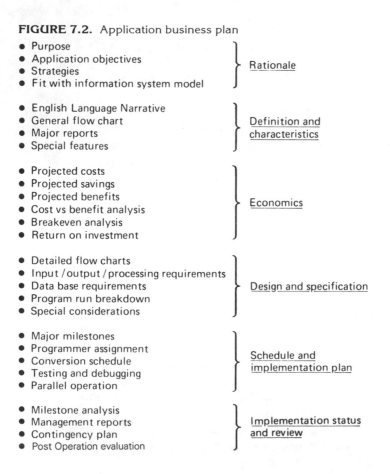

concept with the company's program or project management organization. Many companies have a program management office that assigns program managers to major projects. Although the program managers do not control the departments responsible for implementing the project, they are responsible as catalysts and coordinators to see that the project is completed on schedule and as specified. It is possible that a program manager may be assigned to one of the advisory groups. It then becomes that manager's job to schedule the meetings, see that the written plan is prepared and the schedules monitored, and take action to remain on schedule. Many firms have not as yet considered major IS subsystems as candidates for program management. The contention here is that perhaps they should. More systems have failed because of lack of management direction and leadership than for any other reason. The application business plan and the employment of program management are powerful techniques for ensuring the success of a management information system. Program management in systems development projects is discussed in Chapter 9.

We turn now to a more detailed look at the various subphases. Subphases at the beginning of the cycle are discussed more thoroughly than the others because of their management significance.

FEASIBILITY

Feasibility is a significant phase of the application development cycle. Many companies have launched major programs and moved well along in a dedicated productive effort when someone raised the question: We're making good progress, but are we working on the right problem? This is the purpose of the feasibility phase—to develop a set of selection criteria, a selection procedure, and an effective decision-making organization so that a company can be certain that it is working on the right problem and in the right sequence. The feasibility phase is a vital underpinning of IS. Too often the selection of applications has been left to IS people or has been rubber-stamped by management without real study or analysis.

Figure 7.3 is read from the inside out; thus, the inner ring is broken into categories by the middle ring, while the outer ring gives examples of elements in the middle rings. The figure indicates that there are three general feasibility considerations: (1) technical, (2) economic, and (3) operational. It is important that management carefully consider all three, in addition to establishing their relative weight and significance. The technical considerations are directed at the question of whether the necessary hardware, software, and application tools are available or will be available when required by the particular applications under study. Often there is a risk or probability factor, because one or several of the technical elements may be future items promised by a certain date but not yet available. In this event, management must consider the reliability of vendor claims, whether the particular item is on the critical path, and what insurance if any can be established in case of late delivery. Of course, the risks increase greatly when several key items are in the future category.

Certain hardware items are required, such as input/output devices, communication capabilities, and optical or electronic storage devices. Software items, such as data base

FIGURE 7.3. Application feasibility criteria

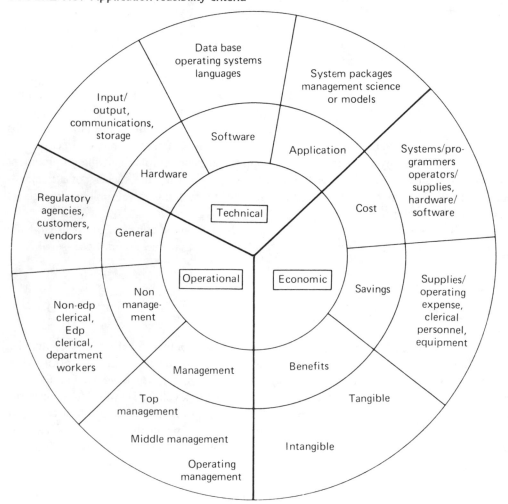

management, operating systems, and special languages, as well as application packages and management science techniques, may be IS requirements. Each of the required items must be carefully evaluated to ascertain its relevance to IS development. The higher the dependence on sophisticated and/or technical items yet to be field-tested, the higher is the risk factor in selecting a particular application for development. Special attention is given to risk assessment in Chapter 8.

A look at the economic and operational feasibility will further qualify application feasibility. Economic considerations represent fundamental feasibility criteria. If a company cannot improve its profit picture or return on investment in the short or long run, then the application should be suspect. In looking at the economics of IS, one must consider this cost compared with the savings that IS can accrue and/or the added benefits derived from the system. It is true that IS can give a company a competitive or strategic advantage, but as the succeeding chapters bring out, it is desirable to place an economic value on the competitive advantage.

A *saving is* a definite IS operating-cost reduction caused by the introduction of the particular application. It could be the reduction of operating costs or the reduction of clerical personnel as the computer system absorbs the routine administrative functions and increases the efficiency, for example, of data entry operation. More often than not, the introduction of IS, although not without some clerical cost savings, will result in an overall cost increase because of the need for added computing capacity and people. Companies have found that computerization pays off, not in reduced costs, but in more meaningful and more timely information.

Turning now to the type of benefits that can be expected from a computer program, we can distinguish two general categories: tangible and intangible. A tangible benefit is one that can be accurately measured and that can be directly related to the introduction of an application. An example is a cost reduction where work formerly accomplished on overtime has been eliminated because of an improved production-scheduling system. An example of an intangible benefit is an improvement in customer service brought on by a more responsive order-processing system. Although it is often clear that the improvement is a result of the application system, it is difficult to place a monetary value on the effect this has on overall company profitability. There are degrees of tangibility in system benefits. Certainly the benefit of improved company image as a result of the automated nature of an application is less tangible a factor than the benefit of improved customer service, although both benefits fall into the intangible category.

In assembling the final feasibility study, the time dimension—when the benefits will occur—is important. If the study encompasses the entire information system of a company, it is clear that such a development will take a rather lengthy period to implement. Some type of phase-in plan must be instituted, which means that the benefits will come gradually, and not all will be apparent during the first year of installation. The feasibility study return-on-investment analysis should reflect this fact.

Placing a dollar value on anticipated computer benefits is a difficult task. An example may illustrate the type of analysis that can be used for this purpose. Many companies have inventory problems that result in a major overstocking of certain items and understocking of others. The key consideration in inventory control is maintaining a balanced inventory that provides the required level of customer service. If asked how much reduction can be accomplished by automating the inventory control operation, most business managers would say, "Plenty." This, however, is hardly a quantified statement of fact. One might look at other companies with similar operations that have computer-based inventory control systems to determine what reductions they have obtained. Another way is to use a computer system to analyze past history of demand and prior levels of inventory. Through a process of simulation (which uses mathematical inventory decision rules), the system can indicate what levels of inventory would have been required in order to meet the desired level of customer service. Comparing these simulated levels with actual levels gives a company a good idea of potential inventory reduction.

An often-overlooked element of feasibility is *operational feasibility.* A particular application may be technically and economically feasible but fail to produce the forecasted benefits because a company is not able to get it to work. This is often perplexing to IS management, who cannot understand why a well-conceived and well-designed system cannot be successfully utilized by the operating departments. There are several reasons for this situation. Some of the problems are motivational and psychological in nature and can be resolved by proper training and indoctrination. Some, however, are serious enough at the outset to warrant placing a lower priority on a particular application area until the problem is resolved. An example is the development of a sales report that shows profitability of sales by item and product line. If salespeople were compensated the same whether they sold item A or item B, the report would be cumbersome and of little value. In this case, it may be wise to assign a lower system priority until specific policies are changed and tested. If this is not done, the computer and IS will bear the blame for the failure, whether they deserve it or not.

It is necessary to assess management, nonmanagement, and general operational considerations as indicated in Figure 7.3. The major focus of the application must be ascertained, and the resulting impact on top, middle, and operating management carefully analyzed. For example, a system may be built on a rather revolutionary approach to production scheduling. This factor obviously has a direct impact on the production-scheduling supervisor and the production manager. If the production manager is a former production worker who has worked his or her way to this current position, is very conservative, and has been antagonistic toward computerized production-scheduling systems, this situation obviously represents a negative operational feasibility consideration. It must either be dealt with and resolved or else recognized as a strong factor in establishing a lower priority for the production-scheduling subsystem. To a lesser extent this is true for nonmanagement personnel as well. A positive attitude and an acceptance of the system on the part of management can be reflected downward to the people who must implement the system. Frequently, the development of IS can impose greater demands on clerical personnel, in the form of their learning new ways of doing business, assuming duties that add to their total work load, or both. These demands are important considerations in operational feasibility.

This area of concern is described by the phrase *technology transfer.* The objective is to transfer the new technology into the company culture. Technology is used in the broad sense to cover the hardware and software components that comprise the system. The important question is not how advanced the technology is, but what impact it has on the organization and the people employing the new system. If it requires organizational change, this should raise a flag that serious attention should be given to preparing the people involved for the changes. Prototyping, a CASE tool, is an example of testing and piloting the system before full scale operation. (CASE tools are discussed later in the chapter.) Prototyping can be a powerful tool for technology transfer if it is used in this context.

The "general" category under operational feasibility is a most significant one and must not be overlooked. Stories of customer reaction and the rigors of converting to a new billing system are legion. Most of us have received notices apologizing for dunning us for bills we have long paid, or for the myriad of other problems encountered because the company was converting to a new computer system. This situation is obviously a consideration in operational feasibility. As an example, if a vendor reordering system requires the delivery of a greater number of smaller orders with less lead time, the vendor must be conditioned to respond to this new policy, particularly if the items in question are in short supply. Similarly, the potential impact of IS on regulatory external agencies must be considered. For example, if the system is designed to provide audit trails, this procedure should be reviewed with the company's auditors and the Internal Revenue Service authorities. This occurs frequently in the development of just-in-time (JIT) inventory systems patterned after the Japanese model. JIT systems reduce inventory by scheduling materials to arrive at the factory just prior to the production lot that requires these materials. Thus it is important to consider carefully the three elements of feasibility described in Figure 7.3. A proper blending, analysis, and weighting of the technical, economic, and operational elements will ensure that the correct priority is placed on application subsystems within an IS and that a company is indeed working on the right problem.

THE SYSTEMS STUDY

As indicated in Figure 7.1, the systems study focuses on the determination of basic business objectives, the establishment of system objectives based on the business objectives, and the development of an input/output processing system specification for the application being implemented.

Figure 7.4 presents a more detailed schematic of the systems study phase. The starting point is the marketplace in which the company competes. Although it is not the responsibility of the systems study group to develop the overall business objectives from the nature of the marketplace, the group must be aware of the development and the policies at this level. Beginning at such a high level may seem presumptuous, but it is essential if the study is geared to improving company operations.

The process outlined here is a microcosm of the long-range IS plan methodology covered in Chapter 2. As the IS LRP must be in concert with the overall corporate business plan, so the new major application systems must be tested against the corporate strategy and objectives of the particular business processes affected by the application in question.

Definitions of terms, business objectives, external and internal strategies, and business system objectives are in order at this time.

Business Objectives

Business objectives state the reason the company is in business. A direct parallel is the job description for an individual, which explains the purpose and nature of the job and the objectives to be accomplished. For a business, the broadest category usually is to maximize revenue, keep costs down, improve profit, and increase the rate of return on investment. These goals normally are quantified by specific dollar figures.

Business Strategies

Of more significance to the systems study group are the specific external and internal business strategies evolving from the business objectives.

External strategies are related to the marketing function and state how the company

FIGURE 7.4. The systems study

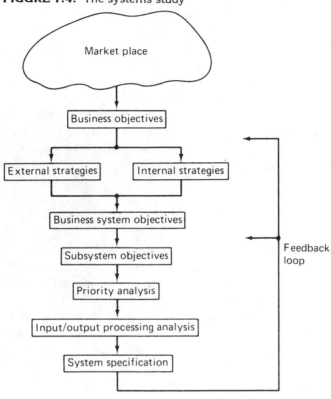

plans to attain the necessary sales revenue from the marketplace in which it competes. The external marketing strategies generally revolve around the answers to three basic questions:

1. With whom do I want to do business?
2. What should I sell them?
3. Why should they buy from me?

The answers will lead to strategies such as extending the geographical boundaries of the marketing area, concentrating a homogeneous product line in a specific marketing area, expanding product offerings to provide a full line, expanding sales 15 percent per year, and so on. These external objectives have considerable influence on the systems study group.

Internal strategies concern those functions related to turning out the product or service offered to the marketplace. These strategies are built around the central focus of providing the product and/or service that meets the external marketing strategies and yet utilizes the company's resources in such a way as to minimize the costs, thus attaining the company's profit and return-on-investment goals. These internal strategies affect the basic production, purchasing, inventory, quality control, accounting, personnel, and engineering and research functions of a company. As a rule, specific internal strategies have great bearing on the systems study group. A strategy might be to level production because of the scarcity of skilled labor or to achieve a 99 percent quality control standard because of the costly impact of product failure to a customer. Another internal strategy might be to institute a standard cost program to control production costs and establish a better basis for pricing. The system study must be aware of these internal strategies, the probabilities of each occurring, and their expected time frame.

The combination of the external and internal strategies is the necessary "front end" of establishing business system objectives. It is true that objectives can be established independently of this type of analysis, and many reasons can be presented for so doing. For example, it is apparent that some companies have ill-defined or undefined overall strategies. The decision then becomes one of waiting until the strategies are determined or of assisting in the establishment of the strategies before embarking on the systems study. This is a tradeoff that a company must face, realizing that a system that is inconsistent with overall company objectives can prove quite detrimental. It is possible to assume on one's own what strategies the company should have and to build a system from there, but doing so can be risky. This is one of the underlying and hidden reasons that a systems study takes so long; often it is not the fault of the systems study team but the result of management's inability to agree on basic business strategies. Systems people, in their zeal to begin, may tend to avoid the major overriding issues in an effort to bypass what they consider top management red tape. The systems group can take this attitude, but in many cases it is like building a house on quicksand. It is better to face the issues, convince management that it must reach decisions, and begin the systems study on solid ground.

Business System Objectives

The next term requiring a definition is *business system objectives.* An information system is defined as the information complex that parallels the physical operations of a company. As explained in Chapter 1, an information system is not the physical operation itself, although the two go hand in hand. For example, a manufactured product is produced by fabricating and assembling various raw materials, piece parts, and assemblies at various work centers. The physical process of bringing together the necessary materials and machines to produce a product is an example of a physical operating system. On the other hand, the process that produces a production schedule telling the plant supervisor which materials and which machines are needed to produce a specified number of products by a specified time is defined as an *information system,* the system that controls the operating system.

Subsystem Objectives

In analyzing a company's operations, it will be obvious that the overall information system can be broken down into a hierarchy of subsystems, and the subsystems in turn into other subsystems. The starting point of the systems study should be an analysis of the hierarchy of business processes that exists within the company being studied. Such an analysis will enable a clearer definition and statement of system and subsystem objectives.

Priority Analysis

After the definition of the system and subsystem objectives, it becomes apparent that the achievement of the entire range of objectives is a gargantuan task and that some type of phasing or priority analysis must be undertaken. The feasibility study should have established some framework for determining priorities. The systems study by now should enable the systems group to present to management various alternatives for its evaluation. The establishment of priorities is a management, not a systems, prerogative.

Once study priorities have been established, detailed data comprising the input, output, and processing requirements of each subsystem are gathered, categorized, and analyzed.

System Specification

The final result or output of the systems study is a system specification. System specs should be developed along the same lines as engineering specs for a specific piece of equipment. The clearer and less ambiguous the spec, the more realistic the proposed computer solution will be. If, for example, the spec omits a requirement to handle a volume up to 20 percent greater by the time the system is installed, the computer configuration will be underestimated, thereby posing a serious problem at the time of installation. The specification, thoroughly understood and with the key measurement criteria (response time, output reports, report content, etc.) signed off by the ultimate users of the system, is the critical output of the systems study.

The development of the systems module concept with its feedback control loop has been described in Chapter 1. Figure 7.4 includes a series of feedback loops. Feedback is extremely important at this stage, because discrepancies not now identified and dealt with can lead to major problems and rework later on, either in the implementation cycle or in actual operation. In many instances, system designers construct a simple prototype or breadboard of the system in order to provide a high level of feedback at an early stage.

The Structured Techniques

A set of methods that have evolved over the past 10 to 15 years, the *structured techniques,* have become more or less the accepted ways to develop application programs. It is appropriate to discuss these techniques here as they are subdivided into structured analysis (the subject we have just discussed), structured design, and structured programming (subjects to be discussed as we move through the development cycle). Like any branch of accepted wisdom, the techniques stem from basic and sound practices that have been followed for years by professionals, many of whom feel there is now a fancy name for what they have been practicing all along.

Structured analysis applies to the systems study subphase and involves the use of tools that define and document users' requirements in a way that they can understand. The output of structured analysis is the system specification. An overall principle of the structured techniques is the top-down concept. It recognizes that systems are developed for users and that the first step is to determine user information requirements and to reflect these in sample reports and response-time projections. The structured approach analyzes systems as one analyzes a company organization chart, in a hierarchical fashion, where subfunctions are combined logically under other subfunctions and eventually become major functions that combine under a single executive or single systems entity. The structured approach mandates looking at the major functions or top boxes first before delving into the subfunctions.

Structured design is built on the divide-and-conquer concept of breaking down a problem into tightly defined, clearly understood subsystems or modules. If the top modules are defined well and in such a way that they are self-contained entities with minimal module coupling or interconnection, then the underlying modules become relatively easy to design and implement. Too often, design proceeds quickly into the detail of lower-level modules, which then all have to be reworked if there is a change in one of the upper modules. Top-down design and modularization make structured analysis and design the accepted way to develop both systems and applications software.

A brief description and illustration of several of the key tools of the structured techniques completes this section. The tools described are:

- Data flow diagram
- Data dictionary
- Structured English statement
- Output report layout
- Hierarchical design organization

Figure 7.5 indicates a typical structured data flow diagram. It depicts physical entities (e.g., store and warehouse), data stores (customer and inventory file), and process boxes (edit and verify order). The objective of the process illustrated is to accept an order from a store and eventually deliver the goods ordered back to the store.

The first process is to edit the particular order form and verify that the proper ordering procedures have been followed. The customer data store (file) is then interrogated to ascertain whether the particular store's credit is within specified limits. Once this has been determined, the order is screened against the inventory data store (file) for inventory availability. If the items are in stock, the quantities are extended based on price, weight, and so on, and an order form is produced. This is the authorization for the warehouse to pick and load the order on a truck or whatever and deliver the goods to the store that originated the order.

This simple, first-level flow diagram does not include processes such as billing the store for goods ordered and collecting the payment. However, these and other processes can be added and described in greater detail in order eventually to flow the total process.

The data flow diagram is a straightforward way to describe the processes of a system—what is going on and the major outputs. Formerly, flow charts with fixed symbols (usually a dozen or so) representing different types of processes and computer resources were used to describe an application. The data flow diagram is simpler, more flexible, and easier for a user to follow and understand. Figures 7.6 and 7.7 are adjuncts to the data flow diagram, describing the contents of each data file (the data dictionary) used by the application and stating in a shorthand sort of English the steps in each process.

FIGURE 7.5. Data flow diagram

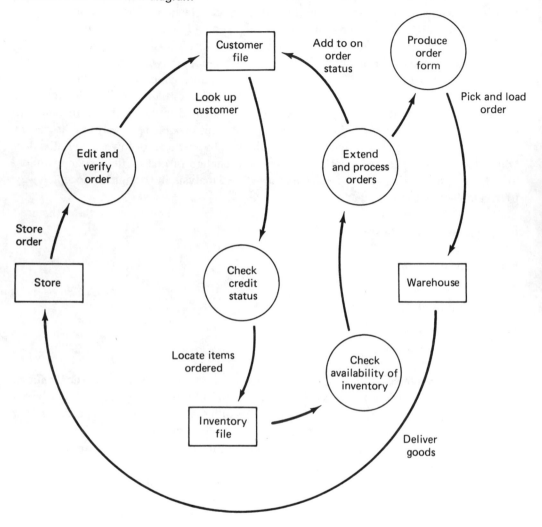

FIGURE 7.6. Data dictionary

CUSTOMER ORDER =
- Customer name
- Account number
- Address
- Credit rating
- On order
- Balance owed

INVENTORY ITEM =
- Item name
- Item number
- On-hand balance
- On order
- Item price
- Item weight

FIGURE 7.7. Structured English statement

Credit Checking Process
1. Check credit category of account
   (a) if A, process order routinely
   (b) if B, ensure that amount ordered plus on order does not exceed amount indicated
   (c) if C, send to sales administration for review before processing.
2. Check accounts receivable balance
   (a) if less than 30 days, process routinely
   (b) if greater than 60 days, but less than 120 days, process but print reminder to sales administration
   (c) if greater than 120 days, kick out for sales administration review before processing.

Very important in the system specification are the output reports, as these are the user-visible portions of the application (they could be printed copy, screen formats, or both). It is essential to review these documents carefully with users. (Figure 7.8 illustrates an inventory report and a billing form.) The result of systems analysis is a user-oriented specification, and one of the keys to successful development is to obtain a user sign-off on the specification. This will involve a careful analysis of the reports as well as an agreement on the response time of on-line transactions and the turnaround time on batch or periodic reports.

Figure 7.9 is a hierarchical diagram used in the design phase. The application is broken down into a process organization showing the various systems modules (processes) and the components of each. This is an excellent technique for ensuring that the total job is understood and divided into logical entities that fit together to comprise the process of the next higher order.

Systems Design

Figure 7.1 indicates that the systems design phase is directed at developing alternate solutions; exploring the various designs; and then selecting, developing, and documenting the one that appears best.

The design phase begins with the hierarchical chart illustrated in Figure 7.9. The particular application is broken down into specific functions—those of lower orders building to create those of upper orders. Structured design requires these functions to be self-contained, so that they can be defined and then coded with the knowledge that they will fit into the total structure. The design phase is the bridge, translating the system spec into a language and structure that can be turned over to programmers for writing the particular machine instructions. Systems design is peeling back the onion, dividing each module into progressively finer and finer modules. Each module is defined, bounded, and given its proper place in the hierarchy.

The interface points between modules are very important. To maintain the focus of structured design, these interfaces or couplings should be minimized and simplified. The more complicated they become, the more difficult it becomes to test and make changes. The highest level of data being transferred from one module to another can be noted on the hierarchical chart. For example, if module A processes a record—that is, it takes the items

FIGURE 7.8. Output report layouts

Inventory Action Report

Inventory action report   Date _____

Item no.	Description	On hand	On order	Total available	Projected demand	Reorder point	Economic order quantity

Inventory action report   Date _____

item no.	On hand	This order	Amount short	% available	Action code	Substitute item no.

Billing Form

Store address   Store copy

Store #   Order #   Date _____

Item description	Item retail	Unit retail	Item number	Quantity	Discount unit and allowance cost	% gross margin

FIGURE 7.9. Hierarchical design organization

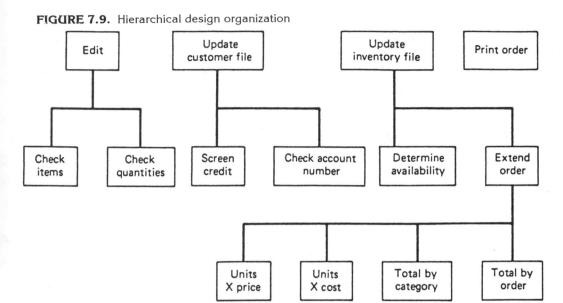

ordered by a particular customer and sums the quantity, price, and weight—and passes the totals to module B, this is the connection or coupling point and should be so noted on the hierarchical chart. The design phase also includes the expression of each hierarchical module in a pseudocode similar to that of Figure 7.7. This then becomes the link between the systems design and the actual writing of machine instructions.

A term used quite often as part of the structured techniques is *walkthrough*. Walkthroughs are review points that take place at periodic intervals throughout the development cycle. They are a way of pulling analysts or designers away from the detail for a time in order to stand back, make a review of progress, and ensure that what they are doing is on track and in line with the original specifications. The purpose of a walkthrough in the design phase is to look for errors, flaws, weaknesses, omissions, and ambiguities in the design prior to commencing the coding. The later an error is found, the more embedded it becomes and the more difficult it is to correct. Walkthroughs are not the formal, management type of reviews that are also part of the development cycle; they are more informal, local, and working-level oriented. In the case of a design walkthrough, the designers would step through the modules of one trunk of the hierarchical chart. The group may consist of two or three designers, with the person who developed the specification also sitting in. The logic of the module, plus the coupling points between modules, would be checked and tested for logic and continuity. Walkthroughs should be conducted frequently at logical breakpoints in the design.

While the structured techniques are intended mainly for professional designers and programmers, many of the processes should be heeded by departmental systems developers as well. For example, many departmental systems do not have a flowchart that describes the application, report formats or the system output. Documentation can be critical to the long-term success of a system.

Resource Utilization

Up to this point we have not considered hardware or software configurations, except in very broad terms to supply costs for calculating return on investment during the feasibility phase. At this juncture, the objective is to verify the ROI or cost/benefit analysis, since we have a better handle on system objectives and the components of the system itself as a result of completing the analysis phase.

During the feasibility phase, we had to guesstimate the hardware and software resources necessary to accomplish the application. The systems study has helped confirm the guesstimates, and the resource utilization phase should enable us to pinpoint the hardware (central processor, disk storage, terminals, printers, etc.) necessary to accomplish the job, as well as the systems software and supporting services. With the advent of distributed data processing, the job of resource selection is a bit more difficult. Systems have more options open to them, such as mini- or microcomputers, shared data bases, and remote work stations. All these elements must be analyzed to come up with the final configuration.

At this point, a good hard look at the resources necessary to complete the design and implementation of the application is in order. If this application has been considered in the long-range plan, we should have already incorporated the necessary hardware, software, and people resources into an operating budget. However, things have a way of changing, so it is important to review the various options. The first consideration is doing the application in-house. If ample application designers and programmers are available, this, of course, is a straightforward solution. More often than not, however, there exists a heavy backlog of application development, and people resources will be tight.

An alternative approach is to see whether an available application package will do the entire job or at least serve as a framework for it. Packages are becoming a more viable alternative to in-house development; potential package solutions should be investigated thoroughly to determine whether they will do the job or whether tailoring and specializing them will take more work than to begin from scratch. One advantage in following the sequence outlined in this development cycle is that, at this stage, you will have completed the systems study and have a good idea of just what the package must accomplish. A note of caution is in order. Although application packages have an allure in that they condense the systems life cycle, their main contribution is in the pre-coded and tested programming modules. This is not trivial, but it should be emphasized that packages do not preclude the need for system feasibility and system analysis. These functions must be accomplished to ensure that the package meets the systems requirements.

Also available are a variety of support arrangements ranging from part-time programmers to "complete outsourcing" firms. This area may involve: (1) basic consultation on a specific subsystem, or (2) full responsibility for the resources (including the computer itself) necessary to accomplish a major system. For example, a company might subcontract the development and implementation of its entire market system to an outside consulting firm.

The proliferation of hardware, software, and service companies presents a challenging dilemma for IS managers. Available to them are a wide variety of alternatives for obtaining computer power. Although there are opportunities for selecting a source or a combination of sources that can get IS managers where they want to be in a faster and more economical manner, they must be careful to base their decisions on an analytical evaluation of the alternatives. There is significant risk in contracting the wrong job to the wrong service company.

OBJECTIVE SELECTION TECHNIQUES

Whether a company is acquiring a new computer system, systems or application software, outside consulting and contracting services, or any combination thereof, an objective method of evaluating competitive offerings is essential. The method need not be highly sophisticated or statistically based to be effective. Often a simple technique of deciding what the decision criteria are and then rating the potential vendors against them will do very nicely. The important thing is to know the job well enough to determine which criteria are important and which are irrelevant. A good systems study should lay the groundwork for determining these criteria.

A basic method, for example, for selecting a potential application package would have the following steps. This technique can be used to evaluate different options, including hardware selection.

1. Determining decision criteria
2. Establishing relative importance of criteria
3. Rating each package (vendor) on how well it fulfills these criteria

1. Determining Decision Criteria

The decision criteria emanate from the basic system specifications. It is somewhat like selecting an individual for a particular job opening: The first step is to have a thorough understanding of the job. Decision criteria usually can be separated into two categories: (1) the necessary criteria, which must be met before further consideration is given, and (2) the desirable criteria, which, though not essential, are considered extremely important in the evaluation. The necessary criteria should be selected carefully, because a hasty selection may arbitrarily eliminate a package at this stage. Examples of necessary criteria are as follows:

Necessary Criteria	Package A	Package B	Package C	Package D
Accomplishes at least 75 percent of job	x	x	x	x
Has been successfully installed	x	x	x	
Is easily modifiable	x	x	x	x
Vendor can provide adequate support			x	x

In this instance, all four packages are deemed suitable for the job, but package D has not yet been installed. Since the company does not want to be a pioneer in an application area vital to its operation, it eliminates package D. All four purport to be easily modifiable, but the vendor of package B is evaluated as not having the necessary support personnel to assist in modifying it. This is considered very important to the company and therefore package B is eliminated, leaving packages A and C as potential candidates for the job.

Next we turn to available criteria upon which to rate the remaining packages. Since we have not placed any relative weight on the mandatory criteria, we want to include weights as well in our rating. Figure 7.10 lists a set of desirable criteria under the categories of functionality, support, and cost.

2. Establishing Relative Importance of Criteria

Figure 7.11 indicates a weighting of the various criteria. This obviously will be a function of a company's situation, its level of resources, and the expertise of its personnel.

FIGURE 7.10. Desirable criteria

General Category	Desirable Criteria	Value	Package A		Package B	
			Score	Wgt.	Score	Wgt.
Functionality	Ability to meet specs Ease of use Ease of tailoring Source code available Audit controls Documentation Maintenance/update plan					
	Subtotal					
Support	Education/training Routine consulting Advanced consulting Assistance in tailoring Responsiveness Proximity Vendor relationship					
	Subtotal					
Cost	Program license fee Installation charge Maintenance fee Customizing charges Training fees					
	Subtotal					
	Grand Total					

FIGURE 7.11. Determining criteria value

General Category	Desirable Criteria	Value	Package A		Package B	
			Score	Wgt.	Score	Wgt.
<u>50</u> Functionality	Ability to meet specs	20				
	Ease of use	10				
	Ease of tailoring	5				
	Source code available	2				
	Audit controls	3				
	Documentation	5				
	Maintenance/update plan	5				
	Subtotal	50				
<u>30</u> Support	Education/training	10				
	Routine consulting	10				
	Advanced consulting	2				
	Assistance in tailoring	2				
	Responsiveness	2				
	Proximity	2				
	Vendor relationship	2				
	Subtotal	30				
<u>20</u> Cost	Program license fee					
	Installation charge					
	Maintenance fee					
	Customizing charges					
	Training fees					
	Subtotal	20				
	Grand Total	100				

For example, if a company plans to do the customizing of the package in-house and there is ample expertise, little weight would be placed on a vendor's ability to customize the package. In this instance a weight of 50 has been placed on functionality, 30 on support, and 20 on cost. The individual items within each category are likewise dependent on the company's capabilities. The items shown here are merely a checklist to ensure that all elements are considered. Cost obviously is the most readily quantifiable of the criteria but the other factors must be carefully assessed as well.

3. Vendor Rating

Figure 7.12 adds the rating score given to each vendor on each of the decision criteria. In this example, a rating scale of 1 to 10 is used. As one goes through an evaluation of this type, it becomes obvious that a good number of value judgments must be made. However, the method provides a consistent framework for evaluating those elements for which

FIGURE 7.12. Rating the vendors

General Category	Desirable Criteria	Value	Package A		Package B	
			Score	Wgt.	Score	Wgt.
<u>50</u> Functionality	Ability to meet specs	20	8	160	5	100
	Ease of use	10	8	160	5	100
	Ease of tailoring	5	10	50	6	30
	Source code available	2	10	20	10	20
	Audit controls	3	6	18	4	12
	Documentation	5	8	40	4	20
	Maintenance/update plan	5	8	40	4	20
	Subtotal	50		488		302
<u>30</u> Support	Education/training	10	8	80	10	100
	Routine consulting	10	8	80	10	100
	Advanced consulting	2	6	12	10	20
	Assistance in tailoring	2	6	12	8	16
	Responsiveness	2	6	12	8	16
	Proximity	2	10	20	8	16
	Vendor relationship	2	10	20	10	20
	Subtotal	30		236		288
<u>20</u> Cost	Program license fee					
	Installation charge					
	Maintenance fee					
	Customizing charges					
	Training fees					
	Subtotal	20	8	160	10	200
	Grand Total	100		884		790

objective methods exist and for pointing out those areas where more subjective evaluation is required. This allows the decision maker to subdivide the problem into individual elements, thereby separating those that can be resolved by objective means from those that require more subjective methods.

In the example used here, package A is superior, offsetting the greater ability of B to train, consult, and assist in tailoring the package as well as the lower cost of B. As mentioned, other factors must be included in the selection, such as the company's ability to tailor the package itself if package A requires it.

Methods are available to qualify your ratings if the degree of uncertainty or risk in your evaluation warrants their use and if time permits. To begin with, this may be the logical time to consider an outside consultant. If the company has a solid awareness of the job to be done and has established its own decision criteria using the described decision framework, a consultant may prove very useful. A consultant may possess the necessary knowledge and contacts with companies using competitive products so that he or she can present a reasonable and fairly accurate competitive appraisal. At the time, the company's internal staff may want to proceed with its own independent evaluation.

Such an independent evaluation would include a careful review of the available literature and presentations made by the prospective vendor. It might also involve a formal issuance of the specifications and request interested vendors to submit a proposal indicating how their product would meet them. Reference accounts are certainly valuable in assessing how the product has performed in other environments. This approach must be used judiciously, as every situation is to some degree unique. Probably the most valid evaluation, although costly to conduct and not always feasible, is a benchmark test. The company develops test input to drive the application system. The vendor then makes whatever arrangements are necessary to demonstrate the application, using the prescribed input data. The company can then measure response time, adequacy of output, and system performance for those vendors who are capable of running the benchmark. While this looks to be the most objective measure of them all, it does place demands on the company to develop a comprehensive set of test data that is representative of the projected workload, and it may penalize a vendor who has a highly functional package but limited resources to conduct the demonstration.

IMPLEMENTATION

Figure 7.1 lists the major functions performed during the implementation phase of an information system. If the implementation involves a major addition of hardware, site preparation work is required. Otherwise, implementation involves the individual programming, testing, and operational running of the programs that constitute the application subsystems, which in turn are part of the system. The postimplementation operational view is an important part of the life cycle. The maintenance and modification phase covers the continued modification, correction, and updating of operational computer programs. It reflects the fact that continued productive running of computer applications, as well as the inevitable changes in business conditions, will necessitate periodic changes and alterations. This important maintenance and modification activity must be anticipated and planned for in advance.

Not much more will be said of the actual coding of applications—the detailed and rather painstaking task of translating the documented design into computer instructions. A particular computer language is selected on the basis of internal standards and the nature of the application. The structured walkthrough is pertinent in the coding phase. Particularly in coding, it is easy to get wrapped up in detail, so that periodic reviews by all members of the team are important to ensure that coding is moving along in line with the original systems analysis and design.

One organizational concept that has become popular is the *chief programmer team,* an adaptation of the division of labor concept. Rather than have every programmer do his or her own coding, documenting, and general administrative work, a chief programmer is made responsible for most of the programming and all of the critical sections. The chief programmer directs the effort of a group whose members are assigned the other supportive duties. The chief programmer and a support team have been compared with a head surgeon leading a surgical team or a pilot heading up a flight team. This division and specialization of duties is said to produce better and faster results.

Testing is a vital part of the implementation phase. The structured techniques also include structured or top-down testing. The key is to test the top modules first to see that they are logical and work before testing their components. This enables dealing with end products and end users—and, since they are the system's final beneficiaries, this is critical. If there is a flaw in an end report, it is certainly better to detect it in the beginning in a top module, rather than to find it in a lower module and have to change all the intermediate modules. In order to test in this manner, dummy routines or what are called *stub modules* must be created to produce output from the lower modules before they are coded so that the higher-order modules can be tested. Individual module or program testing must be supplemented by full systems testing. It cannot be assumed that, because the modules test out individually, they will also test as a system. Systems people have been trying to avoid this trap for decades.

Fred Brooks, a prominent software developer, refers in his book *The Mythical Man Month* to a "9 times" principle. It is observed, much to the chagrin of professional programmers from large corporations, that small so-called garage shops or personal computer programmers can seemingly turn out working programs in a fraction of the time it takes the big shops. In reality, however, as Brooks points out, the programs they develop can be classified as "1 times" programs. To fully document, develop controls, build in error checks, and test a program takes 3 times; and to document, test, and so on as part of a total system takes 9 times. The garage-shop program does a specific job for a specific environment. In a large corporation's IS development, however, applications must be integrated and run in a complex-data-base, distributed-data-processing environment. This is demanding of time, skill, and effort. Whether the figure is 3 times, 6 times, or 9 times, the point is valid that there is a difference between what developers call a "productized" application and a garage-shop, ad hoc application.

Postoperation evaluation is extremely important but is often overlooked completely. Developers, weary from working overtime and handling all the problems that invariably arise with a major implementation effort, do not want to spend the time doing a post mortem on their work. They want to get on with new business. This is why it is wise to employ an outside group, outside the project team, to do a postoperation implementation. The areas to be covered are described in Chapter 9 under the heading "IS Audits and Organizational Review."

THE OPERATION EVALUATION AND MAINTENANCE AND MODIFICATION PHASE

Maintenance and modification is the last phase of the application development cycle. Often this vital phase is not properly considered in IS development. With the pressure of getting the application installed and in operation, the use of short cuts, temporary patches in programs, and a variety of expedients is inevitable.

During the implementation phase, the programmers and systems analysts accumulate a list of changes they know should be instituted. These have been deferred because they do not affect the day-to-day running of the application and can be added later—for example, checking features that increase the accuracy of the input and output but the absence of which does not necessarily prevent the job from running to completion. Besides the internal list of desirable changes and modifications, there are external lists. The users of the system will point out what they think are errors and inconsistencies in the computer reports they receive. Though some such problems may be resolved by additional discussion and clarification, some remedies no doubt will have to be incorporated into the system.

Furthermore, it is inevitable that undetected errors will appear later, as volume running produces unique combinations of transactions and conditions that were not foreseen and therefore not tested.

A prudent course of action is to undergo a period of introspective evaluation before moving on to other applications. This will ensure that there is a solid foundation on which to base further additions and extensions. Thus, the first activity of the maintenance and modification subphase is *evaluation*, which has already been discussed. The evaluation sets the stage for the second activity, called *fine-tuning*, when the problems uncovered in the evaluation are analyzed and resolved.

After the evaluation, the first order of business is to establish priorities among the problem areas. Errors in applications such as payroll or commission payments, which involve monetary payments to employees, represent high-priority items. On the other hand, inconsistencies in a quarterly report that do not involve monetary payment are low-priority items. In these examples it is relatively easy to determine priorities; in practice there will be situations that require considerable judgment before a realistic priority can be established.

It is important to distinguish between two categories of computer problems. The first represents problems that are definite errors and have to be corrected in time. This class of problem falls under the category of *maintenance*. The other category is called *modification*. Modification requests do not represent actual errors but rather alterations or changes that will improve the effectiveness of an application. For example, it might be as simple as a buyer wanting to see the sequence of columns reversed on a particular report for greater clarity, or it may be the addition of a maximum and minimum field to an inventory status report. Although these are desirable changes, they are not errors as such. Most of these modifications are a result of the lack of communication between the systems analyst and the operating department during the design of the application.

Another cause is that the operating personnel begin to see additional benefits, once they receive computerized reports on a regular basis. The IS department should have a procedure for handling the maintenance and modification problems, because these can get out of hand easily and cause a great deal of user dissatisfaction.

Another important consideration is the development of the proper organization to routinely handle systems changes. One must recognize that there is a basic conflict in assigning people to the maintenance function. For the most part, systems designers are creative individuals who are looking for increased systems challenges. They are anxious to work on the advanced or more sophisticated application areas. Therefore, they do not look with favor on reworking and refining applications that are already in operation. A paradox exists, for though the maintenance work may not be the most desirable activity, it requires highly experienced and skilled programmers or systems analysts. The analysts must be able to interpret and understand a program that they were not involved in and that often is not completely documented. It becomes a demanding logical exercise to trace through the problem, find the error, correct it, and test it against a variety of conditions. In addition, it is necessary to ensure that the correction resolves the error but does not cause additional problems in other parts of the program.

For these reasons, many companies establish a separate maintenance section distinct from the new application section. They staff the group with competent junior personnel who can benefit from this experience and can see an opportunity to display abilities in the logic and diagnostic area. It is an excellent training ground for broader systems work.

Whether it be assigned to a separate group or the same group that originally designed and programmed the application, the importance of a sound maintenance and modification program to fine-tune programs cannot be overstressed. The IS department must counter the tendency to move on to new application areas prematurely. System errors have a way of proliferating unless they are caught and corrected early. Outsourcing has become another way to accomplish maintenance.

Throughout the development cycle, it should be apparent that the establishment of standard procedures and protocols is an important element in the process. It is worth mentioning the role of standards at this point.

IS STANDARDS

There is no question that some level of standards adherence is necessary, as standards are indicators of a well-run IS department. A bit of a conflict exists in that the complexity and need for integration demand at least a minimal level of standardization, while at the same time the nature of system users makes them somewhat reactive to standards, particularly if standards are overly confining and restrictive. The degree of discipline and detail depends on the nature of the operation, but a good philosophy to follow is to incorporate only that level necessary for communications and efficiency of operation—standards for standards' sake are counterproductive and can cause a rigid, bureaucratic environment that is not conducive to good morale and productivity.

There are areas where standards are mandatory and areas where they may be desirable, but not crucial, to operations. Generally, standards can be divided into internal and external categories. Internal standards are company specific and relate to how the IS organization manages and controls its own application development. Other standards are broader in nature and are industry-wide. These relate to adherence to a set of standards established by national and international organizations. Both kinds of standards are briefly reviewed.

Internal Company Standards

An important example of an internal standard is utilizing a data dictionary in an integrated data base environment. The major concept of a data base system is that a variety of applications utilize common data. In order to accomplish this (and there are big advantages when you do) adherence to a common definition of data elements is essential. Another area where strict standards should be followed is in change control, whether the changes are in systems software or application software. If changes are not properly documented, tested, and implemented, chaos can occur, particularly since other applications are dependent on the changes. Also, subsequent changes are built on previous ones, thus compounding the problem.

Standards are crucial but not mandatory in areas such as project management, management reports, and organizational matters. While proven techniques can be suggested, it may be better to allow flexibility in these areas, so that a standard that is foreign to those using it need not be imposed when a similar, more familiar one will accomplish the objective.

Here is a sample list of areas where standards (or what in certain areas would be called procedures) might prove very useful:

- Definition of a structured methodology for the planning, development, and implementation of new applications with variation for maintenance or small projects
- Project request and selection procedures
- Project control system
- Systems and programming documentation standards
- Programming standards
- Application internal control guidelines
- Production program change controls
- Production scheduling and control procedures
- Hardware operating standards
- Operations documentation standards
- Personnel and equipment performance standards
- Production problem/incident reporting
- Computer security program
- Management reports
  —systems project requests and backlog (month, trend)
  —project status and performance reports and department summary
  —production schedule performance (month, trend)
  —equipment usage and performance (month, trend)
  —manpower utilization and forecast
  —budget/expense
  —terminal access security violations (month, trend)
  —long-range goals/objectives performance history

Industry-Wide Standards

There has been and continues to be a constant proliferation of new products in the hardware, software, applications, and communications areas. A company has its base of technology, which it continually desires to add to—but in a logical, consistent and compatible manner. This has not been an easy thing to achieve. The answer rests a good deal with the adaptation and adherence to a set of industry standards. Then the selection of new technology is broadened, and the company is not forced to stay with existing solutions or to select from a limited set of potential solutions.

The first level of standards is at the software operating system level. Most large companies have a proprietary operating system, either Virtual Management System (VMS) from DEC, Management Virtual System (MVS) from IBM or another mainframe or mini proprietary operating system. This means that these companies must usually expand their systems using hardware and software from their mainframe and mini vendors. To a certain extent they are locked in. In the personal computer area there are several operating systems from which to choose. There is MS/DOS Windows from Microsoft and OS/2 from IBM which have attained the status of ad hoc standards. Apple Macintosh has a different and incompatible operating system. It is possible to mix systems running different operation systems, but not without extra concern and attention. There are also third generation language standards such as COBOL and C++, and fourth generation language standards such as Structured Query Language (SQL).

This explains why a variety of standards organizations have sprung up and have become very important to the computing community. There are two kinds of standards, ad hoc and industry-developed. IBM has been responsible for many of the ad hoc standards as they have dominated the computer market since its inception, though this has materially lessened in recent years. An example of an ad hoc standard is OS/2. The major industry-wide standards emanate from international standards organizations, U.S. organizations, or collaborative vendor organizations. An example of the first is the International Software Organization (ISO), which is responsible for communication standards like X.25, for those companies and vendors employing packet switching, and a full set of other communication protocols to facilitate networks for worldwide telecommunications (explained in Chapter 5). An example of U.S. standards is the ANSI standard that is the way of representing numbers and characters in binary code. An example of a collaborative vendor standard is UNIX, a set of operating system standards developed by the Open Software Foundation (OSF).

There are hardware and software products on the market that provide gateways and linkages and serve, in effect, as translators from one format to another. However, in the long run these are temporary expedients, and must be analyzed whenever a major addition of technology is anticipated. A company wants to be in a position to add the best hardware and software for its purposes, regardless of brand or make. The company also wants to be protected in the event that a particular product becomes obsolete or its vendor goes out of business. For example, if a particular application runs on a proprietary operating system wedded to a particular hardware platform and the company providing the platform goes out of business, it is a major effort to port the system to another computer, but sooner or later this has to be done. It's a bit more frightening if the application running on the obsolete hardware is a strategic system for the company. Adherence to standards is the prime way of preventing these events from happening. It is a major area of consideration in systems planning and development. It is important to consider standards early in the development cycle.

COMPUTER-AIDED SOFTWARE ENGINEERING (CASE)

CASE is one of the most promising new technologies, and will have significant impact on the development of systems for years to come. Companies find themselves in a situation where major IS applications are 15 to 20 years old. They were written in the mainframe era and have been patched and modified almost to the point of breaking. Furthermore, there is scant documentation, and the application developers have long since left the company. Maintenance costs to keep these programs operable are shockingly high. The maintenance portion of the development budget in many large companies is 60 percent or higher. One might suggest that it is more appropriate to call the department the maintenance department rather than development.

The IS function has been accused of having the shoemaker's children syndrome, that is, of not using their own tools to aid their productivity. This is the promise of CASE. Development costs, primarily people costs, have not followed the same cost curve as the hardware elements in IS. The cost of chips and the hardware they drive has and continues to show a dramatic improvement in productivity per dollar of expenditure. On the other hand, productivity in the labor-intensive application development area has remained about constant, productivity gains just about washing out the inflationary rise in salaries. The promise of CASE is to improve people productivity. Indeed, claims are that some CASE tools provide productivity gains of from 2 to 1 to 10 to 1.

The use of CASE revolutionizes the development process. It is similar to the use of computer-aided design (CAD) in a manufacturing company. CAD helps the design engineer produce the documentation, blueprint, product design, process flow diagrams, and the like. It improves the design, cuts down the time to design a new product, and reduces the cost in the process. The same is true in the use of CASE for designing computer applications. Because it is a rather revolutionary approach to design and changes the way system analysts and programmers do their job, it can meet with a good deal of resistance. Also, there are significant startup costs, not only in retraining, but in the cost of the software tools and the programmer's workstations. However, CASE remains the wave and hope of the future.

Classes of CASE Tools

There are a variety and a growing proliferation of CASE products on the market. They can roughly be categorized as: (1) reverse engineering or design recovery, (2) upper CASE tools, (3) lower CASE tools, (4) prototyping, (5) object-oriented programming, and (6) integrated CASE.

Reverse engineering analyzes the programming code of old systems and produces the documentation necessary to reconstruct the programs for easier understanding, enhancement, and maintenance. Old programs are often classified as spaghetti code; that is, it is very difficult if not impossible to comprehend the beginning or end of specific subroutines or the relationship of one module to another. Reverse engineering makes order out of the spaghetti. The inputs and outputs remain the same so that the system still looks as it did, and retains its original focus to those using it.

Design recovery is a step beyond reverse engineering in that the result of the process provides a linkage into the newer CASE application development environment. From the original code, the process generates the data models, screen formats, process models, and data definitions. These then become part of the data repository for the redesign of the applications in the new CASE environment. This is a little more radical surgery, but it permits future growth and extension and, most importantly, integration with other systems developed using the CASE process.

Upper CASE tools attack the front end of the systems development life cycle. It has been found that a good deal of the time spent on applications is devoted to ensuring that the application meets user requirements, utilizes common data formats, fits with the overall business strategy, and is consistent with the established systems architecture. Problems occur when the developed system is not consistent with these requirements. A major objective of CASE is to build flexibility into the approach to permit later changes and modifications. It is an old myth that systems users know what they want and can specify it at the outset of the project. Rather, the truth of the matter is that the user's view is "Don't do what I said, do what I meant." This is the hard reality of systems development.

Upper CASE starts with the elements described in Chapter 3. It is a top-down approach to development starting with company goals and strategies, and systematically breaking down business processes into data requirements and to information systems that use this data. In effect, one models the business. It becomes a given in developing the model that business functions and the information systems that support them are built around a data base. The key to obtaining the data on which the application depends is a data dictionary that indexes and allows easy access to required data elements. All of this is the province of upper CASE. CASE is software operating on a personal computer that enables one to develop these business models, data elements, and the data dictionary. Above all, the CASE approach is data driven versus process driven.

Lower CASE tools build on upper CASE. Once your data house in in order, specific applications can be designed that utilize specific data elements. The principle outputs of lower CASE are automatically generated documentation and program code on an application-by-application basis. These are the principle jobs of implementing applications, and require a considerable investment of time and talent. The promise of CASE is to increase the productivity of this labor-intensive process, and there are studies that show remarkable gains. Not to be forgotten are the gains in program testing, modification, and maintenance. Because the automatically generated code has already been checked out and tested, the time devoted to these activities is materially reduced. The code generated can be COBOL, C language or a fourth generation language like SQL. The impact on reducing the huge cost of program maintenance is one of the most significant CASE benefits.

Prototyping is such a logical process that one wonders why it was not always an important part of the systems development life cycle (SDLC). Prototyping can be used in the conventional SDLC approach or in conjunction with CASE. Most CASE tools have a facility for prototyping. The concept of prototyping is that it is practical to test portions of the system with the ultimate users before the total system is complete. So the concept is to build rapidly a model or prototype and test it out under live conditions. The model is a quick and dirty implementation such that it doesn't have to have all the bells and whistles replete, for example, with security and backup procedures. You want to see if the principal portions of the system have not overlooked the realities of the actual systems environment. The thesis is that it is easier to make changes at the beginning of the cycle than at the end. It is an application of the principles of quality management to the IS field. The quality process has been used in the design and manufacture of a variety of products; why not adapt these procedures to software development? Software certainly qualifies as products.

Another important software productivity aid in the CASE arena is object-oriented programming (OOP). Another name for OOP is code reusability. Programmers have found through the years that programs often are comprised of the same basic functions, and have developed subroutines consisting of lines of code which can be inserted from a library to perform these functions. It is a very basic and obvious thing to do. The subroutines were applied to those operations that were most often used. So early subroutine libraries were employed in writing operating systems and other systems software. It became clear that things like error handling, input/output routines, and the like could be pulled from a precoded library. The modern reincarnation of subroutines is OOP and the idea that subroutines can be employed effectively in writing business applications.

I will focus here on the benefits and usability of the concept. An object is different from a subroutine in that an object is a completely self-contained unit that includes both data and instructions, while a subroutine only includes instructions. The concept of building a library of objects is valid. These objects would comprise standard functions within the development environment of a particular institution. The application would ideally consist of combining a series of objects to accomplish the desired functions. It makes it feasible to add objects to be used with existing ones to expand and modify applications. For example if a new input media such as optical character recognition is introduced, the basic objects that form the crux of the application can remain the same while adding a new set of input objects. All applications using OCR can employ the new input objects. OOP is an attractive process when used with the graphic interface. An application can be written, dragging (combining) icons into an application window. Many feel that OOP will become the pervasive CASE approach.

Integrated CASE are tools that cover the entire SDLC. A common or standard set of tools can be used in this process. Companies have announced major integrated CASE products. IBM calls their product AD/Cycle and includes a data repository which is a data map and dictionary. It is the unifying element in the catalogue of tools. IBM has agreements with other CASE developers who produce a variety of upper and lower CASE tools, which are compatible with A/D Cycle. The DEC version is called COHESION. Other products marketed as integrated CASE tools are Knowledgeware's Information Engineering Workbench (IEW), Index Technology's Excelerator, and Texas Instruments' Information Engineering Facility (IEF).

DEPARTMENTAL SYSTEMS DEVELOPMENT

The level of detail described in this chapter may be frightening to the small to medium-sized department that wants to implement a set of its own applications. While many of the principles are valid for any size application, the application that focuses on functions that are primarily interdepartmental needn't follow the strict systems development life cycle or incorporate the enterprise-wide modeling and integrated business process techniques of the advanced CASE tools.

The client server approach discussed in Chapter 6 is a good model to follow. The server employs a relational data base that houses the data files required by the department. Either a user-oriented fourth generation language or OOP should be employed to generate the applications required for use within the department. This is the client part of the system. Sometimes existing shells like spreadsheet or expert system shells can be used to tailor specific department applications. Also, application packages should not be overlooked if they are available for the specific area of application. The goal is to be able to concentrate on the functions of the department, not on the technology to support them. Therefore, the technology chosen should be optimized with respect to ease of development and ease of use.

The development environment should include intimate cooperation between the systems user and the systems developer if they are not the same person. Even in larger enterprise systems, a close-knit implementation team consisting of both users and analysts is proving to be the effective answer to successful development. The most crucial elements of a successful system are that it is aimed at aiding the company's competitive position, properly reflects the requirements as specified by the systems users, and fits the cognitive style of the users. The implementation process should reflect these considerations.

SUMMARY

This chapter focused on the application development cycle, with Figure 7.1 depicting its analysis, synthesis, and implementation phases. Top and middle management should be directly involved in the analysis phase. The major contributors to the synthesis and implementation phases are IS management and system personnel, although there still must be a strong management direction and involvement. Since management is most concerned with the feasibility and systems study, a greater proportion of the chapter was devoted to these functions.

Systems feasibility is a most important starting point for IS development. The various feasibility criteria were presented. Technical and economic feasibility have received greater attention than operational feasibility. The last criterion recognizes that every company has a special character, philosophy, and way of conducting business. An information system must fit into this environment. If major organizational changes are planned in conjunction with IS implementation, they must be carefully analyzed and reflected in the overall schedule. Inadequate attention to operational feasibility considerations has been a major cause of IS failure.

The words *management* and *business* were emphasized. Management has been remiss in not applying to IS the same basic business procedures and measurements found successful in other areas of the company's operation, and the tools and techniques described represent excellent vehicles for accomplishing this end.

Case Study

Polaroid Corporation Distribution Division, Needham, MA

From the late 1970s to the mid-1980s Polaroid operated its six regional order entry and distribution centers via local DEC PDP-11s. These systems were independent of one another. Each night they sent transaction data to a central (IBM mainframe) host. Later that night they received data with which to update local files. The systems were free-standing during normal daytime operation. Management needs for consolidated reports could be met only from mainframe files, which were always at least a day old. In addition, because of discrepancies between the inventory processing methods actually used and those reflected in mainframe application programs, the mainframe data were frequently in error.

By 1985 the PDP-11 hardware was showing its age. A decision was made to replace the local computers with a central DEC VAXcluster. The selection decision was easy: Polaroid used a third-party PDP-11 distribution software package, albeit with some custom modifications, and the VAX was the only modern system on which this package ran. Changes to the application programs were initially limited, because there was a high level of compatibility between the PDP-11 and VAX versions of the package. They were, however, far from negligible. Subsequent system enhancement, to take advantage of the VAX environment, introduced further changes.

Polaroid adopted a pilot conversion strategy because the six distribution centers operated independently of each other. The first center was cut over before the Christmas

From working paper "A Practical Framework for Information Technology Conversion Strategies," Babson College, Palvia, Mallach, and Palvia. September, 1990.

shopping rush of 1987. The center used the new centrally located hardware and the converted distribution software package during the ensuing peak load period. Any problems received the immediate and total attention of the programming staff. In an emergency, orders that would normally be filled by the pilot center could have been routed to another center, but fortunately that was never necessary.

An innovative aspect of this conversion was the use of a "speed governor" on the VAX to prevent the first few user groups from developing response time expectations that could not be sustained under full load. As more centers were put onto the new system, the slow-down produced by the governor was reduced. When all were fully on line the slow-down was set to zero, though the code remained in the system for possible future use.

STUDY QUESTIONS

1. Was it wise to use a pilot before converting all six centers? What are the positive and negative factors?

2. Polaroid used a proprietary operating system from DEC. Does this indicate some of the elements in so doing?

3. Do you think Polaroid should use Unix or an open system approach the next time?

4. What do you think of the "speed governor"?

Case Study

Brown Manufacturing Company

Paul Foster is a systems analyst for the Brown Manufacturing Company, manufacturer of a wide range of paper products. Foster had been with the company for two years, serving in the IS department. Prior to this job, he was a programmer and system engineer for a prominent computer manufacturer. He was considered an intelligent, hard-working individual with creative ideas. There was no question that he was a most competent systems analyst.

Foster's major system job was to install a statistical forecasting system to aid the sales, inventory, and production departments. His primary focus was to enable the company's procurement department to base ordering policy on an exponential smoothing type of forecasting, which formed the basis of automatic calculation of reorder points, economical order quantities, and quantity discount analysis. The system would automatically produce a purchase order that needed only the buyer's initials before electronic release to the vendor. Foster incorporated several new ideas in the forecasting and ordering algorithms. He used an advanced seasonality analyzer and also was able to include the effect of known external events such as special promotions and holidays. He was quite proud of the system he had developed and was determined to see its successful implementation. He was sure it would materially aid the Brown Company by better balancing inventory, reducing ordering costs, and eliminating expensive stockouts.

At the outset of the implementation phase, Foster conducted a special seminar for the procurement department. He brought in a leading expert on exponential smoothing from a consulting company. Although the session was quite technical in nature, he detected an enthusiastic response from several of the buyers. He thought they were quite impressed with the degree of sophistication in the system they were installing. Foster followed up the seminar with individual discussions with two of the buyers who appeared rather passive to the new system. He had an additional briefing session prior to productive running. A disturbing element to Foster was the fact that, although he tried, he could never make contact with A. L. Metcalfe, director of purchasing. Metcalfe was a busy man and was either on the road or tied up when Foster held his seminars and briefing sessions. He did speak to Metcalfe briefly during the implementation phase and was assured of the director's endorsement of the system.

Foster was somewhat concerned that his system was a little difficult to comprehend because of the nuances that he had incorporated. However, he was convinced that the techniques were well conceived, had been proven at several companies in other industries, and would work at the Brown Company. He felt that the significant benefits produced by the sophisticated system were well worth the risk. The forecasting and ordering system would put Brown in the leadership position in its industry; the system would be superior to any system then in use.

The system was installed on schedule. A conversion seminar was held prior to installation in order to explain the different forms and operating procedures employed by the new system. Several instructional sessions had to be cancelled in order to maintain the schedule and cut-over schedule that had been established. A postinstallation audit was conducted three months after the system was put into operation. The audit indicated that only two of the ten buyers were utilizing the order forms emanating from the system. The majority had reverted back to the old method of ordering. They used the computer printout on weekly movement to post and update their own PC-based records but chose to ignore the ordering methods. Most buyers were utilizing the same techniques they had used in the past but were comparing their decisions with the computer's suggested ordering strategy. However, when there were significant differences, they followed the techniques that they knew.

STUDY QUESTIONS

1. How did Paul Foster handle the situation? What should he have done differently?
2. Was the Brown operating culture ready for Foster's system? Is his centralized approach unworkable in this environment?

3. How do you rate Metcalfe's role in the situation? Is he typical of purchasing directors?

4. What should Foster do now? Can he salvage what he has done?

SELECTED REFERENCES

Atre, Shaku, "The Scoop on OOPS," *Computerworld*, September 17, 1990, pp. 115-116.

Bachman, Charlie, "A CASE for Reverse Engineering," *Datamation*, July 1, 1988, p. 49.

Brooks, F., *The Mythical Man-Month*. Reading, Mass.: Addison-Wesley, 1975.

Chikofsky, Elliot J., "Can CASE Save Our Aging Information Systems," *Case Directions,* Vol. 2, No. 1, 1990.

Couger, J. D., M. A. Colter, and R. W. Knapp, *Advanced Systems Development and Feasibility Techniques*. New York: John Wiley & Sons, 1982.

DeMarco, T., *Structured Analysis and Systems Specification*. Englewood Cliffs, N.J.: Prentice-Hall, Inc., 1979.

Finkelstein, Clive, *An Introduction to Information Engineering—From Strategic Planning to Information Systems*. Reading, Mass.: Addison-Wesley, 1989.

Gavurin, Stuart, "Where Does Prototyping Fit in IS Development." *Computerworld*, March 18, 1991, p. 63.

Hartog, Curt, Daniel Mosley, and Joe Haspiel, "Object-Oriented Technolgy: A Report to the Board," Working Paper, Center for the Study of Data Processing Staff, Washington University, St. Louis, Missouri, 1990.

Inmon, W.H. *Information Engineering for the Practitioner—Putting Theory Into Practice*. Englewood Cliffs, N.J.: Prentice-Hall, 1988.

Keen, J. S., *Managing Systems Development*. New York: John Wiley & Sons, 1981.

Lin, Chang-Yang, and Chen Hua Chung, "End-User Computing in a CASE Environment." *Computerworld*, March 18, 1991, p. 63.

Loh, Marcus and Ryan Nelson, "Reaping CASE Harvests," *Datamation*, July 1, 1989, p. 31.

Martin, James, *Information Engineering—Volumes I, II, III*. Englewood Cliffs, N.J.: Prentice Hall, 1989.

McFarlan, F. W., "Portfolio Approach to Information Systems," *Harvard Business Review,* 1981, pp. 142-150.

McFarlan, F. W. and R. L. Nolan, Editors, *Information Systems Handbook*. Homewood, Ill.: Dow Jones-Irwin, 1975.

The President and Fellows of Harvard College, "Dallas Tire Corporation, Harvard Business School Case Study," Boston, Mass.: Intercollegiate Clearing House, 1979.

Rubin, Howard, "Dashboards, Waterfalls and Spaghetti Code," *Computerworld*, February 19, 1990, pp. 105-109.

Ruhl, Janet, "How to Survive Post-Implementation Aftershock," *Datamation*, December 1, 1988, p. 77.

Souza, Eileen, "The Impact of CASE on Software Development," *Computerworld*, February 18, 1991, p. 69.

Stamps, David, "CASE vs. 4GLs," *Datamation*, August 15, 1989, p. 29.

Yourdon, Edward, *Managing the Structured Techniques*, 2nd ed. Englewood Cliffs, N.J.: Prentice-Hall, Inc., 1979.

Chapter **8**

Assessing the Value and Risk of Information Systems

INTRODUCTION

The justification of information systems has become a major issue. Interest has been spawned by the rising expenditures on IS and the blitz of new technological developments, making it an area of deep concern to senior managers who find it all quite difficult to comprehend. A dichotomy has developed between the information systems directors and general management. The former, custodians of the new technology, have all they can do to develop and maintain application systems while seeing that new technology is properly metered into the company. The general managers, schooled at a time when computers were not yet part of the curriculum, have developed a suspicious and critical viewpoint about the benefits and value of the rising IS investment.

One would think that this type of feeling is abating as computers have spread into the departments and individual offices of companies. But in a recent survey of over 100 CEOs and other business leaders, *Computerworld* found that 64 percent agreed with the statement, "I do not feel that my organization is getting the most for its information systems investment." It is still true that there is a high discomfort level among senior managers. The nagging question of justification remains.

The John Diebold Research Group originated the term information resource management (IRM). The term implies that information is a valuable company resource, akin to the other more familiar resources such as money, material, people, facilities, land, and investments. Information differs from other resources in that it is extremely difficult to place a value on application programs and data bases developed within corporations. While no one would deny that there is value present, the argument is how much. The premise of IRM is that, if there is long-term value, and most would agree that major application systems have a 5- to 10-year life, then why aren't they capitalized, placed on the balance sheet, and depreciated over time as are other assets of the business? Though the percentage is higher for systems software and acquired application software, the number of companies capitalizing application software is less than 20 percent. Thus, one can see that current IS investment practices do not yet reflect information as a resource of the company, though there seems to be justification for doing so.

SURVEY STUDY: THE ROLE OF IS

The Center for Information Management Studies (CIMS) at Babson College conducted a study of 15 companies, focusing on the role of IS. Two major findings emerged. One was the return to a deep concern over cost control. Almost every company studied was either warding off a hostile takeover, was being acquired, or was looking at the acquisition of someone else. This situation is heightened by the general volatile economic conditions as well as the growing competition from abroad, particularly the Pacific Rim countries. In this environment the IS directors we spoke to are taking a good hard look, not only at future IS expenditures, but at the existing level of investment. Many are recentralizing to reduce cost or are downsizing in other ways. Though not mentioned in this study, companies such as Eastman Kodak are *outsourcing,* that is, employing outside vendors to take full responsibility for the operation of their data centers, telecommunications networks, and application development—in Kodak's case, a multimillion-dollar proposition. Kodak went to this rather radical move to save upwards of 30 percent in running their IS organization.

Another major finding was the importance that IS directors placed on credibility with senior management. The lack of credibility is seen in the turnover that is occurring in the top IS ranks, the fact that managers with non-IS experience are taking charge in a growing number of situations, and in the increased probing and questioning of IS expenditures. Less than a year after the survey, 5 of the 15 IS executives are no longer in their jobs. Many IS departments are returning to internal charge-out systems and strict ROI (return on investment) methods before embarking on any new application. There was a consensus that becoming a member of the management team and a respected member of the senior staff were very important objectives for survival. One IS director stated, "I measure my credibility level by who asks me out for lunch. If an important senior manager wants to talk to me about business matters, not just IS, that's a positive sign."

CURRENT PRACTICES IN JUSTIFYING IS INVESTMENT

There is probably only one thing you can say with assurance about the best process for justifying IS expenditure: There is absolutely no agreement as to what constitutes a well-run IS operation. For example, computer publications like to run listings on the best companies in this and the best in that. Three such listings are published annually, one by *Computerworld,* a second by *CIO* magazine, and a third by *Information Week* magazine.

The *Computerworld* article announced their "Premier 100," the companies investing most effectively in IS. Their criteria of selection were interesting. They looked at companies by industry groups and chose the best in each industry. The criteria for selection follow:

- Annual IS budget as a percentage of revenue (ranked by industry average)   30%
- Current market value of equipment as a percentage of revenue   15%
- Company profitability over the past five years   15%
- Percent of IS budget spent on people (lower percentage gets more points)   10%
- Percentage of IS budget spent on education   15%
- Number of PCs and terminals as a percentage of total employees   15%

Total   100%

This rating is heavily weighted on the level of IS spending. The one value indicator on the list is a very broad one, that of overall company profitability. In a workshop discussing the *Computerworld* study, two IS directors of companies high on the premier 100 list said they were reluctant to show the listings to their bosses or other senior managers. The major weakness to the rating scheme seems to be the thinking that the one who spends most is better. Peter Weill and Margrethe Olson, in their study of "Managing Investment in Technology" reported in the *IS Quarterly*, conclude "that while businesses are investing enormous resources in IT, there is no evidence linking information technology (IT) investment to organizational performance."

Another problem in putting so much weight on IS budgets is that companies differ as to what costs are included—for example, some include voice telecommunications costs while others omit departmental computing equipment not in the central IS budget. These are large swing factors.

The *CIO* magazine survey took a tack that was almost a diametrically opposed to the *Computerworld* approach. They asked a group of "distinguished IS authorities" to name the ten industries that are making the most strategic and innovative uses of IS and then asked "experts in each industry" to select the top ten companies they considered best at using IS to gain a competitive edge within the selected industries. They stated that the 100 companies selected illustrate IS excellence that:

- Demonstrates anew the importance of customer service;
- Proves it's not who you know but how well you are connected to them;
- Declares that current information is as precious as money itself; and
- Illuminates the astonishing shifts that threaten to blur the distinctions among industries.

The panel included some CIOs, but was mainly composed of consultants, professors, trade journal editors, Wall Street analysts, and trade association executives. I suspect this list includes companies that are in the news, and who are not adverse to publicizing and boasting about their accomplishments, or what they think are accomplishments. I can't help but think there are companies, some of them private, that are doing one heck of a job, employing IS in the competitive-edge area, but who have a policy of not going public with their achievements.

A report by *Information Week* ranks the 100 companies where IS is used the most effectively by one easily obtained and simple ratio: profits per employee. The developers of this index indicate it was chosen after scores of interviews with IS chiefs, financial executives, and academics. The premise is that the intended purpose of IS investment is to build a more effective corporation and to serve as an aid to corporate resources, people first and foremost.

Though these reports may be thought provoking and interesting reading, they represent extremes—one trying to be objective in measuring a variety of indices that are thought relevant for IS excellence; a second admits to being completely subjective; while the third uses a single ratio that links effectiveness to profitability. I think there's a little more to it than looking to see whether you are on either of the three lists. I believe we need more rigorous analysis and research in this area. Let's take a look at pertinent research on the subject.

REVIEW OF RESEARCH ON IS JUSTIFICATION

In reviewing a good deal of research that has been conducted on the subject of IS justification, it appears that most has been done by academicians and consultants, but in concert with multiclient study groups. I would like to draw some of the useful points from four such studies. This will be an eclectic approach in developing conclusions on how IS directors can better justify expenditures and thereby improve the credibility level at the senior management ranks. The studies are: (1) Nolan, Norton & Company, (2) the Center for the Study of Data Processing, University of Washington of St. Louis, (3) "A Report; The Benefit of Quality IS" by Edward Rivard and Kate Kaiser, and (4) PRISM, a research service of the Index Group and Hammer & Company.

The Nolan, Norton & Company Approach

The Nolan Norton approach suggests that spending alone does not reflect a quality IS operation. They looked at average IS expenditure by industry in relation to a company's total revenue, but then took another very important cut at it. They developed the concept of the application portfolio, and broke down IS expenditures by major application within each functional area. Thus, while the company might be spending an average of 3 percent of revenue on IS, they may be spending 4.5 percent in engineering and manufacturing and only 1.5 percent in marketing. This could then be analyzed in light of the company's business strategy, with the possible conclusion that the company was missing opportunities for gaining strategic advantage in the marketing area. They also made another cut to show the percentage of revenue spent on: (1) institutional systems, (2) professional support, (3) physical automation, and (4) external support. This was also looked at in light of the company's business strategy.

The Nolan Norton approach draws us away from the idea that "bigger is better." There obviously is more to it than that. Analyzing where the money is being spent is a step in the right direction.

Washington University of St. Louis Studies

From the Washington University studies by Marilyn M. Parker, an IBM researcher, and Robert Benson, director of the Center for the Study of Data Processing at Washington University, comes a method for evaluating a broad variety of application projects. They have developed a ten-criteria assessment list as follows:

Business Justification

    Economic impact

    Strategic alignment

    Competitive advantage

    Management information support

    Competitive response

    Strategic and organizational risk

Technical Viability

    Strategic system architecture

    Definitional uncertainty

    Technical uncertainty

    System infrastructure risk

I believe these are the key factors, a mild concern being that some elements are a close shading of others on the list. Based on the work done by Parker and Benson, Southern California Gas Company has successfully employed a four element evaluation method to make the process more understandable to their management. They place a weight on each factor as indicated in the following, and then rate the project from 0.0 to 1.0 on the basis of how well it satisfies that factor. Thus, the maximum a project can score is 100.

1. *Economic impact—65 points.* This measures a project on its economic value to the company. The present-value method of return-on-investment (ROI) analysis, which recognizes the time value of money, is used. The weighted value of 65 points out of 100 indicates a strong reliance on tangible return at this particular stage in the business. The relative weights can be changed as business conditions dictate. The economic impact is reduced by the degree of risk raised in the definitional uncertainty factor described below.

2. *Strategic alignment—22 points.* This factor measures the degree that a particular application follows the company's business strategy and corporate goals.

3. *Management information support—13 points.* This element measures how much meaningful information it provides management about basic activities of the business.

   Risk or Uncertainty. In addition to the aforementioned business impacts, there
are risks that the project will not accomplish its objectives. This factor rates a project on the
basis of its dependence on new staff skills, new hardware and software components, and the
projected complexity and definition clarity of the application. The risk scores are used to
reduce the economic impact.
   I believe that some form of application or project justification methodology is a
desirable and essential mechanism. The specific format used depends on what is most
effective in a particular company culture. Equally important is a follow-up assessment (post
system audit) to measure actual costs and benefits and to ascertain the degree of project
success. Experience and research show that few companies conduct such a review even on
large, complex, and important projects.

RIVARD AND KAISER REPORT

This report recognizes that there are qualitative benefits and develops approaches for
placing value on intangible or probable returns. These are techniques that are known to us,
but I think have become lost in the broadening of computer application into the strategic and
competitive domains. The authors mention the use of incremental analysis, value analysis,
expected value, and the worst/most likely/best—case method.
   We have a tendency to throw up our hands when we try to scope or at least give a
ball-park estimate of benefits emanating from a system that is aimed at giving a company a
competitive advantage. As an example, one of the techniques reviewed in the Rivard and
Kaiser report is the expected value method. They state that the average annual downtime for
a power plant is four weeks. One week of downtime costs a utility $2 million. The
availability of more timely and accurate information—the objective of a new information
system—will result in improved maintenance decisions that can lower downtime. The
expected value is the sum of probabilities that each reduction in downtime will occur. The
probabilities should be developed by the plant people most qualified to draw the inferences.
The following table is a summary of the expected value calculation.

1 *Possible % Reduction in Downtime*	*2* *Probability of Occurence %*	*3* *Midpoint of Cost Reduction*	*4* *Cost Reduction (Col 3 × Total Cost)*	*5* *Probable Savings (Col 2 × Col 4)*
Total annual downtime is estimated at $8,000,000.				
1–5	25	3.0	$240,000	$60,000
5–10	45	7.5	600,000	270,000
10–15	20	12.5	1,000,000	200,000
15–25	10	20	1,600,000	160,000
			Expected value of benefit	$690,000

There are similar situations where this type of analysis can be quite useful. This is particularly so when an IS project affects product sales or service. Marketing people can be interviewed to solicit their views on what impact the application in question will have on sales and service, or at least the probabilities of different scenarios occurring.

THE PRISM MULTICLIENT STUDY

There is a good deal of pragmatism in the findings of the PRISM multiclient study. Possibly this is a result of the participation of IS directors from companies who were part of the group. The findings emphasize that the processes used must reflect the company culture. For example, performance reports must relate to the business and be understood by management. The fact that this month the IS department turned out a higher function point software total than ever before or that the data center now has 200 MIPS and 60 Gigabytes of data storage are not meaningful statistics for line management. PRISM brings out the importance of improving, not only performance, but also the relationships with users and with management. In other words, it's not just a question of performance reports, it's a question of perception.

On the subject of perception, they believe in measuring user satisfaction, not only via questionnaires, at least annually, but also through focus groups on specific topics. The key is to measure continuously the pulse of your customers. The goal of a measurement program is to develop a partnership with your users so that there is a common understanding and agreement as to what constitutes good performance. The quantifiable elements such as service agreements and user sign-offs have a role, but they must be used in a context of understanding. This is the basis of IS credibility.

Additionally, the PRISM study concludes that you really need a tool kit, not a single measure, to assess the diverse services of an IS operation. Certainly there are capacity and utilization tools for measuring data center performance. But measuring the efficiency of departmental computing or individual computing is another matter. Trying to utilize the same yardsticks in differing operational areas can be disastrous. I remember the statement of a senior manager in reaction to an IS measurement process for a new application that was extremely important to him and his department "if you pull the turnip up too many times to see how it's doing, you kill it." So the PRISM study gives us a much-needed cultural platform that is the base point for a process aimed at improving IS credibility.

DEVELOPING AN IS JUSTIFICATION PROGRAM

What conclusions can one reach in justifying IS expenditures? First, most agree that it has become a very important issue, in fact the cornerstone in achieving credibility with senior management. As someone said, "when the two of us have established credibility, then we can take risks together."

A first step is to decide whether you need to justify what has already been done or whether you want to concentrate on justifying only new expenditures. It is true that what is done is done, but it was the philosopher, George Santayana, who said "those who do not remember the past, are condemned to relive it." A good evaluation of where you are and how you perform presents a solid base point for looking at the future.

ASSESSING YOUR CURRENT IS EXPENDITURES

It is healthy to know what your company is spending on information technology, so that's the first step. This will be an interesting exercise, because the definition of IS has changed; in some companies IS costs include telephone communications, media centers, mail rooms, all departmental and individual PCs, copying equipment, and the like.

Then it will be useful to break the total budget into categories, and by several different cuts. This may be a challenge because many accounting systems have a chart of accounts that is optimized for external reporting or the IRS. It is useful to see the relative expenditures for hardware, people, data center operation, and application development split between new development and maintenance, technical services, telecommunications, education, consulting, and the like. It is also interesting to see the percentage of IS under control of the IS department versus various line departments. In addition, a qualitative analysis of the IS infrastructure should be made, looking into the data and communication architecture, the skills mix of your people, the methods and techniques employed to manage data center operations and systems development, and the program for continuing education and development of people.

One very basic measure of expense is to view budget increases, particularly data center costs, compared with a measure of volume such as the number of transactions handled. In some industries there are one or two key volume indicators for which this may be valid. But this may be a limited measure because there are more important things that IS does for a company, for example, implementing an application that gives it competitive advantage.

The next important cut at IS expense, and this is a good deal more difficult to do, is to break down expense by major application areas like marketing, manufacturing, engineering, finance, and so on. Many applications serve several of the major functions, but it still is possible to get an overview of what areas use IS to a greater extent. Based on the company business strategy, imbalances can be detected.

Along with the foregoing analysis, you may wish to do a qualitative, application-by-application survey of your major systems. The survey could be a rather detailed one, asking multiple questions, or it could be as simple as the following matrix (Figure 8.1), with the IS people rating the cost efficiency (maintainability, currency of the hardware/software platform on which the application runs, etc.) while the end users rate the performance effectiveness (how the application meets their needs, the quality and timeliness of reports, how it improves their productivity etc.). By plotting the applications on the matrix, you can speculate on what it might take to move the ratings toward the upper right-hand column. However, not all need be moved there. For example, if an application producing weekly reports is judged low on the efficiency scale, it may not be worth updating the coding or hardware to make it run faster or on a more modern hardware platform. You may even find that an application or two could be eliminated. This has proved a difficult thing to do (as

FIGURE 8.1. IS evaluation

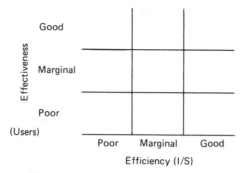

Peter Drucker terms it, "sloughing off yesterday"), but it can save an IS department considerable maintenance money or free up resources for new development.

You may wish to look at industry indicators like IS expenditure per employee or compared to revenue or total expense to see how you line up. However, the caveat is that these numbers can be quite misleading as many studies have shown. As the Nolan, Norton & Company study indicates, you may be spending a lot more or a lot less than industry averages. The key is what you are getting from the expenditure.

ASSESSING FUTURE IS EXPENDITURES

This is probably the more significant arena, because it determines future budgets and future applications, both of which are of concern to management. There is still strong support for measuring IS expenditures in the same way that other expenditures are measured in the firm, that is, by the ROI method. If they can't meet the hurdle rate of the company, they shouldn't be implemented. While it is true that applications are more and more being directed at revenue-producing rather than cost-cutting applications, and some applications, though not showing well in the ROI area, are giving a company a strategic advantage; the ROI approach is still sound for company applications that are a mix of cost cutting and competitive advantage.

RETURN-ON-INVESTMENT ANALYSIS

The assumption is that if a computer is a beneficial tool, it will increase the profits of a company and/or reduce investment and thereby have an effect on improving return on investment. The ROI concept is briefly mentioned here to reinforce its significance to IS projects, many of which have been immune even to the most basic of business measurement tools. Profitability and return on investment are the two key yardsticks of measuring business performance. Figure 8.2 is a simplified schematic of a return-on-investment analysis. The top portion is a profit and loss statement for the company, starting with sales on the first line, subtracting cost of sales to arrive at net earnings before taxes, and then subtracting taxes (a 46 percent rate is assumed) to arrive at net earnings after taxes. Cost of sales consists of variable costs (labor, material, etc.); fixed costs (depreciation, rent, equipment cost, etc.); and administrative costs (legal, personnel, accounting, etc.). Thus, the $1,588,000 is the company profit for the year and forms the numerator of the return-on-investment equation.

The investment or denominator of the equation consists of fixed investment (money tied up in machinery and buildings) and net working capital, made up of current inventory, accounts receivable, and other current assets. The ratio of net earnings to total investment is equal to the company's rate of return on investment. ROI is really what a company is trying to improve, as it is the true measure of how well the company is using the stockholders' money. If a computer can have an appreciable effect on improving this rate of return, then it is most certainly a desirable investment. For illustrative purposes, assume that Figure 8.2 represents the company's ROI at the moment when it is evaluating the possibility of a computer. The figures exclude the last three zeros, so that the company in question is

FIGURE 8.2. Return-on-investment analysis

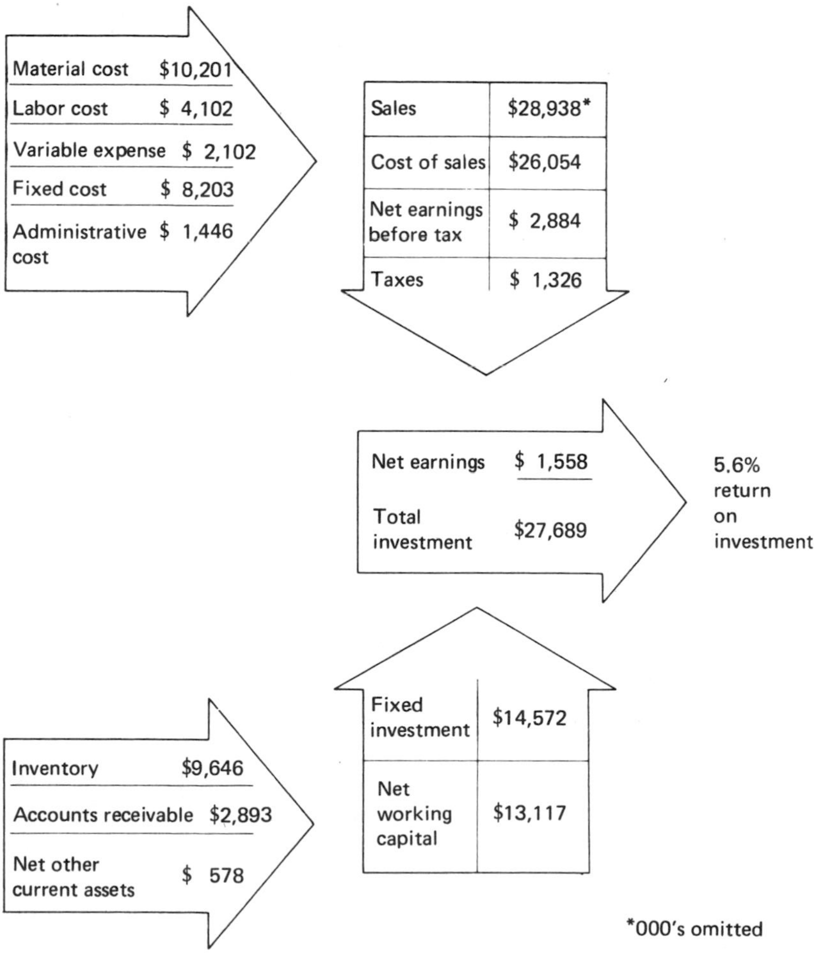

netting $1.5 million on a $27 million investment and has an ROI of 5.6 percent. This is very low for a manufacturer.

The ROI analysis can further determine whether you are working on the right problem or not. For example, a 1 percent improvement in material cost can add $102,000 to profit, whereas a 1 percent improvement in labor cost adds only $41,000. The reason is obvious, for material constitutes a greater portion of the total variable product cost. Consequently, everything being equal, it would seem wiser from an economic point of view to focus IS on improving material costs (e.g., a purchasing system that could take advantage of quantity discounts or a production control system that could reduce material variances and scrap loss). A simple calculation shows that a decrease of material costs of 3 percent through improved purchasing or production control can improve the company's ROI from 5.6 to 6.2 percent.

Another area of real payoff on the investment side is that of inventory. Almost 75 percent of the net working capital consists of inventory. A computerized inventory control system built on just-in-time (JIT) principles, which could better control and balance inventories, would have a significant impact on ROI. A projected 20 percent inventory reduction would amount to $1.9 million. In addition, the reduction in inventory reduces the inventory carrying costs. This reduction in carrying costs (assume a conservative 15 percent) reduces variable costs by $285,000 and adds to the yearly profit. The effect of these changes is to increase ROI from 5.6 to 6.6 percent. The point here is the desirability of looking at IS as an integral part of the business operation, as an element in increasing profit, reducing investment, and improving ROI. These are merely examples of what an ROI analysis can indicate.

DISCOUNTED CASH FLOW

Another approach to ROI takes into account that the development of a major new system requires a long-term commitment by a company. The costs incurred and the benefits realized should be related to one another in such a way as to take account of the time periods in which each is realized.

The discounted cash flow method provides such an approach because it recognizes the time value of money: Dollars spent or earned in earlier years are of greater value to the company than dollars earned or spent in later years. This is so because those same dollars could be invested elsewhere in the company to produce a profitable return.

Figures 8.3 and 8.4 illustrate the costs and savings from an IS investment by a company. The same investment principles apply as well to a company replacing an existing computer, upgrading capability, or adding a new application.

Figure 8.5 indicates that, over the four-year period $797,000 of net positive savings are realized from the investment. Figure 8.6 indicates a net positive savings of $242,000, using tangible savings only.

The ROI technique provides a better measurement for management because it translates the dollar into a common percentage format. This is accomplished by use of financial tables that discount both the positive and negative flows until they equal one another. In the foregoing examples, the ROI is 97.8 percent based on measuring full savings, and 37.6 percent when only tangible savings are measured. This return can now be related to the company's cost of borrowing or other investment yardsticks.

FIGURE 8.3. Cost summary (in dollars)

Cost	0	1	2	3	4
			Year of Installation		
Initial systems and					
programming	66,000	20,000			
File conversion	3,000	3,000			
Parallel operation		4,000			
Other	1,000	1,000			
Total One-time Costs	70,000	28,000			
Hardware rental		62,000	70,000	75,000	75,000
Personal costs		90,000	100,000	105,000	115,000
Supplies and services	12,000	22,000	30,000	30,000	35,000
Other	1,000	1,000			
Total Recurring Costs	13,000	175,000	200,000	210,000	225,000
Total Cost	83,000	203,000	200,000	210,000	225,000

MARGINAL VALUE OF INFORMATION

Marginal value (or *marginal utility*) represents the value (utility) to a buyer of each additional (marginal) unit of a product. It defines the price the end user or consumer is willing to pay for each additional unit of a product. The greater the quantity the user already has, the less, supposedly, the user is willing to pay for an additional unit. The law of supply and demand takes effect, and when the supply reaches a certain point (the saturation point),

FIGURE 8.4. Savings summary (in dollars)

Savings	0	1	2	3	4
			Year of Installation		
Reduction in current data		50,000	110,000	115,000	125,000
processing costs					
Clerical costs outside MIS		10,000	20,000	30,000	50,000
Inventory reduction					
(carrying cost)		40,000	125,000	150,000	160,000
Overtime reduction		5,000	20,000	22,000	32,000
Production variances			5,000	40,000	50,000
Other		1,000	1,000	1,000	1,000
Total tangible savings		106,000	281,000	358,000	418,000
Profit on sales					
(increased customer service)		5,000	50,000	100,000	100,000
Improved sales analysis			100,000	100,000	100,000
Increased management control					
More meaningful data					
Other					
Total intangible savings		5,000	150,000	200,000	200,000
Total savings		111,000	431,000	558,000	618,000

FIGURE 8.5. Net cash flows from computer investment (in $ thousands)

	Year of Installation					
	0	*1*	*2*	*3*	*4*	*Total*
Costs	83	203	200	210	225	921
Savings		106	431	558	618	1718
Net savings	(83)	(97)	231	348	393	797

then demand, theoretically, becomes zero. The supplier must then wait to replace the item as it depreciates or becomes obsolete, or must develop an innovative or attractively priced new item that eventually induces the buyer to buy it. An example is a suit of clothes. The typical businessman wears a suit to work five days a week. He may own three or four suits, but as he buys his fourth or fifth, the marginal value is reduced significantly. He can wear only one per day, and, if he is content with his first five, the sixth offers him little satisfaction. Obvious psychological factors affect this situation (many men for one reason or another own 20 or 30 suits or more), but the preceding analysis holds for the average businessman and explains the marginal value concept.

Let us see if this concept can be applied to information produced by a management information system. Is there a marginal value? What is the point at which the value becomes zero? Some would say that, in the case of information, not only is there a marginal value, there is also a negative value. A condition exists in some companies that might be called "information glut": the organization seems to be choking with information. Reports and analyses have proliferated, partly because of the ease and speed of today's high-speed communications and printing systems. The company may not have made a report utilization survey or study for years. Reports are added on top of reports, and no effort is made to streamline, combine, or eliminate. While formal reevaluation and reassessment may be common practices for the external products the company produces, they are not practiced in the case of computer products (printed reports). The development of IS should serve as a catalyst to trigger the much-needed appraisal of current information outputs. The system should encourage the management-by-exception concept as opposed to management by the ton (referring to mounds of paper spewed out by computer systems). We still await the peerless office.

Although I do not believe the marginal value of information can be determined as

FIGURE 8.6. Net cash flows from computer investment—tangible savings only (in $ thousands)

	Year of Installation					
	0	*1*	*2*	*3*	*4*	*Total*
Costs	83	203	200	210	225	921
Savings		106	281	358	418	1163
Net savings	(83)	(97)	81	148	193	242

precisely as it can be for other economic goods, the general concept does hold and, at a minimum, should serve as a design guide for an information system. In some situations the marginal value of information can be determined fairly accurately, whereas in others it is difficult, if not impossible to determine. The value of information should always be a prime consideration in system design, even in the latter case.

A fairly clear cut example is the value of calculating automatic reorder points and economic order quantities, as mentioned previously. Simulation (later confirmed by actual operation) can illustrate the specific monetary value expressed in lower inventory levels and improved customer service. If the inventory control system can reduce inventory by $200,000, then the value of the information generated by the system that accomplishes it is worth somewhere around $30,000 (15 percent, the carrying cost, × $200,000). Let us pursue this subject a step further. A basic ingredient of an effective inventory control system is a sales forecasting subsystem. Suppose that the current inventory control system utilizes forecasting technique A, whereas forecasting technique B is conceded to be statistically superior. It may well be that the forecast error has minimum leverage on the savings that can accrue from an inventory control system. Simulation may indicate that a forecasting system that is 20 percent more accurate has only a 3 percent influence on inventory levels. If there is a sizable system and programming cost in implementing the new forecasting technique, it may more than offset the value of the information. In this case, the marginal value of information is negative; the cost of acquiring the information is greater than the resultant benefit.

Situations occur where IS affects customer relationships, for example, placing terminals in the offices of a company's key customers, as did American Hospital Supply. Strategic advantage is obtained by making it easier for customers to buy from that supplier than from its competitor. I would ask, How much more will our customers buy from us? Projections of increased revenue can be determined by survey methods, extrapolation techniques, or the assessment of the results of similar systems. If a key customer purchased $800,000 from us in a year at a 22 percent profit margin, a 10 percent increase in sales might be projected due to the new ordering system. This translates into a tangible profit margin benefit of $17,600. Another question I would ask is: How many customers are normally lost in a year and how many fewer will be lost with the new system? If the current number is 10 and the new system reduces that to 8, the tangible benefit would be $44,000 (2 × average profit margin per customer of $22,000).

There are assumptions here, but there are also assumptions in projecting tangible benefits. The assumptions should be made by those with the best knowledge of the situation, in this case someone from the marketing division. To go a step further, the Rivard and Kaiser expected value method can be used to assess the probabilities of different customer buying and retention rates.

In conclusion, although there is no clear cut method of assessing the marginal value of information, the need to do so is important. The value of some information can be accurately determined and weighed against the costs necessary to produce it, whereas the marginal value of other information is difficult to assess. This fact should not preclude the analysis of marginal value; it is certainly more desirable than following the supposition that all information has value. The consequences of the latter concept are often "information glut" and the development not of a management information system, but of a management proliferation system.

RISK ASSESSMENT

Risk (definitional uncertainty) was mentioned in the Southern California Gas Company approach. Professor Warren McFarlan of the Harvard Business School has described a straightforward, easy-to-understand, effective technique for assessing the degree of risk in projects that may be undertaken by a company. This technique has been successfully used by numerous companies and is fully described in a case study called "The Dallas Tire Corporation" (fictitious name for a real company). This technique can be used to assess risks over a range of projects that affect the IS department. The use illustrated here is in application development, an area where the major part of the IS budget is expended.

There are some compelling reasons for assessing the risks in projects. First, an assessment helps you better understand the projects being implemented. An overall idea of its scope and size, its interaction with other projects, and its importance to the company can be better ascertained. Risk assessment helps you compare one project with another, enabling the ranking of projects on a risk scale. This is an important factor in deciding whether to move ahead on a project. Most business-oriented managers opt for a balanced portfolio of risks; that is, they will undertake a high-risk, high-payoff project if they have several lower-risk projects that will come to fruition while they are working on the high-risk one. The balanced portfolio concept sustains management support and tempers the potential of failure of the high-risk project. Probably the most important reason for risk assessment is that it facilitates more efficient management of projects and assignment of personnel to various projects. A high-risk project demands resources and techniques different from the low-risk projects. For example, it would seem prudent to assign your best project manager to the high-risk project. If the high risk is caused by technical considerations, that person should have a good understanding of the project's technical dimension. Stricter control and higher management visibility would be given the high-risk project, with comprehensive reviews and audits scheduled at selected intervals. On the other hand, the low-risk projects can be assigned and managed routinely.

The risk assessment technique utilized divides risk into three categories: (1) size, (2) structure, and (3) technology. In the size category we analyze a project in terms of projected person-years, dollar costs, elapsed time, and other indicators that measure its overall scope. The longer the time span, the more likely it is that the business environment will change during the project's life and compound the timing problem. Projects that have a longer time horizon and require more person-years involve higher risk than smaller projects.

A high-structure project is one for which the company has the required expertise—one that has been done before, is familiar to the company, and is straightforward with few if any design options. A low-structure project is one that requires substantial judgment and perspective, presents many options, and calls for considerable flexibility. In terms of the business activity triangle discussed in Chapter 1; where applications are grouped into three categories of operation control, management control, and strategic planning; applications are less structured as you proceed up the triangle.

The technology risk is related to the company's technological experience and expertise. While a particular technology may be proven in the industry, it has high-risk if it has not yet been applied by the particular company. Projects involving several new hardware devices, such as advanced multimedia workstations or a new type of disk storage, warrant high technology risk. When new software is also required, the risk can be compounded, because experience has shown that it is less risky to apply new software to proven hardware or to apply existing software to new hardware. The users' knowledge and experience, though not normally considered in the technology-risk category, should be included in the assessment.

The next step is to develop a list of weighted questions in each risk category. The selection and the comparative weighting of these questions are subjective elements, but subjectivity eventually becomes a factor in any technique of this type. The real benefit is to force a critical definition and assessment of risk, and to measure all projects with this same yardstick. Consistency of analysis is one of the key attributes of a tool such as risk assessment.

Figure 8.7 includes sample questions used in the Dallas Tire Company case. I have selected six questions from each of the three risk categories. Each question has a weight, as do the various answers. The question weight is multiplied by the answer weight to obtain the score. Thus in the size-risk category, if the total systems and programming person-hours were projected to be over 30,000, the score would be 20.

The absolute value is the minimum and maximum score for the total questions used in each risk category. The score in this case doesn't add up, since only a portion of the questions are given. In this instance project X is a low-risk project, scoring low in all three risk categories; Y falls in the 50th percentile but is high-risk compared with X because of high size and structure risk. The crucial point is that this approach allows you to measure project X against project Y, and, if you decide to implement either or both, it points out the type of project management that should be employed. Figure 8.8 presents a tabulation of the total question set for two sample projects (X and Y).

PRIORITY ANALYSIS IN SELECTION OF INFORMATION SYSTEMS

This section concludes the important area of application feasibility by tying together elements of the four study methods reviewed, and the return-on-investment and risk-assessment techniques just covered. Such a vehicle for establishing application development priorities is considered crucial. The benefits from strategic applications should be scoped by the methods suggested and included in the ROI category.

Return on Investment

This criterion is probably the most tangible and measurable of the four to be used. The ROI should take into account specific cost savings as well as intangibles projected by the marginal value method and expected value approach. The accepted technique for measuring

FIGURE 8.7. Risk assessment

A. *Questionnaire Scoring Sheet — Size*

		Weight
1. Total systems and programming man-hours		(5)

		Weight
( )	100 to 3,000	1
( )	3,000 to 15,000	2
( )	15,000 to 30,000	3
( )	Over 30,000	4

2. What is the estimate in calendar time?   (4)

( )	12 months or less	1
( )	13 months to 24 months	2
( )	Over 24 months	3

3. Length of economic payback: (2)

( )	Less than 12 months	1
( )	12 to 24 months	2
( )	Over 24 months	3

4. By whom will the work be performed?   (2)

( )	Mostly by on-site personnel (MIS and/or outside)	1
( )	Significant portions by on-site and off-site personnel	2
( )	Mostly by off-site personnel (MIS and/or outside)	3

5. Number of departments (other than MIS) involved with the system: (4)

( )	One	1
( )	Two	2
( )	Three or more	3

6. With how many existing MIS systems must the new system interface?   (3)

( )	None	1
( )	One	1
( )	Two	2
( )	More than two	3

B. *Questionnaire Scoring Sheet — Structure*

		Weight
1. The system may best be described as:		(1)

( )	Totally new system	3
( )	Replacement of an existing manual system	2
( )	Replacement of an existing automated system	1

2. If a replacement system is proposed, what percent of existing   (5)
functions is replaced on a one-to-one basis?

( )	0–25	3
( )	25–50	2
( )	50–100	1

FIGURE 8.7. Risk assessment (continued)

3. What is the severity of procedural changes by the proposed system? (5)

( ) Low   1
( ) Medium   2
( ) High   3

4. Proposed methods and/or procedures: (2)

( ) First of kind for data processing   3
( ) First of kind for user   3
( ) Breakthrough required for user acceptance   3
( ) Breakthrough required for data processing implementation   3
( ) None of the above   0

5. What degree of flexibility and judgment can be exercised by the (1)
   system's architect in the area of systems outputs?

( ) 0 to 33%   Very little   1
( ) 34 to 66%   Average   2
( ) 67 to 100%   Very high   3

6. How committed is upper-level user management to the system? (5)

( ) Somewhat reluctant or unknown   3
( ) Adequate   2
( ) Extremely enthusiastic   1

ROI is discounted cash flow, which in essence follows the principle that near-term dollars are worth more than longer-term dollars because of the interest value of money. The table below is based on the company's accepted rate of return. If the company's accepted rate of return is 30 percent before tax, then an ROI of 30 percent scores 10 points; 45 percent, 15; and 60 percent or above, 20. On the downside, an ROI of 15 percent scores 5 points. Point scores are interpolated between these benchmark points.

Weight	ROI
20	Acceptable rate + 100%
15	Acceptable rate + 50%
10	Acceptable rate of return
5	Acceptable rate—50%

Risk

This criterion is based on the relative risk of the application's working and being implemented on time and within budget. As mentioned earlier, three elements of risk are evaluated: (1) size, (2) structure, and (3) technology. This criterion is inverted in that, if the risk is high, the particular weight is low, and vice versa. Size is a measurement of person-years and development dollars. Structure is a measure of the degree of flexibility and how well known the application in question is—the higher the degree of flexibility, the greater is the risk. Technology reflects the extent to which a particular application requires

FIGURE 8.7. Risk assessment (continued)

C. *Questionnaire Scoring Sheet—Technology*

		Weight
1. Is additional hardware required?		(1)

( ) None	0
( ) CPU	1
( ) Peripheral and/or additional storage to mainframe	1
( ) Terminals	2
( ) Mini or micro	3

2. Which of the above hardware is new to your organization?   (3)

( ) None	0
( ) CPU	1
( ) Peripheral and/or additional storage	2
( ) Terminals	2
( ) Mini or micro	3

3. Is special nonstandard hardware required?   (5)

( ) None	0
( ) CPU	3
( ) Peripheral and/or additional storage	3
( ) Terminals	3
( ) Mini or micro	3

4. Is the system software (nonoperating system) new to the MIS project team?   (5)

( ) Programming language	3
( ) Data base	3
( ) Data communications	3
( ) Other—specify	3

5. How knowledgeable is the user in the area of MIS?   (5)

( ) First exposure	3
( ) Previous exposure but limited knowledge	2
( ) High degree of capability	1

6. How knowledgeable is the MIS team in the proposed application area?   (5)

( ) Limited	3
( ) Understands concept but no experience	2
( ) Has been involved in prior implementation efforts	1

new hardware and software or techniques never before used or tested. The following table assigns the risk weight on the basis of the three elements:

Risk Elements	*Weight*
All three factors high	0
Two factors high	5
One factor high	10
All factors low	20

Intangibles

This factor measures the degree of intangible benefit emanating from successful completion of the application, but beyond the measurement of the methods mentioned under return on investment. Although subjective in nature, the intangibles can be quite significant and have a major impact on company success. Intangibles range from improved company image to enhanced employee morale.

The following matrix indicates a method for assigning the ten-point weight of this element.

	Significance	
Benefits	Moderate	High
Short term	4	10
Long term	1	7

Supports Critical Success Factors (CSFs)

This criterion reflects the ability of the application to support the CSFs of key executives and managers within the organization. (CSFs were explained in Chapter 2.) The following matrix seeks to assign the ten weight points to the application.

Weight	Supports CSFs of
10	Three or more top managers
7	The president or key executives
4	Six or more key middle managers
1	A single sponsor

SAMPLE USE OF PRIORITY ANALYSIS

The table below illustrates the use of application priority for a particular company. It is obvious that it takes a good deal of subjective judgment to assign weights to the various factors; nonetheless, the method offers a systematic and consistent approach for beginning to understand which applications should be computerized next and why.

	Factors				
Application	ROI	Risk	Impact	Demand	Totals
Billing/ordering consolidation	18	10	7	8	43
Product-line reporting	14	13	8	5	40
Sales forecasting	12	14	7	6	39
Sales/customer analysis	9	18	5	4	36
Job production scheduling	13	6	6	6	31
Financial modeling	8	8	6	4	26
Factory CAM application	5	9	3	4	21
Truck loading/routing	4	11	3	2	20

It should be noted that this justification procedure applies only to fairly large application developments. A simplified process is adequate for smaller, department-level applications. Obviously one would not want to use this procedure for the acquisition of every personal computer system installed in a department. The intent here is not to eliminate innovation and experimentation. There should always be a place for that in an organization. Too much measurement can be debilitating. The process selected should be consistent with the size and complexity of the proposed application. However, one should always remember that the purpose of any investment in information technology is to add value to the individual or organization commensurate with the investment in product and people required to implement the application.

SUMMARY

This chapter reviewed three studies of the top 100 IS organizations, studies that used diametrically opposed selection criteria. The current IS management climate was then discussed based on the Babson College study of 15 major companies. A review was made of four of the many research projects devoted to suggesting methods for evaluating the performance of information technology in business enterprises. An eclectic set of processes thought to be both comprehensive and sensitive to the specific culture of a company was then presented.

The ROI approach discussed relies on basic financial and cost data, but emphasizes placing a value on benefits thought to be critical to a company's strategic success but not directly measurable. The important element of risk assessment was presented, following a three-dimensional risk categorization methodology. Then an application prioritization approach was described using ROI, risk assessment, intangible factors, and the degree to which the application supports management CSFs.

The era of IS measurement has returned. There is heightened senior management skepticism when discussing the performance and contribution of the IS function to business success. Though maybe a bit painful, this is a healthy situation, and represents an opportunity for the forward-looking IS executive. It is time to start a serious measurement program—to determine what it takes to achieve IS credibility. Management involvement at all levels of the organization is a necessary ingredient in the process. This area is the real "gut" area of the business; it is too important to delegate.

We sweep too many items under the rug with the statement, "You can't measure it, but intuitively I know it's good for the business." Preferred is a thought process that can connect such a statement to a bottom line expression; in other words, to minimize the leap of faith. Even if the degree of certainty is low, the process itself can be enlightening and may serve to bring an added perspective to either a good project that might otherwise die a premature death or a poor project that could roll through the approval cycle on the rhetoric of a single articulate spokesperson.

Case Study

Woodman Products, Inc.

Bob Washington of Woodman Products, Inc. must determine the relative feasibility of three application development projects, ranking them in order of priority. The first application is converting the current order processing application to a more responsive customer-oriented system. It is a far-reaching application that requires a major rewrite of the current system. Intelligent terminals are required that will have access to both a remote data base and a central data base as needed. This application will break new ground for the company. The annual net savings (after additional data processing costs are subtracted) in clerical and administrative personnel is conservatively estimated at $255,000 per year, with a one-time computer and development cost of $400,000. Besides the cost savings, management sees significant intangible benefits in the form of improved customer service. It is estimated that it will take 18 months for the new system to be operational.

The second application is a financial modeling system requested expressly by the company's president. The costs to implement are estimated at $100,000, including the purchase of a software modeling package, the purchase of a color graphics terminal, and the development cost. The benefits are very difficult to measure, but the president is emphatic that the application will enable him and his staff to keep abreast of competitive trends. Washington is a bit concerned that the president was oversold at a recent decision support system seminar conducted by their computer vendor, but he knows that once the president makes up his mind, he is difficult to dissuade. Also, Washington had heard of the success that some companies have had with this modeling package.

The third application involves marketing and had been requested by the five marketing managers of Woodman Products as well as by the product planners. There is common agreement that while the marketing data base is a good one for processing transactions, it has been far from satisfactory for giving the various marketing departments the reports they need on product movement by product line, by salesperson, by territory, and by various marketing divisions. Some reports do originate from the system, but they are inflexible and often require manual calculations and formatting to be of value. Furthermore, the reports are not up to date when received. This application requires a redefinition of the data base and the addition of a graphical interface to the data. Because of the complexity of the transaction data base, a program is needed that will periodically strip summary data from the file to form a simpler management file. Once accomplished, the new file system will be readily accessible by the marketing and product managers in the format they desire. The cost of implementation is estimated at $75,000. The benefits are intangible, but there is common agreement that with the increase in volume and multiplicity of product lines, continued use of the old system is unworkable. Lack of information about product lines can result in emphasizing a line that is losing money while ignoring others that are growing in size and profitability. One market manager estimated the worth to him of a comprehensive product reporting system at $100,000 per year.

STUDY QUESTIONS

1. What criteria should Bob Washington use in determining the feasibility of these applications?
2. How should he rank the priority of these applications and why?
3. What are the constraints in pursuing these application developments?
4. How would you tell the president his application came out third and you didn't have the budget for all three (if this was the result of your feasibility study)?
5. How important is technical risk in the feasibility and priority analysis?

Case Study

An Information Technology Asset Balance Sheet

Any organization can begin to manage information technology costs by creating an asset balance sheet showing all equipment, software, and data resources in use. This report is used to increase management awareness of the capital tied up in information technology resources.

The following is a prototype balance sheet you can adapt. The figures used here are for a large bank that spends about $200 million per year on information technology.

After studying the balance sheet, bank management realized its $2 billion in information technology assets were undermanaged. Furthermore, the organization now reuses its data, has merged decentralized facilities into corporate information technology and makes sure business managers spend time on policies relevant to the biggest capital element in its fixed asset base.

Hardware	Assets	
Centrally managed computers	$120M	This is the most obvious component of the information technology base and the one that accountants track; information technology is just 5 percent of this bank's real assets.
Distributed	$84M	Mainly personal computers. In many

From Peter G. Keen, "Waste Not, Want Not," *Computerworld*, (In Depth), February 25, 1991.

Hardware	Assets	
computers		organizations, PCs, workstations, and departmental systems now account for more expenditures than do central expenditures.
Network equipment	$105M	Telecommunications facilities, often distributed across many different operating budgets
Distributed telecommunications	$59M	Local area networks and departmental equipment
Total hardware	**$368M**	
Facilities (data center and operations)	$192M	

Software	Assets	
Applications development	$420M	Software development expenditures are expensed. The bank had no idea how much it had spent to build the software in use, nor did the accounting system make it easy to find out. This and the figure for "other"software are really educated guesses.
Other, including PC software	$68M	They also ignore replacement costs, which the firm's information technology planners estimated as at least $1.2 billion, three times the original development cost.
Total software	$488M	
Data resources	$1,200M	This is the estimated capital cost of the salaries, processing, and storage incurred in creating the on-line data resources that are the basis for the bank's products and services. It is an indefinitely reusable asset. Data resources do not wear out as they are used.
Total Assets:	**$2,248M**	

STUDY QUESTIONS

1. Does this approach give a more realistic and useful portrayal of IT investment?
2. Are there ways to determine the value of data bases and applications, or is it just a wild guess?
3. Who within the company should be responsible for the classes of expenditures listed?
4. This is the investment in IT for a bank. What would be relative IT investments for insurance companies, manufacturers, and other industries?

5. Do you find it surprising that in many companies, the expenditures for PCs and department systems are greater than central expenditures?

SELECTED REFERENCES

Butler Cox Foundation, "Getting Value from Information Technology," *Management Summary.* Report 75, June 1990.

CIO, Special Issue, "The 1990 CIO 100," August 1990, Vol. 3 No. 11.

Parker, Marilyn M., H. Edgar Trainor, and Robert J. Benson, *Information Strategy and Economics.* Englewood Cliffs, N.J.: Prentice Hall, 1989.

"Profiles of the Top 100 Companies Worldwide," *Datamation.* June 15, 1988.

Rochester, Jack, "Measuring the Value of Information Systems," *I/S Analyzer Special Report.* Fall 1989.

Strassmann, Paul A., *The Business Value of Computers—An Executive's Guide.* New Canaan, Ct.: The Information Economics Press, 1990.

Sullivan-Trainor, Michael, and Joseph Maglitta, "High Pressure, High Stakes," *Computerworld Premier 100.* October 8, 1990, pp. 12-25.

Weill, Peter, and Margrethe Olson, "Managing Investment in Information Technology: Mini Case Examples and Implications," *MIS Quarterly.* March 1989, pp. 3-17.

Chapter 9

Managing IS Development

INTRODUCTION

Chapter 7 described the life cycle of application development. This chapter covers the tools to manage and control the life cycle. Functions to be reviewed fall under the organizational headings of operations and technical support, such as capacity planning, data security, steering committees, and IS audits; as well as functions under the organizational heading of administrative services, such as cost charge-out systems. The first subject covered is project management. Project management is used extensively for application development projects, as well as for operations activities such as expanding a facility, converting to a new hardware system, or installing a communications network.

The premise is that while more of the development and operations of IS are coming under the management and individual departments, there will always be a central data center or operation that provides the backbone networking and data base support. A functional department manager will be involved with IS in two ways: directly with department applications and indirectly with enterprise-wide systems. It is important to be aware of both worlds. Most of the functions covered in this chapter apply whether one is involved in enterprise-wide IS or departmental IS.

PROJECT MANAGEMENT

Management should carefully establish time and cost parameters of IS development. IS development, if not properly managed, can run well over schedule, eating up large sums of money. Although management must be cautious not to apply overly restrictive time barriers for the effort, the overall project must be bounded by a time frame. The IS group should feel that it can ask for an extension, if necessary, but should work under the pressure of meeting a deadline. Periodic status reports can indicate to management whether the study group is working under undue time constraints.

Though broad in scope, IS development is a discrete process, and as such should be controlled by some type of project management technique. Whether the technique be a simple time-based event (Gantt) chart or a more sophisticated PERT system, the need for control is present. The selection depends on the size and scope.

Two techniques are discussed here: (1) PERT, and (2) a project review process that proved quite useful to a large manufacturer.

PERT

PERT (program evaluation and review technique) is a popular technique, principally because of its sponsorship by the U.S. Department of Defense. Most companies that have used PERT find it a most practical and useful tool. However, its popularity has given rise to tongue-in-cheek tales, such as the following:

> When the pharaohs of Egypt were building their pyramids, operating management was already on the scene and firmly entrenched. In fact, although it is not generally known, a worker on one such project, having just pulled a block of stone seven miles across the desert in the wrong direction, suggested a better system. He called it PERT—pyramid erection and routing technique. It is recorded that his supervisor had him flogged to death on the spot.

A prerequisite to using PERT is dividing the overall project into its basic components. For example, if the overall project is hanging a picture, the basic components or activities of the project might be: (1) procure hammer, (2) procure nails, (3) position picture, (4) hammer nails, and so on. The PERT system organizes these project components into a meaningful network showing the appropriate relationship of one to another.

This network of activity relationships is probably the most familiar aspect of PERT. The PERT network is a diagram representing the plan for achieving some goal. It has two basic components: events and activities. An *event is* a point in time in which something is completed or at which some new situation arises. For example, an event might be the completion of a study or the delivery of a computer. An *activity,* on the other hand, is the effort applied to produce an event. For example, it might be the work of the study group or the manufacture and shipment of the computer. By showing the events necessary to complete a project and the various activities leading up to each event, the PERT network portrays the overall schedule of a project. The PERT network, by depicting the interrelation of events, highlights the events that must be completed before other activities can be initiated. Thus, the PERT network serves two important purposes. First, it outlines an entire project; second, it establishes a schedule for that project.

An example of a simple PERT network to depict the project of hanging a picture is shown in Figure 9.1.

Figure 9.2 is a general PERT network outlining the IS feasibility study phase. Keep in mind that this is the schedule for only the broad study and feasibility phase. Similar PERT charts would have to be constructed for the design and implementation phases. It indicates the start point at time D (decision to conduct an IS study). The various activities and the estimated time each will take in relation to the starting point are indicated. As can be seen, the general management guidelines for the study will be established and reviewed (event S) two months from the start date (time periods are in months and fraction of months). The presentation to management (event 14) will be completed in eight months. The interim events and scheduled completion dates are indicated.

The purpose here is not to give an overall picture of how PERT works. A variety of reports and review forms are used. In addition, the completion dates are sometimes stated as (1) most likely, (2) most optimistic, and (3) most pessimistic. These three points are then mathematically averaged to statistically determine the odds of completing a project on time. In addition, critical paths are calculated indicating those events that are necessary for other activities to begin. These critical paths become evident when the entire PERT network of events and activities is completed. Computer programs exist that can develop, process, and update PERT networks, turning out computer reports indicating progress against plan.

PERT can also be used to accumulate costs, measured at each event point. The major expense of application development is normally the salaries and overhead for analysts and programmers, so that a simple compilation of person-months can provide 80 percent of the project cost. However, IS projects involving major costs other than people can entail a more detailed accumulation of cost data against specific event compilation. No matter what project management technique is used, a balance of the need for project detail versus the

FIGURE 9.1. PERT network

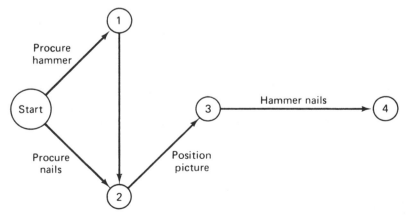

FIGURE 9.2. PERT chart of feasibility study

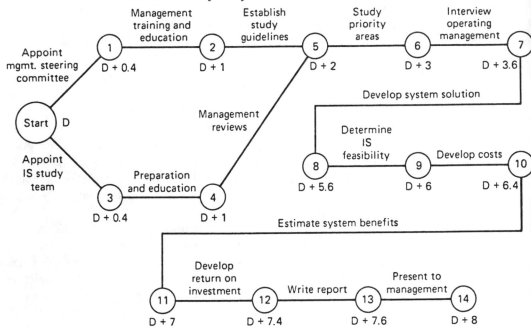

effort of tracking cost and time data must be reached. The level of detail and project complexity will determine whether an automated system is desirable.

An effective technique, whether using PERT or another method, is the employment of a visual project control room. A control room showing key event goals, dates, and responsible persons can have a major motivational impact on the project. Used properly, the room becomes a central location for team meetings, team assignments, and project review. The very existence of the room gives the project importance, and the visual indication of responsible parties applies boss and peer pressure to keep an individual's part of the project on schedule. Also it impresses top management that the team is serious and committed to the major projects.

PROJECT MANAGEMENT AT B&G MANUFACTURERS

We have looked at a widely used control tool. Although tools are important, the process or environment under which project management operates is probably more important. The technique employed by a company to improve project management within an IS organization is now described as the process, and the results are reviewed within the context of an actual application development organization in a real company, which we call Brown & Gordon Manufacturing (B&G).

The IS organization at B&G is responsible for developing and maintaining application software for all operating units of the company. This software is installed at over 20 company locations nationwide. While applications development is centralized, computer operations are decentralized at the operating division level.

To accomplish its mission, IS is structured as shown in Figure 9.3. Under the development director are a total of 80 people. The responsibility for each major system resides with a project manager. Each project manager has all the resources needed to implement an application, though some projects might involve the use of supplemental contract resources. The project manager is responsible for the project from specification through implementation of the application. Representatives from the user departments are involved, particularly during the specification phase.

The IS vice president emphatically felt that no one was really accountable for project schedules in the company. Although he respected the development director, he didn't see the project managers being in control of their projects. He thought his job was difficult because of the inability to develop an environment where managers feel truly accountable for their projects.

On the other hand, the development director felt she had very capable people who wanted to do a good job, but the project managers were either afraid of or just ignored the VP. She thought the VP did not trust most managers or individual contributors.

To improve the situation, an outside consultant was engaged. The VP had requested specific advice on how he could improve the department's ability to develop applications. From his view, they were always late, and he was continuously going from one crisis to another. More significantly, he was always "called on the carpet" by senior management, users, and functional management to explain why yet another schedule had slipped.

The Process

The consultant recommended the approach illustrated in Figure 9.4. The basic components were two workshops facilitated by the consultants, each lasting a half-day. All IS management including the project manager (about 30 people) attended the workshops. The VP of IS opened the first session but did not participate.

The consultant began with a brief discussion of project management in general and some recent experiences. This tended to make the attendees aware that their problems were not unique and that most companies were struggling to optimize their development activities. It also helped establish the credibility of the consultants. In the first workshop the group

FIGURE 9.3. IS organization

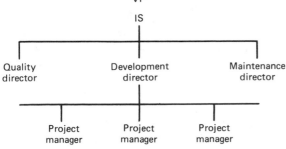

FIGURE 9.4. Critical success factors (CSF) for project success

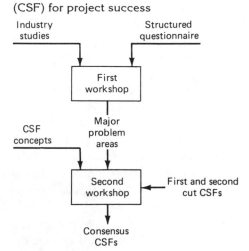

focused on specific projects, articulating why projects had failed in the past. A structured set of 34 questions was administered, the first five of which are shown in Figure 9.5. The questions were tailored to the terminology and environment at B&G. An opportunity to give open-ended responses was also provided so as not to restrict the discussion to predetermined issues. The second workshop, with the same participants, identified those areas where management could improve application development performance.

The VP liked the approach because it didn't appear to take much time and seemed quite straightforward. The development director approved because it involved her entire management team.

First Workshop Findings

Based on a synthesis of: (1) the quantitative rankings of the causes of project failure, (2) the written answers to the open-ended questions, and (3) the discussion that ensued, nine problem areas were identified as the major causes of project failure at B&G. These are shown along with their relative value in Figure 9.6.

The top four deserve some amplification:

1. Lack of communication: Several workshop attendees referred to the lack of communication within management—"what the project managers tells the functional manager, what the functional manager says, and what senior management hears appear to be different." A major problem was that people were afraid to upset the VP by disagreeing with proposed completion dates. And communication with the contract programmers were also cited as a problem area.

2. Unreasonable schedules: The respondents cited unrealistic completion dates set simply as a response to "can you have it ready by?" But often the IS development groups seem unable to credibly estimate time and cost, even if allowed the luxury to do so. It was

FIGURE 9.5. Structured question set

1. Senior management demonstrated the right level of commitment and involvement in the project.

   perception   !   !   !   !   !

   _____

   strongly   disagree   undecided   agree   strongly
   disagree   agree

2. Senior management provided reasonable and timely responses to the problems and conflicts that arose during the project.

   perception   !   !   !   !   !

   _____

   strongly   disagree   undecided   agree   strongly
   disagree   agree

3. Functional managers and supervisors were enthusiastic about and committed to the project at its beginning.

   perception   !   !   !   !   !

   _____

   strongly   disagree   undecided   agree   strongly
   disagree   agree

4. The estimated number of people required to develop the project was just about right.

   perception   !   !   !   !   !

   _____

   strongly   disagree   undecided   agree   strongly
   disagree   agree

5. The actual number of people assigned to develop the project was in the line with the estimate.

   perception   !   !   !   !   !

   _____

   strongly   disagree   undecided   agree   strongly
   disagree   agree

demoralizing to the project team when team members doubted the project schedule could be met. The schedule was viewed as completely unreasonable and the project soon lost "ownership."

3. Lack of right skills at right time: The project team must possess knowledge of both the functional area and the development process. The IS development group at B&G was often distant from the users and basic systems requirements, and was not fully aware of the functional environment in which the application took place. Therefore, the blend of functional and technical know-how at the right levels of the project was not adequate to negotiate effective tradeoffs. A project team will be "requirement rich" and "implementation poor" if it cannot understand and negotiate, both functionally and technically.

FIGURE 9.6. Major problem areas

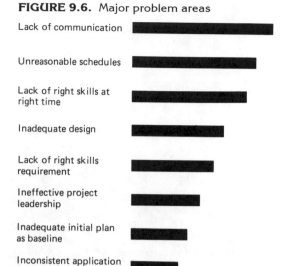

Lack of communication

Unreasonable schedules

Lack of right skills at right time

Inadequate design

Lack of right skills requirement

Ineffective project leadership

Inadequate initial plan as baseline

Inconsistent application of resources

Incomplete testing plan and/or environment

Inadequate monitoring and control system

4. Inadequate Design—Projects that failed at B&G usually involved poor design. A structured method of system design is critical to minimize the interaction between subsystems. This is especially true when the system is large and a number of development subgroups are working on the application. Too much dependence between modules significantly increases the project complexity and testing time, and it makes changes and modifications quite difficult.

Although these were the four prime reasons projects failed in the B&G environment, several other references in Figure 9.6 also contributed to failure.

Second Workshop: Critical Success Factors

After addressing why projects failed and discussing the findings with the participants, the consultant held a second half-day workshop focusing on what is needed to make projects succeed. At this point, critical success factor (CSF) thinking was introduced. As explained in Chapter 2, CSFs are those few (maybe 5 to 7) activities essential to the success of a company, a department, or, in this case, a project. The key is to find the real success determinants and expend energy on them rather than on items of lesser importance. It boils down to asking the participants, "If our objective is to improve the development of systems, on what five areas would you recommend we direct the organization's time, energy, and attention?"

The first workshop on why projects failed prepared the group for consideration of what could be done to facilitate success. The exercise required that each participant develop his/her own first-cut CSFs for the development department. This was followed by discussion of the suggested CSFs by the participants in a group setting. Then each participant developed a second-cut CSF recommendation based on the discussion. This final CSF set became the formal result of the workshop that was then analyzed by the consultants.

Based on the analysis, the consultants recommended that the IS department focus its management attention on the five CSFs that drew consensus:

1. *Define and promulgate functional requirements and control changes:* Strategies (actions) to accomplish this include making the functional manager accountable for the quality and the stability of the requirements, building a better and more credible capability within IS to assess the impact of change on resources and schedules, and obtaining formal acceptance of the application requirements before committing to delivery date. In addition, a formal change procedure must be established.

2. *Develop realistic project schedules:* The ultimate goal is to make the developers feel accountable for the project, to "own" it and its schedule. Developers must be involved in setting the schedule and management must be willing to revisit schedules at various points of the project as more information or real problems come to light, or when a change in project specifications occurs.

3. *Match skills to needs at proper time:* An approach must be put in place so that functional expertise and technical expertise are sufficient, especially during the design phase. The project manager, with the backing of the development director and IS vice president, must be positioned to negotiate the key functional and technical tradeoffs, and to schedule changes with both functional and contractor management. The "right" people must be assigned to the project or be available as advisors.

4. *Know and respond to the "real" status of the project:* "Shooting the messenger" is counterproductive to open communication. Management must encourage honest feedback through the management chain. The system must accurately report project status, identify problems, and assign accountability for problem resolution.

5. *Establish and control the performance of the contractors:* On many projects, IS is dependent on the ability of outside contractors. But it is essential that a baseline be established against which their performance is measured. This also requires the IS has the ability to develop a reasonable plan, be positioned to adjust the schedule if requirements or resources change, and be able to estimate credibly the impact of those changes.

Follow-on Activity

The consultant reviewed the findings of the workshops with the development director. She clarified some written responses and changed the wording of some of the CSFs. The next review was with the IS vice president. His reactions could be characterized by the following statement—"I knew it—these are the areas in which we must do better; I'm surprised that they know it so well and express it so clearly"—a positive response in the consultants' view.

Several items were designated as follow-on actions. First, the same review would be conducted for several levels of management below that of the development director. Second, the VP would appoint a small, select task group with the responsibility to identify specific actions for each of the five CSF areas. The VP insisted that task group participants be credible to both him and the development director, and be recognized and respected by the B&G organization for their experience and knowledge.

Results in Perspective

The development director was pleased that the VP agreed to the task group formation. More important, she felt that the independent consultant had forced the VP to acknowledge negative feedback which, in turn, had set the stage for real change. In addition, the task group formation was an important next step in any long-term change; it provided a formal vehicle to facilitate specific changes. This could not be done without fighting the battle personally or having an outside resource impose ideas or methodologies.

Several additional benefits accrued from the process. First, through the meetings and the follow-up reviews, the message became clear that the company was interested in improving its record of project success. The second, those involved in the project development were able to air opinions and feelings in the workshops. They could become more cooperative partners in the forthcoming changes in project development; they would begin to "own" the resulting strategies.

As a final benefit, all levels responsible for project development, from individual team members to senior management, had improved communications. The process thus enhanced team spirit, which is critical to future project success.

CAPACITY PLANNING

The Institute for Software Engineering defines capacity planning as "that set of functions concerned with determining and monitoring the proper balance between the workload and the equipment configuration at a minimum cost consistent with throughput, response time and reliability objectives."

Distributed processing has radically changed the concept of capacity planning by offering alternatives that heretofore were not economically feasible. The work of large mainframes can be off-loaded to minis or micros, and central data bases can be decentralized or shared with remote processing systems. These changes in system philosophy, together with the growth in volume as new applications were computerized and transaction volumes on existing applications increased, placed a huge demand on computer operations and increased the need for greater sophistication in capacity planning.

Technological and management changes have placed greater emphasis on this area. More often than not, computer center managers project future work from past work without really understanding present utilization or forecasted change in demand patterns. Programs written for a previous-generation machine may still be running in their original mode on the new-generation machine, when, for example, a change in disk access methods or memory

FIGURE 9.7. Capacity modeling

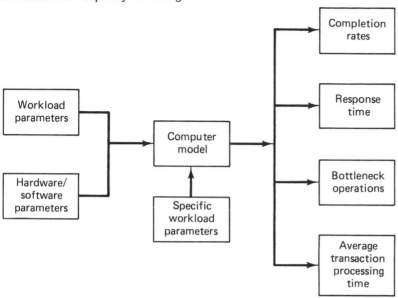

utilization may halve the run time or better. Changes in corporate and systems strategy can make straight-line extrapolation completely misleading.

Since it is unwise to proliferate inefficiencies, the first step in capacity planning is to determine the efficiency of existing operations. It makes little sense to order more hardware when there is a 30 percent waste of existing resources. Software modeling systems are available to evaluate current performance and predict future performance. They operate as shown in Figure 9.7.

The first step is to develop a model of current computer operations. In order to do this, workload parameters are gathered and inputted. These parameters include the number of jobs and whether they are batch or on-line, the average number of transactions; the peak usage rates; number of accesses to storage devices; and so on. Some of these statistics can be determined by analyzing existing documentation; others can be provided by hardware or software monitors. The specific hardware/software device or configuration is the other major input into model formulation.

From these parameters, a software model is developed that can now analyze a variety of workload mixes to determine operational characteristics such as completion time of each job, arrival rate of jobs, response time of different transactions, bottleneck operations (e.g., storage access), and average time per transaction—a very critical element in computer operation. The model utilizes a series of mathematical equations that reflect the mix of jobs being tested. Once the model is tested using derived workload parameters, the model results can be compared to actual results to determine relative accuracy. Though not exact, a well-designed model can represent a reasonable approximation of the daily operation of a computer center. Once the model is verified, a variety of specific workloads can be inputted to determine what will happen under conditions of changed volume, changed job mix, or a change in transaction response time. For on-line systems, the number of terminals is obviously quite important, as well as the amount of time required by operators between transactions or portions of transactions. The model will not only project the future but also point out inefficiencies in existing operations.

An insurance company, for example, was moving into a highly decentralized mode of operation. They wanted to know how many additional applications they could add to each remote facility before having to add capacity. The model in this case indicated the limit of the current configuration performing in its existing mode and also projected the amount of added capacity through additional processors, memory, storage devices, and terminals. Perhaps equally important, the model pointed out where file-access methods could be improved to add 30 percent to existing capacity without adding a single piece of equipment.

Another example is that of a financial institution where the transaction workload had just about doubled over the preceding two-year period, new applications were coming on-line, and the development staff required more test time for the development of new applications as well as for the updating and tuning of old ones. The model in this case indicated that utilization was not the problem, that peak loads were already outdistancing available capacity, and that customer service levels and on-line response time were already affected and would deteriorate with the added workload. The company ran several projected workloads through the model and concluded that by acquiring a new computer processor, initially for development work and then adding storage capacity to the new processor to offload a specific portion of the production workload, they could handle projected peak loads.

Another important consideration is to shield your customers from machine failures. This is particularly pertinent if your are operating in real time. For example any of the trading and reservation applications fall into this category. In electronic funds transfers, banks and their customers must have 24-hour service to effect the multiplicity of transaction types. Large sums of money are changing hands and one day's interest can be a huge sum. In airline reservations, the customer wants immediate feedback on flights, schedules, and costs. These types of real-time applications are growing in number.

Companies with these types of applications are turning to fault tolerant systems. These systems provide redundancy in all units of the system such that if one unit fails, the transaction is automatically shifted to a redundant processor or input/output device or whatever unit is required. This of course adds to the cost of the hardware and software, but it is a well-justified and necessary expense in these instances. In addition, fault tolerant systems have self-diagnosing capability. There is a continual check and monitoring of hardware units, so that if a unit is missing a cycle or has an intermittent failure, this automatically signals that a replacement or repair is needed before the unit breaks down completely. Vendors that specialize in fault tolerant systems are Tandem, Stratus, and Sequoia.

CHARGE-OUT SYSTEMS

IS budgets must be controlled by IS management. Charge-out systems, whereby IS costs are allocated to the using departments on some type of usage basis can be an element in cost control. The purpose of charge-out systems is usually one or several of the following:

1. *Indicate value added for product pricing.* For example, a manufacturing unit prices its product based on overhead costs as well as variable costs—IS is considered part of the overhead.

2. *Facilitate economic tradeoffs.* A department can compare the IS cost to that of its current manual system, an outside service provider, or the development of its own system. Often the IS function is run as a profit center as opposed to a cost center. It quotes prices, and the division can buy the service or can seek a third-party vendor. The growth of alternate services ranging from contract programming to the complete outsourcing the data centers are viable options; so there is choice. Doing it yourself is also becoming a more realistic option with the growth of the distributed system concept.

3. *Modify behavior.* If a department is being charged on a per-transaction basis, it can control its cost allocation by limiting the number of transactions.

4. *Educate users.* Users are more aware of IS services and economic tradeoffs when they understand the basis of cost allocations.

5. *Increase service orientation of IS.* Charge-out systems emphasize the service concept of IS—that its prime role is to serve its users (for a cost, of course).

Keep in mind some basic precepts when developing a charge-out system.

1. Charge on the basis of services rendered or output received, not of internal hardware or channel cycles used. In an article, "Controlling the Costs of Data Services, " in the *Harvard Business Review* Richard Nolan presented the following example of a charge-out system:

Data Processing Services Bill

Resource	Use	Charge per Unit	Total
Elapsed time on computer (minutes)	253,000	$0.04	$9,720
CPU (seconds)	2,430,000	0.0167	40,500
Kilobytes (1 K memory/minute)	14,515,000	0.0016	23,220
EXCP (I/O accesses)	105,000,000	0.0002	21,000
Total Due			$94,440

The user receiving this bill continually fought the system, claimed they were being charged too much, and, after long meetings with IS management, failed to reach any common ground. It is obvious that the user did not understand what a kilobyte or an input/output access was and couldn't care less. Although these measurements may be suitable to measure computer capacity, they are totally inadequate for allocating IS costs to users. The allocation basis should be service oriented, such as report lines received, transactions processed, or inquiries handled.

2. Understand the company organization philosophy. If the IS department is a separately held subsidiary providing services, for example, to independent member banks or insurance agencies, this establishes one cost charge-out framework. The other extreme is a single-product, single-division company with a highly centralized organizational style. A carefully conceived charge-out system is essential for the former, while for the latter the need for a charge-out system is suspect. The degree of concern for charge-out systems increases in companies that have profit centers rather than cost centers.

3. Establish a fit with the company culture. A general concern of this book is the importance of matching management control tools to the company culture. Charge-out systems can be viewed as complicated, burdensome, and useless exercises in companies that are not highly structured or disciplined and that follow the keep-it-simple dictate. Cost systems designed by technicians or accountants must be watched very carefully, lest superfluous detail creep in.

4. Establish goals and objectives at the outset. No one charge-out system can satisfy all the objectives defined for the system. It is critical, however, to establish in the beginning objectives and the relative priority of each. These objectives have been referred to earlier. It should be decided, for example, whether a charge-out system is primarily to add value (costs) to products for pricing purposes or to motivate users to make the most economical use of information. An emphasis on one or the other will have major impact on the system's design criteria.

5. User involvement is essential. The charge-out system should be jointly developed with users, utilizing the accounting department as an advisor. The charges must be viewed as fair by the user or the system will not work. User sign-off on a charge-out system is as important as the sign-off of an application system specification—or more so.

Many IS directors and consultants who have installed charge-out systems have concluded that the best charge-out system is no charge-out system. They feel that it can detract from the mainline responsibility of IS and can lead at best to a great deal of confusion, and at worst to severely strained user relationships. Furthermore, the advent of integrated data bases, distributed systems, office automation, and the like make viable charge-out systems even more difficult. However, there still exist good reasons for charge-out systems, and when charge-out is necessary, the principles discussed here should prove helpful.

DATA SECURITY AND PRIVACY

The advent of distributing systems, data bases, and the concept of information resource management, where data is viewed as a valuable and powerful resource, give new importance to the subject of data security and data privacy. These are separate but related subjects. Data *security is* concerned with the physical protection of data from a host of inside and outside causes, ranging from accidents such as operator or program error, hardware failure, flood, and explosion to willful acts such as fraud and embezzlement. On the other hand, data *privacy is* concerned with ethical and moral protection of data and involves issues such as the right of a company or agency to accumulate data about individuals and groups, the purposes for which that data are used, and the rights of an individual or group to inspect and have access to the data gathered about them.

The issue of data security can be approached by categorizing and discussing four general types of physical encroachment: (1) fraud and theft, (2) systems errors, (3) maliciousness, and (4) accidents and disasters.

1. Fraud and Theft

This category includes events such as the one involving an insurance company, Equity Funding Corporation, where massive collusion resulted in the computerized development of false insurance policies to cover huge cash deficits resulting from thefts by employees. This has been referred to in the literature as the billion-dollar bubble. A series of multimillion-dollar frauds have been traced to computer records and computer programs that access them. Many such losses, estimated to total in the billions, are unreported, but of those that are known, the average loss is in the $400,000 range as compared with $10,000 for bank robbery. The stakes are high in computer theft.

The first requirement to prevent fraud and theft is to control the physical access to the computer room and the workstations that access computer systems. In this regard environmental security is employed in the form of sophisticated lock systems opened by plastic cards; picture IDs; or, in some cases, fingerprints and voice identification.

Security precautions of another kind prevent personnel who have access to the computer facility from committing fraud. This usually involves unique identification codes or passwords. To go a step further, certain user IDs or passwords are restricted to specific terminals and specific working hours or to specific applications or data files. This is an important precaution if IDs and passwords are stolen or given away without authority. A user access matrix may be developed as follows:

	Terminal 43	Terminal 44	Data File 1	Data File 2	Application A	Application B
User A	x		x		x	
User B		x		x		x
User C	x	x	x	x	x	x

Special procedures may have to be established for particularly vulnerable areas. In these cases, data is encrypted and irregular changes of code names and passwords are employed. The more sophisticated the techniques, the more resources, such as people effort and hardware and software facilities, are used. Therefore, management must determine the scope and potential risk in each environment and situation and develop the security measures to match.

A common technique employed by auditors is that of splitting responsibility so that the system requires collusion of two or more people to commit a fraud—like the practice of requiring two signatures on checks greater than a specified amount.

2. System Errors

The second category of security intrusion is system errors. This includes errors caused by hardware, software (both systems software and applications software), and people. System errors can range from a computer failure that causes less than a minute downtime to situations involving millions of dollars. In one prominent instance, improperly placed decimal points on dividend checks actually caused the erroneous payment of some $15 million to surprised stockholders.

Hardware reliability should be a key criterion in selecting a computer system, keeping in mind that the system that never fails has not yet been built and may never be built. Therefore backup must be provided in the form of redundant units, sometimes three or four (or more) deep in the case of electro-mechanical devices, which fail more often than electronic devices. Furthermore, restart and rerun procedures must be established so that in the event of a failure, for example, in hour 16 of a 17-hour run, the operation doesn't have to revert to hour 1 once the malfunction is fixed.

The use of proper audit controls can prevent serious consequences from software failure. Following sound application development procedures such as the structured techniques will materially reduce system errors. Particularly important are the testing and debugging of programs at both the individual program level and the system level. Also, program change control procedures are vital to error-free (or close to error-free) operation.

Personnel are probably the leading cause of system errors. Inept equipment operation can cause system problems and, if proper interapplication protection is not provided, can bring havoc to a system. Training is important, as well as ease-of-use features to reduce the expertise required of many new users desiring access to computer data bases.

3. Maliciousness

An example of maliciousness is the story of a retired civilian programmer in a government agency, who supposedly redressed his grievances in an ingenious way—setting a conditional decision path in a key program that would occur approximately a year after his retirement and would systematically destroy the master data files and programs. There is a fine line between the terms, but *maliciousness* under other circumstances might be termed *vandalism* or even *sabotage*.

Today, maliciousness takes a variety of forms. Computer rooms have even been bombed or set afire by dissident groups, whose causes range from antigovernment to antiautomation. Modern day Luddites are destroying equipment as they destroyed textile equipment in the eighteenth century. The techniques of physical or environmental control described under fraud and theft are pertinent here but must be enhanced to counter potential intruders armed with modern weaponry and technical devices.

4. Accidents and Disasters

This category includes "natural" accidents and disasters, such as fire, flood, earthquake, power outage, and the like, as opposed to deliberately induced ones. There are two areas to discuss: how to minimize or avoid the occurrence of accidents and disasters and what to do in the event of an occurrence.

In the avoidance area, important safeguards are adherence to fire protection principles including fire and smoke detectors; alarms; automatic power-off; generator or battery backup power supplies; and environmental control through air vents, air conditioning, proper false floorings, and outside-wall windows. Proper precautions are needed also for safety and the avoidance of accidents due to electric shock, falling objects, and the like. IS directors should fully utilize the services of corporate facility security and safety officers to provide safeguards in this area.

There are different approaches to disaster backup, starting with a risk assessment estimating the potential losses from different types of disasters. From this base point, various options can be analyzed, ranging from the designation of a selected data center facility of a corporation to back up another, to the employment of a backup center, a service that provides users with total backup including the facility, computer equipment, media, and extensive communications facilities. Companies also provide facility shells, with the user having to supply the necessary equipment. There are also corporations formed by a group of corporations that provide a shared backup facility.

A number of issues are involved, such as the need to back up storage media as well as processing, peripheral, and terminal equipment. Companies with on-line storage in the multimillion- or billion-character range face a particularly demanding challenge. Regardless of the difficulties, disaster backup is becoming an increasingly important matter, not only to the IS executive, but also to the corporate officers of a company.

Privacy

An issue that overrides the entire area of data security is privacy and individual rights. The advent of computers and the ability to build huge, readily accessible data banks has the inherent risk of violating individual rights, leading us toward a "big brother" society. Thus it is technically feasible to have in one location an individual's tax record, credit record, legal record, voting record, and so on. It is not difficult to see the use or misuse of such data by, say, government agencies. In a lighter sense, the proliferation of mailing lists and junk mail is a product of the computer era, and many feel this is an invasion of privacy.

There is a growing concern over privacy in the private, as well as the public, sector of our country. Companies and institutions as well as public agencies can and do accumulate data on individuals and groups. A simple case is the exchange or selling of computerized mailing lists. Individuals have already challenged the legal right of companies to mail unsolicited products to households. Of greater concern is the collection from several sources of data that can serve to affect an individual's credit standing even when the data is erroneous or obsolete. Should the individual be able to challenge and inspect his or her data file as the Privacy Act legislates? This is one of the provocative questions that surround the privacy issue. This subject is discussed further in Chapter 13.

DEVELOPING A SECURITY PLAN

This section on security and privacy closes with a listing of general steps in developing a more secure IS operation.

1. Obtain executive participation
2. Appoint a systems security officer
3. Relieve "suspect" personnel immediately
4. Do not "bury" infractions
5. Organize a cooperative security effort

After a security officer is appointed, as in step 2 above, the following are examples of a cooperative data security program:

1. Organize a security team
2. Prepare a system security plan
3. Provide special training (as required)
4. Implement security operating procedures
5. Design and implement test procedures
6. Document your system disaster recovery plan

This section has touched on the major elements underlying the data security problem. Security is becoming an increasingly serious problem as IS expands to include large data bases and communication networks where data files are accessed from a host of terminal points. One concluding remark: It is essential to think of data security as an integral part of IS development, not a "tack-on" after the system is implemented. Although this may seem obvious, experience indicates that it is worth pointing out.

STEERING COMMITTEES

The IS steering committee has become quite significant in many companies and, if properly utilized and administered, can be an effective tool in developing good user relations and in managing IS development. The steering committee is comprised of a group of key users of information services whose duty it is to act as a review or overseeing body of IS plans and development. A steering committee helps formalize the concept of user involvement that is so necessary for successful systems. It provides a higher-level control that can break logjams or give direction when for one reason or another the IS activity bogs down. A properly comprised steering group can present a broader business perspective to a situation and can help keep system objectives in balance.

Another important function is the sign-off on the specifications of a new major application area. Often the specs or requirements of a new application either are not stated at the outset or are not clear to the eventual users, so that they are major surprises once the application is in operation.

Output and response time of the system should be reviewed at the outset and referred to throughout the production process to ensure that the project will meet its objectives. Things inevitably change during the course of a development cycle. The steering committee can assess the impact of these events and assist in making the most beneficial tradeoff decisions.

Deployment and organization of steering committees vary within a company. Sometimes there is only one general information advisory group, while in other situations a hierarchy of steering committees exists. Figure 9.8 illustrates a hierarchical arrangement of an overall IS steering group and three decision-level groups focusing on the key operating areas of the company—marketing, manufacturing, and engineering. The top group is responsible for approving the business plan for the entire management information system. The group is headed by a prominent member of top management who must be able to devote a good amount of time to the program; in this case it is the executive vice president. The heads or key decision makers of the departments to be affected by IS are also members of the steering group. The director of IS and the manager of systems and programming represent the IS department. This group meets periodically to update the IS business plan as well as to review the status of the three advisory groups working under it.

An advisory group is formed for each of the major application subsystem areas—in this case marketing, manufacturing, and engineering. The group is chaired by a top executive of the department concerned and includes key people within the department as well as the key IS personnel involved in system development. Note that in each group there is a systems analyst representing the department affected. His or her inclusion is extremely important; it ensures that the department's interests and objectives are represented in the detailed implementation steps as well as in the overall planning. They key system designers within the IS department, called the marketing, manufacturing, and engineering project leaders, are also members of the group. They are the IS personnel responsible, together with the department's systems analyst, for the full-time direction of the particular application area. Note, also, that there is cross-representation on each of the committees. The directors of manufacturing, marketing, and engineering are on the steering group, and they also head one of the advisory groups. The director of IS and the manager of systems and programming also sit on advisory groups. Thus, there are continuity and tie-in.

The foregoing example illustrates the ultimate in the use of steering committees. It may well be that a less formal structure will suit a particular situation. Whatever the scope, it is important to follow certain procedures. First, because members of the steering groups all have full-time jobs, every effort must be made to make the meetings crisp, well organized, focused, and pertinent. The purpose of the steering committee is not to cover details or do the work of the IS department, but to review direction, progress toward objectives, and fit of systems to the company culture. The subject matter should emphasize the questions *why* and *what,* not *how.* The group should include respected people from the various organizations and not just those who happen to be available. This is probably the most important success factor of steering committees: The people selected should be able to speak for their division or organization.

FIGURE 9.8. Steering committee organization

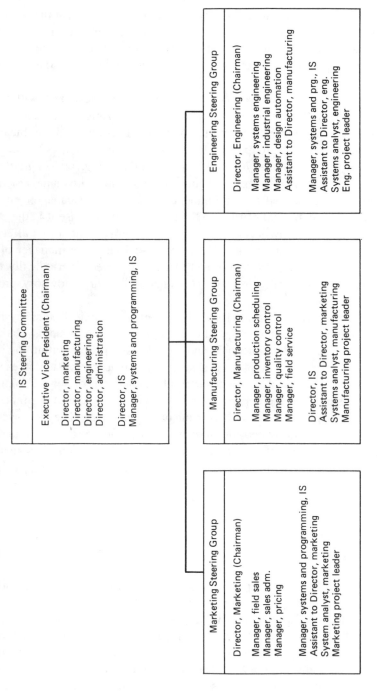

IS Steering Committee

Executive Vice President (Chairman)

Director, marketing
Director, manufacturing
Director, engineering
Director, administration

Director, IS
Manager, systems and programming, IS

Marketing Steering Group

Director, Marketing (Chairman)

Manager, field sales
Manager, sales adm.
Manager, pricing

Manager, systems and programming, IS
Assistant to Director, marketing
System analyst, marketing
Marketing project leader

Manufacturing Steering Group

Director, Manufacturing (Chairman)

Manager, production scheduling
Manager, inventory control
Manager, quality control
Manager, field service

Director, IS
Assistant to Director, marketing
Systems analyst, manufacturing
Manufacturing project leader

Engineering Steering Group

Director, Engineering (Chairman)

Manager, systems engineering
Manager, industrial engineering
Manager, design automation
Assistant to Director, manufacturing

Manager, systems and prg., IS
Assistant to Director, eng.
Systems analyst, engineering
Eng. project leader

While the expanding scope of IS makes cross-functional steering groups essential, the following pitfalls should be avoided if the committee approach is to be effective:

- Group is too large and diverse (six to eight is optimum).

- Meetings deteriorate into vague, wandering discussion.

- Subject matter becomes too detailed and specific rather than focuses on broad direction, strategy, and priority.

- The necessary staff work is not accomplished before meetings.

- Frequency and length of meetings are greater than management can tolerate.

- Substitutes and substitutes for substitutes begin to show up at meetings.

- Low-level chairpersonship or IS domination of the meeting occurs.

IS AUDITS AND ORGANIZATIONAL REVIEW

At periodic intervals, it may prove desirable to stand back and take a good hard look at overall IS operation. Some form of review should be considered on at least a biennial basis. With so much at stake and with business becoming so dependent on IS, periodic audits should be viewed positively by the IS director and corporate management.

Several IS surveys have reached similar conclusions regarding the degree to which companies utilize outside and inside groups to evaluate computer operations. Less than 25 percent of companies with installed small- and medium-scale computers conduct outside evaluations of their computer operation. In companies with large computers, one out of three conducts outside evaluations. Outside evaluation, then, is not the rule even with companies that are expanding upward of $20 to $30 million per year on IS.

On the other hand, more companies subject computer operations to periodic inside evaluations. Two out of five small and medium-sized companies, and three out of five large companies conduct internal evaluations. The surveys indicate that outside evaluations normally are conducted by consultants or auditing firms, and inside evaluations by personnel outside the IS department, usually representatives of the operating department or internal company auditors.

Inside versus Outside Evaluation

There are pros and cons to the use of outside evaluation services for assessing the efficacy of computer operations. A company must determine whether it has the necessary resources and capabilities to carry out its own evaluation and whether the internal evaluation will have the impact of an independent analysis of operations.

A prime consideration is cost. A special audit team formed by the Boeing Company to audit its computer operation included an experienced IS manager, two people who were experienced in systems/programming work, an internal auditor, and a person with considerable accounting experience. After analyzing the job to be done, the five-person group estimated it would take 10 person-years for a complete review and evaluation of all computer systems, including a thorough and detailed analysis of programs. Such an effort can be justified when one considers that possible reduction in running time of just a small percent can mean the saving of thousands of dollars for a company like Boeing, one of the largest users of IS in the country. This estimate provides an idea of the upward boundary of an evaluation effort. It is obvious that the small computer user is not going to conduct such an analysis. In Boeing's case, the company decided to select an application area as a test case before making a final decision to undertake the complete study.

A Booz, Allen & Hamilton study of 108 leading manufacturers using computers points out that 62 percent of those firms employing regular audits confine them to the critical computer operations. The study also indicates the significant degree to which operating managers are involved in the audits. The operating managers usually serve as members of the committee that reviews and analyzes the results of the audit. It is obvious that the involvement of operating management or of people with no direct IS experience depends on the objectives and level of the evaluation being conducted. The performance areas that are most studied are reviewed in the following. The scope and selection of these areas can help determine who should conduct the evaluation and whether it can best be accomplished by inside or outside sources.

Unless the problems seem particularly severe and major directional and organizational changes are anticipated, the evaluation normally can be handled effectively by an inside group. The desirability of having a department evaluate its own performance is open to question. It provides the proper psychological climate for eventual resolution of the problem areas uncovered, but on the other hand it may not result in the most objective kind of appraisal. A compromise solution is to have a person in the IS department assist with the evaluation, since someone with IS experience is required at the detail level. However, the person selected should not have been directly involved in the application under scrutiny. It is wise to include one or more members of a department that is a major user of the system under study. That person need not be the manager or a supervisor of the department, but can be an assistant or administrative aide who reports to the manager. The head of the evaluation team should be a manager of an operating department. This individual will probably not be a full-time member of the team but will direct the activity, maintain the perspective of the study, and see that the objectives of the study are carried out.

An evaluation team consisting of combined IS and operating personnel should be able to point out weaknesses in the system and recommend action to improve the situation.

Performance Areas

It is important to have a clear idea of the objectives of the evaluation before it starts. As an example, the audit team of the Boeing Company had the following general objectives:

1. Assure that computer systems fulfill their stated objectives.
2. Assure that computer systems meet requirements in a cost-effective manner.
3. Analyze all systems costs to see where costs can be reduced and capability extended.

Experience shows that when evaluations are made, companies cover the following performance areas:

1. New application and equipment planning
2. Project schedule punctuality
3. Standards and documentation
4. Systems errors and discrepancies
5. Report-deadlines promptness
6. Computer report usability
7. Overall use to management
8. Operating budget adherence
9. Computer department practices and procedures
10. Audit and systems control within applications
11. Machine room efficiency
12. Programming efficiency

The list is by frequency of evaluation coverage. The rankings differ somewhat among small and large computer users. The first four areas are universal in their significance. Items 5, 6, and 7 are not as important to the larger companies, indicating that those companies have overcome these discrepancies. However, items 8 and 11 receive higher priority from the larger users. This is not surprising, considering the dollar expenditures of the larger user on IS.

Problem Areas

Besides considering the performance areas most often evaluated by computer users, it is significant to view the major problems uncovered by these evaluations. The following list indicates the results of an extensive survey directed to this question. The problems are listed in the order of their frequency of response.

1. Internal communications between IS and management
2. Complex and time-consuming implementation of applications
3. Scheduling and priorities
4. Short- and long-range planning
5. Software performance
6. Equipment performance
7. Equipment downtime
8. Skilled personnel—shortage and turnover
9. Training

THIRD-PARTY ALLIANCES

The make-versus-buy decision is an increasingly difficult one to make as the number of third-party suppliers has increased dramatically. It is possible to contract out pieces of the IS operation or the entire operation itself. There are outside agencies that will do any part of the systems life cycle, from contract programming to application maintenance. There are training organizations; publishing services; companies that will handle electronic data interchange (EDI), acting as clearing houses between you and your suppliers; and there are the outsourcers who will run your entire data center operation for you.

The broadest third-party service is that of systems integration. These are the large consulting firms, as well as the major hardware vendors, who will take over the entire job of integrating your applications into a global architecture. They start from overall corporate strategies and the company business plan, and develop a business model, a data model, a communications architecture, and, indeed, do the entire IS cycle that has been described in this book. It's a big decision to turn over such important chunks of the operation to an outside agency, but it is an option that should be analyzed. If the capabilities are not present and there is no time to hire and train new people, possibly the only outlet is a third party. Also, it is sometimes easier to control and measure outside resources than it is your own.

The big argument against farming out the major IS elements is the growing competitive significance of IS to the enterprise. Do you want to contract out application development that promises to give your company a competitive edge? Many would say that this area is just too important to rely on outside support. The cost factor is another major consideration, for while the hourly cost of consultants and other third-party vendors is much higher than the inside hourly rate, there are other factors that may make the outside route the least costly in the long run. The answer requires a careful analysis of the alternatives and the tradeoffs. There are just as many horror stories of third party implementation as there are of in-house development. One precept to remember is that you can't delegate the final responsibility for successfully completing the project to a third party; it still rests on your shoulders—you have to live with the results. Suffice it to say that you must manage your vendor.

SUMMARY

The prevailing mode of IS organization is hybrid—part centralized, part distributed. The functional line manager is affected by both forces. This chapter reviewed the approaches and techniques that are relevant to both the centralized and the distributed operation of IS. It was stated that the manager must be aware of both.

The ultimate output of any planning process is a list of projects to implement. So it is with IS where the output is a prioritized list of applications. The chapter opened with an explanation of methods for managing the implementation cycle, program evaluation and review technique (PERT). Also, a process employed by a manufacturing company was discussed. The latter process focused on the concept of program management and the elements required to match a process with a particular company culture. This has been a precept throughout the book, that the process must match the culture.

The concept of capacity planning was reviewed. While this is primarily aimed at running the large central IS operations, many of the principles apply to distributed computing as well. The need for fault tolerant systems in certain operating environments was emphasized. Other topics covered were charge-out systems and data security and privacy. Charge-out systems can be a very important factor in establishing a sound relationship with the users of IS services. Data security is a factor whether in the central or distributed operations. It must be an integral part of the planning and implementation process.

The importance of steering committees was stressed, and guidelines were presented for effectively using committees to oversee IS development. Finally, audit and organizational reviews were discussed as a way of ascertaining both the efficiency and effectiveness of the IS operation. This chapter, though maybe not as exciting as those that discuss the technology and the applications of IS, is an important one. Thinking about the subjects covered in this chapter and developing a management approach to implementing and executing applications are essential underpinnings to gaining competitive advantage with IS.

Case Study

Richard Abbott, Applications Development Director

As Application Development Director, I find myself in an interesting position. My people refer to the changes that are taking place as the "D" word, the "O" word, and the "C" word. If these practices are followed, they interpret it as signaling that it is time to be looking for a new job. The practices referred to are Downsizing, Outsourcing , and CASE.

The "D" word, *downsizing*, means that departmental people will be developing their own applications that run on desktop-based client server platforms. The software advances as well as the increase of flexible application packages have reduced the need for professional systems and programming analysts. Yes they could transfer to a department, but they would be throwing away the skills and experience they have built up over the years.

The "O" word, *outsourcing,* is equally frightening. Complete responsibility for the design and implementation of the large, complex applications are being contracted to outside firms. Also, the maintenance of existing applications has been outsourced, and in certain instances, total systems integration responsibility has been given to independent consulting companies. They ask me, "What is there left for the professional?" The nature of the job has changed to becoming an overseer or negotiator, not a doer. These are not the skills they have trained for, and frankly I don't think they are very interested in this kind of assignment, nor do they feel qualified to act in this role.

The few remaining applications we are working on are being implemented using *CASE* tools, the "C" word. My professionals question whether these tools really save that much development time, and they know they execute slower and take more memory than applications developed in COBOL or C. They are skilled third generation programmers. I feel they do an extremely competent job and can probably complete an application in about the same as, or in less time than, a less skilled analyst using CASE tools.

So that's my problem. There's no question that the D, O, and C words are with us. My management is pressing me and the other directors to do much more than we are now doing. But what do I say and do with my professionals, many of whom have been here for 15 years or more, and with whom I have worked and built up strong business and social relationships. As one of my colleagues said the other day at a meeting, "Sometimes I feel we are squabbling over deck chairs aboard the Titanic."

STUDY QUESTIONS

1. Does Richard Abbott have a real problem?

2. What are the circumstances leading up to the problem?

3. What avenues are open to him to resolve it?

4. If you were an application developer at this company, what would your options be?

5. Do you think Richard should be looking for another job?

Case Study

Managing Application Development

The following is a two-dimensional matrix using the risk assessment elements of structure and technology from Chapter 8. For ease of discussion, size is not shown since it is the least significant to the analysis. There is not much one can do about the size, except to break a large project into smaller units.

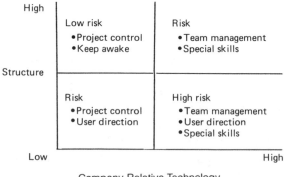

When the degree of technology being employed is low and the project is highly structured and well-understood (high), the project is low risk (upper left quadrant). A simple project control technique can suffice here with the only real risk that the project be ignored and "fall in the cracks." If one stays awake and follows the project, it should most certainly be delivered on time and within budget.

The other extreme is the high-technology, low-structured project (lower right quadrant). These projects can create an experimental, R&D environment. The beginning space flights would fall into this category and, indeed, there were early failures and huge budget overruns. In the information systems application area, installing a nation-wide, all-digital multimedia communication system is another example of a high-risk project. The technology is evolving but is still relatively new; hardware and software standards have not as yet emerged.

Projects in this quadrant must have strong team management. There has to be a good deal of communication and feedback by a close-knit group that works as a team and is capable of reacting and changing quickly as conditions dictate. This is not a "head in the sand" type of project. Because the structure of the project is low, strong user involvement and direction are necessary. This is a good area to produce a prototype or pilot program where a piece of the system is prototyped by a would-be user or customer prior to investing time to formalize the specification. Finally, because it is cutting edge technology, people with special technical skills are required on the team. Sometimes small interdisciplinary ("skunk works") teams are appropriate for this type of project.

Projects in the lower left quadrant require strong user direction on the project team because here is where the risk lies, but require no special skills because they are low-technology projects. A project for a marketing computer simulation model would fall into this quadrant. There are many high-performance, high-quality sophisticated modeling systems on the market today with fully tested hardware and software. The risk here is that the ultimate users of the model are dealing with a relatively unstructured marketing environment based on changing economic, political, and social conditions. Heavy user involvement is necessary in this type of situation to clarify changes that occur over the life cycle of the project.

A project in the upper right quadrant has just the opposite characteristics—the structure is known (high) but the technology is leading edge and therefore high risk. Development of the artificial heart or a complex neuronetwork software system on a massively parallel computer are examples of projects in this area. What the devices must do is well structured, but the technology to accomplish it is not proven.

STUDY QUESTIONS

1. Is this type of analysis helpful in managing projects? How?
2. Are there areas other than technology and structure that are relevant to how a project is managed?
3. Do you think companies tend to use the same project management techniques regardless of the project?
4. What are the advantages of having a project portfolio with balanced risk?

SELECTED REFERENCES

Biggs, C.L., E. G. Birks and W. Atkins, *Managing the Systems Development Process*. Englewood Cliffs, N.J.: Prentice-Hall, Inc., 1980.

Block, Victor, "How Secure Is Your Computer Room?" *Infosystems*. September 1980, pp. 38-52.

Butler Cox Foundation, "Outsourcing Information Systems Services," *A Directors' Briefing*, 1991.

Butler Cox Foundation, "Systems Security," *Management Summary*. Report 76, August 1990.

Canning, Richard G., "Quantitative Methods for Capacity Planning," *EDP Analyzer*, Vol. 18, No. 7, July 1980.

Cash, Jr., James I., Andrew D. Bailey, Jr., and Andrew B. Whinston, "A Survey of Techniques for Auditing EDP-Based Systems," *The Accounting Review*. October 1977, pp. 813-829.

Hodges, Parker, "Charting the Champs," *Datamation*. June 15, 1988, pp. 14-24.

Institute of Internal Auditors, *Systems Auditability and Control (SAC) Study*. Palo Alto, Cal.: Stanford Research Institute, 1978.

International Data Group Publication, "The 1990 CIO 100" (special issue), *CIO*. August 1990, Vol. 3 No. 11.

Kass, Elliot, Bruce Caldwell, Thomas Hoffman, and Diane Medina, "N.Y. Blackout 'Darkness' Data Centers," *Information Week*. August 20, 1990, pp. 12-13.

Kelley, Albert J., Ed., *New Dimensions of Project Management*. Lexington, Mass.: D.C. Heath, 1982.

Konsynski, Benn R., and F. Warren McFarlan, "Information Partnerships-Shared Data, Shared Scale," *Harvard Business Review*. September-October 1990, p. 114.

Lewis, Peter H., "Being Ready for the Day When the Lights Go Out," *The New York Times*, August 26, 1990, p. 11.

Leibs, Scott, "The Value of Security," *Information Week*, June 4, 1990, pp. 53-56.

Lobel, Jerome, *Foiling the System Breakers: Computer Security and Access Control*. New York: McGraw-Hill Book Company, 1986.

Maciariello, Joseph, *Program Management Control Systems*. New York: John Wiley & Sons, 1978.

Matteis, Richard J., "The New Back Office Focuses on Customer Service," *Harvard Business Review*. 1979, pp. 146-159.

Murray, John P., "Retrofitting the Data Center," *Computerworld*. 1982.

Nolan, R.L., "Controlling the Cost of Data Services," *Harvard Business Review*. 1977, pp. 114-124.

Nolan, R.L., "Effects of Chargeout on User/Manager Attitudes," *Comm. ACM 20*, 3 (1977), pp. 177-185.

Toigo, Jon William, "Security, Biomentrics Creep into Business," *Computerworld*, June 11, 1990, pp. 75-78.

Chapter 10

Management Science and Decision Support Systems

INTRODUCTION

"Management science" and "decision support systems" are not absolute terms that can be defined with precision. Management is part science, part art. These two disciplines attempt to put the science element into management decision making. Management science emanates from the concept of operations research, which uses mathematical methods to describe and to solve a variety of problems. Examples are given in the chapter. While these methods are usually employed by specialists within the company, it is important for the manager to have an idea of the areas of application and to know something about the underlying process that produces the solution. The principal management science applications of linear programming, queuing theory, simulation, and statistical analysis are illustrated with basic examples.

While using some of the mathematical models of management science, decision support sytems are used for less structured problems, in other words, where the art of management is blended with the science. Experience shows that this is the more prevalant environment in business. While the management science applications would provide the final decision, decision support systems, as the name indicates, would support the decision made by the manager. Management intuition and perspective are still key ingredients in the decision process. The two terms overlap and, indeed, some of the software tools that are termed decision support systems have the ability to do linear programming and to create mathematical models. The important thing to keep in mind is that this chapter discusses how information systems, building on management science and statistics, can aid in the mangement decision-making process.

THE THREE LEVELS OF BUSINESS PROCESSES

Figure 10.1 shows three levels of business processes: operational control, management control, and strategic planning. Computers employing management science techniques and decision support systems (DSS) are capable of aiding the decision-making process at all three levels. However, as has been indicated, computer systems have had greater impact on the management control and operational levels than on the strategic level. A principal reason is that job functions at the lower levels are more structured and thus easier to translate into programmed logic. Indeed, many lower-level decisions become automatic, with no management intervention required.

A very basic example of computer-aided decision making at the operational control level is a sales-order processing system that suggests substitutes or options if the item ordered is not in stock. For example, a grocery store manager may order ten cases of 12-ounce cans of tomatoes. The system, finding that there are no items in inventory at the closest warehouse, might shift the order to another warehouse, another brand, or substitute the 10-ounce can. These substitutions could be made automatically by preprogrammed logic or could be suggested to a merchandising manager who would then select one of the options.

An example of DSS at the operational level is the production-scheduling function in a manufacturing plant. Based on such factors as sales forecasts, setup costs, inventory levels, factory load, workload, and other elements, a balanced factory work schedule is produced.

FIGURE 10.1. The business-process triangle

Again this can be automatic, based on a preprogrammed computer algorithm, or semiautomatic, with the intervention of the production manager, who may have knowledge of variables not part of the computer model.

DSS at the strategic level often involves an interactive dialogue between user and computer via a terminal screen, frequently having graphic capability. Because top management is concerned with the impact of decisions across the entire organization, business models are optimized (or at least targeted so) at the corporate level. An example was described by the director of management information systems of Northwest Industries, one of the earlier adaptors of DSS for strategic planning. He indicated their DSS as providing a "comprehensive business analysis and planning system, not only in the financial sense, but for strategic planning and econometric modeling of our formal four-year business plan."

MANAGEMENT SCIENCE APPLICATIONS

Management science takes its roots from operations research (OR), which began in England during the late 1930s, when a group of scientists were asked to help the military use their then newly developed radar in locating enemy aircraft. It was called operations research because it originally involved scientific research on the operational problem of radar. This successful activity led to the establishment of OR sections in the Royal Air Force, Army, and Navy. In 1942 the United States introduced OR into the military, and the postwar years brought OR to industry.

The original concept of OR was to assemble a team of experts from diverse disciplines to integrate their expertise to solve a complex problem usually involving sophisticated mathematic models and simulation. As OR spread to business, the name *management science* gradually came into vogue in an attempt to make the activity less imposing to management. OR connotes a think-tank concept where a group of scientists get together to mull over abstruse problems. Management science is the business reincarnation of operations research.

The remainder of the chapter is devoted to describing the methodology and presenting examples of management science and DSS at all levels and illustrating the tools used in developing these systems.

Figure 10.2 describes the process or methodology of management science. The first step is to analyze the problem, whether it be the balancing of production machine centers, the location of a new warehouse, or the optimum sales mix of products. The next step is to isolate the key elements, those factors that are significant in increasing profits or reducing costs. Next, a mathematical model is constructed that expresses the interrelationship of the variables and simulates the effect of different combinations of them. The model is then tested and the results measured against desired standards or against previous simulations. If the results are not satisfactory, the model is modified. This continues until the model's performance is satisfactory. Then actual conditions and facilities can be changed to conform to the model. If the model was a good one, the actual results should be the same as those obtained by the simulation.

Business and professional people make decisions every day. Facts and data are gathered, arranged, sorted out, sequenced, assigned relative weights, and evaluated to form

FIGURE 10.2. Steps in management science

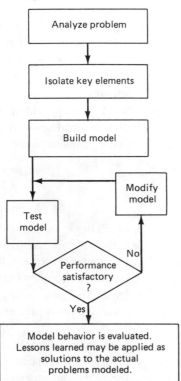

the basis for decision making. At some point decisions become very hard to make because the factors and decision criteria have become too complex. This is to a large extent due to the highly efficient and interrelated industrial organization that business has created. Today's decisions generate countless more ripples than they used to. As a result, business people pay more for incomplete, off-center, or "seat of the pants" decisions.

Companies on the leading edge of their industry are making effective use of management science methods. A prominent paper company has developed a computerized model of its timber and wood products division to gain the most efficient use of timberland and to plan site location for new plywood plants. The model consists of 8,000 equations and 15,000 variables. A major chemical company uses a computer model to simulate an industry segment and the company's potential for a share of market and profitability. A glass company has a corporate financial model that allows executives to test the impact of ideas and strategies on future profitability and to determine the needs for funds and physical resources.

Other examples described in business periodicals and trade publications indicate where companies, in addition to simulation, have used computer-risk analysis, gaining a composite picture of the key factors involved in implementing a new policy, determining the probabilities of each event occurring on time, and determining the composite odds of success. Another area is sensitivity analysis, the measurement of the effect of the variation of individual factors on the final result. For example, in certain instances the leverage of an individual factor is high—a 5 percent increase in sales may trigger a 30 percent increase in inventory and may have a major impact on the overall result of a program. In another case a 50 percent fluctuation in one element has minimal effect on the final outcome.

The development of management science has led to a classification of different techniques that are applicable to particular classes of problems. These techniques include linear programming, queuing theory, simulation, and statistical analysis. Each of the four techniques is described and illustrated.

Linear Programming

Linear programming (LP) is a mathematical technique for deciding among competing demands for limited resources. A series of linear equations evaluates each factor in the problem in relation to the other factors. The classic example of a problem solved by LP involves a number of warehouses throughout the country, a limited quantity of product, and a large number of distributors with a given demand. Knowing the cost of transporting goods from each warehouse to each distributor, the problem is to schedule shipments so as to minimize transportation costs. As the number of factors in problems of this type increases, manual procedures become inadequate.

A linear solution can be used for a product-mix problem, in which a company wants to produce the maximum profit from set of raw materials that can be combined in a number of different ways to satisfy finished-product specifications. Blending of gasoline is an example of this type of application.

Linear programming is used in a "cut-and-trim" situation to decide how to cut standard-size rolls of steel or paper into various widths and sizes to satisfy specified customer demands and to minimize trimming waste.

Another example of LP is its use by an advertising firm as illustrated by the following example adapted from a press release:

Audience Buying Habits and Media Rates
Are Combined in a New Media Service

A computerized service that combines research data on the buying habits of media audiences with published media rates to provide advertising agencies with analyses of consumer audiences, rather than total audiences of various media, was demonstrated by a New York advertising firm.

The firm also unveiled a data communications system for the advertising industry. The system, which links a computer to a nationwide personal computer network, permits agencies anywhere in the U.S. to obtain immediate media market research and other information.

The service describes the audience characteristics of some 200 different media vehicles, including newspapers, magazines, and radio and television, in terms of the actual users and purchasers of any of 50 different product categories.

By defining media audiences in terms of their purchases, the system provides evidence of which media deliver the largest numbers of prospects for a given product. Through the combination of this information with current media rates, ad agencies can determine with greater accuracy the best media to use for advertising specific products, and the lowest cost for obtaining maximum coverage. A technique called linear programming combines these factors into the mathematical model necessary to produce the desired results.

During a press demonstration, data from the New York market area in six product categories, combined in a four-step process with rate data from four local media, were shown. Within five minutes the computer analyzed the data and produced a two-medium combination that represents the best media mix for each of the six products, based on the lowest cost to reach the largest unduplicated audience of prospective buyers for each product.

The product categories shown were dog food, cigarettes, cleansers, facial tissues, wines, and automatic washers. The media used were the *New York Times, New York News,* NBC-TV, and CBS-TV.

Although the New York market was used for the demonstration, every major market area in the nation, as well as the entire U.S. market, eventually will be included in the surveys.

Queuing Theory

This technique (less widely used than linear programming) is applicable to solving problems where it is desirable to minimize the costs or time associated with waiting lines, or queues. These problems occur, for example, at a checkout counter, at a receiving dock, or at a turnpike entrance. Given that, on a Saturday, 200 people randomly enter a supermarket every hour, and the average checkout time is five minutes, queuing theory can help schedule the number of checkout stations to minimize waiting time and labor cost.

The following example shows one practical application of queuing theory to a business problem:

Department Store Chain Uses Computer
to Consolidate Warehouses and Optimize Dock Facilities

A prominent Midwest department store chain has employed the concept of operations research and a high-speed digital computer to help it consolidate its warehousing activities. The chain formerly supplied its retail outlets from three warehouses located in the greater Chicago area. A series of changing conditions led management to consider that one warehouse could do the job in a more economical fashion and still maintain the desired delivery cycle.

An initial consideration was the addition of dock facilities necessary to handle the increased truck traffic. The additional dock facilities could be planned realistically if three factors were known—the number of trucks, their arrival time, and the time to service each truck. In addition there were economic considerations involved in the problem. The trucks were leased, so waiting time had a definite cost associated with it. However, additional dock facilities, while cutting down waiting time, necessitated a considerable monetary investment. The problem of cost factors in economic conflict with each other and the waiting-line principle is a classic case for the application of queuing theory. Here's the way the company went about solving the problem.

A study analyzed the existing traffic flow at the three warehouses, and the results were projected to that expected at a single warehouse. The study involved a sample seven-week period in the spring. The effect of seasonal variations was projected from the basic data, using historical company records. It was discovered that the number of trucks increased only 5 percent during the Christmas rush but that the number of pieces handled increased 50 percent. In addition, truck servicing time was found to vary within certain bounds, depending on factors such as size of truck and type of merchandise. A service time pattern was found to be a combination of a fixed time interval and a variable time interval dependent on the number of pieces being handled.

While the number of truck arrivals had certain patterns and frequencies (for example, an average of 105 trucks arrived in the morning, while 65 arrived in the afternoon), there was a chance relationship that precluded a simple arithmetic solution. An additional element was added to the classical queuing theory solution—the use of the Monte Carlo method. The name *Monte Carlo* implies the presence of chance. Using the frequency distributions produced by the studies as boundaries, the Monte Carlo technique randomly selected a time of arrival and a service time for each of the arriving trucks. This is where the power of the computer comes into play. The computer simulates a day's operation by totaling the waiting time and length of queue for each truck serviced that day. The computer runs through a full year's operation using random numbers to simulate actual conditions while assuming a varying number of docks. These iterations are repeated to the point where computer output indicates to management the tradeoffs of waiting time and investment in new dock facilities. This then forms the basis for the most economical solution to the problem.

Problem solving is greatly enhanced by the processing power of the computer, running through massive simulations and arithmetic operations in a fraction of the time it would take to do them manually. In fact, the job would be so burdensome to do manually that it would never be attempted in the first place. Combining three warehouses into one and doing it in the most economical manner is a classic example of the use of advanced mathematical techniques and the power of modern computers.

Simulation

Simulation is used in business to determine the effects of decisions. Simulation reduces the risk and expense of decision making by using hypothetical or historical data instead of trying out decisions on live data, a risky and expensive method. This process is similar to using a wind tunnel to simulate wind velocities and pressures to find the effect of flight speeds on the fuselage of an airplane model. This is certainly far more expedient than building a full-scale plane to test a design. Likewise, businesspersons can project the effects of their decisions through the use of mathematical models that react as the real world reacts.

An example of simulation is an inventory simulator that accepts product demand for particular items over prior sales periods, together with details concerning lead times, quantity discounts, and inventory and buying costs. Alternate inventory policies are simulated and measured against the resultant inventory levels, stockouts, and inventory and buying costs, to determine which policy best meets management's objectives.

Business models are being used by a growing number of companies. These models enable management to view the impact of a variety of policies and decisions on the profitability of a company. Sometimes the result of a decision or policy goes against the intuitive expectation. A computer-based model can point this out by reflecting the mix of a variety of alternatives on profitability.

Corporate Financial Model
Directs Company Activities

An oil company has developed a corporate financial model that may be the largest and most complex corporate model yet. The computerized model takes into account the production, transportation, manufacturing, and marketing operations of the company. The working version required thirteen person-years to complete and an additional ten person-years to familiarize management with the operation of the model, to solicit comments and suggestions for improvement, and to incorporate some of the suggestions into the model. (Note that it took almost as much time to get the model into effect as to build and implement it in the first place.) The model puts pertinent information into an analytical framework that aids the management decision-making process. It performs the following functions:

- Forecasts net income for one year, accurate within 1 percent
- Prepares short-term profit plans and long-range (ten-year) projections
- Provides preplanning information in budget preparation
- Calculates variances between budgeted and actual results
- Triggers revised forecasts if not proceeding in accordance with plan
- Acts as early warning system for monitoring activities and signaling necessary reactive plans
- Indicates effect on income and cash flow by following alternate investment strategies
- Assists in planning the addition of new facilities and a host of special studies
- Accomplishes all the preceding items with great speed (for example, the computer processing time to simulate one year of operation is 14 seconds)

The corporate model is the core of the company's management system. The model can reflect the impact of a variety of company plans and actions on profitability. One of the major attributes of the system is the turnaround time for a simulation. Exploding a gross sales forecast into the components necessary to produce a particular volume and then ascertaining profit and loss from the mix formerly took ten days. With the computer model, this can be accomplished in several hours. The previous methods discouraged changes or the testing of different forecast mixes on profitability; now management is encouraged to experiment and to innovate.

Statistical Analysis

This technique is probably the most widely used of all the mathematical techniques available to business. While the general topic being discussed is management science, keep in mind the fact that these techniques can form the foundation of decision support systems. There is a fine line between the two disciplines. This becomes more significant as we discuss statistical analysis, for it is the basis of decision support systems. Statistical analysis covers a broad range of problems and is useful wherever large amounts of data or information must be evaluated. A typical application is sales forecasting, where the history of item movement is used to forecast future demand.

The following write-up of the computer studies performed by the Public Health Service illustrates typical applications of statistical analysis:

Public Health Service Collects and Analyzes
Data to Monitor the Air and Water

The Public Health Service has installed a computer for use in a variety of radiation, water purification, air pollution, and other environmental studies. The computer is used in reducing to summaries large amounts of data in the study of environmental pollution. The summaries can be used to evaluate the hazards to health caused by the various pollutants. The computer also performs statistical analyses of data to support investigative research in areas such as water pollution, air pollution, radioactive contamination, and food sanitation. Data reduction and analysis are required for the many national sampling networks involved in the collection of information about pollution.

The source data in most cases are readings of the density of bacteria, chemicals, and particles in air and water. These readings are taken at numerous locations throughout the United States on a 24-hour basis. These data are converted to digital form and sent to the center.

The computer converts the raw data into usable units (e.g., parts per million), rejects data beyond predetermined limits, and generates a report of the readings.

Applications of the computer in this area can be divided into the following categories:

Air studies. A typical application involves the analysis of gaseous air pollution measurements in connection with the Public Health Service's National Air Sampling Network. At ten different urban centers, measurements are automatically recorded around the clock at five-minute intervals for several different pollutants. Pollutants measured include carbon dioxide, nitric oxide, nitrogen dioxide, and sulfur dioxide. Over 150,000 readings per week are recorded.

Data are received from operators of the data recording equipment in the field. These give information about periods when the recording equipment didn't work, when data were erroneous, when the equipment drifted in measurements, and when the equipment had to be recalibrated.

The data are then processed by a program that refines the raw data by adjusting it according to drift points, calibration, etc., and converts the data to units such as pollutant parts per million parts of air.

Every month the collected data are used to prepare a series of statistical summaries, for example, the daily average concentration for each pollutant for each city. Techniques of statistical analysis are used to calculate means and maximums for hourly and daily periods and to plot trends. By examining these reports, public health officials can spot areas in which pollutant readings are unusually high and can observe trends in different areas of the country. Reports on this subject are forwarded to Congress.

Water studies. The water study programs receive data from laboratories doing analyses of water pollutants. For example, rivers are sampled to determine whether industrial plants are discarding industrial chemicals. The data are then used in the same manner as the data on air. Statistical studies point out valuable trend information.

Radiological studies. Radiological studies use another method of statistical analysis, called matrix algebra, to estimate radioactive pollutants. For example, an analysis of the feces of infants is made to determine how much radioactive material in various foods is absorbed by each child. In the area of animal physiology, experiments are made on guinea pigs to determine the effect of auto exhaust fumes. Statistical routines such as multiple regression, orthogonal polynomial curve fit, and confidence limits are also used to analyze data.

STATISTICAL INVENTORY CONTROL

The foregoing described the use of rather advanced mathematics to analyze data in a public health setting. Some of the same processes can be used in a business setting, but more simple mathematics can be used to achieve some significant results. In inventory control, transactions are processed against an inventory master file to produce an updated inventory status report showing the current balance of each item. This is really nothing more than inventory accounting and hardly deserves the name *inventory control*. Let's now add the control dimension and see the practical application of statistical analysis to a familiar problem.

The major objective of inventory control is to buy for the least total cost consistent with customer service requirements. To do this, you must know when to buy and how much to buy. This is all that is required, but it takes certain mathematical calculations to answer these questions. The first calculation is a forecast, or best estimate, of what we expect to sell of each item.

Forecasting Methods

There are various methods of forecasting. One is the *moving average* method, in which an average is taken of the last six months, each month adding the current month and deleting the oldest month. Another method is the *weighted moving average* in which a specific weight is given to particular months, normally to current months. The following is an example of a weighted moving average:

Month	Demand	Weight	Weighted Demand
6 (current)	140	50%	70.0
5	130	25%	32.5
4	120	12%	14.4
3	110	10%	11.0
2	90	2%	1.8
1	80	1%	0.8
		Forecast	130.5

Both of the foregoing forecasting techniques have shortcomings. The weighted moving average method is a little more sophisticated, but human judgment must still determine the relative weight for each month. A third technique is called exponential smoothing. Exponential smoothing is a weighted moving average method that places the heaviest weighting on the most recent demand. It can be thought of as the learning curve representation of past demand. It continually measures actual demand against previous demands to determine the error and correct it. Exponential smoothing uses three factors to forecast demand.

New forecast = forecast for last period + α (forecast error for last period)

The first factor is the forecast for the last period. The second factor is the forecast error for the last period; and the third factor, represented by the Greek letter α, is called the *smoothing constant*. This smoothing constant gives exponential smoothing its name. The smoothing constant gets its name because it "smooths" out a demand curve projection by considering previous errors. The derivation of the term *exponential* comes from the fact that the weights assigned to the demands experienced in past periods vary exponentially with respect to the number of periods they are away from the current period. In the case of a smoothing constant of 0.5, a 50 percent weight is placed on the last period's demand, 25 percent on the previous period's demand, 12 1/2 percent on the next previous period, and so on. Although not a panacea, exponential smoothing can automatically establish the best demand trend for an item based on prior experience, and continue to evaluate its selection by measuring the error or distance away from the trend line of each succeeding period's demand. It can adjust the trend based on these errors and forecast probable demand for a wide range of items with varied demand patterns.

Forecast Error and Safety Stock

In discussing forecasting, the concept of forecast error was continually mentioned. It is obvious that forecasting depends on the theorems of probability, where there is no such thing as a sure bet. If we knew the forecast was accurate, knowing when to buy would be easy. The order point would be determined from knowing the quantity of the item we expect to sell over a lead time or procurement time. If it takes five days to procure the item and we sell at a rate of 50 per day, we should always order when our inventory balance shows 250. If we order 500 at a time, the order would arrive exactly as inventory hit a zero balance. This is shown graphically in Figure 10.3.

FIGURE 10.3. Ideal reorder curve

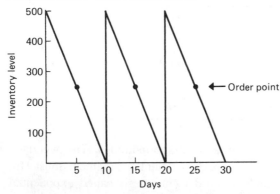

This, however, is an ideal situation. In reality, demand would not always be 50 per day. Safety stock is required to cover forecast errors and unforeseen situations. The level of safety stock can be determined statistically by knowing the forecast and forecast error of a given item and the desired customer service or percentage of stockouts that can be tolerated. A smaller safety stock is needed to ensure a 95 percent customer service level for an item with a stable demand pattern than is needed for an item with a fluctuating demand.

Figure 10.4 superimposes the safety stock requirement on the previous chart. We assume a need of 100 units as safety stock. The order point is now 350 units. The broken line indicates how safety stock is consumed when demand does not follow the forecast.

Calculating Economic Order Quantity

Let's now direct attention to the second major question of inventory control, "How much to buy?" In the foregoing example, the order quantity [or economic order quantity (EOQ), as it is called] was a ten-days' supply, or 500 units. This amount was determined arbitrarily and could be either too much or too little. Here is where the concept of

FIGURE 10.4. Reorder curve with safety stock

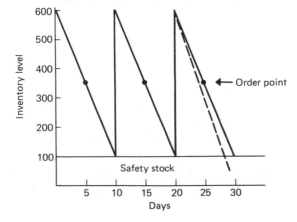

economical order quantity comes into play. The problem is to minimize both inventory carrying costs (capital, taxes, insurance, storage, depreciation, etc.) and reorder costs (check writing, receiving, purchase order preparation, etc.). Inventory levels, and hence inventory carrying costs, can be reduced by a larger number of smaller purchases. But as the number of purchases increases, ordering costs increase. Likewise, any quantity discounts are lost. The EOQ formulation balances these opposing costs and defines the most economical quantity to purchase. The behavior of these two cost factors can be viewed graphically in Figure 10.5.

As the order quantity lot size increases, the cost of carrying inventory increases because greater inventory will be on hand at any given time. As the order quantity increases, the cost of ordering will decline because fewer purchases will be required throughout the year. The total cost line (broken line) is the sum of the carrying cost and ordering cost. The low point of the curve, where total costs are at a minimum, is the economic order quantity. This can be stated arithmetically by the following formula:

$$EOQ = \sqrt{\frac{2AO}{I}}$$

A is the annual demand for an item; O is the ordering cost; I is the inventory carrying cost.

In summary, we have considered the basic elements involved in inventory control and have illustrated the required statistical analysis. The forecasting technique described is basic to inventory control. The question of when to buy led to a discussion of safety stock and the use of safety stock as a buffer to ensure a desired level of customer service. The question of how much to buy led to the economic order quantity and the statistical analysis involved in minimizing the opposing costs of ordering and carrying inventory. This is a basic and straightforward example of a system that can assist buyers and merchandisers in making decisions. There are additional factors that cannot be captured in the model, such as the merchandise manager's knowledge that one of the company's competitors will be introducing a product that will take market share away from the company.

FIGURE 10.5. EOQ determination

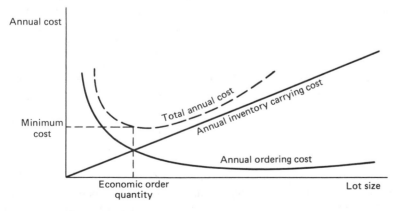

MAKING DECISIONS UNDER CONDITIONS OF UNCERTAINTY

The preceding discussion for the most part has assumed a "black-and-white" world; that is, either something is known or it is not. In actual business operation, however, obviously there are certain risks or probabilities that a certain course of action will be successful. The technique of risk analysis is called *decision theory* and is being linked to a computer system in a growing, but still select, circle of companies. This technique falls more under the label of decision support systems. A basic example of the technique and its benefits to decision making may help qualify its future use.

The problem to be solved by the use of decision theory is the evaluation of prospects for the purchase of a high-value durable goods item that entails a good deal of presale effort. The selection of prospects that hold greatest profit potential is of prime significance in order to focus a limited sales force on an expanding marketplace.

In analyzing the situation, the following questions must be tackled one at a time and an economic evaluation made of each.

What is the payoff or profit potential of each prospect?

What are the costs involved in bidding for the account?

What are the odds of getting the account?

The profit potential is based on the revenue that can be expected over a five-year period. A five-year period is selected because a customer can be expected to contribute add-on business after the initial sale. If installation is not anticipated before 12 months, the profit potential must reflect this factor. For example, a multidivision company expecting to sign a contract for one machine ($110,000 revenue) to be installed in 12 months, with two similar machines to be installed two years after the first, would have a five-year revenue potential of $880,000 ($110,000 × 4 + $220,000 × 2). The revenue potential must then be viewed in light of its profit contribution (based on the company's accounting methods) and must be discounted in light of the fact that revenue does not all accrue the first year. The resultant discounted contribution margin for the aforementioned sale might be $170,000.

What presale effort must be expended in an attempt to sign the account? This figure covers the cost of special engineering, systems analysis, special training courses, demonstration programs, proposal preparation, and other support needed to bid for the business. For example, if an elaborate proposal, plus considerable special engineering, is required, the cost might be as follows:

2 engineers for 2 months (4 person-months × $5000)	$20,000
1 illustrator/designer for 3 months ($2500/person/month)	7,500
Supplies and proposal material	1,500
	$29,000

The next step is the determination of the betting odds or the probability that the sale can be closed. This is a rather subjective evaluation, but an analysis of competitive factors, plus past experience, can be used to establish the odds. The result is stated in terms of a percentage probability.

To see how decision theory works, assume that there are two prospects and that it is desired to rank them according to priority, for it is not possible to expend a major sales effort on each. The following decision table (Figure 10.6) indicates that prospect B holds the greater profit potential. It brings this out by comparing the expected monetary value of the two accounts. Prospect A has higher potential but with less probability of realizing it and with a greater selling expense. If prospect A is signed, a profit return of $170,000 will result, whereas a loss of $29,000 will be incurred if the prospect is lost. If prospect B is signed, a profit return of $90,000 will result, whereas a loss of $6,000 will be incurred if the prospect is lost. The expected monetary value of B is $32,400 as compared with $10,800 for A. These figures are obtained by multiplying the probability of getting the sale (20 percent in the case of A) times the profit if the sale is made ($170,000) and subtracting the amount obtained by multiplying the probability of losing the sale (80 percent) times the sales cost or loss if the sale is lost ($29,000).

Decision theory is a systematic method of facilitating decision making under conditions of uncertainty. The example used here has but a few variables and there are only two alternate courses of action. As the variables and alternatives are multiplied severalfold, as is the case in most business decisions, the need for techniques such as decision theory becomes more apparent.

Decision theory analyzes the factors underlying decisions and allows decision makers to quantify the major parts of problems so that they are free to concentrate on those factors that cannot be readily quantified. The human mind has a difficult time handling multidimensional problems. Decision theory divides a problem into its logical parts, analyzes each part separately, and then puts the parts back together in their proper perspective in order to reach a decision. Decision theory follows the philosophy of divide and conquer—that is, divide a problem into its logical components, analyze and quantify each component, and thereby conquer the overall problem.

FIGURE 10.6. Decision table statement of problems

Account A (the account described in the foregoing)		Account B
Revenue potential	$880,000	$560,000
Profit potential	170,000	90,000
Sales cost	–29,000	–6,000
Net profit potential	$141,000	$ 84,000

Alternatives	Bid on Prospect A	Probability	Bid on Prospect B	Probability
Get the sale	+$170,000	20%	+$90,000	40%
Lose the sale	–29,000	80%	–6,000	60%
Expected monetary value	+10,800		+32,400	

DECISION SUPPORT SYSTEM COMPONENTS

This section helps tie together the discussion on decision support systems. Figure 10.7 outlines the components of a DSS. The DSS generator is the software hub of the system. It provides the program logic to interface to the management user of the system. We say "management user"; however, it could be a professional or IS person. More and more, the user is a management person because the interface program is becoming more in tune with the management cognitive style, that is, more graphical and intuitive. The use of object-oriented programming as explained in Chapter 7 is one of the tools that is becoming very attractive to non–IS professionals, and DSS generators are beginning to employ this methodology.

Other components of DSS include a data base and a tool base. The data base includes the data needed to feed the applications in use. For example, it may include sales history for the last five years, consisting of sales by geographical territory, by product, by salesperson, and by any other category that is relevant. It may also include sales of competitors' products and their market share by product or geographical territory. Also included would be data from external data bases or the ability to tap a pertinent group of outside data bases via telecommunications.

The tool base or kit includes the mathematical models and analytical techniques to process and manipulate the data base to produce the desired output. The tool kit would include the normal functions provided by spreadsheets, including a library of mathematical and algebraic functions ranging from simple square root formulas to sensitivity analysis, regression analysis, optimization models, and financial functions such as present-value calculation. The tools range from a simple single arithmetic function to complex multi dimensional models, for example an airline model which takes into account factors such as scheduling, seating capacity, air craft utilization, traffic patterns and statistics, financial considerations and the like.

The components for the system can be housed within a single workstation; that is, the software program and data base can be part of a management workstation on the desk, or the data bases could be located at a central or remote site. The considerations determining whether the system is a centralized or distributed one are the same as those discussed in Chapters 5 and 6 under the distributed systems model and IS organizational factors.

DECISION SUPPORT SYSTEM (DSS) TOOLS

In the evolution of most technologies, there is a period when the technology is new, complex, hard to learn, expensive, and seemingly useful only to a handful of specialists. This has been true of DSS. In the early days when DSS or management science were

FIGURE 10.7. Decision support system components

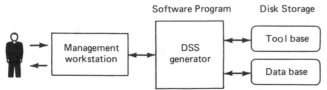

called operations research (OR), we had the image (I should say the reality) of a group of scientists working the back room developing complex mathematical models that only they could even begin to comprehend. However, the advent of the powerful desktop workstations with lower price tags, and, most important, the availability of packaged DSS generators incorporating ease-of-use features are having the effect of democratizing the use of DSS, bringing the systems out of the labs and into the hands of management.

The earlier models were written and customized application by application in programming languages like FORTRAN, ALGOL, or PL/1. The process was tedious, took a very long time to design and implement, and the costs were extremely high. The designers had to be highly experienced and skilled individuals. Most importantly, because there was minimal user involvement, the resulting models often did not reflect the actual business conditions or were so difficult to understand that managers were afraid to use them. While today's DSS generators are not yet the exclusive domain of management, the new interactive, graphical interfaces make it possible for managers to get into the act, sometimes writing their own DSS, but more often collaborating with IS people to design systems based on their requirements.

The first-level DSS is the widely used spreadsheet. Advances have been remarkable and today's LOTUS 1-2-3 offers integrated graphics and a set of built-in mathematical functions in addition to the ability of users to write their own macros. LOTUS is mentioned, as it is the most popular spreadsheet, but a host of other packages that can accomplish the same functions are on the market. There is no question that the spreadsheet can accomplish the most widely used application, that of executing a series of "what if" commands. For example, a company's profit and loss statement can be projected out five years, and can then be modeled to show the cumulative effect of key variables such as inflation rate, price of product, market share, product margin, and the like. Menus and graphical commands make the spreadsheet the operating province of just about all levels of management. Yes, the manager can have an assistant do the work but, as many executives are finding out, there is value in rooting around in the data, in experimenting, and in seeing a variety of future scenarios.

Other DSS generators, and there are quite a few of them on the market, include Express, Focus, and IFPS/Plus. These packages run on a gamut of computer systems ranging form large supercomputers to small PCs. There is also an assortment of packages that specialize in linear programming, modeling, or statistical analysis. They are more powerful in concentrating on a specific set of functions, but most of the general-purpose generators have capabilities that can satisfy the requirements for the majority of users.

DSS generators can be compared on a common criteria set, the most important of which are:

- *User interface*—A key question being how well the package satisfies a heterogeneous set of users with widely varying skills and experience.
- *User support*—What documentation and training programs are available.
- *Input capabilities*—DSSs use a good deal of input, so the ease of entering that input, including the ability to use data from already existing data bases, is quite important.

- *Output capabilities*—the versatility of reports and the ability to utilize multiple media to show results.

- *Expandability*—the abilities to add more power and larger data bases and to link with existing and future networks become key elements in selecting a DSS.

- *Cost*—one, alas, cannot overlook the hardware and software cost of installing such a system, nor overlook the people cost to design and implement.

These costs must be consistent with the benefits and returns of these systems, which, though often difficult to measure, can be quite significant and could provide the difference between the success or failure of an enterprise.

IMPACT OF DSS ON DECISION MAKING

There are some important considerations in the development of DSS. The first is that the data required for the decisions faced by top management are external and unstructured. The second is that decision support systems are not well understood and have been slow to gain acceptance. The third reason is that much management decision making relies on intuition, executive sensitivity, "gut feel," and other unquantifiable data. Although more and more of the elements are being quantified, and more of the management process is becoming understood and programmed, there is still a factor of intuition with which the computer is incapable of dealing. Management has been defined as part science, part art. Many feel the art overshadows the science and that the world of management is one of dealing with ambiguity. The following are factors to consider in assessing the role of decision support systems in a company.

Unstructured Data

Much of the data required by management are unstructured, nonprogrammed, future oriented, inexact, and external. This information is the most difficult to acquire, update, and process. Another factor restricting the development of decision support systems for top management is the lack of definite cause-and-effect relationships among data. An example is a sales forecast for a planned item. In order to project a forecast, the company must know the market in which the product will compete, the market saturation for the product, and the impact on existing products in the line. Whether it is more reasonable to forecast by an extrapolation of how similar items have behaved in the past or by a competitive share of market analysis is open to question. The method selected is crucial to the forecast. Even if the necessary data are available (for example, sales history by item), there may be no logical basis by which to show the effect on sales of the introduction of a new item. There are many other situations where management decisions must be made in the absence of quantified cause-and-effect relationships. This is not to say that these relationships will never be known. However, the problem of obtaining the unquantified data required for top management decisions, combined with the unstructured decision rules, presents formidable challenges for computerized decision support systems directed at strategic planning.

Unfamiliarity of Management with DSS Techniques

Many managers are still leery of using sophisticated (to them) mathematics as a basis for decision making. First they may not understand the models that are constructed to analyze the specific situation. Management may be skeptical of making a decision based on a set of poorly understood equations, and often the IS specialist is incapable of explaining in management terms just what the mathematical processing will accomplish. Furthermore, if a manager recognizes that the data used as input to the model do not have a high degree of accuracy, the results may appear suspicious. Managers may feel more secure with a complete "seat of the pants" decision than with depending on the model. At least it is cheaper, they rationalize. What management fails to realize is that although neither the management science solution nor the "seat of the pants" solution may prove to be wholly accurate—the odds on the management science solution (if the technique is properly used) are a good deal better.

Reliance on Intuition

Many top managers feel that good strategic decisions are made more by intuition than by a quantitative analysis of the available data. They do not ignore data when they exist but rely on intuition when little or no data are available. An article by Professor John Mihalasky of the Newark College of Engineering points out that the higher people are in an organization, the more incomplete are the data on which they base decisions, and the more they rely on intuition, hunches, or instinct.

Professor Mihalasky feels that we may be putting too much faith in machines and data—on the logical decision maker versus the so-called nonlogical decision maker. He further points out that studies suggest that some managers have more precognitive ability than others. This ability gives these managers a better batting average in making decisions intuitively. The study divided 25 chief executives into two classes according to their proved performance based on profitability. For one of the tests, managers matched a series of numbers (0 to 9) printed out randomly by a computer. An average score is 10 percent. The successful executives outscored the nonperformers in 22 out of 27 tests. Statistically, the chances of this happening by accident are fewer than 5 in 1000.

Some people have extended the thesis suggested by Professor Mihalasky and used it as a rationale for ignoring quantitative and logical approaches to management decision making.

This study does not claim to justify the role of intuition in decision making, but it does raise some intriguing questions. If there is such a thing as intuitive ability and if the ability can be tested, to what degree should the intuitive decision be valued in contrast to the logical decision (based on advanced management science techniques)? Granted that the logical decision is the preferred one when the data are known and quantifiable, what degree of data reliability is the breakeven point, where the logical decision becomes preferred?

SUMMARY

This chapter has dealt with the applications of management science and decision support systems to business problems—a leading trend in computer usage. Classes of management science problems were described and examples given to illustrate the major categories of linear programming, queuing theory, simulation, and statistical analysis. The inventory control application was used to show how statistical analysis can aid management decision making. Management considerations were reviewed to explain why these techniques have been relatively slow to become accepted within the business environment. Much software has been produced that aids in the development of DSS solutions. Some of these aids were described in this chapter.

There is no question that presidents of companies still have to make the important business decisions and be the driving force in business success; they will not be replaced by computers and business models. More and more, however, their decisions will be tested and validated by the techniques described in this chapter. The rationale of decisions will be greatly enhanced. Computers, management science, and decision support systems will not assure business success; however, these tools will improve one's odds. As someone has said, "While you can lie with statistics, it's far easier to lie without them."

Case Study

Decision Support System at Frito-Lay

Every business manager I know shares one frustration: the difficulty of obtaining fast, accurate, and comprehensive market information. Whether selling mouthwash, disk drives, or, in our case, snack foods, a manager needs to know whether a product is giving the competition fits, or if it's a clinker. And you need to know quickly or the competition will kill you.

Until recently, Frito-Lay had a centralized decision making structure common to many corporations. Product information crept upward through the organization on what I thought was a timely basis. I soon discovered it wasn't timely enough.

It did not, for example, provide Frito-Lay enough time to respond quickly to its rapidly changing and complex markets or to fine-tune its inventory. It also did not allow us to shorten our business cycle enough to stay ahead of the competition. And it did not allow me, the CEO, to have the latest sales and profit information on the 14 million snacks sold weekly through our 400,000 sales calls.

So we changed—radically.

The catalyst was our Decision Support System, brought on line last year. DSS kicks

From Robert H. Beeby, *The Wall Street Journal*, June 11, 1990.

back to 200 managers detailed sales and inventory information fed into it by 10,000 route salespeople equipped with hand-held computers.

For example, one of our salespeople who handles more than 50 stores for us in New Jersey no longer spends hours writing orders, invoices, and sales reports. With his palm-sized computer, he now completes his "paperwork" in a minute or two at each stop, running through a programmed product list complete with prices. At the end of each day, his sales report is transmitted in seconds to headquarters in Dallas. Even conservatively, if we estimate that our route salespeople save just three hours a week, that's 30,000 hours a week for the entire sales force, and untold savings in clerical, postage, and forms costs.

Here's how the system serves us:

Helps in tracking new products. In this area, DSS is invaluable. This spring, for example, Frito-Lay launched its new "Light" line of snack foods. DSS allows me to see if this new line is cannibalizing other Frito-Lay brands—and I get the information in a matter of days, not weeks as was previously the case. I also have easy access to data showing our performance vs. competitive brands'. For Ruffles Light Potato Chips, I can determine the total sales from the previous week supermarket sales vs. smaller accounts, average sales on a particular route, and the success of our promotions. Most important, the data allows me to make midcourse corrections to ensure the success of the Light line.

Facilitates faster, more accurate decisions. Recently, I noticed red numbers (indicating reduced market share) for tortilla chips in our central business region. I punched up another screen display and located the problem: Texas. I kept punching up new screens and tracked the red numbers to a specific sales division and finally the chain of stores. The numbers pinpointed the problem area and, after additional research, revealed the culprit: the introduction of a generic store-branded product. We quickly formulated a counter-strategy and sales climbed again. Time invested: a couple of weeks. Before DSS, finding such a problem and correcting it took the better part of three months.

Through information technology, even cardboard cartons that were used to transport our products become a business opportunity. Last year, 88 percent of all cartons shipped to our distribution centers were returned by our sales force for reuse. If we push the percentage up a single point, it saves Frito-Lay $700,000. So, through DSS, we are now tracking cardboard returns by individual sales route and by store, and we hope to push returns above 90 percent.

Assists in "management by walking around." When Tom Peters coined that phrase he wasn't thinking of a computer tour of operations by the CEO. But that is what DSS allows me and other senior executives to do. I can, at a glance, view the performance of each of our managers and salespeople around the country. If I see something I don't like, I can fire off an electronic mail memo. Conversely, if there is a good news, I'm likely to contact the manager and congratulate him.

Helps us to decentralize. I never thought a computer would be responsible for a total reorganization of Frito-Lay, but it has been. Last year we decentralized, breaking the company into four geographic business areas, each with its own business plan, structure, and profit-and-loss responsibility. We did so because DSS, and the detailed information it provides allow middle managers to have a complete picture of what is happening in their regions. Now approximately 60 percent of the decisions that used to be made by top management are made by regional managers, leaving the decisions affecting the company as a whole at corporate headquarters.

As a result, top management can see within a few days which products are hot and which are not, enabling it to devise its strategy on the spot. But most important, DSS gives us the information we need—not what someone wants to give us after it has been massaged and sanitized. And we get it when we want it, which is usually immediately. While DSS currently operates through 200 terminals, it will reach 600 managers before fall, many of them via satellite transmission.

A note of caution, however: When incorporating an information technology system, do so step-by-step. Computers as a strategic marketing tool may still be unfamiliar to lower and middle management, and may require a breaking-in period. Let your people feel the impact of the system, so that, as additional programs are incorporated, the process will seem evolutionary. The results will be revolutionary.

STUDY QUESTIONS

1. What do you think of the Frito-Lay system?
2. Do you think there's a justified return on investment?
3. Project what might have been the problems in implementing the system—both technological and people-wise.
4. Would you expect there would be a heavy investment in training field managers?
5. Which parts of the system are the most significant and why?

Case Study

Ross Togs Department Stores

A prominent Midwest department store chain, Ross Togs, had employed operations research to help it consolidate its warehousing activities. The chain formerly supplied its retail outlets from three warehouses in the greater Chicago area. A series of changing conditions led management to consider that one warehouse could do the job in a more economical fashion and still maintain the desired delivery cycle.

An initial consideration was the addition of dock facilities necessary to handle the increased truck traffic. The additional facilities could be planned realistically if three factors were known—the number of trucks, their arrival time, and the time to service each truck. Economic considerations were also involved. Since the trucks were leased, waiting time had a definite cost associated with it. However, additional dock facilities, while cutting down waiting time, necessitated a considerable monetary investment. The problem of cost factors in economic conflict with each other and the waiting line principle is a classic case for the application of queuing theory. Here's the way the company went about solving the problem.

A study analyzed the existing traffic flow at the three warehouses, and the results were projected to that expected at a single warehouse. The study involved a sample seven-week period in the spring. The effect of seasonal variations was projected from the basic data, using historical company records. It was discovered that the number of trucks increased only 5 percent during the Christmas rush but the number of pieces handled increased 50 percent. In addition, truck servicing time was found to vary within certain bounds, depending on factors such as size of truck and type of merchandise. A service time pattern was found to be a combination of fixed time interval and a variable time interval dependent on the number of pieces being handled.

While the number of truck arrivals had certain patterns and frequencies (for example, an average of 105 trucks arrived in the morning, while 65 arrived in the afternoon), there was a chance relationship that precluded a simple arithmetic solution. In addition to the classical queuing theory solution, the company used the "Monte Carlo" method. (The name Monte Carlo implies the presence of chance.) Using the frequency distributions produced by the studies as boundaries, the Monte Carlo technique randomly selected a time of arrival and a service time for each of the arriving trucks. This is where the power of the computer comes into play. The computer simulates a day's operation by totaling the waiting time and length of queue of each truck serviced that day. The computer runs through a full year's operation using random numbers to simulate actual conditions while assuming a varying number of docks. These iterations are repeated to the point where computer output indicates to management the tradeoffs of waiting time and investment in new dock facilities. This then forms the basis for the most economical solution to the problem.

STUDY QUESTIONS

1. Do you think management would be convinced that computerized simulation and the Monte Carlo method helped them resolve the dock problem? Are there any potential pitfalls in the logic?

2. Can you see other opportunities for this type of approach to assist a company in decision making?

3. Compare this dock and truck model with a financial model that a company might employ. In which are there more variables and more assumptions?

4. Why aren't these types of approaches more prevalent in business?

SELECTED REFERENCES

Alter, S., *Decision Support Systems: Current Practice and Continuing Challenges.* Reading, Mass.: Addison-Wesley, 1980.

Beeby, Robert H., "How to Crunch a Bunch of Figures," *The Wall Street Journal*, June 11, 1990.

Keen, P. and M. S. Morton, *Decision Support Systems*. Reading, Mass.: Addison-Wesley, 1978.

Knowles, Thomas W., *Management Science Building and Using Models*. Homewood, Ill: Richard D. Irwin, 1989.

McClatchy, Will, "Executive Support," *Informationweek*, December 10, 1990, p. 66.

Nelson, Theron R., *The Management Science System*. Homewood, Ill.: Richard D. Irwin, 1988.

Oberstone, Joelee, *Management Science Concepts, Insights, and Applications*. New York: West, 1990.

Chapter 11

The Impact of IS on Management: Managing with Information

This is a key chapter of the book, since the foundation or fundamental premise is that tomorrow's managers must possess the capability to manage with information. Information will become *the* most valuable resource for decision making and for building competitive enterprises.

In the last chapter, making decisions based on mathematical models was covered, and the importance of understanding these types of systems was emphasized. This chapter broadens the use of information for management effectiveness. First, the environment in which managers will find themselves is explored. Alvin Toffler's "third wave" or "information age" will set the background for the twenty-first century manager. Then the management process is reviewed, as one perspective of this book is that understanding the role of management is a prerequisite to understanding how information can support that role. The management function is divided into the three general categories of administrative, leadership, and conceptual thinking. The use of information is discussed in each of these three areas.

It has been found that people at the management level (people at any level for that matter) have different cognitive styles; that is, they respond better to certain types of approaches than they do to others. Information systems must take this into account and develop multiple interfaces to systems which reflect this diversity. The chapter discusses this important factor.

The focus of the discussion is on the dual role of managers, not only as users of information systems to support their own management functions, but as leaders/supporters in introducing the right level of IS within the company. With the latter in mind, the chapter develops a set of guidelines for senior managers who want to establish the most dynamic IS environment within their company.

THE THIRD-WAVE: THE INFORMATION AGE

Alvin Toffler, in his provocative book *The Third Wave*, categorizes the development of a society into three waves. During the first wave, the agricultural age from 8000 B.C. to 1700 A.D., the majority of people worked the earth as farmers, living primarily off what they produced and trading or purchasing the few items they didn't produce or make themselves. The second wave, the industrial age, changed all that with the introduction of different forms of energy and machinery. The second wave brought with it bureaucracy and the hierarchical management style that still predominates: standardization, specialization, and synchronization; concentration, maximization, and centralization. Order, discipline, and assembly line mentality are the foundation of the second wave.

The third wave, the information age, beginning about 1950 with the advent of the computer, is built around four clusters of industries that Toffler thinks will be the backbone of what he calls the new technosphere:

1. *Electronics and computers* (the focus of this book).

2. *Space industries.* Toffler projects that we can accomplish things in space not possible on earth. For example, with no gravity in space, there is no need for containers, nor is there any problem in handling highly poisonous or reactive substances. TRW has identified 400 alloys we cannot manufacture on earth because of gravity.

3. *The oceans* will become the source of much-needed food, of minerals (silver, gold, zinc, copper) and of phosphate ores for land-based agriculture. We will have the aquavillage under the oceans and the floating factory in space.

4. *The biological industry.* Toffler feels this area could be the most important of all. Metal-hungry microbes will mine valuable trace metals from ocean water while genetic engineering will be employed to develop people, for example, with cow-like stomachs to digest grass and hay, thus alleviating the food shortage. We will use bacteria to turn sunlight into electromechanical energy and use microorganisms to eliminate the need for oil in plastics, paint, and so on. The cloning of mice and the test-tube conception of babies are actual examples of what is to follow.

The technosphere will be blended with the *infosphere*, which will have an equally profound effect on society. Information in the new infosphere will be demassified with the advent of more local newspapers, regional newscasts, the additional selectivity of cable TV and its myriad of channels, and personalized, computer-based information for business use. Toffler sees a shift away from second-wave temporal rhythms of working a prescribed shift to a more flexible, individually tailored work pattern and style. The epitome of this trend is the electronic cottage, where, because of home computers and terminal links to corporate and other data bases, activity can again center on the home as it did in the agriculture or first wave. The words are flexibility, diversity, and personalization, with the accent on flexible working hours, individually customized compensation packages, participative management, matrix management, and the like. Figure 11.1 illustrates the changes brought on by the third wave.

Toffler suggests that second-wave leaders today are like passengers on the *Titanic* squabbling for deck chairs—the dying order trying to hold on to their position and power while their world sinks under them. He points out that our institutions were designed in a pre-Marx, pre-Darwin, pre-Freud, and pre-Einstein era, and before the airplane, automobile, factory, computer, nuclear bomb, and birth control pill.

Third-wave managers feel IS can have a major influence on their decision making. They see an evolving innovative and highly individualistic management style being abetted by personalized executive decision support systems. They see computerized decision models to which they will supply parameters in the form of "what if" questions, with the model spilling out the results of various options, thus enabling executives to select from among them while adding the subjective and intuitive elements that only they can. The third-waver envisions the ability to personally browse through a data base for specific performance data and projection of future performance based on a variety of selective factors.

Third-wave managers are on-line executives in that their style is consistent with the personal use of an executive terminal. They see office automation in the broad sense—not only as a help to a secretary in typing memos and reports and communicating them electronically to predefined distribution lists—but also as a personal productivity tool. They

FIGURE 11.1. Shift in third-wave thinking

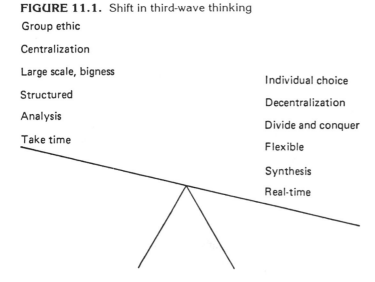

Group ethic

Centralization

Large scale, bigness

Structured

Analysis

Take time

Individual choice

Decentralization

Divide and conquer

Flexible

Synthesis

Real-time

are the electronically aided executives who run nearly paperless offices because their correspondence, departmental instructions, meeting schedules, and the like are computer produced through the use of electronic filing and communication systems.

They believe in a team management style in conjunction with IS. Their companies have organized around market segments or niches, wherein products and markets have been pinpointed and selected because of each company's particular expertise and desire to penetrate and dominate. No longer does competing across the board make sense. The successful companies are those that specialize in growing and profitable segments and subsegments of a specific marketplace. Third-wave management views decentralization as essential in achieving the necessary entrepreneurial thrust and motivation. This means that managers must control as much of the information flow and support for their departments as it logically makes sense to control. Highly defined and distinct market segments make this a viable approach. Third-wavers believe in carrying into the business world the political viewpoint that the government that governs best, governs least.

Finally, third-wave managers feel that IS will have a major impact on their future jobs, probably more than any other single force in their companies or in society. They sense that a manager who does not recognize this will probably be obsolete in five years. With this in mind, it behooves executives to be heavily involved in IS projects that affect their operations. Not only will they become involved when asked to, they will be taking greater leadership in directing the IS efforts. They see the impact on their jobs not just in the operation and control areas, but in the strategic area as well. Future third-wave managers will be on-line executives tapping their personal, as well as company and outside data bases, for information. They will need to have this capability to compete against companies whose executives operate in this mode.

All managers must act as change agents, understanding the trends of society, the culture of their companies, and their own proclivities and then metering third-wave thinking and techniques into their world. With this framework, let us take a look at the relative impact of IS on the various levels of management.

Figure 11.2 is an illustration of the management process as described by R. Alec MacKenzie ("The Management Process in 3-D," *Harvard Business Review,* November-December, 1969). Although this article was published some time ago, the basic management process has not changed a great deal and MacKenzie's analysis of the management process remains quite valid today. I am most impressed with the framework that MacKenzie has developed; and as I compared it with my own management role and those above and below me, I realized how much thought went into what appears to be a rather simple schematic. My purpose here is to explain the elements of the manager's job in enough depth to ascertain the effect that a management information system can have in helping managers carry out their job responsibilities.

Figure 11.2 indicates that the manager basically deals with three elements—ideas, things, and people. These elements are reflected in the tasks of:

Conceptual thinking, where one formulates new business ideas and opportunities.

Administration, where the details of the management process are handled.

Leadership, where people are motivated to accomplish business objectives.

FIGURE 11.2. The management process

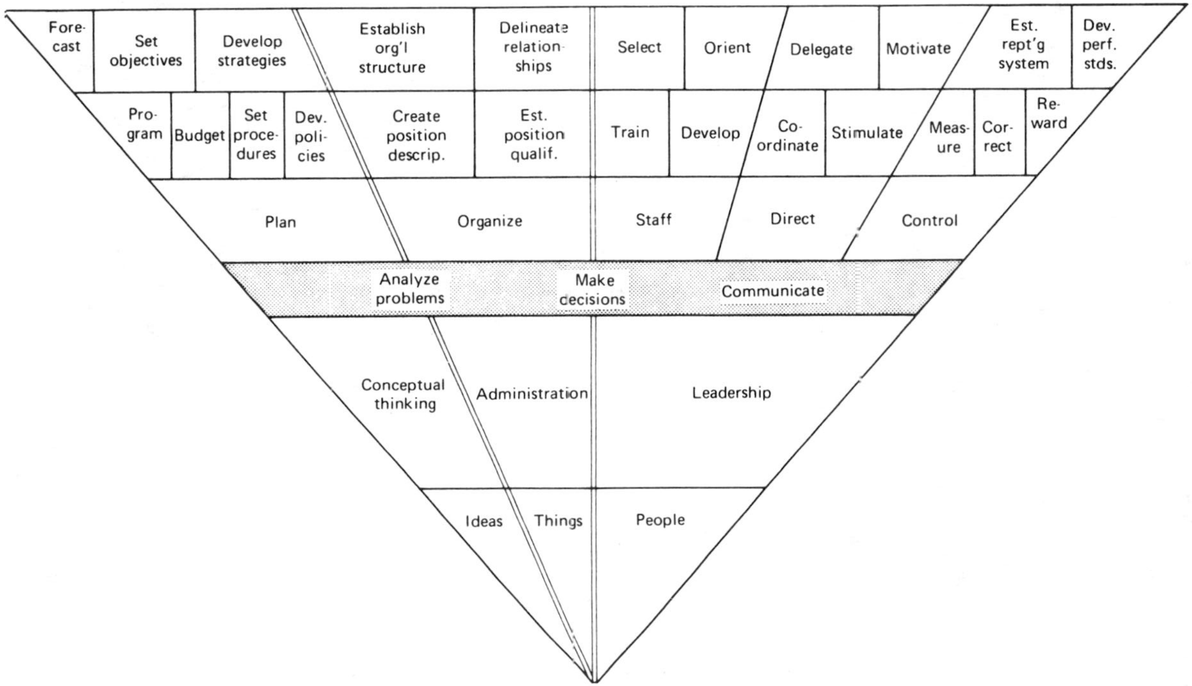

Analyzing problems, where facts are gathered and alternate solutions are evaluated.

Making decisions and *communicating* the decisions to the people who must implement them are termed *continuous functions,* for they occur repeatedly rather than sequentially throughout the management process.

The *sequential functions* consist of:

Planning, where a course of action is selected.

Organizing, where the work is arranged for accomplishing the plan.

Staffing, or the selection and allocation of the work to the people who will perform it.

Directing, the commencement of purposeful action on the work at hand.

Controlling, where the plan is carried out and satisfactorily completed.

The activities indicate what constitutes the five sequential functions of the management process. In order to develop a plan, one must:

Forecast, or determine the effect on future sales, costs, or profit.

Set objectives, the end results.

Develop strategies on how to achieve the end results.

Program, or establish a priority and sequence of the strategy.

Budget, or allocate resources.

Set procedures, or arrive at standardized methods.

Develop policies ensuring that rules and regulations exist to govern significant recurring matters.

An example might serve to bring the planning function into perspective. My experience as a planning manager in developing a product business plan follows the seven listed activities. In planning the introduction of a new item, a forecast of the future marketplace and impact of the product in the market are important starting points. Then, objectives such as desired market share and revenue and profit goals are established. The strategies for achieving these goals involve statements such as the following: We will go after new markets, we will offer the lowest-priced products, we will offer the best-quality product—or a combination thereof. The programming involved is to indicate which products with what features will be offered first and why. The budget for the project must be established at this point, and it must be consistent with what it will take to carry out the objectives and strategies, and yet it must not affect on-going programs to any great degree. The procedures and policies begin to blend into the organizing function because they involve statements stating, for example, that PERT will be used as a project control technique with monthly status reports prepared for top management.

The organizing function is more straightforward and, following the foregoing example, includes *establishing the organizational structure* for the production of the new product. If the product is to be produced by the existing line organization, this position is stated; or it may be that a new operational unit is organized to design and produce the new product. If a new organization is set up, top management must *delineate relationships* between the new and the existing structure and define communication and liaison points. The *creation of position descriptions* and the *establishment of position qualifications* will indicate whether the plan can be carried out by the existing organization or whether additional people with specifically required skills are needed.

This leads into the *staffing* function, where the qualified people for the required positions are selected; oriented to the plan objectives, strategies, policies, and so on; *trained* in the necessary tasks to be performed; and *developed* to the extent of making them feel a part of the company and the project on which they are working.

The *directing* function involves the steps that are normally associated with getting things done through people. These steps include *delegating,* or assigning responsibility and accountability; *motivating* to persuade and inspire; *coordinating* to ensure that the efforts of one group are consistent with the efforts of the others; and *stimulating change* when differences occur, conflicts arise, and it is necessary to resolve these differences before proceeding with the task.

The *control* function completes the cycle and involves the *establishment of a reporting system* that is consistent with the total reporting structure but that reflects pertinent milestones and progress against a schedule; the *development of performance standards*, to set the conditions that will determine whether the job is properly completed; a technique to *measure results* to ascertain whether the desired quality was attained and the extent of variance from the goal or standard; the taking of *corrective action* to get the task back on schedule and up to standard when deviations occur; and, finally, to *reward*, whether by recognition or remuneration for the accomplishment of the job and the meeting of goals.

Again, the message is that it's important to start with the things a manager does to ascertain the degree to which information systems can help him or her. It is important to avoid computerizing the insignificant or nonfunctions of the job; that is, to avoid helping the manager get to where he or she doesn't want to be faster than ever before.

THE BENEFIT/BENEFICIARY FRAMEWORK

Another framework that is close to that used by MacKenzie is the benefit/beneficiary matrix, as described in the book *The Information Imperative* by Gibson & Jackson. Figure 11.3 shows the categories of efficiency which, on a general scale, equate to administration; effectiveness, which is a combination of administration and leadership; and transformation, which is analogous to conceptual thinking.

The *x* axis indicates whether the particular system in question has impact on the individual, the functional unit in which he or she is engaged, or the total organization. Several examples will serve to show how this operates. In the upper left-hand box, the use of electronic mail by an executive is an example of using IS for individual efficiency—doing what was done before but faster. In the individual/effectiveness box, an example is the personal use of a spreadsheet to monitor a critical commodity process. An example of individual/transformation is the use of the personal "information lens" concept where the individual's interest profile has been analyzed such that any change to issues deemed critical

FIGURE 11.3. Benefit beneficiary matrix

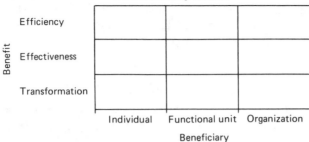

is transmitted from external data bases to the executive's PC in thirty-second intervals. Information applications in the other boxes have been discussed throughout the book.

While the big blockbuster applications are those aimed at enterprise-wide and functional unit effectiveness and transformation, much can be gained from application in the efficiency and individual areas. Normally a company needs a good balance involving activity throughout the matrix.

THE ELECTRONICALLY AIDED EXECUTIVE

We have divided management activities into three general categories: (1) administrative, (2) leadership, and (3) conceptual thinking. The first and second categories can be aided by electronic means as an extension of office automation; the third, by executive support systems and decision support systems as discussed in the last chapter. We now discuss these areas.

The first application in automating the office is usually word processing, and this is no surprise. Typewriting has been with us for decades, and word processing, which provides functions such as automatic paragraph insertion, simplified editing, spelling verification, and the like, is a natural extension. Also, there is a fairly well-defined cost/benefit resulting from either pooling the typing or increasing the productivity of typists. However, there is potentially a bigger payoff in automating the office—and that centers on automating the managers as well as the secretaries. As much as 30 percent of a manager's job can be spent on administrative matters, such as letters, memos, reports, expense accounts, meeting, travel, and telephone calls. If electronics can reduce the time it takes to carry out these administrative duties, it is obvious that more time can be spent on the conceptual thinking portion of the job, where the real payoff is.

Figure 11.4 builds in stages the accoutrements of the electronically aided executive. The terminal device can be used either directly by the executive or by a secretary or aide. The first stage is to be able to write letters and memos and store them on electronic media. The terminal can be a typewriter, a dictating device linked to a telephone line; or even, in the future, voice messages electronically interpreted directly into electronic storage, thus bypassing the typing or keying by an intermediate. Because of communications lines and networks, the origination point can be any site where a communication linkage exists. Thus, executives are freed from their offices. They can initiate memos or letters from home, the

FIGURE 11.4. Electronic administration

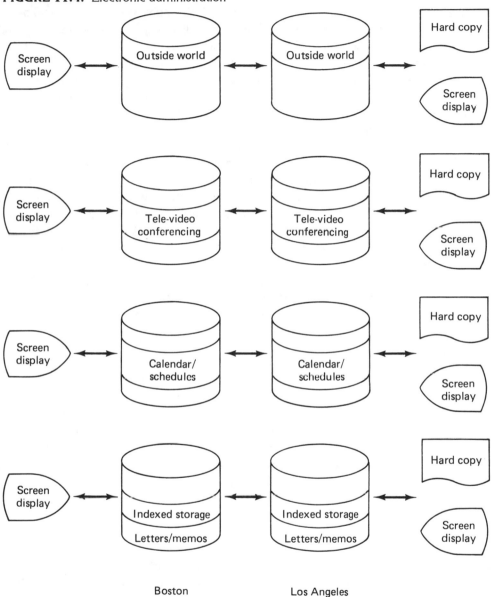

Boston   Los Angeles

airport, or a hotel room. The inputted data are transmitted to a personal file, where they can be accessed by a secretary for further processing or can be sent directly to individuals at various destination points. Figure 11.4 shows that the executive's office is in Boston, where she is communicating with executives in Los Angeles. She sends a memo to the electronic file of a Los Angeles executive, who can receive it either on a PC screen or on a hard-copy printer. Fax machines can also be used to augment electronic mail and voice mail.

Letters and reports are maintained in indexed storage for retrieval at a later date. The key element is a proper indexing system, usually involving cross-indexing so that the executive can retrieve, for example, the Jones letter, or the letter on chemical waste, or the letter written last Wednesday. The file can include graphic material, voice messages and digitized pictures, and illustrations. Thus, the executive begins to build an electronic file system that can be accessed directly via a communication link.

The next stage of automating the executive is the addition of personal calendar and schedule processing. A personal time calendar is maintained on the file with meetings, appointments, and the like noted. The executive's subordinates, peers, and superiors do the same. It is akin to a schedule board in a sales office; in this case, however, the schedule board is electronic and can be changed or updated on-line from the home, the airport, or the hotel room. Reminders, memory joggers, and the like can be part of the file. It works this way. You want to call a meeting of the plant steering committee on July 8 from 1 to 3 P.M. The personal files of those on the steering committee are checked for availability, the appropriate meeting room for the size of the steering committee group is selected and reserved, and a list of the preparatory materials necessary for the meeting is indicated. Once the meeting is scheduled, the personal calendars of each of the participants would also be reserved.

At this point a particular management style and work ethic come into play. A workaholic executive can have a field day with this type of system. He has an idea at 3 A.M. and has orders in Jones' file when Jones arrives at 8:30 A.M. that day. He can easily stay in the act while traveling or on vacation. This can be both positive and negative. The real benefit, as always, comes from judicious use of the new media. When one realizes how long it takes to personally contact six people (telephone call, executive out of town, secretary at lunch, and so on), the productivity benefits of this type of communication are evident.

Stage 3 of Figure 11.4 adds teleconferencing and videoconferencing to the electronically aided executive's array of tools. Many companies now have teleconferencing rooms for "many-to-many" communication to and from remote locations. A meeting is convened in Boston, but there are neck microphones and an audio link so that voices can travel to and from the Los Angeles area where the other half of the meeting attendees reside. Charts and other visual exhibits can be transmitted and displayed when necessary to clarify a point. Also, access to electronic files can be made. Though this form of communication may not be as effective as face to face, it saves so much time and cost that it becomes a viable substitute in many instances.

Optical fiber and satellite transmission are making videoconferencing a cost-effective medium. Whether tele- or videoconferencing, it is apparent that productivity of the executives can be increased dramatically by the reduction of travel and the ability to hold meetings without the delay of travel. It is a particularly effective medium with the rise of global companies and global business.

The final stage of Figure 11.4 adds the outside world to the electronic file. This extends the effectiveness of the system, since, for example, market data bases or competitive market share statistics from data service companies can be accessed. Executives can also add their personal files to the media, thus maintaining bank accounts, assets, stock records, reminders of birthdays, physical exams, and the like. This is an alternate to having a personal computer in the home. The privacy of this data could be maintained by having a special password for access to this portion of the file.

It is interesting to speculate on the ramifications of this mode of operation—aside from the obvious productivity improvements and the impact on work style, motivation, and the work ethic. Currently, the office is the locus for the executives. They spend perhaps the majority of their working hours there. They write, phone, meet people, read, look up things in files, and so on. But if the scenario described here comes to pass, the locus can change to wherever there is terminal access—and this could almost be anywhere. We not only have the paperless office, we also have the officeless office. We have removed the geographical boundaries of where business can be conducted and begin to see why Toffler's electronic cottage becomes a reality.

The electronic cottage is a metaphor for being able to work from your home because of all the electronic hook-ups from your PC to the computers of your company, supplier, and customer. This concept can broadened to include the hotel room, the automobile, and the airplane, because of laptop or note pad PCs and the further reaching out of communication networks.

EXECUTIVE SUPPORT SYSTEMS

The time is 2:15 P.M.

A senior executive has just taken a call from a client who's confirming delivery of a major order. While she speaks, the executive touches the screen of her computer terminal to bring up the status information she needs. Seeing a delay in production, she assures her client that the order will be sent on schedule and calls the production manager to expedite the delivery and discuss the delay. What she hears convinces her that a meeting of certain executives is in order.

Using her keyboard, she types a short message calling a meeting in 35 minutes— and with two touches the message has been distributed to eight colleagues.

At 3:00 P.M. the executive opens the meeting by explaining the need to solve the production bottleneck before orders are lost. Heads turn as a large screen at the side of the room lights up, changing as the executive touches a computer terminal to create data and colorful graphics that appear instantly on the large screen display. Computer terminals rise out of the conference table in front of the executives...and they begin to enter data. Potential solutions are immediately displayed on the large screen. After a short discussion by the executives, the ideas are revised, ranked, and narrowed to two approaches, which all approve. The executives receive a printout of the final data as they leave. It is now 3:52 P.M. as the plan is put in action.

This is from a report by the University of Georgia Executive 2000 Project where a fully-functional, electronic boardroom has been created to demonstrate the advanced uses of executive support systems, as well as to collaborate with support systems and electronic presentation systems. The project shows, as in the foregoing example, how executives can use information, not only to see past results and performance, but also to make business decisions in a fraction of the time it would take without electronic support. Studies have shown that executives spend over half their time in meetings. Even a small savings of meeting time can free up significant executive power.

Right off there is a definition issue in describing a term as broad as *executive support systems* (ESS). First, the term *executive* normally refers to the most senior or top management of a company. In the context of ESS, the term usually includes other levels of management at the middle and operation level. Thus, ESS can be focused at senior management, at lower levels, or at all levels. Generally speaking, however, the major thrust is at one of the two higher levels.

The term *support systems* also has implications. Earlier, three general categories of management responsibilities were described: administrative, leadership, and conceptual thinking. ESS normally does not center on administrative functions (i.e., e-mail, scheduling), although these can be integrated into the ESS. ESS mainly centers on duties within the leadership function, particularly those involved in controlling (measuring, reporting, correcting) and directing (coordinating, delegating, stimulating). The decision support systems described in the previous chapter provide support in the conceptual thinking area (forecasting, developing policies and strategies), but certain ESS designs can incorporate elements of conceptual thinking as well. For example, business models based on past history, external events, and future indicators can be used to forecast potential strategies.

The ESS Model

Figure 11.5 indicates a general model of an ESS. The voluminous by-product data from all the company's transactions—be they sales, vendor orders, production lots, inventories, or the like—are captured. Management is interested only in summaries and various compilations of these data, such that, at prescribed times, these data are extracted from the transaction files into a format that facilitates the development of management reports. Similarly, outside data emanating from data sources such as Dow Jones and Reuters are captured and extracted into the summaries required by management. Most of the ESS software systems on the market have what may be termed a *management lens*. This translates the data into meaningful management formats as prescribed by the executives using the system. The information is then passed onto the executive screens. As mentioned, the administrative systems, including e-mail and the like, can be integrated into the system as well, via the management lens.

FIGURE 11.5. Model of a ESS

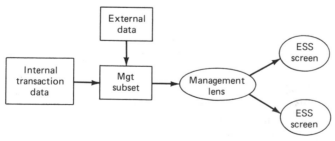

Defining ESS Needs

Management has had problems with information over the years. The information age has in many cases accentuated the situation. Managers complain on one hand of not having enough information or the right kind of information. On the other hand, they bemoan the glut or surfeit of information. They receive reams of performance data when what they want are summaries and variance reports. In many situations this is not directly a result of the technology, but the result of the people responsible for IS just not systematically asking about and analyzing the information needs of management. The technology is present to produce reports or ad hoc information in a variety of tabular, graphical, or other multimedia formats. The key issue remains the content.

The concept of critical success factors (CSFs) has already been explained. It is particularly applicable to defining the information needs of management. Figure 11.6 establishes a framework for the CSF process.

The process usually begins at the level of the CEO and his or her direct reports. Individual CSFs are developed, those five to seven areas where outstanding performance is absolutely necessary to achieve one's stated goals. Then, through various interactions with the corporate staff, the individual CSFs are analyzed to form the CSF set for the organization. This is a very important step, and involves serious discussion, because consensus as to what drives the business is a vital underpinning for any ESS.

The next step is to develop the measures that will track the CSFs to see that they are being followed and met. Once these measures are determined, the ESS design begins to locate, or create if they are not available, the data bases that contain the information. The design of the ESS then proceeds to develop the reports that provide the measures to track the CSFs. This process is repeated for as many levels as desired, but the other management-level CSFs and their measures must be consistent and supportive of the corporate CSF set. The CSF process is a unifying force that focuses the entire corporation on common goals

FIGURE 11.6. Using CSFs to define ESS needs

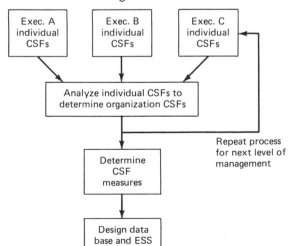

and objectives. The ESS supports the process. Most importantly, it ensures a top-down implementation, and this is one area that demands it. Many failures of ESS can be traced to improper attention to using executive needs as the mandatory front end. It is obvious that top management support is the sine qua non of ESS. It must be more than a commitment, however; it must include involvement. Most successful systems have management champions who drive and influence others by their example to spend the time to learn and use a system. In the case of ESS, the champion is the CEO.

THE CSF DISCOVERY PROCESS

One way to determine individual CSFs is via a structured survey form. The interview form in Figure 11.7 has been used for this purpose. The form can be completed in private, or an interview process can be utilized.

The interview process should, in general, answer the following seven questions:

1. Who are you?
2. What do you do?
3. What is important to be successful?
4. What information do you need?
5. What difficulties do you have obtaining it?
6. What would be the benefits if you had it?
7. What information do you expect to need in the future?

A questionnaire consisting of 14 questions has been found effective in gathering the type of information required. Figure 11.7 is a sample interview using this set of questions. The questionnaire has been developed so that the information can be synthesized at the conclusion of all the interviews. The example is a second-level manager, the central operations sales director.

THE CONTENT OF EXECUTIVE SUPPORT SYSTEMS

Computerworld published the results of an intensive study of ESS users. The study mostly reported on users who were employing packaged ESS solutions from three major suppliers, Comshare Inc, Pilot Executive Software, and Execucom Systems Corp. The prices of these packages range from $100,000 to $200,000, and all offer software that provides excellent color graphics; easy-to-use menus (some employ touch screens) that allow access to data bases (both internal and external to the organization) for retrieving various levels of detailed information about operating results and for showing exception reports and analyzing trends.

There are also PC-based systems that sell for as little as $595, but these are far more limited than those from the three companies mentioned. Home-grown systems can be produced using enhanced versions of spreadsheet packages or powerful 4GLs and relational

FIGURE 11.7. Information planning questionnaire

INTERVIEWEE: Ralph Jones   INTERVIEWER: Bob Harper
JOB TITLE: Sales Director   RECORDER: Harry Benson
JOB FUNCTION: Manage Central   DATE: 10/28/91

Division Sales Operation—30 Salespersons

JOB FUNCTION/EXPERIENCE

1. *Principal Job Responsibilities, Place in Organization*
   Has 30 salespeople covering the eastern states. Also responsible for sales support, administration, and entering of orders. Goaled on basis of bookings, revenue, and shipments. Reports to sales VP who has responsibility for overall sales and support of US. He, in turn, reports to the CEO of the company. The product is numerically controlled machine tools.

2. *What Are Your Job Goals?*
   Must meet yearly quota for bookings, revenue, and shipments. Must also stay within expense budget. Also expected to do a certain amount of long-range planning with customers and to provide support in the way of education and training.

3. *Time with Company, Years/Experience in Current Job*
   Has been in sales 20 years, has been a salesman or sales manager all working career. Ten years of the 20 have been spent with industrial products. Started as junior salesman and worked way up to senior account representative and then manager. Has had current job for 3 years. No staff experience.

4. *Experience with Data Processing, Computers, IS People*
   No experience in IS. Took no courses in school and has scant knowledge. Took one three-day course 5 years ago. Has seen IS evolve but feels he doesn't have time to get involved. Has little or no contact with IS people. Sometimes calls when a report is late but otherwise doesn't get involved. Several years ago, he was contacted by an IS systems analyst who was going to install a terminal in the office for on-line reports. However, with organizational change, this project was delayed twice and never got off the ground.

5. *Critical Success Factors (few areas where, if things went well and results were there, the business and you would succeed)*
   A. Must keep about 10 key accounts that constitute about 50 percent of the business and maintain their growth.
   B. Must keep good salespeople. Turnover is high and competition for people is rampant in the industry.
   C. Must get share of emerging markets. New name business is important for remainder of 50 percent. Must target accounts and obtain prospects.
   D. Must meet yearly goals and know how he's doing at specific time of the year.
   E. Must maintain strong education group and see that accounts are well trained.

6. *What Information Do You Need to Support Your CSFs?*
   A. On key accounts, must know installed value of equipment, on order, projected activity, probability of close and when, competitive actions, etc.
   B. Turnover rates not really helped by information. It is a motivation, management concern.
   C. Needs help here but is not getting it. Needs prospect lists, opportunity list by company size, number of employees, etc.

FIGURE 11.7. (continued)

D. Information critical. Must be up to date so he can answer questions raised by boss and boss's boss.

E. Doesn't see much here though report by account listing education taken and status could be useful.

PROBLEM IDENTIFICATION & PRIORITY

7. *What Problems Do You Have in Getting this Information?*

A. Account information is nonexistent. Does not have a good reliable inventory of customer equipment. The only way he knows about prospective activity is to call individual salespeople of sales managers. It's sometimes embarrassing when he gets calls from important staff people at the home office.

B. No reports on turnover. Does receive listings of salespeople; their goals and actual against goals on a quarterly basis.

C. Thinks that competitors have Dun & Bradstreet file analysis to the extent that salespeople can call on specific prospects that are suspects because of specific size and business parameters. His group makes cold calls, which are expensive and frustrating to the salespeople. Also could use direct mail advertising or lead into new customers.

D. Big shift to measure, not only by account and salespeople, but also by product. Company is becoming product oriented but reporting and measurement are very rudimentary. Must produce product cut on a manual basis—is expensive to do and is too late.

E. Doesn't see a problem. We usually know where we stand. Other—Needs forecasting system. The boss asks how the year will be and it's embarrassing because we can only give gross or estimate that has little to back it up.

8. *Of the Problems Identified, Prioritize Items on a Scale of 1 to 7 (with 7 highest).*

	You	*Boss*	*Boss's Boss*
A. Account info	7	7	7
B. Turnover reports	2	2	3
C. Prospect info	6	4	4
D. Product performance reporting	7	7	7
E. Education data	2	2	2
F. Other forecasting	4	6	7

For Each of the Problems, What Benefit Would You Attribute to Their Resolution?

A. Account info

Good reporting system could save one administrative person. Possibly could increase revenue 5 to 50 percent from these accounts—would know where to concentrate.

B. Turnover reports

Useful but we have a feel for this without formal reports.

C. Prospect info

Really a must. If we are to stay in business and grow, the business must have new accounts. Could get 5 percent more market share with good system. Improve sales productivity 20 percent.

D. Product performance reporting

Though profitability isn't a direct goal, it is vital to the company. Selling better margin items is essential for good bottom-line results. Also sees goaling changing to key off products.

FIGURE 11.7. (continued)

    E. Education data
       Will help but can't quantify.
    F. Other forecasting
       Have doubts about how this could be developed—but if it could, could have major impact, though hard to quantify.

10. *In Your Opinion, Describe the Degree of Difficulty in Resolving Each Problem.*
    A & B should be easy; C requires outside information and this may present a problem but other companies are doing it. D & E should present no problems but thinks forecasting is high risk because the company doesn't know how to do it.

11. *In Your Opinion What Role Could Be Played by You, Your Boss, Corporate, and IS in the Solution to the Problems?*
    IS has to take leadership; will spend time if it's specific but his job is to motivate and manage salespeople and sales managers. However, because of the potential benefit of some of the solutions, quite possibly people will have to get more involved.

FUTURE INFORMATION NEEDS
12. *What Changes Do You Foresee in Information Technology that Could Alter the Way You Do Business?*
    On-line systems where reports could be processed at the press of a button. Spend an inordinate time in paperwork and administrative matters in lieu of direct selling. Needs information data base to keep home office off the back of sales.

13. *Focus on the Future and Try to Project Information Needs in that Time Frame.*
    With rate of change in industry (CAD/CAM and robotics), it's hard to foresee the future and what might be the makeup of the business. Know they need more competitive data and data on prospects so that they can maintain and improve market share. Needs data quickly in order to respond and get the competitive edge. Also needs to reduce lead time from order to shipment.

14. *What Would You Like to See Happen as a Result of this Interview Process?*
    Appreciates opportunity to talk and to express his needs—no one really asked before. Doesn't expect miracle overnight and frankly has been skeptical of IS but maybe this is first step in improving things. If so, he is all for it.

---

data bases. One important caveat that is often overlooked is that the cost of the software package does not include the time to assess executive needs, the time to agree on the type of information that will drive the firm, and the time to computerize the data if it is not in the form required by the package or if it is not in electronic form to begin with. These factors are why some of the respondents to this study (more than a few) reported the cost to get their ESS up and running from $500,000 to over $1,000,000.

    The *Computerworld* study indicated the following as the most common applications within ESS:

    Financial: The executive may monitor profitability, analyze expenses, or look at the breakdown of revenue—whether by region, corporate division, department, or product.

Marketing: The system may display market share, demographic makeup of the customer base, and product popularity in various geographic regions.

Operational: The executive may view productivity variation across a number of plants, how the actual production rate compares with the plan, and how a strike would affect productivity.

Human resources: May include executive succession planning, number of employees that fit into certain categories according to their skills and experience, actual head count versus planned head count, and background information on individual employees.

Competitive: May include news stories regarding the competitors' financial performance and product mix.

External factors: Executives may want on-line access to interest rates, government regulations, indicators of the general economy, and industry trends.

Any of these applications can also be viewed simultaneously; for instance, executives can look at head count versus financial performance, or internal versus external factors.

ESS OUTPUT REPORTS

The following illustrates a few of the more common outputs of ESS. Three of the most prominent uses are drill-down, trend analysis, and exception reporting. The system's main menu looks something like Figure 11.8. The upper right and upper middle buttons are for external information from outside data bases. The upper left displays results information that has been defined as critical by the senior executives, those indices by which performance is measured. The lower left and lower right tie in the administrative functions of mail and schedules on a single screen. The lower middle button produces reports, highlighting areas that exceed a predetermined number, either positive or negative. The exceptions are usually color coded so that they are immediately visible to the executive.

Figures 11.9 and 11.10 illustrate the drill-down capability. Figure 11.9 shows, by its four divisions, a company's budget statement compared with forecast. Touching the screen on the proper line or clicking a mouse on the line will drill down into the next level of detail, in this case showing which products are responsible for the variance for Division 1. Further drill-down could highlight detail on any of the four products.

Figure 11.11 shows a sales trend based on results for the first three months of the year. This information, or similar information, can be displayed in graphic form in a variety of ways. Exception reports can be developed to appear at the touch of a button. Color codes can be used; for example, you may have instructed the system to code positive results from the plan in green and negative results in red, with anything over 10 percent negative in yellow. That way a quick scan of successive reports will immediately highlight the areas on which you will want further information or where you want to take immediate action. Figure 11.12 shows a multimedia display of numeric as well as graphic display of the same information. There are a multitude of different types of reports and representations of the information, but drill-down, exception reporting, and trends are the principal types.

This, then, is the substance of ESS. Such tools are very important, in fact, they

FIGURE 11.8. Main menu (From the Comshare Commander Executive Information Brochure, Comshare, Ann Arbor, Michigan.)

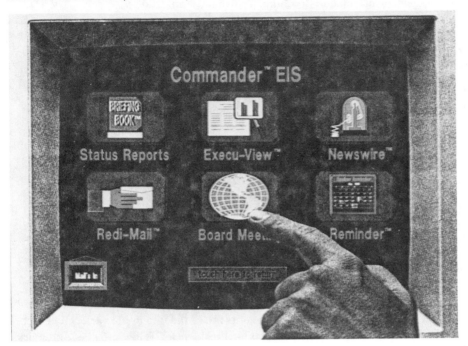

FIGURE 11.9. Drill-down by division (From the Comshare Commander Executive Information Brochure, Comshare, Ann Arbor, Michigan.)

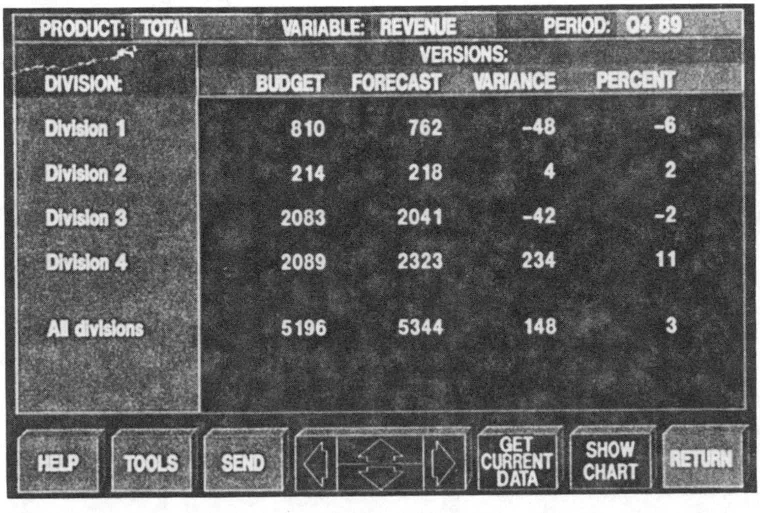

PRODUCT: TOTAL	VARIABLE: REVENUE		PERIOD: Q4 89	
	VERSIONS:			
DIVISION:	BUDGET	FORECAST	VARIANCE	PERCENT
Division 1	810	762	−48	−6
Division 2	214	218	4	2
Division 3	2083	2041	−42	−2
Division 4	2089	2323	234	11
All divisions	5196	5344	148	3

HELP | TOOLS | SEND | ◁ ⬍ ▷ | GET CURRENT DATA | SHOW CHART | RETURN

FIGURE 11.10. Drill-down by product (From the Comshare Commander Executive Information Brochure, Comshare, Ann Arbor, Michigan.)

DIVISION: DIVISION 1	VARIABLE: REVENUE		PERIOD: Q4 89	
	VERSIONS:			
PRODUCT:	BUDGET	FORECAST	VARIANCE	PERCENT
Product A	189	185	-4	-2
Product B	150	151	1	1
Product C	352	304	-48	-14
Product D	119	122	3	3
TOTAL	810	762	-48	-6

| HELP | TOOLS | SEND | | GET CURRENT DATA | SHOW CHART | RETURN |

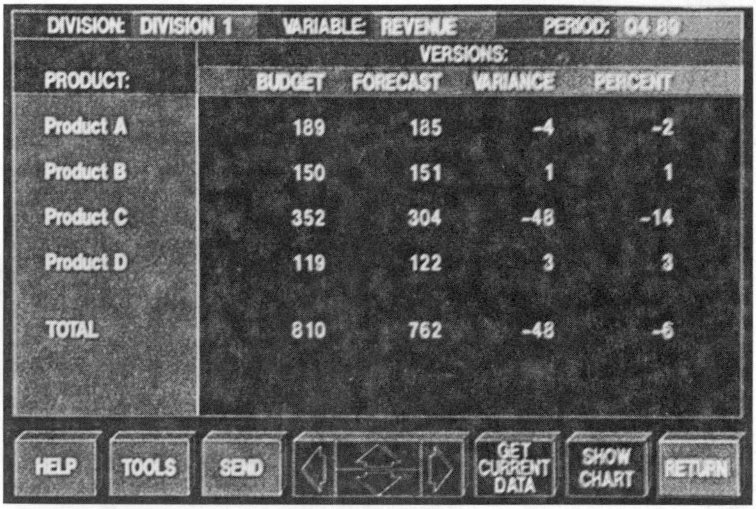

represent the essence of this chapter—managing with information. Here is one area that demands top management's attention. The benefits are of the intangible variety, but there is no doubt that they are present. William Glavin, President of Babson College, remarked when he was vice chairman of Xerox:

> A key to the success of the Executive Support System has been its usefulness. The last thing in the world that I need in my office is a piece of hardware that does not help

FIGURE 11.11. Trend chart (From the Comshare Commander Executive Information Brochure, Comshare, Ann Arbor, Michigan.)

VERSION Act/Fcst	LINE ITEM Sales		REGION U.S.	
	TIME PERIOD			
DIVISION	January	February	March	
Avionics	27.67	37.19	36.40	42.48
Fuel Tanks	11.29	13.30	13.74	15.24
Hydraulics	10.98	12.17	10.03	10.10
Landing Gear	20.09	18.21	21.46	21.29
Axles	10.92	10.15	6.91	5.32
Bearings	27.02	28.38	30.34	31.90

| HELP | TOOLS | SEND | | GET CURRENT DATA | SHOW CHART | RETURN |

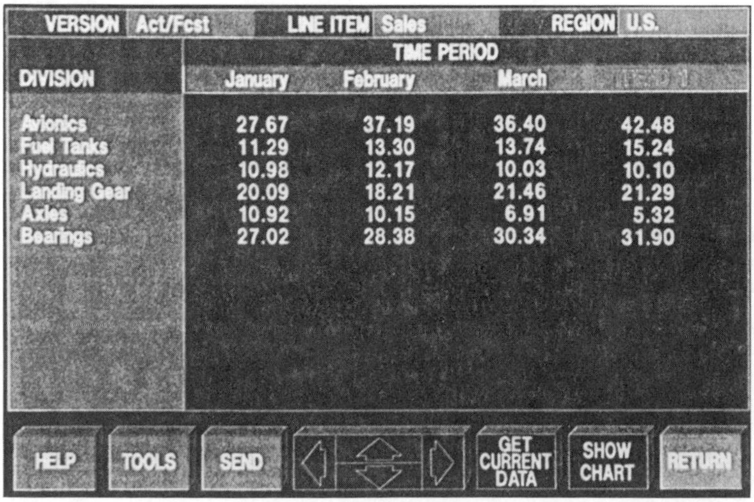

FIGURE 11.12. Multimedia display (From the Comshare Commander Executive Information Brochure, Comshare, Ann Arbor, Michigan.)

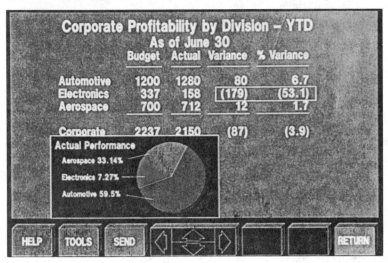

me manage more effectively. Technology for the sake of technology is both unneeded and unwanted. The Executive Support System is neither. It provides me with easy access to the corporate management data base.

The system is embedded in the business process of our senior management and is an integral part of our business planning process and our operations reviews. Frankly, the Executive Support System is so ingrained in the way we manage the business that it's difficult to imagine life without it. (From Executive Support Systems, Rockart & DeLong, Homewood, Ill.: Irwin, 1988.)

All of the above analyses have focused on historical and current data. ESSs also have the ability to incorporate the "future" using the decision support techniques described in the previous chapter. "What if" projections can be used to project year-end results based on the extrapolation of performance to date or based on external factors such as forecasted share of market and future price structures. While producing a common set of performance indicators shared by the management team can be extremely effective in focusing attention and action, the development of future scenarios based on models and "what if" analyses can be of even greater value. It is like comparing benefits in the "effectiveness" category with those in the "transformation" category. The latter, when purposely analyzed and acted on, are the blockbusters that can give the company competitive advantage.

MANAGEMENT AND COGNITIVE STYLE

There is an ongoing debate whether senior executives should or need be direct users of information systems, that is, have a PC in the office for personal use. It is true that voice recognition devices and touch screens are making it feasible to avoid using the typewriter keyboard, but there is still the question of whether this is the best use of executive time. The question remains, Would it be better use of time to delegate the actual communication with the computer to an assistant? The conclusion here is that that decision depends on the management and cognitive style of the executive.

Most CEOs or senior managers, now in their late forties or fifties rarely took information systems courses during their college years or personally performed word processing or spreadsheet analysis. What they have learned has been acquired on the job or through a variety of continuing education programs. The important thing was that computers were not a normal embedded process; as is the case with more recent graduates, it was a tacked-on capability.

Whether direct users or not, the important thing is that managers must understand IS well enough to act as overseers of the employment of IS in the major functions of the business that they manage. It is the individual's management style or cognitive set that dictates whether he or she will be comfortable using a PC. There are left-brain managers (structure/analytical) and right-brain (intuitive) managers and there will always be. The latter may still be leery about the direct use of a PC, even though they may have even been introduced to them early in their business life.

Assessing Management Style

This assessment is an important first step since business managers operate in a variety of ways.

Henry Mintzberg, a well-known pragmatic management researcher, challenges the common view of managers as reflective, regulated, rational, and scientific professionals. Rather, he emphatically describes what management is really all about:

> The facts show the manager works at a relentless pace. His activities are characterized by brevity, variety and discontinuity. He is strongly oriented to action and dislikes reflective activities.

Mintzberg says that if there is a single characteristic in the practice of management, it is that:

> The pressures of his job drive the manager to be superficial in his actions—to overload himself with work, encourage interruptions, respond quickly to every stimulus, seek the tangible and avoid the abstract, make decisions in small increments and do everything abruptly.

John Rockart of MIT describes the antithesis of the Mintzberg model in relating the work style of Ben Heineman, then president and CEO of Northwest Industries.

> Northwest's Executive Information System with its extensive and continually growing data base is now used by almost all managers and executives at corporate headquarters to perform their monitoring and analytic functions. But the driving force behind the system and its most significant user remains Heineman. Working with the system is an everyday thing for him, a natural part of his job. With his special

knowledge of the business and with his newly acquired ability to write his own programs, Heineman sees great value in working at a terminal himself rather than handing all assignments to staff personnel.

"There is a huge advantage to the CEO to get his hands dirty in the data," he says, "because the answers to many significant questions are found in the detail. The system provides me with an improved ability to ask the right questions and to know the wrong answers." What is more, he finds a comparable advantage in having instant access to the data base to try out an idea he might have. In fact, he has a computer terminal at home and takes another with him on vacations.

With these two models in mind, it is wise to determine your management style and that of other managers contemplating ESS—is it more the Mintzberg model or the Heineman model? This will prove a crucial factor in how and for whom the ESS is designed and implemented.

Assessing Cognitive Style

In addition, research indicates that humans have different cognitive styles, "intelligences," with different parts of the brain controlling different abilities. For example, we are so constituted that some of us learn better from pictures than from words.

Howard Gardner suggests there are six intelligences—linguistic, musical, logical-mathematical, spatial, bodily-kinesthetic, and personal. Drawing on Gardner's work, Theodore Reid and Richard Dooley note that poets, writers, and public speakers have exceptional linguistic skills; composers, conductors, and musical performers have exceptional musical skills; engineers, mathematicians, and computer programmers have exceptional logical-mathematical skills; artists, sculptors, and architects have exceptional spatial skills; while athletes, mimes, and dancers have exceptional bodily-kinesthetic skills. The sixth ability, personal intelligence, allows one to be in touch with one's own internal feelings as well as to notice and distinguish motivations and intentions in others. Those occupations where personal skills are important cover a wide gamut, but include diplomats, sales professionals, labor negotiators—and business executives.

Dr. Reid correlates types of intelligence and effective computer-learning techniques. He claims that the logical-mathematical and the musical do best with programmed instruction; the linguistic, with written documentation; the spatial, where the overall picture is shared first and the various tasks overviewed; the bodily-kinesthetic with a hands-on, do-it-yourself, trial-and-error approach. Those with personal intelligence—most of the CEOs by the way—will learn more effectively with personal, individual, one-on-one instruction. While this is an oversimplification and it is apparent that most of us have more than one intelligence, the theory does seem to hold up in practice.

Though the business schools of our country may be turning out progressively more Ben Heineman's with enhanced logical-mathematical intelligence, experience finds Mintzberg-model executives with strong personal skills still a dominant model. As with management style, establishing the dominant intelligence mode of an executive can be very valuable to the approach used in the selling and training of either administrative, leadership, or conceptual-thinking information systems.

THE ROLE OF SENIOR MANAGEMENT IN IS

The previous section discussed computer literacy—defined as the ability directly to employ PCs in your work and to possess the requisite hardware and software knowledge to do so.

Of greater importance is information literacy—the facility to recognize that information is an asset and a strategic commodity to a company. Executives must also realize the cost and energy that must be expended to capture, store, maintain, and communicate that information throughout the organization. They must have an "information perspective" to know when an information demand should be handled within minutes and when it's going to take years. (They must be able to distinguish the trivial from the blockbuster.) They must know that they have to play a part in being able to use information strategically. And they must set priorities, place some sort of value on the information requested, and be able to specify what they and the company need in the way of IS.

Experience indicates that senior management has some or all of the following concerns or questions about information systems:

- Is the technology running away with us?
- Are we spending too much or too little?
- What return on investment are we getting or should we be getting?
- How should we measure the return?
- Is my IS director qualified to meter the technology to best support the company?
- How does our IS function compare with those of competition?
- Do we have a comprehensive long-range direction and strategy?
- Are we treating information as a resource?
- Do our senior managers use information systems?
- Can I use information systems to greater strategic advantage?
- What should be my knowledge/involvement level?
- Am I part of the problem or part of the solution?

A common belief is that the CEO and senior management are less informed about the IS function than any other major function in the business. If, indeed, information is viewed as a resource at least as valuable as the other resources of the business—cash, inventory, people, and facilities—then there is solid rationale for increased understanding and involvement.

The senior management team is placing the IS executive in a most precarious position. Turnover has accelerated in the IS profession to where the tenure in these high-burn-out positions is three to four years or less. This is not a healthy situation. More and more top management is filling the job with proven managers rather than proven technicians. While there is much to be done on the part of IS executives to improve the perception of their service, the CEO must also play a major role, first by a better understanding of the IS function and then by the top office involvement with and the backing and support of the IS executive and the information systems he or she produces.

THE PAYOFF FROM TOP MANAGEMENT INVOLVEMENT

There is a lack of solid research into the correlation of top management involvement and IS success, though conventional wisdom certainly supports the correlation. It is for this reason that I was impressed with the research conducted by Professor William J. Doll and reported in *MIS Quarterly*.

Doll studied 33 firms and characterized them as having successful or unsuccessful IS based on a 6-criteria, 37-question survey aimed at evaluating the results of application development. A high value was placed on completing projects that met design and benefit objectives, were delivered on time and within budget, were adaptable to changing management needs, and were developed in a rational sequence based on expected payoff potential and probability of success.

Then both IS directors and CEOs were interviewed using a structured question set. It was found that in firms with successful IS, top management made more effective use of the following four processes:

Yes to:	Firms with Unsuccessful IS Development	Firms with Successful IS Development
Executive Steering Committee Do you have a system policy committee, comprised of managers from functional areas of the organization, involved in setting priorities and/or allocating resources for systems development?	23.1%	55.0%
Written Plans Do you have a written overall plan for systems development which (1) covers all major functional areas of the business, and (2) clarifies inter-relationships between applications (systems)?	23.1%	60.0%
Development Priorities Do you and higher level management have a mutually agreed upon set of criteria for deciding which applications (systems) to implement first?	46.2%	90.0%
Funding Committee Has top management made a long-term commitment to provide stable funding for system development activity?	38.5%	70.0%

Though the author is quick to note the sample is small and the results, therefore, tentative, the conclusions suggest, for both IS executives and top management, significant guidelines that appear consistent with successful IS development activities. The proper level of management involvement is not just another way to consume valuable management time; it pays off as the successful IS departments in this study illustrate.

DEGREE OF TOP MANAGEMENT INVOLVEMENT

CEOs of large companies have stated that people have been preaching to them all the time about their involvement in IS. Publications and seminars hammer home the theme that information and the management of it have become so critical and strategic that CEOs must get involved. But they plaintively ask the question, "How and where should I get involved? I have to pick the shots carefully because I'm already putting in 12 hours a day and I don't see too many things dropping off my agenda."

As a starter kit for this process, the following matrix (Figure 11.13) is presented. A variety of activities associated with the IS function are listed, while four gradations of CEO involvement are indicated. First is a level that says this activity is so important to the business that the CEO should personally approve the activity. Second is a level that suggests that CEOs should insist that the company do it, though it may or may not be necessary for them to approve the result of the activity. Next is a level that indicates the CEO should review the activity but not necessarily personally approve; and, finally, a fourth level that says that, though the CEO may have an interest in the activity, it should be delegated, usually to the IS executive or to user management. It is felt that this type of thinking can begin to build the business partnership between the CEO and IS executive that is so vital to effective information systems.

Referring to Figure 11.13, CEOs should insist that there exist an IS long-range plan; furthermore, they should approve it and should ensure that it is consistent with corporate

FIGURE 11.13. CEO involvment levels

Activity	Approve	Insist	Review	Delegate
Long-range IS plan	X	X		
Determinitation of application portfolio			X	
CEO decision support system specification	X			
IS budget and resource allocation			X	
Security/backup plan		X		
IS mission statement		X		
Selection of IS executive			X	
Technological risk assessment	X	X		
Design of systems				X
Hardware/software selection				X

strategies. This is probably the most significant area for CEO involvement; yet it is far from an accepted practice.

The determination of the application portfolio suggests a prioritization process for directing information resources to different functional areas of the business. For the most part, the CEO should not be asked to approve either the process or the resulting portfolio. However, the CEO should have influence in key application projects that have a far-reaching effect on the company. Certainly a new reservation system for an airline; for a distributor, an on-line ordering system that links customers with the company's data base; or the entry of a financial institution into electronic cash transfer are applications worthy of the CEO's involvement. At a minimum, the interest of the CEO will impress the implementors with the importance of the project—but, more ideally, the CEO can add his or her perspective to the overall direction of the application. The application areas under question are large, complex ones usually involving multi–person-years of effort.

Certainly for an executive decision support system that he or she will personally use, the CEO must demand final approval. Survey results of decision support systems, conducted by the Society for Information Management, support the conventional wisdom that those systems that were initiated by executives and in which there was heavy executive involvement were the most successful; yet this occurred in only 12 of the 56 systems studied.

IS budgets should have CEO review, particularly since the application focus in many companies may place cost containment above application effectiveness as the major guiding force. Overemphasis of this approach can result in overlooking emerging opportunities in the information systems field that offer strategic advantages. It may be prudent to allow the IS operation to grow at a rate faster than other operations; for this reason the CEO perspective may be a necessity.

As has been mentioned, with so much riding on information systems, and with the increasing importance of information as a resource, information resources and assets must be protected. The CEO should insist there is a formal plan and program in place for information security and backup.

A mission statement, outlining the overriding strategic direction of IS within a company, is a vital but often missing element. This statement is the charter on which the IS long-range plan is based. As with a security plan, the CEO should insist there be such a charter though he or she need not approve it.

The selection of an IS executive is a very sensitive and extremely vital activity. If the position reports directly to the CEO, then obviously the CEO should have the final decision; but even if the IS executive reports through an executive VP, administrative VP or controller, the incumbent should know that he or she is there with the full cognizance and approval of the CEO. The position is so important that the confidence and respect level of the top office is essential for success in this role.

With the rapid changes in technology that have been described, it is important for the IS executive to know the company's propensity for risk, that is, whether the strategy should be a "following" one rather than a "pioneering" one or somewhere in between. For example, employing leading-edge satellite communications is an expensive proposition with fairly high risk but with considerable benefit once implemented. This type of decision warrants the direct involvement and approval of the CEO, who must insist that his or her views are known on this matter.

There are obviously many matters in which the CEO should not be involved; often a problem arises when a preponderance of activities hit the top office which have no business getting there. Two such matters are listed as examples on the chart. They are the design of systems and hardware/software selection—activities to be handled by professionals using state-of-the-art methodologies.

This matrix is not an all-inclusive list, but it does indicate important areas of executive concern. More important, it is meant to generate a reflection on the part of the CEO—a pause to question the adequacy of his or her personal IS involvement level.

SUMMARY

This is a very important chapter. It deals with the impact IS has on management, and the impact that management has on IS. The chapter opens by characterizing the information age, mainly via the metaphor of Alvin Toffler's third wave. Next, the management process is reviewed focusing on the three major elements of the managers job that deal respectively with ideas, things and people. The similarity to the benefit/beneficiary matrix was noted— ideas being akin to transformation, things to efficiency, and people to effectiveness.

Then, the effect of IS was explored in each of the three areas. E-mail, personal scheduling, and tele-videoconferencing were examples of IS support in the things arena; electronic support systems (ESS), in the people arena; and certain types of ESS as well as decision support systems (the previous chapter), in the ideas arena. ESS was discussed in some depth, reviewing a general model of an ESS, consisting of the compilation of a management subset data base extracted from the company's internal transaction data and from relevant outside data, and then the production of meaningful screens of information based on individual management lenses.

The concept of critical success factors was reintroduced indicating that this provides, in the case of ESS, that very important top-down approach to designing the system. A structured questionnaire was reviewed which assists in the CSF discovery process. Examples of the type of information emanating from ESS were covered, illustrating the three general types of reports including drill down, exception, and trend.

The degree to which managers deal with ESS directly or for administrative IS support depends on their personal cognitive styles. Two diametrically opposed management styles were reviewed. Six "intelligences," or ways in which managers best digest information, were discussed, as was their relevance to ESS. The role of senior management in IS concluded the chapter, making the point that this role implies a comprehensive understanding of IS (sometimes called information literacy), which is considerably more important for senior management than computer literacy. This type of comprehensive understanding is essential if the company is to use IS for effectiveness, to transform the organization, and to manage with information.

John Preston, Director of Marketing Support

I am reasonably versed in computers, and have been trying to use my PC for word processing even though I don't type well. I also am on the electronic mail system and have attempted to learn LOTUS 1-2-3. It has been six months since my computer was installed. Keep in mind that my job as Marketing Director involves the management of our entire sales support activity from market analysis to product planning to product support including the education function.

My reason to try a PC was rather a negative one, I must admit. Frankly I had received little support from the the central IS group. I needed summary reports and either got too much or not the right stuff, or it was so late that it lost its relevance. I complained for a while, but then didn't bother.

My introduction to the PC came through the information center that we established about a year ago. I dropped in on a LOTUS training class. Frankly it wasn't suited to my taste; that is, it assumed a higher familiarity than I had, and also I didn't feel comfortable with the different levels of people who attended.

But now I find myself in a bind. If I honestly appraise my experience, I know I have put in a great deal of time in learning to do some rather mundane things. Though the whole concept may be called user-friendly, it hasn't been that way to *this* user. Maybe it's the training or lack of it, maybe it's the fact that I've been preoccupied with the company reorganization, or maybe it's just me. But whatever, on balance I would question the amount of time I've spent that has detracted me from doing real work which is to manage and motivate my people. I seriously question the presence of the PC in my office, which is not to say they shouldn't be used by my people. My secretary can handle my electronic mail, and my staff can provide me with the reports and analyses I need.

STUDY QUESTIONS

1. How reasonable is John Preston's view of the PC world?
2. Who is at fault for getting him into this dilemma?
3. You are the IS person responsible for providing information support to John Preston. What steps would you take?

Fact-Based Thinking

Permeating each of Sandy Sigoloff's (CEO and President, Wickes Companies) critical components was an underlying concept: fact-based thinking. Sigoloff's mind moves quickly, but he had to feed his creative and decisive intellect with the facts to make well-structured, well-founded decisions.

As step 1, Sigoloff had to get access to the facts. In a crisis, fact-finding is time critical. The normal reporting cycles of a large business were far from adequate. He offers an example:

> The one-year business plan was reviewed quarterly by the board and monthly by the staff. A hard [final accounting] closing might come two or three weeks after the month was over. If you are basing the operating of your business on that, you're out of phase the three or four weeks it takes to close a month [and analyze results]. We couldn't, in our judgement, run the company effectively with all the things we were doing—very heavy investment in capital equipment, strategic redirections of the business—by looking at closing information so infrequently.

Sigoloff needed a means of spotting problems much sooner. "That meant we needed two kinds of closings: a flash closing and a hard closing. [To do that] we had to get the information directly from the field. So we used electronic mail to communicate. [E-mail] became our source for getting the preliminary program data very quickly. Then we integrated it into the [executive system]."

Sigoloff also needed a means of insuring the accuracy of the facts he received. "Someone might say to me, 'Oh, that's probably not a problem. Just an abort on sales because of rain, or something like that.'" To see past the easy explanations, Sigoloff directly accessed raw operational data. "It's always nice to know that, in those circumstances, you can look at both ordered information and raw data. I would work with the numbers myself [on the computer] and say, 'Umhum! The overhead in the G&A smells.' When I saw something like that, I sent an electronic mail message asking for clarification of line item number 26 or 27. Then I would have discussions with others."

Did raw data bring information overload? Just the opposite, Sigoloff explains. "It was so easy to stay informed that you really didn't feel [overly] dependent on anybody, and I think that's very important. Not that you don't trust everybody that works for you, but it was there for you to evaluate yourself if you wanted it."

From: Mary E. Boone, *Leadership and the Computer,* Rocklin, Cal.: Prima Publishing.

By staying on top of the facts, Sigoloff cultivated a sense of what he wanted people to pay attention to. Over time he got better data, and more problems were handled at a lower level:

Many times you want to check the conclusion with the raw data . . . not to embarrass [people], but to train them to do a better job. The real test is to create a manager—to develop people. That's what this is all about. The question is, has this manager really been effectively trained to produce usable information?

I wanted to train the managers to ask all of the questions before the information gets into the systems. I want them to think through the contingencies like: What happens if energy prices go up? What happens if we have a flood or tornado? What happens if I have a water shortage? I wanted to train the manager to do all of this stuff before I got to it. [Access to information] is a coaching tool because what you're really trying to do is make people better managers without [discouraging them].

With facts in hand, Sigoloff had to consider many alternatives and their implications for the future. He wanted to see the situation from as many points of view as possible. Listening was the means to this end. "The flip side [of communicating] is listen, listen, listen. You have to understand what people are telling you in order to sort the truth from fiction."

Listening involves encouraging healthy dissent, according to Sigoloff. If people do not feel comfortable disagreeing, then a leader is not listening properly; the leader will not get different perspectives on a problem. Here, too, Sigoloff saw the information system as a component of his leadership strategy. By equipping his people with the means of disagreeing with him, the computer improved his own decision making capabilities. "[Providing others with access to internal information] gives the person you interact with the knowledge base to disagree with you, and the more disagreement you can have to evaluate a problem, the more likely you are to get a successful answer."

With access to facts, in the form of clear and timely data, and people's opinions, Sigoloff was well positioned to make decisions. He elaborates on why he felt it was important to do much of his thinking and decision making on line: "Many times, a decision is one where [a CEO] wants the privacy of reflection on things—even though he's been advised. My computer system was extremely important in reviewing the progress of the company."

STUDY QUESTIONS

1. How important is it that the CEO is involved in executive support systems? Is this necessary to give the signal to the rest of the organization?
2. Of the ways Sigoloff uses computers and data, which is the most significant?
3. Do you think Sigoloff is typical of today's executives? Tomorrow's executives?

SELECTED REFERENCES

Boone, Mary E., *Leadership and the Computer*. Rocklin, Cal.: Prima Publishing, 1991.

Gibson, Cyrus F., and Barbara B. Jackson, *The Information Imperative: Managing the impact of information technology on business and people*. Lexington, Mass.: Lexington Books, 1987.

Paller, Alan, with Richard Laska, *The EIS Book, Information Systems for Top Managers*. Homewood, Ill.: Dow Jones-Irwin, 1990.

Rockart, John F., and David W. DeLong, *Executive Support Systems: The Emergence of Top Management Computer Use*. Homewood, Ill.: Dow Jones-Irwin, 1988.

Rockart, John F. and Michael E. Treacy, "The CEO Goes On-Line," *Harvard Business Review*, November-December 1982, pp. 82-88.

Rockart, John F. and Michael Treacy, *Executive Informaiton Support Systems*, W.P. 1167-80. Cambridge, Mass.: Center for Information System Research, Sloan (MIT), 1981.

Schoderbek, Peter P., Charles G. Schoderbek, and Asterios G. Kefalas, *Managment Systems Conceptual Considerations*, 4th ed. Homewood, Ill.: Richard D. Irwin, 1990.

Toffler, Alvin, *The Third Wave*. New York: Morrow, 1980.

Chapter 12

New Information Technologies

INTRODUCTION

Living with a high rate of technological change has been and continues to be a way of life in the IS field. Such a rate of change affords a surfeit of opportunity, as well as presents a series of new challenges. There is general agreement that the rate of change has accelerated over the life span of computers and the volatility is higher than it has ever been. And all this comes as the business world is evolving toward a service-oriented, knowledge intensive, global society. This chapter covers the emerging technologies that will have the greatest impact in the next ten years. Some have been discussed or mentioned in previous chapters, but this presentation serves as a summary. Then, one of the most promising technologies, expert systems, is illustrated by a comprehensive case study. The introduction of this particular technology presents lessons for the introduction of other new technologies into a company.

The world of technology and information systems is an exciting one, and the products are coming so fast that, as someone has said, "IS is an industry facing insurmountable opportunities." This oxymoron is a timely one as there is no question that the unexamined employment of technology is not a healthy pursuit. The key is to meter the technology to suit the organizational culture, background, and specific company strategy. While this chapter discusses some of the leading-edge technologies, the caveat remains to be aware of what is available and will be available, remembering the important statement that the key objective is competing not computing.

CONTINUATION (ACCELERATION) OF MORE CHIP POWER

The chip is the computer component that provides the underlying power, the fundamental platform for all the information processing that occurs. The Intel 80386 and 80486 chips are commonplace, and the 586 and beyond will come in rapid succession. All this is putting the equivalent of 5 to 7 MIPS (millions of instructions per second) on a desktop, or in the attache case. And in the engineering/scientific arena, Digital Equipment Corporation, IBM, and Sun are delivering workstations that exceed 25 MIPS. Coprocessor and multiprocessor systems add additional power. Reduced instruction set computing (RISC) provides another added power source. RISC systems work on the basis that about 20 percent of the instructions are used 80 percent of the time, so only the frequently used instructions are implemented; the less commonly used ones are emulated by a combination of the extant instructions.

But sheer speed is not the only advancement on the horizon. Memory capacity will grow dramatically, as will storage with erasable optical disks. Nippon Electric Company (NEC) in Japan is designing a one-gigabyte (billion-byte) memory chip using a super-computer for design and employing a laser etching process for manufacture. Optical disk storage won't just be data storage, but will include graphics, images, and voice as well. Optical storage providing 650 megabits of data having a ten-year life span will be available at a cost of $250. The PC will have multimedia capabilities, utilizing a chip that compresses the bits representing a video frame to give the PC the power to perform high-resolution video. The user will be able to work on video images or high-resolution graphics while compact-disk-quality sound plays in the background.

One may ask why you need such power on a desktop. The reason becomes apparent when you realize that it takes about 100 MIPS to interpret continuous speech and one million bytes of memory to store a high resolution color photograph, not to mention video.

A principal manifestation of chip power and miniaturization is the portable computer that permits use at home, on a business trip, in a hotel, or in an airplane. From the size of an attache case, PCs have been reduced to the size of notebooks or note pads, and will get smaller yet. A current model is as high and as wide as a sheet of paper, just more than two inches thick, weighs 7.4 pounds and runs for three hours on batteries. It has a high-resolution monitor, a 60-megabyte hard disk, and 10 megabytes of memory. Palm-top (fits into the palm of the hand) computers are also becoming available. Current prices, still relatively high, might one day approach those of the former hand-held calculators. Also, the weight will be materially reduced, and, via cellular communications, you will be able to communicate from your personal computer while in a car or hotel room.

Miniaturization means that power can be more easily decentralized, and, although power alone does not necessarily cause a revolution in computer usage, the sheer magnitude of the change eventually results in a shift in the kind of applications employed, not just in doing things faster. If prognosticators missed anything ten years ago it was the impact that microcomputing power would eventually have on computer usage. It dramatically changes the tradeoffs of who does the computing; where computing takes place; and, eventually, how computers are used. When combined with the blitz of an ever-improving foundation of PC-based software, it all adds up to a revolution.

INTERCONNECTION AND NETWORKING

Marshall McLuhan said it many years ago—that with the full incarnation of television, the media will become the message; that is, the process of communication will be more influential in what we perceive than the communication or message itself. Though maybe a bit extreme, there is truth in the statement. In time, the connection of your computer to other computers or to outside data bases could be as standardized as the threads of a screw or the prongs of a plug. Furthermore, fiber optics will radically change the speed and costs of communication. AT&T currently can transmit at a rate of 1.7 billion bits (or a 30-volume encyclopedia) in a second. The predictions are that the United States will be "glassed" by the year 2010. This means that all our voice and data communications between businesses, institutions, and homes will be via optical fiber. The cable that currently brings you 25 channels of television will be replaced by fiber that can bring you two hundred channels of high-density TV. On the international scene, current undersea cables that transmit 560 megabits per second (the equivalent of 80,000 simultaneous voice channels) will be replaced with fiber transmitting 5 billion bits per second. Most prognosticators in this area predict the slowdown of satellite transmission with the ascendency of fiber optics.

All of this requires the development of a group of standard interfaces to allow compatibility between the plethora of computing equipment brands in use. The future will bring these standards into universal use so that it will become as easy as picking up a telephone and connecting with anyone in the world. However, because there are a host of special interest groups, this development will not come easily; but inevitably standards such as UNIX, X.25, OSI, and ISDN will help create this environment.

In order to play in the interconnect world, companies must develop the IS and telecommunications architecture that can incorporate this type of integration. It seems to be a growing conclusion that most of the old applications, many designed 10 to 15 years ago, will have to be rewritten as part of a rearchitecting strategy. This is a hard bullet to bite because the expense is very high while the benefits are long range. It's like installing a new furnace when the old one is still limping along. The old adage, If it ain't broke, don't fix it, may not apply here. The real gains will come from what is being called "reengineering," a revolutionary new look at what IS can really accomplish in making a company more competitive. In most cases this will involve completely new applications of IS causing big changes in the way people accomplish their tasks. IS will not just automate what heretofore was done manually or by rudimentary computer application, it will tackle completely new areas. The phrase has been coined "obliterate, don't automate."

The foregoing will change the way we communicate, giving us options that previously were technologically or economically infeasible. We are seeing this in the development of interoperational systems where companies are linked electronically to their customers and to their suppliers via EDI (electronic data interchange) applications. Improved connectivity will abet worldwide funds transfer and worldwide trading in general. And it may come to pass that personal electronic communication could substitute for travel and face-to-face contact. I have used the qualifier "could" because it still must be shown that these second-level contacts are as effective in the long run as the personal ones. One can speculate about the arrival of McLuhan's global village of electronic junk mail and artificial intelligence.

John Naisbitt, popular futurist, points out that transportation suburbanized America while electronic technology will further disperse us, this time to the rural areas where we can experience an improved quality of life. Naisbitt himself lives in Telluride, Colorado, in the San Juan Mountains, and indicates that with his computer, telephone, and fax machine, he is in touch with the rest of the world as if he lived in downtown London or Tokyo. Whether tomorrow's business folk follow the Naisbitt model is subject to management style and individual motivation, but at least the option for spending more of your life in the high-quality lane will be there.

Beyond the individual proclivity for mountains, it is possible for entire businesses to be located in "high-quality" country. As we move to a service economy, proximity to natural resources or sources of supply will become less important than they are today. The days of industrial belts and huge shopping malls could be behind us. So there will exist the option to work individually, part time or full, in an area remote from the main locus of your business or if your business is labor intensive, to move the business to a living area where it is easier to attract the required people skills.

The Travelers Companies have 300 telecommuters who work from their homes. Many of these workers are skilled people, knowledgeable in handling medical claims. They have gained this experience and expertise over many years and they cannot be replaced easily. So these people, many of them women, get up at 5 A.M. to connect to the home-office computer and handle a half-dozen claims before their children arise. Then, after they are off for school, the home worker processes other claims, is interrupted again, and finishes the day's activity in the early evening. This is the type of flexibility that permits this scenario in an increasing number of instances. But, again, it should be emphasized that the presence of the enabling technologies is not the only motivation for change.

DATA NAVIGATION, MULTIMEDIA, AND HYPERTEXT: RECOGNIZING OUR INEXHAUSTIBLE RESOURCE

Someone has said that the only resource you can tap and use without depleting or losing value is data. That's true even though one who has the data first can often use it to reduce its value for the next user. The United States has a vast reservoir of data in business enterprises, libraries, and research centers. The Harvard Business School is spending $50 million to bring its business library on-line and to be part of a network of information sharing. Technological advancements will allow major improvements in the use of this data resource.

First, multimedia integration will facilitate the electronic capture of data, not only as text, but in graphic, pictorial, and voice format as well. Today less than 5 percent of business data are in electronic form and of the 5 percent, over 90 percent of the data are text. Clearly, there is much to be done. Figure 12.1 illustrates the newsletter of the future, utilizing a personal computer and multimedia to describe the events of the day. Figure 12.2 shows a continuum, starting on the left with the media that would appeal to the logical intelligence of an individual and proceeding to the right where the media used appeal more to the emotional feelings of a person. This corresponds to the characterization of left-brain people who are more logical and analytical versus right-brain people who are more intuitive and

FIGURE 12.1. A multimedia newsletter (from David S. Marshak, Senior Analyst, Patricia Seybold's Office Computing Report)

A Multimedia Newsletter

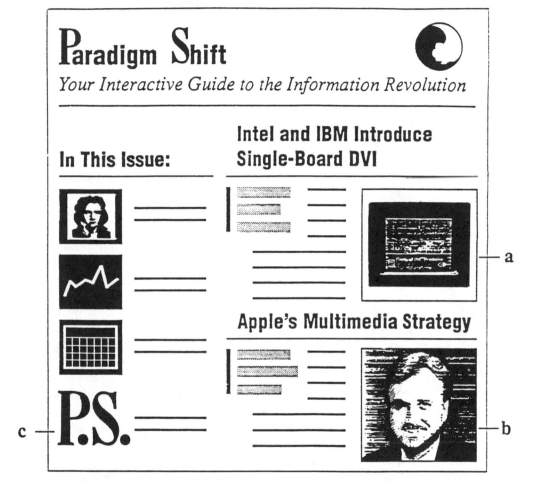

One of the opportunities provided by the integration of multimedia into our workplace will be the ability of information providers like ourselves to use our audio and video sensitivity to increase the human bandwidth upon which we receive information. Multimedia information sources can also provide a high level of interactivity, allowing the user to comment back to the publisher using voice or video annotation, to manipulate a live graph or data set with his or her own numbers, and to enter an interactive, multimedia conference to discuss common issues with other readers of the publication.

If you were now reading a multimedia newsletter, this particular article would appear very differently. For example, you could select the picture marked (a) and see a video of a demonstration of the new DVI board introduced by Intel and IBM. Selecting (b) would bring you an interview with Tyler Peppel on Apple's multimedia plans, including his presentation on how video will be integrated into a future release of the Mac operating system. For more interactivity, selecting (c) would bring you into an online conference run by the publisher, where you could exchange ideas with other readers about, for instance, the future of multimedia. And, at any time, you could send a comment to the publisher or editor about the content of any article.

We do not provide this type of report—yet. Stayed tuned to this station.

FIGURE 12.2. The logic-emotion continuum (from David S. Marshak, Patricia Seybolds's Office Computing Report)

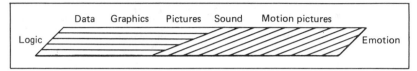

are swayed by the feel and look of a situation. In many cases both brains are needed to make sound and responsible decisions. This is the promise of multimedia.

There will be a host of new data bases and data base software. The levels of use of the new data base technology range from personal and group data management systems to national libraries. In the former area, advancements in the development of erasable compact disks and hypertext data bases will allow individuals to integrate and connect otherwise separate and disparate blocks of data within their working domains. Hypertext looks at data as sets of chunks and links. A chunk is a basic unit of data that is associated with other chunks via pre-established linkages. For example, in Apple's HyperCard system, a box of file cards is viewed as the basic metaphor. With HyperCard, a chunk is a file card worth of data. Other technologists are projecting an all-encompassing public electronic library system based on hypertext principles. This could allow the linkage of internal and external data searches.

A simple example may illustrate the approach. A product planner is working on the introduction of a new product and wants to analyze recent announcements of products in the same category as that which she is planning. She knows she has read about such products but can't remember where. With hypertext, she can link to chunks of data in her company files pertaining to that product category and can also access outside public or private sources that are using hypertext principles. Hypertext is a powerful concept, sometimes referred to as data navigation or data mining—metaphors that suggest the use of computers and communications to tap a resource that can be more valuable than the ores and minerals in the ground. It is a megatrend to watch closely.

The "data lens" concept will be a future application. Based on the individual's personal and business interests and what he or she needs to accomplish the work at hand, an information profile is developed. This may be thought of as an expert systems front end to data navigation. The individual lens continuously scans current information from worldwide data bases and brings that information in the media suggested by the individual's cognitive style to his or her personal computer workstation. The lens is adjusted regularly based on changes in interests or work patterns.

HUMAN INTERFACE TECHNOLOGY

The predominant way to enter data into a computer system or to access data already stored remains the keyboard. This has always been a deterrent to individuals who are not comfortable with typing data and commands into a computer system. This group includes factory workers, salespeople, police officers, and construction people, as well as a good number of managers and executives. However, technology will assist in this important area and open up IS to a vast army of new users. The solution is really quite simple, but not so simple to implement. The solution is to make the machine more like the human, to adapt to the way humans communicate. And that is by voice, by handwriting, and by touch.

Speech recognition devices have been on the market for many years. They are able to recognize up to 5000 words, but they still require a pause after each word and this is limiting to people who are accustomed to rattling off sentences at breakneck speed. The early systems are used by doctors who state patient symptoms and input other data verbally so that patient records are available immediately and can be sent to other doctors or specialists as required. This is an instance of an important application that has impact on efficiency as well as effectiveness. There are other examples as well. The system recognizes the words and converts them into digital signals that can be processed as if they had been entered by a typewriter into a word processing software package. Other uses would be for applications by the factory workers and managers, aforementioned who could enter and access information the way they do it now—by asking for it verbally.

Systems will be available that have a vocabulary of 10,000 or more words and can process continuous speech. An expert systems front end will, in effect, develop a voice print of an individual's unique dialect and accent and will store it in the computer. The voice print will be established via a ten-minute interaction with the system. Also on the horizon is automatic language translation where a person will speak in French and the system will be able to translate the sentences into English, which would then be available for editing and reproduction. The industry has developed a host of excellent decision support systems and executive support systems that arc not used because of the unavailability of a simple interface. Voice recognition will be a big assist.

Another development is handwriting recognition. Currently there are systems (called pen-based) that can recognize printed block letters and numbers but not the variety of handwriting styles that would make for more broader use. But, aided by such techniques as neural networks, unique handwriting can be interpreted and provide the basic input for the processing of transactions or used as input into word processing systems. Portable note pad systems without keyboards will be available. Census takers, inventory clerks, production schedulers, and fast food restaurant workers, as well as executives on airplanes will find appeal in this type of machine.

We see touch screens today where people can point to a specific icon on the screen, and by so doing break an X/Y light beam to signal the execution of the function represented by the icon. Increasingly, these types of applications will be seen in shopping center kiosks or in travel centers where customers can order products, obtain airline tickets, or get quotes on different insurance policies or investment opportunities. Additional uses will be by executives using executive support systems.

Touch, voice, and handwriting (symbol manipulation) are really a return to the fundamental ways people have been communicating since civilization began. I have always felt that the computer should be a tool for humans and adapt itself to us, not the other way around. These fundamental modes of communicating are finally enabling this concept to be carried out. There will always be two kinds of people, those who are comfortable with the keyboard and those who are not. While the percentages may change a bit in favor of the former, there will still be enough of the latter to make the capabilities discussed here viable alternatives.

CLUSTER MANAGEMENT VIA GROUPWARE

The cluster management concept is a departure from our hierarchically oriented, second-wave company structure where the organizational backbone is chain of command. We see this in the high-tech startup companies that have been so successful. Small groups of people, representing different functions and different organizational levels get together to solve a problem. The criteria for membership is the knowledge or experience to contribute to the solution—not where you fit in the organization. Members of the cluster may be geographically distant, but technology allows them to be productive contributors.

Groupware is the software that acts as the central clearinghouse for making pertinent information available to members of the cluster. The technology described in the foregoing such as interconnection and networks facilitate the linking of members. Multimedia enrich the ways that people can communicate. These linkages allow on-line meetings, the development of project data bases, on-line bulletin boards for use by members, and the hardware and software necessary to hold group meetings via videoconferences or a hook-up of personal computer screens. Of course, groupware can utilize the hypertext capability to access outside data resources that can then be shared with the cluster.

While electronic mail, voice mail, and FAX provide technology for communication, groupware is a broader solution for people who need to share information and ideas. Using the information lens concept, members of a group can be kept informed of items within the company and outside it that bear on their work. The software package Lotus Notes is an example of the beginning of this new class of software. The following description appeared in their announcement packet:

What is Groupware?

Some industry observers define groupware as any networked application. Others have narrower definitions requiring, for example, a higher level of user-to-user interaction via the application in order for a product to be deemed true "groupware."

Lotus sees groupware not as a product category per se, but as a horizontal concept that is as wide and ubiquitous as today's vast library of stand-alone PC applications. However, there are certain fundamental characteristics or minimum performance criteria that should be used to gauge the quality and degree of groupware functionality of an application.

Groupware applications should allow users to:

- organize, assemble and distribute information;
- act on behalf of a group;
- interact within a group;
- transcend location and time;
- create, maintain and access long-term records;

- reorganize information for relevance and meaning;
- communicate without face-to-face meetings;
- shape the system's conformance to the workgroup's style, and manage the system's evolution as the workgroup's needs change;
- reduce needless paperwork and duplication; and,
- greatly improve communications.

Conquering Space and Time

Researchers in this pioneering field refer to groupware as "computer-supported collaborative work." Some use the term "coordination software." But whatever it's called, the groupware concept offers major benefits in building new applications.

Perhaps the most powerful advantage is the ability of members of the workgroup to transcend space and time. That is, despite any differences in the time of their communication, or their individual location, group information sharing is enabled.

Space and time considerations can be divided into four categories: same time/same place; same time/different place; different time/same place; and different time/different place. The first scenario is best represented by a face-to-face meeting. The second could be a coast-to-coast phone call. The third could be a printed memo left in a local in-box. The fourth, the most difficult and remote, is most commonly handled in business today by a mailed letter.

It is in this last, most difficult category that groupware's impact can be extraordinary because it can give different time/different place communication nearly as much impact as a personal meeting—certainly four or five times the impact of a letter. Like electronic mail, groupware communications are personal and immediate. Unlike today's character-based electronic mail, groupware communication can include graphics, spreadsheet files, or other numeric data as well as text, and allow the receiver to exercise presentation choices such as hypertext. Notes allows organizations to manage information for effective access and distribute it broadly, yet maintain appropriate control and security.

One of the most serious challenges a company faces is to compress or shorten the length of time that it takes to make something happen. It could be as simple as getting an agreement on the timing and location of a company meeting or it could be the process that transforms a market requirement into a commercial product. Company organizations are complex and the communication process heightens the complexity because of increasing intercompany alliances and global operations. Problems arise if the organization is clogged and unable to move information in a timely manner to the ultimate decision makers. Cluster management and groupware offer a way to condense the cycle.

Image Processing and Image Management

As stated before, less than 5 percent of business data are in electronic form. The majority of the remaining 95 percent resides on paper. People have been talking about the paperless office and paperless society for quite a while, but we seem no closer to it than we were ten years ago. Electronic data interchange (EDI) and image processing are in a way conflicting technologies. The ideal way to reduce paper is to capture transactions and data in electronic (digital) form at the exact point of the transaction, and then to maintain the data in their digital trappings through processing and into history files. This is the goal of EDI. On the other hand, image processing or imaging is the process of optically scanning paper documents and placing the images into electronic or optical storage. As EDI applications grow, there will be less and less need for imaging. However, there is already enough paper around from pre-EDI days that will be there even as EDI expands to create a demand for imaging.

Figure 12.3 illustrates the components of an image-processing system. We are talking about mass production and considerable expense, as today's systems range from $50,000 to $1 million depending on the configuration. These prices will be reduced with the general lowering of chip costs and the machines powered by chips. The types of documents that are commonly digitized are checks, credit card statements, and insurance policies. The documents are passed over the scanner and converted into a series of binary 1s and 0s. A data compression process ignores white space between the letters or numbers, which reduces the number of bits stored by a factor of about 35 to 1. Bear in mind that the stored document is an image, and not a text file. Therefore in order to retrieve it, software must be used that assigns identity (location and addresses) to the document.

With the identification capability, we are talking about image management. Image management systems are software that provide data base–type functions, such as indexing, and accessing by multiple methods (name, account number, date of transaction, and so on). The form of storage is usually magnetic or optical disk depending on the cost/performance tradeoff. We will see more optical disk as the price plummets because speed of access is normally not that crucial with historical records. The workstations in the systems diagram permit interrogation and display of records from the image file. These can be connected via local area networks (LANS) or if access is required from locations in the United States and around the world, via wide area networks (WANS.)

It is estimated that the number of documents stored by U.S businesses is currently 545 billion and expected to grow to 800 billion by 1994. We are literally drowning in a sea of paper. Image processing and management offer a way to make a dent in this paper deluge.

Artificial Intelligence

Artificial intelligence (AI) refers to a class of applications that in a major way require some form of intelligence. I say "in a major way" because it is true that many computer applications not specified as AI have elements of intelligence. For example, Figure 12.4 indicates that transactions, receipts and orders, are automatically entered into the system by a scanner in a store or in a warehouse. Based on a forecast of future activity, an economic order quantity is suggested to the buyer. A conventional program that accomplishes this has been written and resides in the computer. But when we refer to AI we are thinking of another class of problems and solutions. The intelligence required is beyond the traditional scope of business problems that comprise business applications today.

There is no absolute definition of AI; rather, it is an evolving field. Generally, the field is thought to include the functional areas of natural language processing, robotics, machine

FIGURE 12.3. (From an International Data Corp. [IDC] white paper, Farmington, Mass.)

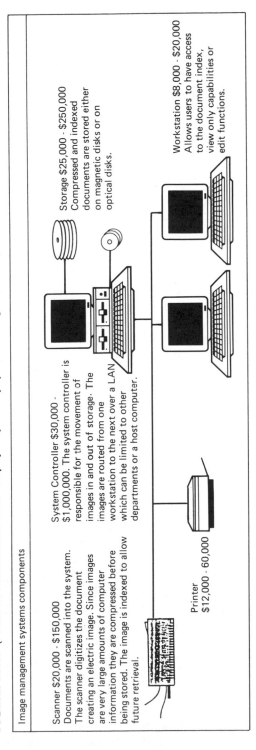

Image management systems components

Scanner $20,000 - $150,000
Documents are scanned into the system. The scanner digitizes the document creating an electric image. Since images are very large amounts of computer information they are compressed before being stored. The image is indexed to allow future retrieval.

Printer $12,000 - 60,000

System Controller $30,000 - $1,000,000. The system controller is responsible for the movement of images in and out of storage. The images are routed from one workstation to the next over a LAN which can be limited to other departments or a host computer.

Storage $25,000 - $250,000 Compressed and indexed documents are stored either on magnetic disks or on optical disks.

Workstation $8,000 - $20,000 Allows users to have access to the document index, view only capabilities or edit functions.

329

FIGURE 12.4. Conventional computer decision making

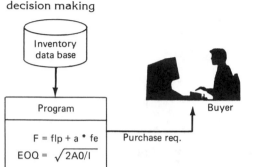

optics, expert systems, and neural networks. Natural language processing means that a person can speak to a machine in his or her own unique accent in the language of choice and the individual dialect can be recognized and put into machine language for further processing. Thus, the system could interpret a deep southern accent requesting airline flight information from Atlanta to Los Angeles with all possible flights and costs.

Computer-aided manufacturing (CAM) and design (CAD) have already been mentioned as rapidly growing areas of computer applications. Robotics is an extension of CAM. CAM allows computers to control and drive manufacturing processes such as drilling, lathing, and milling. Robotics extends the range of machine-aided functions to die casting and welding, among others.

The Robot Institute of America (RIA) has developed a definition of *robotics* as follows: "A robot is a reprogrammable multifunctional manipulation designed to move material, parts, tools or specialized devices through variable programmed motions for the performances of a variety of tasks." This definition helps, because the public image of a robot is a device with anthropomorphic qualities that walks around on two legs, speaks, and emulates a human being in its actions. Most robots are used in factories, don't walk or speak, and don't look humanlike at all.

In industrial use, the robot must bring some form of intelligence to the work, have a form of power and control over the work, and be able to lend a strong and capable hand. In fact, the latter may be the best way to think about the functions of a robot. A robot can emulate the functions of the hand—grasping, gripping, lifting, moving, and positioning items.

Many feel that computer-driven robots will mark the next significant stage in the industrial revolution. The Japanese have embraced robotics and currently have more robots than the United States. Sweden, which has always had a penchant for technology, is also among the leading robot producers. Robotics experts feel the next wave of robots will be more sensitive and more intelligent than those in use today, being able, for example, to employ an artificial sense of touch and to make decisions based on the texture of an object—also to use a complex vision system to recognize objects on the basis of their shape without the requirement of special lighting. Several leading-edge companies are developing what they call "factories of the future" based on advanced robotics.

Machine optics is an extension of robotics in that the machine now begins to emulate the workings of the human eye, and can scan for position, shape, size, and other physical attributes that we normally detect with our eyes. This adds a major dimension to industrial robots, enabling them to react to conditions that are encountered during the process and are therefore not dependent on knowing exactly what objects the machine will encounter before the process commences. A simple version of machine optics is the ability to scan handwritten documents and turn them into machine code that can be manipulated by a computer program, such as a word processing application.

The two most far-reaching technologies in the AI camp appear to be neural networks and expert systems, so we devote time to explore each. We look at neural networks first, then explore expert systems in depth, since this branch of AI will be more prevalent in the foreseeable future.

NEURAL NETWORKS

The human brain does not process and act on data in a purely sequential way as conventional computers do. Also, the human brain is extremely adaptive to new stimuli and input. Neural networks process data by emulating the human thinking process. A neural network is built from a mass of single processing units, each unit attempting to model a biological neuron. The collective behavior of the multiple processing units is aimed at modeling the complex functions of the human mind.

Neural networks differ from expert systems in that it is not necessary to first express the logic and decision rules into a completely specified computer program. Neural networks have a learning capability in that it is possible to generalize from previous data and to make conjectures based on this experience. In expert systems, you would expect the same answer to a problem if you enter the same data. With neural networks, however, you can receive a different result depending on how many iterations you make with similar data. Thus, the answer is a learning process based on changing conditions. The technology has the ability to learn from its mistakes.

Parallel processors, such as those produced by Thinking Machines Corporation in Cambridge, MA, work on the "divide and conquer theory," which argues that maximum processing speed can be achieved by getting multiple processors to work together rather than by relying on the power of a single supercomputer. For example, they have linked 65,000 microprocessors together to achieve a speed of 2500 MIPS. This is the type of architecture and speed that will prove very effective in powering applications like neural networks.

Neural network applications include human pattern recognition to convert handwriting into a format suitable for input to word processing software. The United States hopes to use neural nets to read and sort handwritten ZIP codes. The Chase Manhattan Bank is developing systems to spot patterns in financial transactions. For example, there is an enormous cost in stolen credit cards. With historical data on credit card transactions, the Chase neural network uncovered specific trends and tendencies; for example, transactions most likely to be questioned involved the purchase of women's shoes in the range of $40 to $80. The Butler Cox Foundation has reported on the use of emerging neural networks to indicate commercial applications in credit checking systems geared to detect likely loan defaulters, to build a predictive model for customer demand and allocation of seats for an airline, and to design an intelligent camera to monitor safety hazards at railway crossings.

EXPERT SYSTEMS: A CASE STUDY

One of the best ways to understand a concept such as expert systems is to follow a case study or the successful implementation of one. This case covers a class of problem that has been receptive to ES solutions—that of a troubleshooting maintenance program.

The Product and the Marketplace

A page printing system (PPS) is a complex computer device that is employed to produce large volumes of printed output. It can produce 18,000 lines of print per minute. The system consists of a high-speed tape unit, an electrostatic printer, and a sophisticated paper cutting and collating device. It has 25 subsystems, over 2000 electro-mechanical components, and is considered difficult to troubleshoot. Furthermore, these systems often are run around the clock with many problems occurring during the difficult-to-service second and third shifts.

Purchasers of page printing systems are Fortune 1000 companies with manuals, order catalogues, parts listings, and large documents to produce. It is not a volume item like personal computers, but rather a specialty one; thus the location of units is rather diverse throughout the United States and Canada. Approximately 400 systems are installed. The U.S. government is a major customer. Service and response time are vital elements in the marketing strategy of the product.

The reason that an expert systems solution was sought in this situation was that the product was complex and it was becoming increasingly more difficult and expensive to hire and train maintenance experts to the necessary quality level. In addition, equally complex new models were planned for announcement in subsequent years. These models, though similar, were sufficiently different so as to require a continued update of skills and knowledge on the part of the field engineers and place even greater demand on the few experts available.

Problem Assessment

The aforementioned characteristics appeared to fit the model of an expert system solution in the general area of diagnosis or troubleshooting; that is, we have a situation where:

- The problem is sufficiently complex but narrow in scope.
- There is at least one recognized expert who is willing to act as a source of information and who is articulate enough to be effective.

- It takes an expert minutes to a few hours to solve a problem.
- The expertise is scarce.
- There appears to be a logical process to diagnose the problem which does not require a great amount of intuition.
- There is high pay off in problem resolution.

Figure 12.5 is a general schematic of the problem-solving process from the initial customer complaint. As can be seen, a difficult problem can result in three on-site visits, by the field engineer, the specialist, and the expert, respectively. Obviously there are cost savings to be made if, in a number of instances, the field engineer, via the expert system,

FIGURE 12.5. Page printing systems: problem-solving process

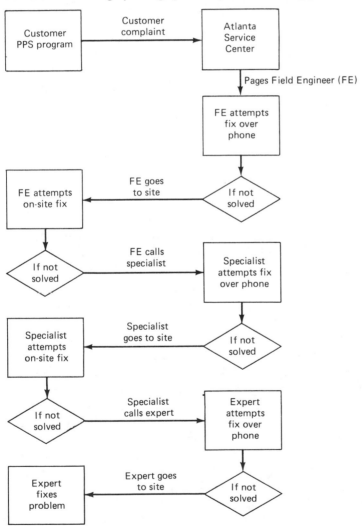

can preclude interaction or visits by the specialist or expert. More importantly from the customer's view, considerable time can be saved that otherwise would be expended in matching the required people to the specific problem.

The Approach

Once the problem domain was identified, a three-stage development process was laid out. The first stage was problem definition and statement of objectives. The objective, simply stated, was to aid the customer service engineer in troubleshooting the page printing system (PPS). The system must be available as a 24-hour diagnostic aid, must be a training aid (akin to a flight simulator) in lieu of hands-on experience, and must provide a reservoir (knowledge base) for PPS product knowledge and know-how. The cost goal was to reduce the mean time to repair (MTTR) by 30 percent, a cost savings of $950,000 over a five-year period.

The second stage is the gathering of knowledge (the knowledge acquisition and assimilation process). This is the crux of an expert system solution. The problem was well bounded, and the logic and knowledge rested in the head of a single expert. Unlike other systems domains consisting of a great deal of output and input with minimal processing crossing multiple departments and functions, this application did not tap many minds for a variety of details. The key to an expert system is to leverage depth rather than breadth. This presents both positive and negative elements. In the case of PPS, there were few experts, and one was selected based on proven knowledge and expertise through actual experience.

The methods used were to read available manuals on PPS system maintenance and to build a preliminary knowledge base, through a general question-and-answer process with the expert. A knowledge base is a set of rules, mostly of the if-then variety—a sort of decision logic tree. For example, a problem symptom—erratic paper motion—is indicative of paper not being fed evenly, causing double printed lines or unplanned spacing. Figure 12.6 illustrates the potential causes of this problem and the chances of each cause occurring.

An expert system can be classified by the number of rules in its knowledge base. A rough categorization is that small problems have under 350 rules with large problems having from 3000 to over 10,000 rules. The PPS expert system is classified as a medium system with the equivalent of about 2000-plus rules.

After the preliminary knowledge base was developed, the logic, control, and protocol analysis was reviewed by the principal expert as well as by other groups for verification and testing. However, the backbone of the knowledge base and rules reflected the problem-solving ability of the single expert based on background, experience, and problem expertise. The expert's opinion became the final word.

The next stage is recursive, to complete the design by implementing and reimplementing. Tackle the simplest and best understood versions of critical tasks first, deal with the most familiar and accessible portions of the process, and get a subset working as quickly as possible. The output of this subset is then tested and evaluated by the expert to ascertain future direction. This technique, called prototyping, is a standard and necessary part of artificial intelligence software. The implementation evolves from prototyping to fine-tuning.

FIGURE 12.6. Interface network (symptom and causes)

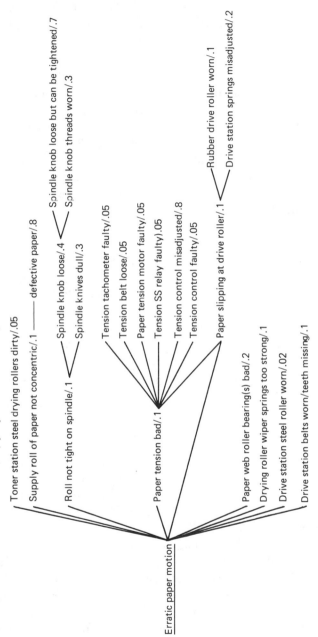

User Interfaces

Effective user interfaces were a most important element of the PPS system, as they are in all expert systems. End users range from professional experts, to a variety of semi knowledgeable people, to trainees. During the development stage, users are the system developers (knowledge engineers) and implementors. The key questions to be answered were: Just who are the other classes of users? How do they view the system? To what information do they need access? What do they need to be able to do with the information? There is nothing as demoralizing to an expert as having to step through a host of procedures that are basic and completely unnecessary. On the other hand, too precipitous a leap into the subject will lose the neophyte. The modular approach adopted kept the user interface separate from the functioning of the expert system itself. This allowed a variety of user interface modules to be developed without significant changes to the expert system. The user interface is the most volatile and unpredictable part of the total process. By modularizing the interfaces, work at several user levels could be conducted in parallel. Development time was thereby reduced substantially.

Four major user-mode functions were developed. The first and probably the most important is for the field engineer who troubleshoots and maintains the equipment. The main system criterion was an easy-to-use default operation that could limit the amount of input by defaulting to a standard set that operates in the largest majority of cases. The interface had to allow for help and feedback facilities and had to give a good deal of control to the field engineer. The other classes of user interface were the expert who must be able to review easily, adjust the rules as necessary, and add to the knowledge base; the knowledge engineer who uses expert system tools to develop the system; and the programmer who must be able to change and alter the system software as conditions dictate. Without these the desired level of user acceptance and effective system employment could not have been reached.

Some Generalizations

Figure 12.7 illustrates the components of an expert system such as the page printing maintenance program. The steps of problem definition, development of a knowledge base, and prototyping/implementation are the three stages mentioned. The inference engine is the heart of the system, the program that executes the decision logic and interfaces to the variety of users as mentioned in the case.

Expert system software is increasing in sophistication and also broadening to run on a variety of hardware platforms. If the developer feels that a completely custom system is needed, the application can be programmed by languages such as Lisp and Prolog. However, shells are available to ease the development process. These operate in the same way that spreadsheets do; the parameters that convey the decision rules are entered and the programming to construct the knowledge base and inference engine are automatically generated. There are a number of expert systems shells on the market, including Intellicorp's KEE, IBM's Expert System Environment (ESE), and Information Builder's Level 5 Object.

Hardware platforms have evolved from specialized hardware with the requisite number-crunching speed such as those made by Xerox, Texas Instruments, and Symbolics,

FIGURE 12.7. Expert system components

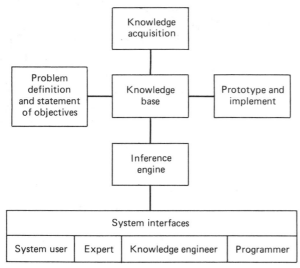

to mainframe platforms, to a growing number of expert systems running on 386- and 486-processor personal computers. The downsizing to PCs of all but the most large, complex ES applications will be a continuing trend.

Status and Future Enhancements

Phase I of systems implementation commenced with management approval of the project and the selection and funding of the design team. The design/implementation process required four and one-half person-years plus twelve weeks' involvement of the expert. The process featured an early prototype with a preliminary user interface design and the acquisition of 20 to 30 percent of the decision rules comprising the knowledge base. This phase took seven months, with the remaining five months (phase II) spent on interfaces and continued testing and verification of the rules. Phase III is the use of the system in specific sites, with its gradual incorporation at all the sites. It should be noted that developing expert systems for follow-on products took far less time than the original effort. As in any major systems development, the initial process must be expanded and modified as actual usage increases. The current priority list of modifications includes incorporating the rules for new versions of the page printing system as they are announced, and adding and modifying rules as experience dictates. Relating back to the original system objective, the system provides an effective 24-hour diagnostic aid that continues to build user confidence. Moderately trained field engineers are using the system based on previous experience and records, and analysis shows the MTTR (mean time to repair) has been materially reduced. The implementation approach was a laissez-faire one where field engineers could opt to use the system or not. Most are now using the system, and experience shows that the engineer, once introduced to the system, becomes dependent on it as a primary source of diagnostic information.

DEVELOPING AN EXPERT SYSTEMS STRATEGY

Expert systems are no different from any other sweeping new technology; the "front-end" probing and analysis are essential for deciding the extent of technology employment. The first concern is to understand the problem domains and to determine how important these are to the company's competitive stance or bottom line. Information systems are being used more strategically in a growing number of industries and companies. The Michael Porter framework suggests that companies can gain a competitive edge if they can: (1) reduce the cost of the product or service, (2) differentiate a product or service, or (3) develop a new market niche. If expert systems can affect any of these three areas in a major way, they must be considered seriously.

A prominent force in expert system strategy is the commitment and leadership from the top. In all major systems development, it has been said that top management commitment is crucial. It applies even more to systems where the technology is new and still in a test mode and the system gestation period is lengthy.

An organized search for key application areas and the determination of strategic areas of opportunity where competitive edge is apparent are prerequisites for the employment of expert systems. Relative payoffs or justification of alternate opportunities should be carefully evaluated. Several insurance companies are developing expert systems to qualify prospective policy holders and, through an on-line interactive dialogue, to be able to write a policy at an unattended kiosk in a shopping mall. Oil companies have developed expert systems to analyze geodetic factors and to direct oil-drilling operation. Expert systems-based financial analysis systems are projecting cash flow and future profit and loss scenarios for new companies and are analyzing investment portfolios. These are instances, and there are many more, where expert systems afford competitive advantage by reducing costs dramatically, differentiating a product, or opening up a new market niche.

The classic applications have been a medical system called MYCIN which diagnoses bacterial infection; XCON, a hardware configuration for the Digital Equipment Company; and Dipmeter advisor to help geologists determine geological structures from a variety of measurements. More and more, smaller expert systems are being used by companies in a variety of ways, such as front ends to complaint departments, sorting mail, or providing an "information lens" that culls data bases and news reports based on interest patterns of individual managers.

DuPont is the model of a user of the small expert system. They started this approach in the mid-1980s, launching a six-person AI task force. The approach was to develop small expert systems using simple shells running on personal computers. Three years after the formation of the group, some 200 systems were in use and another 500 in development. An expert systems user community numbered 1500 and a report indicated expert systems were saving the company $10 million per year! Once described as computer toys, these expert systems burgeoned throughout the DuPont organization.

A typical expert system application was the "packaging advisor," which helped DuPont customers select appropriate materials for specific packaging needs. Customers would input their requirements such as shelf life, temperature of the storage compartments, and so on, and the expert system would access a number of possible options including the price and features of each. Over 20 systems were designed for a variety of material control applications. The PPS system described earlier was a medium system with 2000 rules. These packaging advisor systems contained 100 to 200 rules, so they were able to be built by the hundreds and installed over a short period of time. They were not as encompassing as the PPS expert system as they focused on a more narrow and simple task, but the composite benefit to Dupont was impressive.

This example of a successful implementation says a good deal about expert systems. It is a typical type of problem that is receptive to this evolving new technology. There are lessons to be learned that are helpful to a company that is considering expert systems. As in any new technology there are risks to be evaluated, namely that the project will fail, the project will be late and well in excess of cost estimates, or the project will fail to fully meet the specifications. Another type of risk inherent in an expert systems' implementation is that the system will work, but the algorithms may be so constituted that they do not accurately reflect the expert's thought process. This may be difficult to detect and may only be seen after mistakes have been made. Although this problem may not have been severe in an application such as the page printing system where there is an immediate feedback loop (Does the printer work after repair?), it can be more serious in implementations such as the medical diagnosis. An expert systems strategy must carefully consider, weigh, and evaluate these risks.

SUMMARY

This chapter has focused on emerging technologies that are expected in the next ten-year time span. Not all technologies have been covered; rather, those that promise to have the most impact on business and management are reviewed. It is interesting that much of the new technology centers on the word *extensibility.* An overriding trend has been the lowering of the cost of computing because of the evolution of chips and other components. This has extended technology into areas of society that were not even imagined twenty years ago, bringing tremendous computing power to the factory, to the store, and to the desk. It has caused the technology developments just described to fall into two categories: those with added power and sophistication, and those aimed at making it easier for a wide range of users with different cognitive styles to employ them. Thus, on one hand we have expert systems, neural networks, networking, and image processing; while on the other we have groupware and simpler human interfaces.

I was privileged to hear C. P. Snow discuss the two-culture milieu concept in the Godkin lectures he delivered at Harvard in the early sixties. Snow, an Englishman trained in physics with a doctorate from Cambridge, was a scientist and worked in a variety of government agencies; he was also a prolific author, writing more than a dozen novels. He was knighted in 1957 and died in 1980. He was a man for many seasons.

Figure 12.8 illustrates his basic concept: a continued confrontation between the scientist and the humanist. He referred, for example, to the decision on strategic bombing in World War II, wherein the thinking was that bombing a city's population centers as well as its military and support centers would remove the will of the people to resist. This thinking proved to be incorrect. Snow used this issue to show the danger inherent when a prime minister (in this case Winston Churchill) relies almost completely on a scientific

FIGURE 12.8. Two-culture milieu.

source (F. A. Lindemann) on which to base a complex technical decision with such far-reaching effects. Snow elaborated on the necessity for the humanist and scientist to reach the proper level of communication and understanding.

Progress comes from a meeting of the minds of the scientist and the humanist. The real challenge is for the scientist to provide the technology in a way that can be utilized and understood by the humanist. I like the phrase "elegance in simplicity." A good tool maker keeps the user in mind and understands the workings of that user's mind.

Case Study

Fielding Electronics

Wallace Lott joined Fielding Electronics, a designer and manufacturer of semiconductor memory and processor chips for the computer industry, some six months ago as director of IS. He was stunned to find that a company developing products in the forefront of technology would have internal computer systems that were (in Lott's words) hardly in the twentieth century. Though no one had expressed major concern with the information systems within Fielding, Lott felt that upgrading the hardware was one of his first priorities.

Lott was a graduate of MIT and had worked in their computer lab upon graduation. After a two-year period in which he concentrated on advanced simulation models, he became a salesperson for Digital Equipment Corporation (DEC) and sold minicomputers and microcomputers on an OEM (original equipment manufacturer) basis to large engineering houses, who in turn would add software and applications for resale to end users. Lott was very successful at DEC, never needing home office support, as he could provide his own technical expertise. He had a reputation of really knowing his product and what made it tick.

Lott's new company was running a large mainframe with a peripheral array whose age averaged eight years from time of first industry introduction. It was obvious to the new IS director that Fielding was certainly not a leading edge computer user; in fact it was at the trailing fringe.

His first major proposal to management was a plan to upgrade hardware. It called for a replacement of the mainframe with dual 32-bit, high-powered minis. The latest high-density disks would be added, even though Fielding would be a test site for them. Micro-based intelligent work stations would replace the current five-to-ten-year-old CRTs that were controlled by the mainframe. Graphic terminals would gradually be installed in key executive locations and a communications network established so that an electronic mail feature could be added to the current word processing applications.

Lott's plan was greeted enthusiastically by the management of Fielding. They had always felt the existence of the "shoemaker's children" syndrome, and it was a bit embarrassing to show visiting customers their antiquated computer hardware. This was the major reason bringing Lott in. They were particularly excited about the machine room model that an engineering design firm had developed for them. It featured a completely glass-enclosed computer room with model work stations and automated office modules. The telecommunications control center was particularly impressive, replete with screens, monitors, and switches. Each piece of equipment had its model number, capacity, and speed characteristics noted on a panel directly above it. There was no question that this installation, representing the state of the art in computer hardware, would be a showcase and give Fielding the high-tech image they sought.

The installation went like clockwork; a PERT chart in the information system control room plotted every step along the way, and management could enter the room and ascertain the status via a specially conceived color code.

Nine months after the installation, Lott was summarily relieved of his duties and replaced by a senior IS professional with fifteen years' experience in the field. The new director found a 24-month application backlog, a bevy of irate vendors who had been either not paid or paid erroneously, and a multitude of outraged internal users.

STUDY QUESTIONS

1. What went wrong with Lott's well-conceived plan?
2. What elements might Lott have overlooked or downplayed?
3. Was Lott the real problem, or was he a scapegoat?
4. What challenges face the new IS director? What should be his strategy?

Case Study

Taking Stock of EDI

Wal-Mart Stores, Inc. uses EDI integrated with an inventory ordering application to eliminate the need to manually reorder much of its merchandise in its 1400 stores nationwide. Wal-Mart, with 1800 EDI trading partners, boasts one of the largest EDI programs in the U.S.

From *Network world.* January 8, 1990.

The department store chain uses scanning machines at the point of sale and in distribution centers to track inventory depletion accurately.

When stock levels fall below a predetermined point, computer systems in the stores or at distribution centers generate an electronic purchase order. That order is then sent via EDI to the appropriate supplier, according to Mark Schmidt, senior director of Information Services at Wal-Mart in Bentonville, Arkansas.

EDI is a critical element of Wal-Mart's Quick Response strategy, which enables the general merchandiser to streamline inventory and speed the delivery of goods to stores in response to consumer demand. Wal-Mart currently uses Quick Response to order high-volume items or goods from suppliers that are extensively automated. The company will expand its Quick Response program by adding suppliers that automate their operations.

"EDI had enabled us to change the way we do business, making us more efficient and productive," Schmidt said.

But integrating EDI into existing applications is not always as easy as many companies would like.

Gregory Harter, Director of Finance at Cummins Engine Co., Inc. in Columbus, Indiana, said successful EDI programs require a good deal of coordination among corporate departments that traditionally operate independently. They also require companies to work closely with EDI trading partners.

"EDI won't solve a company's communications problems; it will only magnify them," Harter said. "Companies need to chart and then simplify the flow of communications between departments and trading partners before implementing EDI. Otherwise, they are doomed to encounter problems."

Cummins Engine spent more than six months integrating a variety of applications used to manage customer orders, such as shipping, accounts receivable, and invoicing. An interdepartmental task force at the company determined that all internal applications should use the same code number when referring to individual customer orders. In turn, Cummins' customers would use the same code number when processing the orders at their end, Harter said.

Standardizing code numbers throughout all applications eliminated the need for clerks to rekey information from one application to another, Harter said. The standardization also enables applications to automatically pass new information concerning a shipment among multiple applications without human intervention.

"EDI is the application-to-application exchange of data, not the computer-to-computer exchange of data," Harter said. "If data just flows between computers and not applications, somebody has to read, print and reenter the data, which nullifies any benefits of EDI."

STUDY QUESTIONS

1. Note that Wal-Mart adds suppliers only if they automate their operations. What does this say for those wanting to do business with Wal-Mart?

2. Do you think that the reengineering of business processes is a prerequisite to effective EDI?

3. Explain what is meant by the difference between application-to-application and the computer-to-computer exchange of data.

4. What are some of the pitfalls of EDI?

5. Are the benefits of EDI more in the efficiency or effectiveness area?

SELECTED REFERENCES

The American Association for Artificial Intelligence, *Proceedings Eighth National Conference on Artificial Intelligence*. Cambridge, Mass.: AAAI Press, 1990.

Brody, Herb, "The Neural Computer," *Computerworld*. October 1, 1990.

Ditlea, Steve, "Welcome to Virtual Reality," *Sourcebook*. Fall 1990, pp. 58-61.

Eckerson, Wayne, "Leading-Edge Users Merge EDI, Existing Applications," *Network World*. January 8, 1990, p. 2-8.

"Emerging Technologies, Annual Review for Managers," Management Summary, Butler Cox Foundation, London, England, 1990.

Fisher, Marcia, "Digging Out with Image Technology," *Datamation*, April 15, 1989.

Gallagher, John P., *Knowledge Systems for Business*. Englewood Cliffs, N.J.: Prentice Hall, 1988.

Gibson, Richard, "Japan's NEC Corp. Unveils Its Fastest Supercomputers," *Wall Street Journal*. April 27, 1989.

Harbert, Tammi, "Uniting Nations on Networks," *Computerworld*. May 28, 1990, p. 98.

"Image Management Systems," IDC White Paper, Framingham, Mass., 1990.

"Intel to Unveil Supercomputer with Low Price," *Wall Street Journal*. January 8, 1990, p. B2.

Kanter, Jerome, Barbara Braden, and David Kopcso, "Developing an Expert Systems Strategy," *MIS Quarterly*. December 1989, pp. 459-467.

Kanter, Jerome, "New Tools, New Rules," *Information Strategy: The Executive's Journal*. Winter 1990, pp. 51-54.

Keen, Peter G.W., "Business Integration Through Technology Integration," *Advance*. Vol. 4, No. 1, 1991, pp. 1-6.

Leibs, Scott, "The Promise and the Pitfalls," *InformationWeek*. February 11, 1991, pp. 38-40.

Lewis, Peter, "Radio Waves That Really Bend, From Motorola," *The New York Times*. February 24, 1991, p. 8.

Markoff, John, "An Aging Dancer Fights to Keep Up," *The New York Times Business*. February 10, 1991, pp. 1-6.

Mockler, Robert J., *Knowledge-Based Systems for Managment Decisions*. Englewood Cliffs, N.J.: 1989.

Rifkin, Glenn, "Putting 65,000 Processors to Work," *Computerworld*. July 18, 1988.

Runyan, Linda, "Hot Technologies for 1989," *Datamation*, January 15, 1989.

Savage, J.A., "Taking the 'Place' Out of Workplace," *Computerworld*. May 14, 1990, pp. 67-69.

Snow, C.P., *The Two Cultures: A Second Look,* 2nd ed. Cambridge, England: Cambridge University Press, 1963.

Straub, Detmar, and James C. Wetherbe, "Strategic Information Technologies for the 1990s: Organizational Needs and Technological Fit," *Managment Information Systems Research Center Working Paper*. February 1989.

"Superconductor Efforts to Lead to Devices Soon," *Wall Street Journal*. June 7, 1989.

Sviokla, John J., "PlanPower: The Financial Planning Expert System," *Harvard Business School*, 1986.

Williamson, Mickey, "Neural Networks: Glamour and Glitches," *Computerworld*. February 15, 1988, pp. 89-92.

Xenakis, John, "Deloitte & Touche Counts On Neural," *InformationWeek*. November 19, 1990, p. 22.

Chapter 13

Information Systems and Society

INTRODUCTION

To this point, the emphasis has been on the impact of IS on management in a business setting. In this chapter, the focus shifts to the effects that IS has had, is having, and will have on society and the individual—a broader look than has been taken in previous chapters. Issues to be explored include ethics, invasion of privacy, computer crime, legal issues, and quality of life, as well as physical and environmental concerns. Also included is a look at the profession of IS and what opportunities exist for people either specializing in the field or who seek a position where the emphasis is on managing with information. Finally, the education and training dimension is reviewed. With technology coming at society at an ever-increasing rate, how people are trained in the new technology and the new ways of managing with information become very crucial subjects.

THE RISE OF THE KNOWLEDGE WORKER

Generally speaking, as indicated by Figure 13.1, there have been three industrial eras, the first centering on man's use and mastery of material (preindustrial revolution), the second centering on the use and mastery of energy (the Industrial Revolution) and the third focused on the use and mastery of information (postindustrial revolution). The Industrial Revolution

FIGURE 13.1. Technology and the industrial revolution

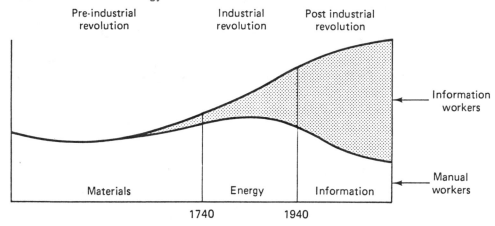

is thought by most to have started with the use of steam power in the mid-eighteenth century. The onset of the information era is more difficult to pinpoint, but is probably tied to the development of the first of the electronic computers in the 1940s.

Before the nineteenth century, most work was performed manually by farm workers and unskilled laborers. The man mainly associated with the development of modern technological principles that drastically changed the character of work was Fredrick Winslow Taylor (1856–1915). He applied what is now called scientific management or systems theory to manual tasks. By studying and analyzing physical movements and the sequence of activities, a streamlined and improved method was developed, resulting in the production of more goods or products in a shorter period of time. Automation, or the use of machines in this process, was a natural extension, replacing people power with machine power.

Peter Drucker indicates that "the substitution of knowledge for manual effort as a productive resource in work is the greatest change in the history of work." He points out that in 1900, 18 of every 20 Americans were manual laborers, 10 of them farmers. By 1965, only 5 of the 20 of a vastly increased work force did manual labor, only one being a farmer. This trend continues today and is the cornerstone of the information revolution. Manual workers are being replaced by knowledge workers. People learn how to accomplish work in schools or by reading books and manuals or taking correspondence courses. They do not learn in the factory, on the farm, or at the work bench. Computers and information systems are the tools of today's knowledge workers, as the hammer and saw were the tools of the manual worker. This is not to say that every knowledge worker uses a computer or advanced information technology. Knowledge workers span the gamut of sophistication from clerks and cashiers to systems analysts using computer simulation to project the future or business strategy of large corporations.

An example brings out the evolution that has been taking place, as first a machine with an operator replaces several manual workers and then, in turn, the operator is replaced by a computer. The objective is to drill several holes of a specified pattern into a metal surface. In the beginning, the worker drilled holes in metal by hammering a boring-like device of prescribed size through the metal. Later a hand drill with an adjustable bit was used. Then a drill press was used to position the work piece under the drill and a button was pressed to lower the drill through the work piece. These evolutionary drilling developments removed the physical portion of the job from the worker and reduced direct contact with the machine. The advent of numerical control removes the worker still further from the machine, indeed, almost all the way.

In numerical control, a machine such as a drill press or lathe is controlled by a computer [computer-aided manufacturing (CAM)]. The computer control unit, attached to the machine tool, generates the necessary impulses to control the drilling of a hole in a specific spot in a piece of metal. The reason that the process is called numerical control is that the movements of the drill and the work to be drilled are controlled by numbers representing the shape of the desired finished part. It is more accurately called *symbolic control,* because the actual machining process is described by symbols, some of which happen to be numbers. Now we have machines under robotic control; a robot accomplishes the positioning of the part and its movement through the drilling process.

These stages parallel the three areas already mentioned. The first stage of the manual drilling corresponds to the use of materials and manual operation of the preindustrial revolution; the use of the drill press is a feature of the Industrial Revolution with the use of steam or electrically powered machinery; and the advent of numerical control is an example of the postindustrial period with the productive use of information and the advent of knowledge workers.

There is also a parallel evolution that has been occurring in the home and in the world of the individual. Cooking and cleaning were accomplished without machines and by manual effort exclusively in the preindustrial era. The use of vacuum cleaners, dishwashing machines, and the like are commonplace today. Programmed utilities such as the microwave oven or the intelligent temperature control device are forerunners of the postindustrial processes.

Figure 13.1 shows the period prior to 1740 as the preindustrial revolution, when manual workers predominated. In fact there were but a few knowledge workers as the shaded area indicates. The Industrial Revolution spawned the concept of knowledge workers with the substitution of machine power and the development of the steam engine, electrical power, telegraph, telephone, radio, automobile, and airplane. Today we live in the information era where knowledge workers abound. Workers now deal with the symbols of work rather than the work itself. All of this is not without its impact on society.

THE LUDDITE SYNDROME

The Luddites were an organized band of English rioters who campaigned against and destroyed labor-saving equipment in the early 1800s as a protest against lost jobs and the poor quality of work produced by the machinery. Their leader was called Captain Ludd and the aftermath of his activity was a series of shootings and hangings and then strict legislative control before the movement finally came to an end. Today the term Luddites is used to refer to an individual or group who are against automation or the use of machinery to replace people or even to augment individual effort.

Modern day Luddites and Captain Ludds are prevalent in the computer age. The

FIGURE 13.2. Twenty-first-century gravestone

original Luddites attacked the initial products of the first industrial revolution, namely, textile machines; modern-day Luddites find computers, and the information systems they power, targets for their twentieth century fear and anxiety. Today's Luddites do not use physical destruction as their means, but rather more subtle methods geared to the information era. As described earlier, one government worker embedded in a computer program a condition that would occur exactly a year after he retired. The date would trigger the execution of a program subroutine that would destroy the department's program file and central data base. In this case, a backup file system prevented this sabotage from becoming a complete disaster. Worms and viruses are much in the news, and several classic stories are related later in the chapter.

Other business people, including some high-level executives, secretly resent the intrusion of computers into their business sphere, changing the way they perform their functions and causing them to learn complicated new procedures whose effectiveness they question in the first place. The mode of battle here is often to avoid involvement altogether or subtly to withhold key information parameters that are vital to successful system operation.

Still others fear the encroachment of machines into the areas of personal freedom and flexibility of life style. Consumers who have done battle with a company's computer system while attempting to clarify an erroneous billing or a paycheck discrepancy are modern day consumer Luddites. Figure 13.2 personifies what this group thinks the advances in computer technology will lead to.

There is nothing unusual about this computer reaction; resistance to change has been a psychological fact of life since the beginning of time. None of us is completely immune. However, there is something to say about resistance to change. In his book, *Father, Son & Co.,* Thomas J. Watson Jr. tells this story of his father: Once in the early fifties Dad visited a research lab at Columbia University that was experimenting with high speed circuits.

Upon leaving the lab, he remarked that the engineers didn't seem to know what they were doing but they were doing it at 200,000 times a second. (As an aside this is still true of a good deal of computing today.) In a similar vein, an analyst proclaimed on seeing a printout of complex mathematical equations spewing from a high-speed computer printer, "amazing...it would have taken 40 scientists 40 years to make a mistake like that."

It is obvious that we should be as interested in what computers can do for us as well as what they can do to us. The answer is not resistance, recalcitrance, and sabotage. Everyone is aware of what technology brings to a society, in transportation, communication, medicine, industry, education; yet there are urban blight, traffic jams, pollution, radiation, crime, juvenile delinquency, schizophrenia, depression, and loneliness. As Peter Drucker says, "The only positive alternative to destruction by technology is to make technology work as our servant. In the final analysis this surely means mastery by man over himself, for if anyone is to blame, it is not the tool, but the human maker and user. 'It is a poor carpenter who blames his tools' says an old proverb."

INFORMATION SYSTEMS AND THE INDIVIDUAL

Information systems have changed the way corporations compete and the manner in which people manage in the information age. IS has also changed the private world, the world that is experienced outside the working hours of the day. It is useful to take a look at this world.

Figure 13.3 places the individual at the center of the sphere that describes the interactions of the individual with information systems. The inner ring circling the individual indicates that money is a common denominator of the future system scenario, though it will not be money as we now know it. The cashless society will slowly evolve as it is doing now with the proliferation of credit and money cards. A single money card or the individual's fingerprint or voice will serve as the exchange agent for the transactions that take place. The next ring indicates the six major systems, which will be computer powered and will have major influence on the individual. One overriding approach to all of the six major systems will be to obtain the services from the individual personal computer in the home or via wireless contact (e.g., cellular phones) in cars, airplanes, or hotels.

The outer ring lists the functions or subsystems of each of the six systems. The first major system, a consumer system, includes the grocery store, drug store, department store, and other shops where automatic scanning of price and identification code will create simultaneous offsets to the customer's bank balance. The consumer system will be a growing information system contact point for the individual. The consumer will play a more involved role and in a growing number of cases, will effect the transaction him- or herself as is done now with automatic teller machines.

The second major system is leisure time, which will be a growing arena as information systems and other technological advances reduce the hours of work. Contact with travel agencies for hotel, travel, and entertainment reservations will be on a sophisticated, information system basis. Individual preference profiles will be part of the central file for each subscriber, so that accommodations can be tailored to individual requirements including such things as aisle or window seats, special diet, deluxe or economy accommodations, and the like.

FIGURE 13.3. Information system and the individual

In the public and private service system, library access and retrieval will be under computer control, while there will be automatic links to fire and police departments via home and car sensor devices. Accounting, legal, insurance, and brokerage services will be individualized and maintained in computer records; personalized insurance and stock portfolios will be under computer control and updated automatically as conditions dictate. The individual will be bumping into information systems more and more in this area.

The home information and control system, centering on the three major subsystems of entertainment, environment, and security, will be a major contact point for the individual. While in the other systems the individual will be an external user, in the home he or she will be a principal designer and operator of the system.

A fifth system focuses on education and medical practice, each of which has a significant influence on our lives. Information systems will have a great deal of impact on these functions with the aims to improve service, reduce costs, and make better use of scarce educational and medical expertise. Information technology such as computer-aided instruction, videoconferencing and the like, will dramatically change the way we learn and interact with others.

Finally, financial—the sixth system—will center on a money card and integrated individual financial file. Banking will be conducted differently than it is today; the service will be ever present, but we will not be making visits to banks. Electronic funds transfers will occur at the sale or transaction point, automatically debiting or crediting a central account based on the transaction type. Savings, loans, mortgages, trusts, and the like will be handled as part of an individualized integrated central data base. For better or for worse, the individual will maintain a consolidated up-to-the-minute financial status.

Progress around the circle will be uneven; that is to say, the computerization of these functions will not take place simultaneously. Depending on economic and technical feasibility, some systems will represent the leading edge while others will lag in development. It is also unlikely that these systems will develop as an integrated whole, as some are dependent on others. One thing is certain and that is that these systems will be with us in the years ahead.

One would hope a key criterion for development priority would be the needs of the consumer or individual. A theorem that has existed since automation began, though not always followed, is that systems should serve people and not the other way around. Greater IS literacy can provide knowledge and perspective in seeing that the individual can play a role in seeing that systems do serve people both in the short and long run.

THE IMPACT OF TECHNOLOGY—ELECTRONIC HIGHWAYS

The foregoing scenario will be built on a micro-based telecommunications network that will drive digital signals for voice, text, video, and graph (maybe even smell) across fiber optic cable or through the air to any place where humans are located.

Electronic highways will replace concrete highways. Rather than drive an automobile, we will bank at home, order merchandise at home, work at home via videophone and teleconferences, and obtain our news and mail at home through electronic mail. Furthermore, we will spend much of our leisure time at home because we will have video games, videoconferences and education classes, a wide selection of video movies, and will be able to pursue a variety of home hobbies and pastimes via our in-house computer system.

We will be able to have medical check-ups via video and sensor links and even have illnesses diagnosed (house calls are back). We will be able to vote at home and have a say in important referendums (the town meeting form of government will be back).

Think of the cultural impact of such a scenario. People could work in the suburbs and even in small cities away from the metropolis. The urban problems of pollution, congestion, and blight would receive a major assist, and, because we would carry no cash on our person and have automatic sensor links to police stations, crime would be reduced. People in small cities would have access to medical treatment as good as that available to big city folk. Culture would be shipped to the small towns via optical cable television; the days of the eastern or western establishment would be gone.

The ultimate in electronic travel might be as stated by a West Coast professor in a quote from an article entitled, "21st Century: A World of Artificial Men," published in the *LA Times* and *Washington Post*. Though I don't subscribe to the concept of telecloning, the thought is provocative. "It may be possible by 2067 for man to travel by 'teleportation'; that is, the cells of the human body, and even its personality and memories will be transmitted from one place to another by radio. This could be done by feeding an individual's entire genetic code into a computer, and sending the information to another computer, perhaps on the moon or Mars. The information then would be used to reconstruct the individual out of the essential materials in storage at the destination. This would amount to creation of exact replicas."

SOCIAL VALUE AND THE QUALITY OF LIFE

The foregoing scenario brings out a plethora of social issues and social consequences. It makes one think that everything that can be done is not necessarily worth doing. A simple criterion that can prove useful in sorting out the worth of the burgeoning new products and capabilities is the question, "Does it improve the quality of life?" Quality of life has both an individual and societal implication, and, of course, there will be individual judgments. The following article (Figure 13.4) articulately brings up the quality of life issue.

COMPUTERS THAT MONITOR THE WORKPLACE

There is always a downside to the employment of technology, and the computer is no exception. Office workers, particularly those that spend time handling company transactions, have complained about the new "electronic sweatshops." The workers who are most affected include telephone operators, reservation clerks, and people handling telephone orders and customer complaints. These workers spend a good deal of the day, if not all of it, behind computer screens handling an array of repetitive transactions.

Every week employees are given report cards that emanate from their "computer supervisors." These reports show the number and type of transactions completed, the time per class of transaction, a comparison with past performance, and an analysis of where the person stands in relation to peers. It is also possible to score the percentage of transactions in which procedures were not followed or errors occurred. Knowing they are being constantly measured places enormous pressure on the workers. In some instances they are paid on the basis of transactions handled correctly. These same computer supervisors can keep track of time away from the desk, including coffee breaks or lunch breaks, and can advise if the times are exceeding prescribed norms.

Many issues are raised by this type of operation. There are issues of the validity of the computer programs to measure accurately; then there are issues of privacy and intimidation. There may be some who look at these types of systems as fairer than the normal subjective performance measurements, but there is also a cadre who resent the "Big Brother" intrusion into their work. At any rate, there are federal and state committees on employment and productivity and organizations like Nine-to-Five, a Cleveland-based unit, that looks into the variety of employee complaints. These issues emanate when work patterns are changed

FIGURE 13.4. The cordless tie that binds people to work (1990, The Boston Globe Newspaper Co./Washington Post Writers Group. Reprinted with permission.)

I am standing in the lobby of a large office building when the man beside me starts talking into his briefcase. The fellow looks buttoned up and rational, so I assume if he is hearing voices, they are real ones. There is a phone in his briefcase.

I am sitting at a red light in traffic, when the car beside me starts ringing. The driver picks up the receiver and begins a now common routine. She steers her car with one hand and her business with the other.

I am somewhere over Connecticut on a one-hour shuttle from Boston to New York when my companion sticks his credit card into the chair before us and calls his office to find out if there are any messages. At 22,000 feet, he leaves a phone message in Boston about where to forward his phone messages in New York.

Once upon a time, a sitcom hero named Maxwell Smart used to talk into his shoe, and we laughed. But somewhere along the line, the high-touch gadgetry of the spy films got transformed into the tools of everyday trade.

Today there are people within reach of a phone every moment of their lives except takeoff, landing and a long tunnel ride. The work-world is now an interlocking network of communications and messages, a proliferation of phones, a great babbling overkill of touch-tone technology.

We live from call-waiting to call-forwarding, from answer machines to voice mail. We are surrounded by cellular phones and portable phones. We even have a little pocket phone to form a "personal communications network."

In theory, this population explosion of phones and their fax-similes has sprung into being to offer mobility and freedom from the office. Indeed, people who take phones to the gym, the restaurant, even the bathroom, swear by the freedom they gain with this telephone tether.

But watching my colleagues-on-call, I have become convinced that this network is a tie that binds more and more people to work.

The executives who go to the beach with a towel and a telephone aren't liberated from the office: They are only on work-release. The cellular commuters haven't changed the work environment; they have turned every environment into workspace. The new touchable class reminds me of parolees let out of jail after being collared by a tracking device.

I admit to being somewhat phonephobic. One of the great pleasures of life is being out of touch. If I were to devise a home voice mail, it would say: Touch 1 if this a life-threatening emergency. Touch 2 if your are a family member with a flat tire on a dark corner. Touch 3 if you are a junk-phone call and would like to be immolated.

But even by normal standards, we've gone too far. In the work-world, we are increasingly seduced by the notion of how efficient it is to be in constant contact with each other. The phone in all its forms has become a kind of endless meeting that entices us to spend more time communicating than producing. And the operative phrase is "more time."

The Bureau of Labor says that Americans are working longer hours than we used to. Twenty million or so have bumped the workweek over the 49-hour mark. There are no figures that tell us how many of those hours are spent leaving messages to call. Nor do we know how much time is spent responding to questions that we're asked only because of the availability of the instant-information-gratification system.

In the constant-contact future, it's easy to see an insidious extension of work and a more insidious extension of the workplace. In the industrial age, the factory foreman controlled his workers from nine to five. In the information age, workers are always available.

Today it is possible to begin work with the first commuting mile on a cellular phone, continue it through a lunch accompanied by a "personal communications network" and end with a bedtime chat into your briefcase.

In 24-hour contact, we haven't missed a thing. Except, of course, the time for rumination, the solitude and space for the work we call thinking.

For years the pitch of the telephone company was "Reach out and touch someone." Now we're all tied up, workers of the world united by the touch-tone, and we need a new slogan. How about this one: "Let my people off the hook."

without considering the personal ramifications. It is a certainty that future technology, possibly driven by expert systems, will be able to monitor and supervise office workers to a far greater extent than is currently done. The social and human elements remain crucial considerations.

THE PRIVACY ISSUE

"Last spring, the long arm of American Express reached out and grabbed Ray Parrish. After getting his credit card in January, the 22-year-old New Yorker promptly paid bills of $331 and $204.39 in February and March. Then he got a surprising call. His credit privileges were being suspended, an American Express clerk informed him, because his checking account showed too small a balance to pay his April charge of $596" (*Business Week* cover story of September 4, 1989).

This story is similar in some ways to the federal government attempting to root out what they termed *double dippers* by comparing files of welfare recipients with government payroll records. The thinking is that, if you are drawing a salary from the government, you shouldn't be drawing welfare at the same time.

A major issue in both of these cases is whether it is legal or ethical to use personal data to build cases, either true or contrived, that affect the individual, perhaps even convicting them of crime and sending them to prison. Does it matter whether the data in question assist or hurt the individual? For example, many companies sell mailing lists that have been developed as a by-product of another business they are in. Some make more money from the by-product mailing lists than from the main-line business they are in. If it is known that people who buy four-wheel-drive campers are good prospects for buying camping equipment, the list of people buying Chrysler Jeeps would have value for L.L. Bean. An individual joins the Audubon Society and soon thereafter is receiving requests from a variety of ecological foundations. What is the value of knowing everyone in the Denver area who earns $100,000 or more and has $10,000 available on a credit card? Is it of interest, and to which business leaders, to know the number of X-rated movies rented from the local video outlet. Is it upsetting to know that your airline reservation system is responsible for your receiving 20 different mail order catalogues each month?

Another class of potential invasion of privacy is illustrated by the following example. An employee is looking for a position in another company. His supervisor finds this out in her routine perusal of the company's electronic mail network. She has a routine of checking messages between employees. The supervisor fires the employee, indicating that looking for new job on company time is not a proper thing to do.

There are laws that protect the individual. For example, the use of your social security number as a universal ID is not allowed, but this is a moot point because your name and address can be almost as effective, particularly with the processing power of today's computers, data bases, and communication networks. There is no question that laws must stay in step with the power of technology that affords new ways to violate a person's privacy and civil rights. The Privacy Act of 1974, approved by Congress, is one attempt to answer some of these issues, and is the broadest on the books. Other laws are the Video Privacy Protection Act of 1988, which prohibits retailers from disclosing video rental records, and the Computer Matching and Privacy Protection Act, which regulates some computer matching of federal data but still leaves many potential matches unaffected.

The Privacy Act of 1974 applies only to the public sector, but its content is relevant to the private sector. Its basic contents are: (1) Congress, finds that an individual can be directly affected by the collection, maintenance, use, and dissemination of personal information by federal agencies and that the right of privacy is a personal and fundamental right protected by the Constitution of the United States; (2) the increasing use of computer and sophisticated information technology has greatly increased the harm and potential harm to an individual; (3) the purpose of the Act is to provide safeguards against the personal invasion of privacy by federal agencies; (4) no agency may disclose any record to any person or another agency without the prior written consent of the individual to whom the record pertains; (5) each individual has access to his or her own record; and (6) each agency will maintain only that information relevant and necessary to accomplish a purpose of the agency.

The Privacy Act stipulates civil remedies, fines, and criminal penalties for violating a person's privacy rights as indicated under the Act. It also establishes a Privacy Protection Study Commission to further study data banks, automated data processing programs, and information systems of government, regional, and private organizations in order to determine the standards and procedures to protect information and recommend relevant courses of action to the president and Congress.

Possibly, a set of laws of this type is required in the private sector. However, the expense and effort required of companies to comply with a strict interpretation of the law would be considerable. Data files pertaining to employees, customers, and suppliers would require a different type of file organization and protection scheme. Also, third-party audits at prescribed times might well be required to insure compliance.

Data privacy is not only a domestic issue, it has become an international one as well, as indicated in this *Wall Street Journal* report of July 20, 1990.

The European Community and Personal Data

The European Community Commission is seeking to protect personal data against abuse.

Five European Community Commission members—Italy, Belgium, Spain, Portugal, and Greece—lack legislation protecting an individual's right to control personal information in private or public data banks. Worried that varying levels of protection throughout the European Community Commission may obstruct the flow of information, the commission has proposed a directive based on a Council of Europe convention already ratified by seven European Community Commission states.

The directive would give individuals the right of access to information about themselves and the right to correct erroneous data. Data relating to race, health or political opinions would receive extra protection against unauthorized use.

Filippo Pandolfi, commissioner of science and research, says he fears that modern telecommunications technology means there is a greater risk that sensitive information will be misused or stolen.

The gathering of huge amounts of personal data in digital form and the ability to transmit those data have opened up all types of opportunities, both positive and negative, which challenge the laws developed for protecting individual rights in the preinformation era. George Orwell's classic, *1984,* about future society envisions "Big Brother" as a political dictator. In our twenty-first century society, "Big Brother" may appear as a data base expert.

COMPUTER CRIME AND HACKING

Computer crime and hacking fall into the general category of unauthorized intrusion into information systems. Computer crime includes theft whereby individuals have tampered with records, for example, to set up fictitious suppliers to obtain payments for bogus services rendered. The Equity Funding Corporation scandal many years ago was the forerunner of a run of computer crime. At Equity Funding, massive collusion resulted in the computerized development of false insurance policies to cover huge cash deficits, resulting from theft by employees. This was referred to as the billion-dollar bubble.

The crimes can be more subtle, such as gaining access to internal data files that can then be sold to competitors under the guise of consulting assistance. Also, computer programs can be copied for sale or for individual use. The theft of data or programs has a different connotation, at least to some, than where the objective is hard cash. There is a rationalization that says that data or programs are intangible products that can be used by others without exhausting the original source. That is, when one takes a copy of the data file, the original is still there for the owner to use. Except in rare cases, this is, as indicated, a rationalization—and an indefensible one at that. Copyright laws now protect software as they do to other forms of intellectual property. Court cases have upheld software copyrights.

The copyright law has existed for years to foster and protect the inventor's ideas for innovative concepts that eventually influence the development of new products. The advent of the information era and the concept of software have challenged the law and provided a type of product that is unique. That product can be defined as intellecutal property.

Computer crime can also take the guise of espionage. Such was the famous case covered in the book *The Cuckoo's Egg: Inside the World of Computer Espionage,* in which the author, Clifford Stoll, traces a seemingly trivial 75-cent accounting error to an international espionage plot formulated by a foreign intruder who gained entry into more than 30 supposedly secure military and research computers. Stoll uncovered a spy ring in West Germany linked to the KGB in the U.S.S.R. that was paying for classified information about the U.S. space program and other military matters. This started out as if it were the work of an innocent hacker who wanted to prove he was clever enough to gain access to secure military computers, but it turned out to be a different kind of story.

In the spring of 1990, Robert Morris, Jr., a Cornell graduate student, was sentenced to three years probation and a $10,000 fine for unleashing a worm that temporarily disabled several thousand computers that were linked via Arpanet, a network that connects many educational, government, and business computers. This is an example of hacking that is not done for material gain or for espionage. At best it is creative play that has the positive aspect of showing innovation and brings out the lack of security precautions in computer systems throughout the world. This, many claim, is a positive aspect of hacking.

On the negative side, a worm or virus (a virus modifies other programs, copying itself and changing the host program, while a worm copies itself into other computer systems, but does not change host programs) can do irreparable damage by destroying files and programs that are worth millions of dollars. Backup files can recreate the data, but not without major interruption and cost. Hacking can also create an atmosphere in which institutions must spend inordinate amounts of money and energy developing full-proof security systems that actually impede the free exchange of information that can benefit society in the long run.

On the more playful side of hacking, the following appeared in *Information Week*:

Virus Attack

Last Friday, the 13th of July, at least one Novell Netware site was hit by the Jerusalem B software virus. The virus apparently entered through an MS-DOS program and then entered other programs to delete images that were programmed to execute on Friday the 13th.

The advent of computer crime and hacking have raised some very significant ethical issues. *Harvard Magazine* wrote about the Morris affair (Morris was a Harvard graduate), and prominent people in science and law had their chance to air their views on the Morris case (see the following). It is apparent that the advent of modern information systems has created new conditions and new situations that require looking again at our laws and regulations to see what changes must be made to equitably handle these types of situations.

Crime and Punishment: Five Views of the Morris Case

Jeffrey Schiller, network manager at the Massachusetts Institute of Technology: "This is the first serious situation to telegraph the message that these computer networks are considered part of the national infrastructure, and, therefore, abusing them is considered a crime rather than a clever hack. Ten years ago there would never have been a felony conviction for this—it would probably have been handled as a local matter at Cornell."

Clifford Stoll, space scientist at the Harvard-Smithsonian Center for Astrophysics and author of *The Cuckoo's Egg: Inside the World of Computer Espionage*: "Not funny. Our department couldn't do any work for two days. He did it as a research project? Suppose I went around the city and let the air out of 6000 people's tires as a 'research project'? My computer costs run twice what my car does and I don't use it just to go to and from work, I use it all day long. And if the worm *had* worked exactly as he had planned, it would still be around today in people's computers, causing problems."

Lewis Lee, director of computer operations in the Faculty of Arts and Sciences: "I think he did something that was stupid and he should have realized what the consequences were. You don't play about on a production network. I'm not sure that he should go to jail, but if it's not made clear that there are dire consequences, it'll just happen again. It was a very immature thing to do—and that's putting it mildly."

F. Warren McFarlan, Walker professor of business administration: "The issues raised by this case are absolutely fundamental and paramount ones. In our private-sector networks we are inadequately prepared to defend against a concerted attack by a determined, knowledgeable hacker. As a society we are increasingly dependent on our computer networks. Perhaps a reasonably stiff sentence would be a powerful deterrent.

"As with any kind of fraud, the mind of the criminal is somewhat more imaginative than the internal controls. You are always building a defense against the last war."

Charles Ogletree, assistant professor of law: "Our laws have to be broad enough to come up with some kind of sanction, both to deter future crimes and to establish some form of rehabilitation. I think that a stiff punitive sanction, not necessarily involving incarceration, would be appropriate in this case. I would not be surprised to see the judge require Mr. Morris to apply his knowledge, skills, and experience in preventing future problems of this type. Or he might be required to work with young people, to introduce them to the world of computers, and to show how they can be used in positive, productive, and educational ways."

PHYSICAL AND ENVIRONMENTAL CONCERNS

Many reports and studies focus on the office of the future. In most of the scenarios, a strong role is played by computers and attendant equipment driven by computers. Tomorrow's office workers will spend an increasing amount of time working with comptuer systems. There are a number of concerns that are precipitated by increased interaction with computers. First, there is a concern about excess radiation caused by video display terminals (VDTs). Several isolated studies brought out the potential increase in miscarriages to pregnant women who spend a good deal of time in front of a video screen, but I think it fair to say that an absolute connection has not been scientifically proven. Another hazard is the stress on wrists, elbows, and shoulders caused by the positioning of the body when entering data into a personal computer. Serious numbness and pain have been reported in a number of cases. However, ergonomics specialists continue to study the office and the impact of computers on work patterns. They point out that relatively minor design changes can materially improve the situation and alleviate any major concern in this area. However, these human factors must be seriously considered in designing new systems and laying out work space. Probably, having a work environment in which employees sit eight hours per day is not a desirable thing regardless of possible VDT radiation and repetitive strain injury (RSI).

On a positive side, tehcnology is assisting people with a variety of handicaps to enter the workforce and be productive. One man with a disabling neurological problem uses a laptop computer and special software that drives a speech synthesizer, enabling him to deliver a speech and to answer questions despite the fact that he can't speak. The individual types the words, which are then interpreted and fed to the synthesizer that voices the words. On the other side, individuals who can speak but do not have hand motion can speak into a computer and have their words printed and disseminated. Quadriplegics can activate a computer with the blink of an eye or a nod of the head. There are a great many examples of how the handicapped are assisted by some ingenious inventions or adaptations of existing technology. The technology is opening up new opportuntites in our work community every day. It provides business with a source of competent and useful individuals who have significant brain power which is now able to be harnessed. These devices are expensive, but the Americans with Disabilities Act and some active proponents for the handicapped can see that we use all our resources to the fullest.

EDUCATION AND TRAINING

IS education has become a vital concern to the profession. It is important both inside the IS department and to the IS users. Studies tell us there will be fewer college graduates majoring in IS in the years ahead; yet the demand for systems analysts and programmers continues to increase rapidly. The responsibility of a company's training function is to establish educational programs that satisfy both the need for an increased cadre of trained systems analysts, whether they are assigned to IS or to user departments, and the need for intelligent involvement of the user community.

Educational facilities include the following:

Schools

Secondary schools

Colleges

Business schools

Graduate schools

Internal on-site company training

IS department

Computer vendor

Consultants

Private educational institutions

External training

IS professional societies

IS educational agencies

Seminars and business meetings

University continuing education programs

Self-study courses

IS Education in Schools

I see the computer programming in preparatory schools, and in many colleges as well, as fitting into the mind-stretching capacity. Most students will not be computer systems analysts or programmers in the future, just as most will not be biologists or physicists. Computer programming is an excellent mental discipline that forces the individual to think logically and rationally and to focus on solving a specific problem. Furthermore, it can be an enjoyable educational experience and an educational motivator to many students. In addition, it should be noted that the basic computer programming courses given in secondary schools, particularly those schools with PCs that can communicate with a remote computer, also aid in the understanding of information processing and data communications in general. The students gain an awareness that data, like voices, can be transmitted over telephone lines and that the computer at the other end will act in accordance with prescribed rules.

The responsibility of business schools, both graduate and undergraduate, is to train students for business and professional specialization. A distinction must be made between training: (1) the student who plans to be a specialist in data processing, and (2) the student who plans to pursue a general business career, specializing in a field other than data processing. Figure 13.5 illustrates the span of curriculum—at the top, those courses of study suited for the specialist, and, at the bottom, those geared for the generalist. Depending on the type of program and professional focus, courses can be selected from the top or the bottom half. The more the twain meet—that is, the greater the extension of the technical specialist into the general manager area and of the general manager into the technical area—the more effective will be the interaction level of the two groups in a real-life business setting.

Though change is occurring at the leading IS universities, there is still a tendency to emphasize the technical subjects at the expense of the managerial ones. A major reason has been that many of the instructors and professors are themselves technically oriented and have an unbalanced view of the technical versus the general business aspects of computer training; they stress the former. This situation is accentuated by the fact that they are most familiar and comfortable with the technical. Furthermore, the technical aspects are easier to teach. The gap exists because the older faculty, who are more experienced in general business requirements, did not learn computers in school and did not encounter them them

FIGURE 13.5. Relative education priority

Basic Technology
Hardware/software/programming languages   MIS
Computer Operations   Technical
Terminal use/debugging/machine-room operation
Basic Technical Concepts
Batch, on-line, time-sharing, networking
System Development Cycle
System analysis and design
MIS Managerial Techniques
Project management, risk assessment, planning
User Interface Languages
Terminal access; nonstructured, English-like language
Conceptual Framework
Stages theory, information as a resource
Key MIS Application Concepts
Integrated data base, distributed processing
Pivotal Managerial/Organizational Issues
Decision support systems, centralization/decentralization   General, or User
Societal/Individual Issues   Business Manager
Privacy, ethics, computer literacy

much in their business careers. They have handed over computer training to the computer specialists and now suffer the same communication and interface problem that exists between the general manager and the IS specialist within a company.

An in-depth study by Babson and Bentley College professors based a forecasted shortage of IS professionals on the University of California's ongoing survey of college freshmen's interest in computer careers versus the Bureau of Labor Statistics' projected demand for computer programmers and systems analysts through the year 2000. They offer reasons for the drop in student interest in the IS major. Among the reasons are the impression on the part of students that IS is a technical field, often requiring a math background, and that a career in IS involves working by one's self in isolation from other departments within the organization. To support this finding, the authors point to studies that show that IS professionals require less social interaction than any other profession.

One may cast suspicion on the Bureau of Labor Statistics as not reflecting to the proper extent the trend of easier-to-use technology that does not require professional programmers and systems analysts to develop and use. Also, the heightened awareness of IS in the elementary schools may establish a different perspective; that is, that IS and computers are an embedded part of most everything we do, and are no longer the domain of the techies and asocials. Furthermore, more enlightened marketing of the IS curriculum in colleges can do much to dispel the myth that IS is not for those who seek jobs in marketing, accounting, finance, or other functions within a business. Rather, it can be a vital part of their jobs in these areas, enabling them to manage with information and to improve their effectiveness in major ways.

Business schools should be educating *tweeners,* a word used to classify the growing importance of a group of people who are the buffers, translators, facilitators, consultants, or whatever term you want to use. They are business trained, but are also comfortable with the technology. This indispensable group translates the needs of various layers of management into systems that concentrate on the human factors. They operate by the dictum "elegance in simplicity" in that they are creative in shielding system complexity from the users of the system. They don't get their kicks out of designing a system that is unfathomable and so complex that only a nuclear physicist would feel comfortable using it.

In the educational and business institutions, these types of people have fallen between the cracks. The students majoring in computer science wind up programming and running the complicated mainframe transaction systems and the telecommunications networks of Fortune 1000 companies. The finance, marketing, and manufacturing majors go into the management of these line functions within the corporations of their choice. There are no training programs available for the important "tweeners." A new function is required that would call for a strong information systems background but in a context of understanding line business functions and human and organizational behavior.

From the company viewpoint, positions and growth paths should be provided (probably of the dual-ladder variety) for these internal business information analysts. This can ensure that computers are used for their highest calling—that being their use in strategic areas of the business and in providing executives with information support for the things that are really important to them.

The education process must train managers for this type of role. Information systems should be embedded within the regular functional disciplines such as marketing and finance.

The problem is that the teachers of these courses are not that familiar with computers and the information systems people are not that familiar with the functional areas. The solution could well be combination courses cotaught by IS professors and functional discipline professors. This would involve a collaboration and a sharing of the responsibility for curriculum development; the combination would be powerful. Babson College, for example, has a course called Accounting Information Systems. This course, which is jointly taught by accounting and information systems professors, covers how accounting information systems (i.e., general ledger, accounts receivable and payable) are controlled, maintained, and, more important, used. Other such courses are offered or planned in manufacturing, marketing, and finance.

INTERNAL ON-SITE COMPANY TRAINING

Since many business managers went to business school before computers were properly brought into the curriculum, today's management needs training. It is also apparent that those managers who did receive IS training need continual refreshing and updating. A common method of obtaining this training is for a company to conduct its own on-site education program tailored around its individual requirements. The larger, more experienced users of IS may have a training department for this purpose. In most firms it is a by-product responsibility of the IS department. Training is so important that it is beneficial to establish a training group or possibly a training steering committee consisting of non-IS as well as IS people. Doing so make sense, because the majority of the people being trained are not part of the IS department.

Most companies look to the IS department as the primary source of educators. Although it is quite possible that talent of this type exists within the department, the company must guard against too technical a focus. As has been illustrated, the general manager requires more than a basic hardware and software course. Other sources of on-site training are computer vendors and consultants. The major computer vendors have been in the education business for many years and have the talent and the course material to assume a good deal of the training burden for a company. However, like the business schools, they, too, have specialized more in technical training, and their basic system and computer management courses may not be geared properly. Most vendors will tailor a course or an entire educational program for a particular company. The computer vendor has the advantage of having a full set of instructional aids, complete course outlines, and educational documentation, all of which are extremely important. However, a company should carefully review the course objectives, course content, and instructors to ensure that the course is suitable for its own requirements.

Consultants and private educational institutions can provide the same types of services offered by the computer vendor. These two sources usually have the advantage of not gearing the education around a specific piece of hardware, as might be the case with the computer vendor. These courses can be given on company time or in the evening, or a combination of both day and evening sessions can be utilized. It is important to state clearly the objectives and background expected for each course and to have individuals with roughly the same backgrounds and interests in the sessions. Management's enthusiasm for computers can diminish quickly during a highly technical session with highly technical people. If the company resorts to the use of consultants or private educational institutions, course objectives and capabilities should be thoroughly evaluated before a contract is signed.

EXTERNAL TRAINING

A wider variety of course offerings and educational opportunities exists if the company is willing to go outside for its training. Professional societies either present courses on a variety of IS subjects or can help organize and arrange outside training sessions. IS educational agencies can be utilized for training outside the company just as for internal training.

The outside courses offer the opportunity for managers and personnel to mix with their counterparts from other companies, to exchange ideas, and to broaden their appreciation of IS. Most of the sessions put on by these agencies are well constructed and tested and clearly state the objectives and purpose. Many are aimed at management-level people. However, a caution is in order, because some courses are not what they look like on paper. It is wise to spend time evaluating the offerings before signing up. Several telephone calls to prior attendees in a position similar to your own might help qualify the particular session. It is also desirable to discuss the seminar content with someone from the company's own IS department in order to qualify it further.

In addition to the paid courses discussed in the foregoing, there are good opportunities to attend seminars and business meetings devoted to specific IS subjects. Special-interest groups on either an industry or functional basis (sales, finance, etc.) are adding computers and IS as subjects at their regular business meetings or holding periodic seminars on these subjects. These sessions offer excellent opportunities to further one's IS education and have the added benefit that the people attending are in the same line of work and have similar IS background.

Most universities have credit and noncredit courses as part of their continuing education programs in computer and computer-related subjects. These courses are presented in the evening and can offer an attractive method of acquiring IS background. Again, people should be aware of what they are getting into, and a call to previous students or to the instructor is often a good idea. Some colleges and universities offer membership in IS centers associated with the school, where workshops, conferences, research, and working papers are the media for keeping companies current on new technologies, new IS applications, and effective management techniques.

Finally, the executive should not rely completely on organized classroom study. Outside reading of books and periodicals should be used to supplement the formal training. A subscription to one of the IS journals may prove a good investment, or the occasional reading of a management-based computer book may be worthwhile. Libraries offer video tapes that can be utilized along with packaged documentation as self-study programs. The programs range from basic systems concepts to data base and telecommunications.

SUMMARY

This chapter has stressed the human factors side of information systems. John Naisbitt has said that successful adaptation to the information age involves a balanced blend of high touch with high tech. We must keep in mind the people dimension, which includes the consideration of such things as personal benefit, quality of life, and ethics.

The elements of the changing information era were described, emphasizing the rise of the knowledge worker and the decline of the farmer and manual worker. Resistance to change and the modern reincarnation of the Luddite were then considered. Since the chapter focuses on society, the impact of the computer on the individual was presented, illustrating the six general areas where individuals are and will be affected by technology. The criteria of social value and quality of life were discussed.

The potential invasion of the computer in our private lives was introduced. Issues centered on whether individuals have a right to know what information is carried about them in data files, both public and private, and whether they should have the right to preclude use of this information without their consent. The legal and ethical considerations were both reviewed. Various laws aimed at providing a level of individual protection, including the U.S Privacy Act of 1974, were discussed.

Computer crime was distinguished from computer hacking as revealed in the computer espionage case as described by Clifford Stoll, and the computer hacking case wherein Robert Morris was given a fine and a commuted prison sentence. The difference between a virus and a worm was discussed, with the ramifications of both. Different views on the social impact of hackers were presented. Also discussed were physical and environmental issues caused by the increasing presence of computers in our offices and homes.

Finally, the subject of education and training was explored. Any approach to improving the social aspects of IS use must be based on sound educational principles and a sound educational program. The various avenues for acquiring education were explored, ranging from business schools to professional associations to continuing education programs to doing it yourself. The changing role of IS in society and business must be matched by a changing approach to IS education. More often than not, this requires a blending of IS into the other functional areas of study—more of an integration rather than a view that IS is a specialty or highly technical and separate area of study. One may call this the democratization or socialization of technology.

Case Study

Ethics Quiz

For each statement below, indicate whether you think it represents ethical or unethical behavior.

1. A company employee uses his home computer to access the company's administrative computer. The worker doesn't make any changes in data stored on the computer; he simply checks to see if a bill has been paid to a friend's company.

2. A home satellite dish owner builds equipment that will allow him to uplink to a communications satellite. Just to see if his equipment works, he broadcasts the message "Aha! It Works!!!" interrupting HBO and Showtime programming for about 30 seconds.

3. A college student uses his home computer to access the college's administrative computer. He leaves the message, "Your security system isn't as good as you thought!" in the system administrator's directory and then exits from the college's computer.

4. A graduate student working her way through school is loaned a PC by a friend to use while she writes her thesis. The student can't afford to buy a word processor, so another friend gives her a copy of WordPerfect.

5. A homeowner discovers that the pay TV channels on the cable coming into his home are unscrambled, even though he has never ordered those channels and is not billed for them. He says nothing to the cable TV company and occasionally watches those channels.

6. An investment counselor uses his PC to access the computer at a local bank. He looks at the bank balances of several companies, companies he is about to recommend for his clients. He makes no changes to data stored on the computer and leaves no traces that he has even been there.

7. A homeowner buys a "black box" that will unscramble scrambled cable TV signals from a friend for $300. He then uses the box to unscramble the pay TV channels coming over his cable without notifying the cable TV company.

8. A high school student discovers that the program development for his favorite game software is being done on a mainframe in the city where he lives. He accesses the mainframe with his home computer and transfers the software from the mainframe to his own computer.

9. An employee discovers the electronic mail password of another employee and plays a practical joke by sending out a crazy message to several departments under that password.

Some of these issues are from a Bentley College paper given to incoming freshmen.

10. A supervisor scans several employee electronic mail files because he suspects they are using the system for personal purposes.

Case Study

The Cuckoo's Egg by Clifford Stoll

The book, *The Cuckoo's Egg,* has caught on because viruses, worms, and computer intrusion are very much in the news, and also because the story is a computer age version of a cop-and-robber chase. It is a suspenseful tracking-down of the "Hannover Hacker," a German named Markus Hess who sold classified information about Western technology to agents of the Soviet KBG that he obtained from secure data bases.

This true story involves us in the nomenclature of computer intrusion, explaining that a worm copies itself into computer memory, differing from a virus which embeds itself in computer programs. Thus, with a worm your programs remain intact after you have cleaned up the damage done by the worm. With a virus, however, you have to clean up your programs or in some cases completely reconstruct them.

The story begins with a 75-cent accounting error, which intrigues Clifford Stoll enough to initiate an investigation, an investigation that becomes an obsession, driving him to spend a year in tracking down the hacker, tracing him through Milnet, Arpanet, and Tymnet and into Army, Airforce, and Navy computer systems throughout the United States. The hacker would steal or create passwords to enter the systems and then use techniques to obtain super-user status, meaning he had access to any program or data file in the systems.

Because he took such a circuitous route through the various networks, it took persistent tracing to eventually track down the hacker in Germany. Also frustrating Stoll's chase was the reluctance of the CIA, NSA, or FBI to take an interest in the case or to help in any way until quite late in the game. Many prominent, secure, and classified research centers insisted to Stoll that it was not possible for a hacker to penetrate their systems even when he had evidence to the contrary.

As we follow the mystery, we are introduced to hacker language like trapdoor functions, password encryption, super-user, the Gnu-Emacs hole, and trojan horses. Also, we encounter the networking terms of ethernet, fiber optics, satellite links, as well as the operating systems nomenclature, Unix, VMS, TSO, VM, MVS, and so on. It isn't necessary to fully understand these terms in order to follow the plot. They are merely the accoutrements of computer crime, as the mask and gun are to bank robbery.

The interesting part of the story is the discussion of the legal and ethical considerations that are raised by the incident. One can certainly surmise by reading the book that Stoll is quite liberal in his outlook. He points out that the liberals have a tendency to excuse hackers, and feel that too strict a policy or the threat of legal redress can thwart innovation and interfere with freedom of speech and individual rights. However, it is interesting that after this tedious ordeal of over a year, Stoll developed a real distaste for the German hacker and hackers in general. Here are his statements:

> These break-ins are far more insidious. They're technically skilled but ethically bankrupt programmers without any respect for others' work, or privacy. They're not destroying one or two programs. They're trying to wreck the cooperation that builds our networks.
>
> It's damned well exactly like a house ... Breaking into these systems is trespassing without permission. It's wrong no matter what your purpose is. And I have a right to ask these government agencies to help me get rid of this bastard. That's their job!
>
> I learned what our networks are ... a fragile community of people, bonded together by trust and cooperation. If that trust is broken, the community will vanish forever. Other programmers sometimes expressed respect for hackers because they test the soundness of systems, reveal holes and weaknesses. I could respect this view ... but I could no longer agree with it. I saw the hacker not as a chess master, teaching us all valuable lessons by exploiting the weak points in our defenses, but as a vandal, sowing distrust and paranoia.

STUDY QUESTIONS

1. How serious is hacking? Should we stiffen laws and penalties?
2. Some organizations defend hacking as an exercise of creativity and see it doing no harm as long as it doesn't destroy records. Discuss the pros and cons of this statement.
3. Does it surprise you that some of our top secret agencies do not have secure data bases?
4. What does this say about the need to build security into our systems?

SELECTED REFERENCES

Alexander, Michael, "Hacker Trial Begins in Chicago," *Computerworld.* July 30, 1990, p. 8.

Bell, Daniel, *The Coming of Post-Industrial Society.* New York: Basic Books, 1973. For a more recent version, see Daniel Bell, "The Social Framework of the Information Society," in *The Microelectronics Revolution*, Tom Forester, ed. Cambridge, Mass.: M.I.T. Press, 1981.

Burston, Harold L., "RTM and the Worm That Ate Internet," *Harvard Magazine.* May-June 1990, pp. 23-28.

Cale, Edward G., Charles H. Mawhinney, and David Callaghan, "The Implications of Declining Enrollments in Undergraduate CIS Programs in the United States," *Journal of Information Systems.* June 24, 1990.

Couger, J. Daniel, "Motivating IS Personnel," *Datamation*, September 15, 1988, p. 59.

Davis, Gordon B., "The Knowledge and Skill Requirements for the Doctorate in MIS," *Proceedings of the First International Conference on Information Systems*, December 8-10, 1980, Philadelphia, Penn.

Gabor, Andrea, "On-the-Job Straining," *U.S. News & World Report*. May 21, 1990, pp. 51-53.

Guisbond, Lisa, "Ergonomics Awareness Piques," *Computerworld*. November 12, 1990, p. 138.

Hoffer, Jeffrey, Alan G. Merten, and John F. Rockart, "Teaching the Current or Future General Managers: A Critical Function for the MIS Faculty," *Proceedings of the First International Conference on Information Systems* (Dec. 8-10, 1980), Philiadelphia, PA.

Hooper, Laurence, "For Data Security, Computer Virus Is Least Problem," *US Journal*. August 15, 1990, p. 8.

Kanter, Jerry, "The Stagnation of Videotex," *The Business Week Newsletter for Information Executives*. October 28, 1988, p. 8.

Kantrowitz, Barbara, "Casualties of the Keyboard," *Newsweek*. August 20, 1990, p. 57.

Lefkon, Richard G., "An Ounce of Prevention," *CIO*. February 1991, pp. 20-21.

Leibs, Scott, "Hacker Tracker: 'Be Eternally Vigilant,'" *InformationWeek*. May 7, 1990, p. 58.

Leibs, Scott, "Judgment Day," *InformationWeek*. May 7, 1990, p. 57.

Lewis, Peter H., "Are Computer Safety Laws Taking the Right Tack?" *The New York Times*. January 6, 1991, p. 8.

Lewis, Peter H., "Privacy: The Tip of the Iceberg," *The New York Times*. October 2, 1990.

McCusker, Tom, "Why Business Analysts Are Indispensable to IS," *Datamation*. January 15, 1990, pp. 76-78.

Nunamaker, Jr., Jay F., Daniel J. Couger, and Gordon B. Davis, "Information Systems Curriculum Recommendations for the 80's: Undergraduate and Graduate Programs," *Communications of the ACM*. November 1982.

Rifkin, Glenn, "Technology Offers Disabled a Chance to Make Their Mark," *Computerworld*. February 11, 1991, p. 25.

Rifkin, Glenn, "A Wider Work Force by Computer," *The New York Times*. December 16, 1990, p. 11.

Schwartz, Evan I., Jeffrey Rothfeder, and Mark Lewyn, "Viruses? Who You Gonna Call? 'Hackerbusters,'" *Business Week*. August 6, 1990, pp. 71-72.

Zuboff, Shoshana, *In the Age of the Smart Machine—Future of Work and Power*. New York: Basic Books, 1988.

Chapter 14

Business, Management, and Information Systems in the Twenty-first Century

INTRODUCTION

This final chapter views the technical and managerial trends that will effect companies in the future. The chapter opens with a look at the business environment of the twenty-first century, speculating on what types of businesses will be successful and what will be the profile of the successful managers of these businesses. Eight management IS trends are presented. It is important to present changes in this category because it has been a premise of this book to think about technology and management, not to emphasize the former at the expense of the latter. Technological trends were presented in the previous chapter.

Special emphasis is placed on the trend to global business and the new role of the CIO to succeed in this setting. The concept of the global information officer (GIO) and his or her responsibilities are outlined. Events are creating a global economy and society such that most companies will face an environment similar to one of the three presented in this chapter.

The chapter concludes with a discussion of the impact of information technology in education. We have moved more slowly in this area than in others, which may be surprising because most feel education should lead rather than follow. Examples of approaches using technology for learning are presented.

A LOOK AHEAD

At the beginning of a decade, it is inviting to look out at the next ten-year period to forecast the culture and environment in which we will be living and working. It becomes particularly inviting when it's the 1990s, and you are looking out at the new millennium, the year 2000.

From an overall business view, three questions are pertinent: (1) What will be the business environment in the twenty-first century? (2) What will be the profile of successful companies in that environment, and (3) What will be the profile of successful managers in this time frame? In addition, managing with information requires an answer to a fourth question: What will be the IS environment necessary to support and shape this business environment?

The book focuses on managing *with* information, but it also includes the study of those that manage the information, the IS professionals. It is the thesis that these two functions are merging, though it is believed they will never completely merge. However, the understanding of both roles is vital, whether your objective is functional management or IS management.

Figure 14.1 indicates that an understanding of the overall business environment is a prerequisite for what successful businesses will have to do, and understanding what successful businesses will have to do is a prerequisite for what successful managers will have to do. The future IS environment will play a role at all levels in shaping and supporting these domains. This leads to an understanding of the level of IS knowledge required by the business manager, which is the focus of this book.

Business Environment in the Twenty-first Century

A number of prominent authors and research reports focus on the future business environment. John Naisbitt's book *Megatrends 2000* opens with a chapter on the global

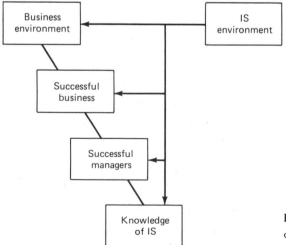

FIGURE 14.1. Business and management climate

economic boom of the 1990s. He indicates that, at the turn of the century, we will witness the line up of North America, Europe, and Japan to form a golden triangle of free trade. He believes that the future of the American economy is positive and will grow with this emphasis, not deteriorate and lose ground. He sees, for example, the fact that the Japanese are investing in the United States not as a sign of Japanese strength over U.S. weakness, but just the opposite.

Finally, he believes that, as dean Lester Thurow of MIT's Sloan School has also emphatically stated, we will look back at Europe 1992 as the single most significant economic and political event of the decade. Naisbitt says that " a single-market Europe by the end of 1992 is a strategic vision like John F. Kennedy's vision, 'we are going to put a man on the moon by the end of the decade.' He points out that more countries than the original twelve are organizing themselves to bring it about. This is heightened by the new democratic shift of governments of Eastern Europe. A new global lifestyle will emerge.

Most analysts agree on the following set of business environmental elements as we approach the twenty-first century:

- Changing demographics; more women and minorities in the work-force
- More geographically dispersed work force
- Heightened sense of ethics and community
- Environment, ecology, and health care become serious agenda items
- Globalism and increasing international alliances and connections
- Networking/alliances between business, government, and education
- Added complexity in doing business in a global marketplace
- Information technology will become embedded in everything we do

Successful Businesses in the Twenty-first Century

Successful businesses will recognize the global environment and will set up organizations that optimize global resources. Being global means more than opening sales offices in foreign countries; it means taking advantage of the unique talents and capabilities that exist in different cultures, knowing when to standardize across national boundaries and when to specialize on a company-by-company basis. The successful company will be fast, flexible, and focused, and will have an entrepreneurial spirit. Large, bureaucratic, authoritarian organizations will not be able to maintain competitiveness; those that excel will operate in a more decentralized, consultative manner with virtually everyone having the opportunity to provide input. Organizational structure will be more flattened as compared with today's hierarchical style.

The twenty-first century organization will take a more holistic approach to issues. Problems will be more complex and multifaceted, requiring a management that is both specialist and generalist, not exclusively one or the other. Increased interdisciplinary and cross-functional approaches will be necessary, as well as as an understanding of the rapid and radical technological changes that are becoming increasingly a part of the environment.

Successful Managers in the Twenty-first Century

This leads to a discussion of the attributes of the successful twenty-first century manager. The *Management Practice Quarterly* annual survey of the career backgrounds of top company CEOs projects that the manager of the future should master a foreign language and culture; know how to negotiate; have polished business manners; speak and write well; understand the uses of technology; be familiar with the political, economic, and regulatory situation; and have an entrepreneurial spirit and the capacity to innovate.

As Stanford University professor Harold Leavitt sees it: "A business leader must have three major talents: problem solving, implementing, and pathfinding—meaning visionary and entrepreneurial talents. Business schools teach the analytical tools needed for problem solving, but almost ignore the other two. These are the skills businesses look for more and more."

Professor Noel Tichy of the University of Michigan believes that business education needs a transformation, and suggests that new priorities be established; students should gain a global perspective, for starters, and acquire knowledge of a foreign language and culture, and gain a good respect for ethics. He believes that students must sharpen their speaking, writing, negotiating, and other "soft" skills, and that more emphasis must be placed on managing and using technology. Students should be prepare for a "cross-functional" role that doesn't fit neatly into academic classifications.

In summary, successful managers in the twenty-first century will be flexible, self-managing, cosmopolitan, continued learners, and problem finders, as well as problem solvers. Performance will be enhanced by strong analytical skills and the ability to deal with ambiguity; by being an integrator; by being numerate, as well as literate; and certainly by the capacity to deal with technology and IS.

THE IS ENVIRONMENT OF THE TWENTY-FIRST CENTURY

A understanding of IS is an element common to the business environment of the future as well as to the successful business and successful manager of the twenty-first century. In addition, IS plays a role in supporting many of the other elements in the aforementioned scenarios. For example, businesses must be able to communicate rapidly and effectively over a global network. IS is the cornerstone of this capability. The following discusses the key management IS forces, of which future managers must have understanding and perspective. Most have been mentioned in the book, and, thus, this serves as a summary. The technical forces were discussed in the previous chapter.

IS Management Trends

1. IS as a competitive weapon. Tomorrow's manager must understand the importance of information as a valuable resource and the use of IS to gain competitive advantage. As we move to a service-oriented economy, companies will turn more to technology for serving customers, and for compressing the delivery cycle of goods and services by electronically connecting customer and supplier. This has been stressed through-out the book, but remains a key perspective for innovative companies and managers.

Yes, there are benefits in developing efficiency-and-effectiveness computer applica-tions—that is to do the things we are doing now more productively and with more relevance to the users of information. However, the real benefit comes from what is called *transfor-mation,* those strategic systems dedicated to changing the way a company operates or manages. This requires commitment, involvement, and vision from the IS professionals, but particularly from the senior managers of the particular enterprise. It also requires a willing-ness and an ability to change.

2. The line manager takes charge of IS. This is a major finding of MIT's Management of the 1990s project. Innovation springs from the minds of those who know the business. With the increase in ease of use of packaged software and the development of advanced languages, line managers will control more of the computing resources and directly control the development of applications in their areas of the business. This is a principal cornerstone of this book, and is the meaning of its title, "Managing with Informa-tion."

This may be called the "democratization of technology," but that is just what is happening. The personal computer will become as commonplace as the telephone; it will be embedded in everything we do. The spreadsheet provides this democratization for accoun-tants. It is a natural adjunct of the work; they use it to embellish and create new ways of manipulating numbers, of developing future forecasts and models for improving company performance. These are not done by IS professionals, but by the accountants themselves. In a similar manner, the technology discussed earlier will place the computer into the hands of managers where they will use it to do the things that they are best positioned to do. The important thing is that the technology will be transparent to them, allowing them to focus on improving and repositioning the business process.

3. Information literacy will be mandatory. There are more pressing reasons than ever for the educational and business emphasis on education and information literacy. The "extensibility" of computer usage and the dispersion or democratization of the use and management of computers to the line departments make it essential for a company to have an educational strategy. Historically, it has been far easier to obtain budget money for hardware expenditures than for the training to use that hardware. The emphasis must be on information literacy—that is, an understanding of the general concepts of information processing; how computer systems support and shape a person's job function, the tradeoffs between investment and benefits, time expended, and time saved; and the application areas that will give a company a strategic advantage. Information literacy is a stage above computer literacy, the latter usually implying the ability to use a personal computer.

The phrase "elegance in simplicity" is a pertinent design principle for IS. In many instances, the most effective computer applications are those that are straightforward and easy to understand and operate. Yes, there is sophistication and elegance in the approach, but it is skillfully hidden from the user. This may be another word for the popular phrase "user friendly." The Apple Corporation is noted for the innovative introduction of the Macintosh graphic interface. Many mainframe and minicomputer designers scoffed at the idea of using a third or so of the computer's memory for simplifying the user interface; the key, they thought, was optimizing the execution cycle. IBM's alliance with Apple is an example of this recognition. Look for software in the future to be more Mac-like and to feature elegance in simplicity. This phrase also has meaning when designing the education curriculum for achieving information literacy.

4. Pragmatic planning. Management has become a bit leery of the tedious long-range planning processes that takes key managers out of circulation for weeks at a time—the final result of which is a huge tome placed on a shelf where it gathers increasing layers of dust. U.S. managements often adopt a binary approach to doing things: either it's a 100 percent effort or no effort at all. Planning and the intensive quality circle programs of recent years have received a tremendous amount of attention, but the very intensity of these efforts has made many managers skeptical. Although there is a recognition that the complexities of business in our increasingly merger-minded, internationally focused, and deregulated world calls for the development of more long-range thinking (as the Japanese do), the appetite will swing to what is termed *pragmatic planning*.

From an IS planning perspective, it is a given that the plan must be in sync with the business, must reflect the vision of how senior management sees information technology in shaping the business, must be built on a flexible architectural base, and must transfer responsibility into the hands of line management whether it be in approving the specifications for new applications or in actually implementing and operating applications that are pertinent to their business segments. There is no question that the overriding necessity for successful planning is a process that is in tune with the management style and culture of the company. That process should answer straightforwardly six basic questions: Where are we? Where do we want to go? How do we get there? When will it be done? Who will do it? and How much will it cost? Pragmatic planning is an important facilitator in the nineties and beyond.

5. Recognition of the human factor. As mentioned earlier, the human factor remains critical. Visionary thinking, strategic directions, and long-range planning are useless unless they can be translated into meaningful development projects employed by management and the work force to improve the company's product and services as perceived by customers. Those two forces, the management/work force and the customers, are still what it's all about. Ultimately, success for IS is how well the systems support the clients. IS Executives will spend a good deal of their time, not only with their internal customers— but with the real customers—those who buy the company's products and services. It is important to realize that there is still an abundance of technophobes in the world and always will be. A recent report on Japan indicates that while the Japanese flood the market with computers, semiconductors, and computer components, they are surprisingly illiterate in the employment of computers in their own country. A prime reason for this, say educators and researchers, is the ancient value system and tradition that emphasize creation and development of ideas in informal group settings, not before a computer terminal.

The successful IS executive of the nineties will be a combination businessperson and technician. The complexities of such elements as rearchitecting systems, use of expert systems, parallel processors, and the like require an in-depth technological awareness; while the dispersal of more of the control of IS to the line functions and the use of systems for competitive advantage call for an enlightened business perspective. And, coming from business schools is a new cadre of managers who are more independent, desire more options and choices, have a higher level of self-interest, are entrepreneurial, and seek greater participation in decision making. These people will be the new users of information systems of the nineties. John Naisbitt called this megatrend "high touch—high tech" some five years ago. It's more pertinent now than ever.

6. Third party alliances. Companies are recognizing that, not only can't they do everything themselves, in many cases it is better to let someone else do it—even if the in-house capability is present. Vertical integration used to be the watchword of successful businesses, that is, a company should have the capability to produce the entire product. For example, if you were producing a computer system, one should aim to manufacture and assemble one's own hardware, including processor, disks, and peripherals, as well as the software. In addition, the company should provide its own support and maintenance functions, as well as its own sales force. Now we see companies that do one thing or several things well and rely on third parties to provide the complementary products and support.

This is becoming true in the internal operation of an information system function. It is necessary for a company to establish the overall technical architecture, that is, the telecommunications and data base standards and the way systems will interact and achieve compatibility. Once that is established, outside vendors and suppliers now have the opportunity to provide part of the solution in a more effective way and at a more attractive cost than doing it in-house. Previous discussion has covered the range of services from farming out the entire data center operation, called outsourcing, to doing it yourself with minor contracted systems and programming help. Also, services can be obtained ranging from part-time or ad hoc consulting to systems integration, in which a single company or unit takes over the entire job of designing the architecture and applications systems needed by the company and selecting the hardware and software components to execute the plan.

7. Executive support systems that aid the decision process. We have reviewed executive support systems (ESS) that have been primarily aimed at providing status and performance information. Tomorrow's systems will model and forecast based on both internal factors and external factors. ESS will transform into proactive rather than reactive tools. ESS will combine with expert systems and other artificial intelligence–based approaches to project alternate scenarios that optimize the strategy the company is pursuing, whether it be to increase share of market, reduce the cost structure, or differentiate products and services.

Telecommunications networks will provide the current information on operations in a global setting, and this information will be used in concert with current external information from a battery of outside sources. The composite data will be analyzed by decision models that reflect the long-range strategy of the business. A selected cadre of senior executives will be able to base decisions on the model, and thereby materially condense the decision-making process. Data-sharing via videoconferencing will allow executives in global locations to participate fully in the decisions.

These are the IS management forces that will influence the manager of the twenty-first century—the IS awareness that twenty-first century managers will need to succeed.

8. Business reengineering. In many instances IS systems of the past were aimed at automating previously manual operations or using more advanced technology to reautomate processes making them more efficient, that is, faster and more accurate. The concept of business reengineering is to dramatically change the way work is performed. You don't do the same things faster, you do it in a completely different way. You challenge the established rules, you rethink the entire process. Your goal is to materially change the way you do things.

At a large transportation company, when they didn't find a faster way to handle invoices within the accounts payable department, they in effect "obliterated" the invoice and used shared information that was entered directly by the customer via electronic data interchange (EDI) into a database. A greeting card company found dramatically different demand patterns for its 150,000 cards at stores even within the same neighborhood. Rather than keep inventories of cards in warehouses and try to forecast item movement, they "obliterated" the warehouse and used advanced imaging technology to print the cards at the store. A provider of health insurance cut the number of people in customer service required to handle a new contract from seven to one. This was accomplished through the use of an on-line data base and an individual knowledgeable in the steps necessary to complete the transaction.

In all these cases, information was used to empower the individual, to simplify and expedite a particular business process. Though business reengineering can deliver some major improvements to routine jobs, the concept, when innovatively and creatively used, can provide companies with major competitive advantages. Most of the dramatic breakthroughs are a synergistic result of senior managers and IS people working together. A management champion is the sine qua non of success. Reengineering almost always causes significant change in the way people perform their jobs. Without strong management support and leadership, the changes may never happen.

THE CHIEF INFORMATION OFFICER AND
THE GLOBAL CHALLENGE

Thus far in the chapter we have centered on the role of functional managers, and what they must know about IS to be effective. In this section we discuss the role of the IS professional who provides the architecture, data bases, and telecom network so that others have the information with which to manage. One overriding trend that has been mentioned throughout the discussion of business and management in the twenty-first century is the evolution of the global company and the realization that most companies are already involved in this transition. The focus now shifts to the changes in the role of the CIO brought on by the global dimension of the job.

As organizations grow beyond national boundaries, their communications and information management requirements have become increasingly vital to their operations. IS managers of global organizations must define their roles in the context of the larger, geographical focus. More specifically, the organizations' chief information officers (CIO) must look upon themselves as the catalysts and facilitators of a process involving transnational teams of IS systems designers and implementors, working under the aegis of a set of unified strategic objectives. The end product of their effort must be the establishment of a user-driven "information utility" that can respond quickly to shifts in the global environment and to the business strategies of the parent organization.

The operational requirements of a truly global organization significantly increase the difficulties faced by the CIO. As a global information officer (GIO), this person's responsibilities and performance expectations are transformed—both quantitatively and qualitatively.

Domestic, Multi-National and Global Organizations

It is readily apparent that organizations in both the public and private sectors are migrating from domestic (national) to global entities. It is important to differentiate three distinct operational environments as they affect the responsibilities of the CIO/GIO.

A *domestic* business operates locally, regionally, and/or nationally within a single set of national boundaries. It may obtain materials from a foreign country, outsource production, or sell abroad but the domestic organization remains rooted in its home country and does not, therefore, have significant operational requirements in other nations. For that matter, it tends to be managed by and recruits from the domestic market for its executive leadership.

By contrast, multinational corporations have one or more operations of their own in foreign locations. These overseas entities either evolved from startup operations or came into being as the result of the merger/acquisition process. Typically, the overseas components of a multinational corporation function as semiautonomous enterprises with their own management, sales, production, and information technology teams. They may operate under the same banner, but as business enterprises they are often quite different in terms of what they do and how they do it. Business organizations along these lines have been in existence for decades. Indeed, one finds examples of French, British, and U.S. multinational corporations as early as the middle to late nineteenth century.

Today's *global* corporation may be distinguished from its multinational predecessors in that it makes every effort to integrate its foreign and domestic operations into a unified enterprise. Typically, such an organization functions under the aegis of a common strategic plan, draws its leadership from all over the world, rotates its management team among its various locations, and strives to meld its common corporate identity with those of its host cultures. Thus, a global company balances its need for centralized control with its desire to adopt a "domestic" image and exploit competitive advantage in respective national customer bases.

The Challenge of Global IS Management

The following three vignettes illustrate different aspects of the global information officer's duties and concerns. Their purpose is to serve as a vehicle for the exploration of the challenges confronted by any senior IS professional operating in a global context.

Scenario I. The Barkley Company is a manufacturer and distributor of cosmetics and toiletries in the United States. They have developed a multibillion-dollar business and have one of the top names in the industry. But now they have acquired a company, Chateau, Inc., headquartered in Brussels, a firm that manufactures a similar line of products for the European market.

Chateau had been planning to exploit the EEC in 1992 and also plans to expand into Asia and other parts of the world.

Tom Brooks is the CIO of Barkley and has been responsible for the operation of the Information Technology Group within Barkley for five years. In one stroke of the pen, he has become a GIO. He must now bring Chateau, a European entity, under the Barkley IT umbrella.

Scenario II. Ralph Jones is the vice president of information systems for the Global Banking Corporation headquartered in New York. He has domestic and international responsibilities for the management of multiple information systems development and implementation activities in ten countries throughout Europe, Asia, and Australia. He oversees the systems development and the operation of ten field data centers in London, Rio, Paris, Brussels, Madrid, Tokyo, Rome, Sidney, Singapore, and Manila.

He recently installed a new communications system to ensure that all data centers are current as to one another's activities, maintain systems standards, employ the most recent releases of commercial software packages, and develop applications in concert. Ralph is also responsible for the development of a strategic plan for the bank's use of IT on a global basis.

Scenario III. In 1975, Jeans, Inc., an outdoor/casual clothing retailing company, opened its doors in Toronto. Since that date, its growth has been meteoric, with over 700 sales outlets throughout Canada and the United States. Now, Jeans, Inc. is preparing to enter the European and Far East markets in a big way. A marketing team has identified 80 new store locations overseas while operations has geared up to deliver product in accordance with customer needs.

As the CIO for Jeans, Inc., Terri Schwartz must install point-of-sales and inventory control systems in each new store. She must also engineer the adaption of the corporations' centralized financial control system to accomodate a multitude of different currencies, tax laws, and home-country reporting requirements. In addition, Jeans, Inc.'s European and Far East management teams want their own customized executive support systems and enhanced voice/data communications.

A Summary Analysis of Scenarios

The first of our case studies identifies what is becoming an almost commonplace occurrence, namely the expansion of an organization overseas through the acquisition of a foreign firm. The Barkley Company buys Chateau, Inc. In a typical multinational business plan scenario, Barkley could have run Chateau as a separate entity, skimming off profits and possibly cross-selling products. However, the strategy of the parent company is global in nature; that is, the Chateau acquisition is viewed as an entree to Europe in 1992. To fulfill its objectives, Barkley must integrate Chateau into its U.S.-based marketing, sales, manufacturing, and distribution programs. It must also adapt its own practices to complement those of Chateau.

These business needs in turn drive the development of Tom Brooks' IS efforts. In the first place, the CIO (now GIO) must establish a common basis for the communication of vital financial and operational data between the U.S.-based parent and its European-based acquisition. He must raise questions about the design, functionality, and communications standards employed by the existing voice/data networks within both organizations. In this process, he and his IS team will access the merits of the company's newly expanded base of installed software and hardware, and make changes as necessary. When settling on a common global strategy for IS, the CIO/GIO will need to establish more rigorous criteria for system selection and design so as to accommodate the business requirements of the European, as well as the U.S. marketplace.

Furthermore, to avoid confusion, redundancy, and wasteful conversion costs, he must participate more directly in the key decision-making processes of the corporation. In brief, the CIO/GIO can no longer sit back and concern himself exclusively with computer- and telecommunications-related issues. More than ever, his organization's sales, operations, and distribution strategies will drive his team's priorities and limit its options. The additional burden of coping with the IS complexities brought on by the acquisition of Chateau compounds these difficulties, underlining the importance of CIO/GIO access to and participation in the highest levels of corporate planning.

Clearly in the case of our second scenario, the Global Banking Corporation of New York, this type of organizational structure is already in place. Ralph Jones manages worldwide information technology operations, oversees standards, and prepares global IS strategic plans for his company. In this regard, his position is certainly helped by the industry within which he works. Traditionally, financial services institutions, including banks, insurance companies, and brokerage firms, have been at the leading edge of IS systems development and deployments. Indeed, these businesses are driven largely by the vast amounts of sensitive data that they must collect, store, process, and communicate on a daily (even minute-by-minute) basis. They therefore spend heavily on high-tech delivery systems and associated products, but for this investment, they expect rapid response times, fault tolerant computer systems, and a high level of data integrity.

For his part, Ralph Jones must manage ten data centers around the globe to performance standards set by his bosses, Global's CEO and executive committee. As key elements of this assignment, the corporation expects the CIO/GIO to ensure that all of its data centers run current versions of the corporation's software; that all security, auditing, and backup/contingency planning systems are in place and fully operational; and that communication standards and procedures are followed at all times. Because a particular locale might impose special operating considerations on a data center operating in that country, the CIO/GIO needs to be sensitive to cultural differences and environmental conditions. Finally, he must keep an eye on developments within the information industry and among his competitors so that his company can maintain a competitive edge in IS.

In developing a profile of GIO, the experiences of Ralph Jones at the Global Banking Corporation are illustrative in a number of respects. First and foremost, while Mr. Jones enjoys access to the top, this in and of itself may not prove sufficient to ensure his success. To manage effectively, he also requires local knowledge of each of his operating units. He works to position the IS function strategically within the corporation and to ensure that his group's plans evolve in concert with those of the parent company. But he must balance stability and reliability with flexibility because both he and his superiors recognize the need to respond rapidly to changes in the external environment.

Perhaps most important of all, the CIO/GIO recognizes an ongoing need to scan the technological horizon in search of new hardware, systems, and services. His approach in this regard might be twofold. In the first place, he could encourage and evaluate home-grown IS solutions from any of his own operating sites for deployment throughout the global organization. Second, he could look for applications elsewhere in the banking industry or in some allied business for use at Global.

By contrast, the challenges faced by the CIO of Jeans, Inc. are quite different from those of Global or Barkley. Global is already an established global player; Barkley purchased an existing European network to become a global organization. As a young upstart, Jeans must create an infrastructure and related delivery systems in keeping with its expansion plans. To achieve these objectives, executive management at Jeans appointed two independent development teams—one for Europe and one for the Far East.

Each of these teams is headed by a senior salesperson and has been allotted a budget with which to acquire sales and distribution locations, identify key markets and define product lines and sales strategies. In addition to the team leader, each team includes operations, financial, marketing, and legal specialists. However, neither team includes an equally senior IS expert. Instead, the CIO is an *ex officio* member of both teams. This was done by senior management because they recognized the importance of voice/data communications standards and well-integrated IS solutions. They have decided, therefore, to keep the responsibility for these functions in one set of hands.

While the reasoning behind this decision is perhaps laudable, it places Terri Schwartz in a difficult position. She must establish and maintain a close working relationship with both teams. And, at the same time, she must balance their demands and expectations with those of the parent company, operating in the United States. Unlike the team leaders, who are understandably caught up in the excitement of their respective assignments, Ms. Schwartz recognizes the many difficulties, potentially high costs, and considerable risks that she and her IS group will face in addressing the expectations of Jeans, Inc.'s expansion teams.

In this instance, the CIO must balance competing demands for her group's limited resources. This situation is further complicated by the fact that the decision-making and priority-setting context is clouded with uncertainties. Simply put, Jeans, Inc. has never ventured overseas before. Yet, rather than build strategic alliances with businesses already operating in the firm's targeted geographic locations, Jeans management has decided to go it alone. To mitigate the dangers inherent to the plan, the CIO must marshall her team to limit the uncertainties. In particular, she will need to prototype and test the company's expanded financial and inventory control systems prior to their formal implementation. She must build consensus around networking and reporting standards both at headquarters and at the global periphery. Furthermore, she must ensure that the systems so deployed meet the multicurrency, multilingual, and diverse regulatory environments as identified by the two business development teams. The ultimate success of the enterprise depicted in scenario III will depend largely upon the CIO's ability to win general support for a unified IS strategy in light of these factors.

Attributes of the CIO/GIO

Now that three possible IS globalization scenarios have been reviewed, it is appropriate to ask what these examples suggest about the role of the CIO/GIO. From the outset, let us set aside as given those capabilities that one would expect to find in any CIO regardless of the global scope of his/her responsibilities. Chief among these would be a broad understanding of and fluency with information technologies, computer and phone systems, and voice/data networking strategies. In terms of operating environments, the CIO ought to have a working knowledge of both centralized and distributed data services; a familiarity with personal computers, intelligent workstations, and hardware peripherals; and experience in managing the personnel who run these machines, systems, and services.

However, CIOs need not be technologists in the strict sense of that term. Rather, they should know how to exploit IS resources, cope with the issue of standards, and plan in a constantly evolving IS environment. More than anything else CIOs must be strategic in the way they manage the parent organization's information utility. It is also essential that the CIOs be user driven and as informed about the business and operational requirements of the firm as they are about the application of IS. Indeed, it is quite common for CEOs to select experienced line managers as their CIO, allowing the appointees to develop the necessary technical expertise on the job.

Last, but not least, CIOs require the capacity to administer complex, multifaceted projects effectively and through consensus. Here, staff development and delegation are the keys to success. CIOs cannot afford to be "hands-on" all the time; they must rely on trusted lieutenants to implement programs that emerge from the planning process.

All the aforementioned characteristics are necessary to transforming a CIO to a GIO. What distinguishes the global player, interestingly enough, is not that person's level of technical expertise. Rather, it is the GIO's capacity to place the information technology requirements of the organization in the proper context and to exploit highly distributed resources to get the job done.

In all of the foregoing scenarios presented, the CIO/GIOs' first assignments in line with the corporations' global expansions had two primary focuses. On the one hand, they focused internally to review and value the operational requirements of the organization as driven by its strategic plan and the resources available—both from within the parent company and its acquisition(s)—to address these needs. Like any other executive manager, CIO/GIOs must master these issues if they are to perform adequately.

On the other hand, all of these representative information officers also treated the external environment as a key element in their planning efforts. To the extent possible, they addressed the cultural differences, language issues, infrastructural and business practice variations, and technology limitations prevalent in each of the host countries in which they operated. They were sensitive to the nuances of multinational/cultural IS systems development and exploited this diversity in formulating responses to the challenges posed by corporate management.

THE USE OF TECHNOLOGY IN EDUCATION

We switch gears and conclude our discussion of the future with a look at technology in education. There have been critical reports about the use of technology in education. Two briefing papers from the Hudson Institute point out that education (tied with social work) is the most labor intensive of activities. They indicate that labor costs are equal to 93 percent of output value compared with 54 percent for all private business. They also point out that productivity in education has not shown any considerable rise while costs as reflected in tuition have been rising at a rate above that of inflation. The other interesting fact is the low investment in technology, an average of $1000 per employee in education versus $50,000 for the U.S. economy as a whole. One could argue that there are good reasons why these statistics are so—for example, it is in our best interest for education and social service to remain intensively human activities. The issue appears to be the extent to which technology, particularly IS technology, can be used to enhance education and affect its cost.

Letter From a College Founder

The following letter, written in the very beginning of the computer era by the founder of Babson College, Roger Babson, provides a very interesting point of departure as we look at education and technology in the twenty-first century.

November 5, 1955

Mr. Ralph May
50 Congress Street
Boston 9, Massachusetts

Your letter of November first received. The goal, of course, is to give better instruction for less cost. This will partly be accomplished by using such machines as the UNIVAC.

The goal of any improved instruction must be smaller classes—not over 20. The instructors must be the ablest and most up-to-date who will command huge salaries—like movie actors—of $60,000 to $600,000 per year, each serving through these machines a hundred or more colleges, at a cost per college no greater than the price of records. Each class will be monitored by a girl paid $100 per week trained as a piano player. She will operate the UNIVAC for this small group, working eight hours per day, serving several different classes, changing the memory drums as needed.

The UNIVAC will be fed at a central studio by recording over a period of one or more years all the answers to questions which have been asked of these famous men during the past two or three years. Every possible question will be in the index book, and every possible answer will be in the famous man's own voice in the UNIVAC. The students will argue with these famous professors, and the UNIVAC will answer. It will be a round table far exceeding in intelligence and interest anything now at conventions or on television. The presiding young lady will only operate a dial—like a telephone dial. She will call any number, which will give the answer to any question. The result should be more effective than the present "human touch" idea. We have been misled to believe we must have a visible human teacher.

Most Sincerely,

Roger Babson

Roger Babson, the founder of Babson College, was a fascinating gentleman. In his letter to the chairman of the board of Babson College, written when he was eighty years old, we gain a glimpse into the mind of the visionary educator and financier. Mr. Babson presents a revolutionary concept for education wherein the wisdom of the greatest thinkers and teachers of the day would be recorded and stored in a computer data base. Students in classrooms throughout the country could ask questions and, in effect, carry on an electronic dialogue with these famous people. The computer would serve as their tutor, a cloned Socrates, simultaneously enlightening a world of would-be Platos.

Mr. Babson's perspectives are truly amazing if one considers that it wasn't until 1954 that the first commercial computer, the UNIVAC I was installed at General Electric's appliance plant in Louisville, Kentucky. During those early years, there was no disk storage as we know it today and no communication links from remote locations. On-line systems with remote access to data bases were many years off.

The "presiding young lady" Mr. Babson refers to is the computer operator, accessing the memory drums (data base). The piano player metaphor is no doubt associated with the fact that the early UNIVACs stored information on drums, much like the music rolls of early player pianos. Personal computers, telecommunications, and on-line data bases can now replace the "$100-per-week girl," but the year was 1955. One would think these views would emanate from the laboratories of Harvard and MIT, not from the conservative mind of the man who ran for president on the prohibitionist ticket in 1940.

It is interesting that despite some outstanding examples of the use of technology in education, overall, we still are asking the same questions Mr. Babson asked. Videoconferencing can bring to the campus speakers from remote places, and telecom networks can provide remote interaction with the speakers. Data bases can store huge amounts of information that can be queried from distant locations. Also, multimedia can be used to simulate live experiences using combinations of voice, text, video, and graphics in an integrated fashion. And computer-aided instruction (CAI) modules exist that employ multimedia.

There has been resistance to the widespread use of technology in the educational setting. Educators feel, and with good logic, that face to face is still the way to impart ideas and get people to think. However, the argument can be made that CAI could properly address certain portions of the study matter, say 20 to 30 percent of course material, thus improving teacher productivity and eventually making a positive contribution to lowering the cost of education.

There is no question that there is danger in losing relevance when electronic communication is used as a substitute for human contact. There is an analogy in the use of electronic mail. The electronic medium is a good one for certain types of communications, a primary example being the delivery of what might be called emotion-free information. Thus, the on-line search for financial or demographic information from stored data bases is becoming quite widespread and quite useful. Likewise, the delivery of messages to announce meetings, schedule public events, and communicate other static information is another positive use of the medium.

However, electronic mail is not desirable for communication that might be termed people-intensive—that which requires negotiation, debate, gaining commitment, or where the matter is controversial. It is of little value for establishing a relationship, for motivating, for leading, for sparking interest, for gaining credibility, or for developing trust. It is difficult to observe body language electronically, and that is often the real message.

The same principle applies for concepts such as Mr. Babson's on-line Socrates. Is this the most effective medium for the specific educational objectives that are sought, and what are the cost/quality tradeoffs? These are the penetrating questions that should be raised in assessing the role of technology in education.

New Uses of Educational Technology

It is accurate to state that the computer has not made a significant inroad into reducing the cost of educating today's students, and that holds for elementary school right through to higher education. Possibly the correct approach is to use computer assisted education for those courses or portions of courses that impart raw knowledge, the kind that don't require interpretation or discussion. As technology improves, and as we become more computer and information literate, the balance will gradually shift to innovative uses of technology in education. It is instructive to take a look at several examples of advanced uses of technology in education.

Distance learning: a live example. Though it is probably too early to judge its success, the International School of Information Management (ISIM) offers full courses and IS degrees without stepping into a classroom. This may afford one model for the future, and may prove to be the logical extension of Mr. Babson's concept. Figure 14.2 consists of excerpts taken from ISIM's catalogue.

Computer-aided instruction. We are seeing more and more exciting examples of the use of multimedia to enhance the learning process. The following examples cover three different subjects, but each illustrates the power of the media to enhance the message. *Harvard Magazine* November-December 1990 issue describes three interesting implementations at Harvard University.

The Perseus Project. This venture utilizes three of the newer technologies to provide a three dimensional view of Greek history. The three technologies include the videodisk which brings to the computer screen 15,000 images including still pictures, diagrams, photographs and full motion video. Another technology employed is Compact Disk, Read Only Memory (CD-ROM) which holds fifty megabytes of textual material comprising poetry, a classical dictionary, a lexicon and an assortment of scholarly articles. The third technology is HyperCard software, referred to in the previous chapter, which the student uses to access the data by pointing to a series of linked objects.

Examples of how the student uses the system to enrich the normal single dimension learning process are described in the article. Examples include a student who sees Herakles mentioned in a Greek play and can instantly look up references to him in other texts, call to the screen pictures, drawings, and sculptures of Herakles, look up the Greek characters for the word Herakles in the lexicon, and check out a reference in a classical dictionary. This is truly a multi-dimensional approach to learning and may illustrate the cliche that a picture is worth a thousand words.

FIGURE 14.2. International School of Information Management Santa Barbara, CA.

The ISIM Learning System

The Electronic Campus: A Participatory Learning Experience

ISIM does not offer classroom instruction in the traditional sense. Its "campus" is provided by an electronic network, ISIMnet, through electronic mail, electronic bulletin boards, and electronic seminars. ISIMnet is the basic vehicle for instruction and for faculty/student and student/student contacts. Each student and faculty member has an electronic "mailbox" that serves as the channel for interaction with the network. The faculty member who teaches the course provides general instruction and individual assistance, and encourages participation in student/faculty and student/student discussions.

To function in this learning environment, students must have access to a computer with communications capability, that is, a computer equipped with a modem and ISIMnet communication software.

The network facilitates self-paced learning and enables faculty members to monitor students' progress without requiring them to congregate to a designated place. Students are free to pursue their studies where they work and live. They can build upon their life experiences and, with the help of the faculty, they can design their study plans to serve their personal and career goals.

The Electronic Classroom (E-Class)

The electronic, or virtual, classroom is an exciting new medium for educational delivery, ideally suited to meet the needs of adult, employed learners. It permits students and teachers living and working in widely dispersed geographic locations to interact asynchronously, that is, at times most convenient for each.

For example, a student may find the evening hours most productive for class participation or study, whereas the teacher may choose the early morning hours to post instructions, read and respond to students' questions, or answer mail. Both are in close contact with one another, even though each individual is free to select the best time for her/his participation and response.

In the E-class, lesson plans, texts, and assignments are communicated to the student via a central computer through ISIMnet. The central computer stores the messages in sequence, along with other communications by members of the class. These communications are available to all participants in the E-class each time they "sign on." After signing on, members of the class "download" these messages with their telecommunications software and modem. After receiving these messages, students sign off, and then study each message whenever convenient.

After preparing their questions or comments "off line," students then "upload" their messages to the central computer. The entire process permits a relaxed and thoughtful preparation of all class interchanges. This has not generally been possible in the traditional learning/teaching milieu.

The article goes on to describe other examples: "The Perseus interactive software allows a student to "walk around" sites such as the Acropolis, calling up photographic vistas from different points on a plan, and zooming in to examine details of the Parthenon. While studying a poet of the Olympic Games, one can inspect the actual locale of Olympia. If you're dealing with ancient oral poetry, why not include recordings of this poetry in modern performance, along with pictures of Greek art objects that depict people speaking poetry?"   We have come a long way from the one-room school building and the blackboard. While content is still the essence, form is also significant to the learning process.

Three Mile Island.   Harvard has employed the case method of teaching in many of its graduate schools. Using multimedia approaches can materially enhance and give an added sense of reality to a case study. The John Kennedy School of Government has used this approach in a case involving the nuclear accident at Three Mile Island. The participant becomes a senior manager of the plant and the regular office tools are available to phone experts, consult with scientists, and speak to supervisors in the reactor control room. In addition the individual communicates with outside media, politicians, and interested third parties.

This simulation uses multimedia techniques to transform a computer workstation into your office at Three Mile Island. The time dimension is simulated as one must respond in a certain amount of time or lose the "window of opportunity." The real world is emulated by busy telephone signals or led astray by false leads. Actual footage from news reports is accessible, and one must make decisions with the then available information. Thus, this approach, utilizing multimedia-based software, enables an individual to gain an emotional as well as an intellectual experience. It appears to be a powerful learning tool.

Medical Diagnosis.   As the preceding example simulates a nuclear accident, Harvard also employs multimedia software to simulate a medical diagnosis. A medical student is asked to diagnose a patient with various symptoms. He or she can hear a digitized recording of a heartbeat, which may indicate a specific kind of valve blockage. The student has the ability to compare the heart beat to a normal one.

As the student develops a tentative diagnosis, he or she can get a listing of potential diseases that could cause the problem. The student can order an x-ray and observe it on the workstation monitor, with the ability to zoom in on specific areas. He or she can then call up medical textbooks and research data to further test the diagnosis. The student can call for more tests and observe on the monitor, such as the heart beating with iodine contrast dye. Each test can be reviewed visually or aurally. This is another impressive example of multi-dimensional learning.

These projects are from Harvard University, which is not considered a leader in the field of computer-aided instruction. Yet these are impressive examples. One can see the extension of these multimedia, interactive combinations of video and the computer to a wide area of science and liberal arts. These sessions evoke a wider "psychological bandwidth" than can be incorporated by a live teacher and the written words on a page or via a simple audio-visual. The idea, as pointed out in the Harvard examples, is that the wider, broader, and more extensive the involvement of the senses, the greater the impact of the learning experience. It is even possible through a new medium called artificial reality for a student to experience an operation using his or her own hand in a multidimensional simulated operating room environment. You actually see and experience the effects of the scalpel. This is a technological extension of the flight simulation teaching students receive to learn how to fly an airplane.

These and other computer-aided learning experiences hold exciting promise, but must be kept in perspective as Harvard president Derek Bok said in a report on computers in education:

The important thing is to provide a climate in which people are encouraged to experiment with technology for educational purposes. Machines are wonderful if they do help learning. But technology is a subject which produces people of great enthusiasm who, because of the power of these machines, are inclined to confuse technological virtuosity with their real quality of impact on students. Because of the high expense involved, we need to move very carefully in a time of strained resources.

The subject of using technology in education is a vital one. Not only is it important in elementary and institutions of higher education, it is important for continuing education as conducted by schools, training agencies, or by business. Education is a vital underpinning for living and competing in the coming global economy. The proper employment of IS technology will provide for improved education to a wider audience at less cost. Education and technology are inextricably linked.

SUMMARY

In the final chapter, we stand back and view IS in light of the changing business, management, and overall economic climate expected in the twenty-first century. Management trends in the IS domain are presented and serve as a checklist for contemplating the future. The global aspects of the CIO's job are covered with the advice to change one's vision and scope, to understand cultural diversity, and to react to the challenges of the new job dimensions. This will transform a CIO to a GIO. The impact of technology on education was presented as an important issue for our entire society.

As the book's theme and title is "Managing with Information," so this final chapter centers on a discussion of business and business management; the starting point being management. While managing with information by itself is not a new or revolutionary concept, the advent of the technology supporting and surrounding the computer provides new dimensions of information availability and use. Coming within a time window of less than forty years, it can rightfully be called a revolution—managing with information in the 1990s is a quantum leap over managing with information in the 1960s. It is not the same ball game. Management now realizes that information is a resource equalling or exceeding the worth and power of the other more widely accepted resources—people, material, facilities and money. Having stated that, the book closes on a humble note.

Although computers can do wondrous things and can materially aid management in conducting its business, I think we must retain the perspective to realize that the discipline of management still remains part art, part science. There are still things people can do better than machines, and still things that only people can do. It will always be that way. I think the point is made clear by a book called *The Analytical Engine*, in which the science writer (and my college classmate) Jeremy Bernstein recalled the career of Charles Babbage, the nineteenth-century English mathematician who invented the analytical engine that was the forerunner of modern computers. Bernstein mentions the time that Babbage wrote to Lord Tennyson as follows:

Sir, in your otherwise beautiful poem "The Vision of Sin" there is a verse which reads

Every moment dies a man
Every moment one is born.

It must be manifest that if this were true, the population of the world would be at a standstill, In truth, the rate of birth is slightly in excess of that of death. I would suggest that in the next edition of your poem you have it read—

Every moment dies a man
Every moment $1\frac{1}{16}$ is born....

I am, Sir, yours etc.

May art continue to thrive with science.

Case Study

Computers in the Year 2001

The turn-of-the-century Sam Curtis has reviewed his data processing needs with several vendors and has selected the Alpha system. Sam's manufacturing business had reached a stage where paperwork was beginning to pile up and he knew a computer system was required. The Alpha system features a customized turnkey system that requires no programming or systems personnel on the part of the user. Sam and his controller indicated their particular application requirements, and via a menulike selection process the relevant application chips were plugged into the processing unit and the system customized for Curtis's unique requirements. The chips are chosen from a program library and can be exchanged or updated as conditions dictate. This feature is important to Sam, as he anticipates growth from inside and also from acquisition. The application chips provide economical processing power that is optimized for Curtis's particular method of operation. Thus the software is bent to serve the user and not the other way around. The application chips offset the increasing people and programming cost that has paralleled the inflationary economy since 1980. The Alpha system is customer-installable and comes equipped with self-diagnosis and maintenance routines such that the average machine failure is once per year. Sam is looking forward to the installation of his first computer system.

When the investment counselor, Carole Harrison, enters her office one morning in the year 2001, her duty for the day is to review the customer portfolios assigned to her and the stocks under her surveillance. The portfolios of her clients are under continual computer control. The stocks were selected based on the individual investment profile, income status dependencies, future objectives, and the like. Each day the closing prices of the various stock exchanges are screened against the updated customer profiles. When change points are hit, automatic buy and sell orders are issued to maintain the desired profile of the portfolio. Harrison has access to a computerized econometric input/output model of U.S. business. The model immediately reflects the various investment factors, such as new housing starts and inventory positions. The model projects the impact of these elements on current and future stock market prices and investment decisions. In addition, Harrison can obtain a projection of future economic patterns based on her own judgement of what she thinks is likely to occur. The model can simulate the complicated interaction of many variables and print out the results in a matter of seconds on Harrison's office terminal.

The twenty-first-century Dr. Lloyd Carson is able to spend far more time in medical research and in enjoying his family because of the patient monitoring system installed at his hospital. Every patient is continuously monitored for thirty different biological functions, from temperature and blood pressure to brain wave patterns and metabolic balance. Between visits a two-way video screen enables Dr. Carson to communicate with his patients. After reviewing the monitors, he then indicates the various medication and tests for each patient via a special terminal. To request a test or medication he need only point with a light pen to the name of the requested test or prescription. Dr. Carson's orders are transmitted immediately to the on-line terminal in the lab or clinic where they are queued by priority and then carried out. Patient records are automatically updated when the drugs are dispensed. Diagnostic tests also are conducted via an on-line telemonitoring system that projects the most likely diagnoses along with the statistical odds of each possible diagnosis based on case histories. The computer can suggest courses of treatment and project the duration of the illness.

Helen Swindell looks at the calendar and sees that today is May 26, 2001. Helen is an early riser and often sits down at the family computer control center with her first cup of coffee to get chores out of the way before the rest of her family stirs. The kitchen is already comfortable, because the house temperature has been programmed to respond automatically to the outside environment. First she asks the computer to list the notes and reminders for today on the display screen. (The family uses the computer as a message board.) Helen finds a note she left herself that she needs to buy a few clothing items for her daughter. Helen decides to order them via the terminal, since she has a business luncheon in conjunction with her job at the bank. Monday is grocery day, so Helen asks for a price update and then checks off the items she wants. Pressing a transmit button delivers the order to a terminal at a local supermarket. Because of the home computer control center, it is no longer necessary for one member of a family to devote full time to running the household. The Swindells are living in what was called the "cashless society" back in the 1980s. For every purchase made, whether at home or in a store, Mrs. Swindell inserts an ID card and her index finger into a special identifier unit. Her social security number and fingerprint provide the necessary identification. The computer checks her credit status and automatically debits or credits her bank account.

STUDY QUESTIONS

Relative to these four twenty-first-century information systems users:

1. Which seem to be the most likely to occur?
2. Why do you think they are most likely to occur?
3. Do you think the quality of life will be improved if the vignettes come to pass?
4. Are the information systems that are used in business harbingers of the type of systems to be used in people-oriented institutions such as the hospital, school, and home?

SELECTED REFERENCES

Drucker, Peter F., "The Coming of the New Organization," *Harvard Business Review*. January-February 1988, pp. 45-53.

Drucker, Peter F., *The New Realities*. New York: Harper & Row, Publishers, 1989.

Halberstam, David, *The Next Century*. New York: Morrow, 1991.

The Index Group, "Europe in 1992, Winning Through Technology," *Indications*. Fall 1988.

Kanter, Jerome, and Richard Kesner, "The CIO/GIO as Catalyst and Facilitator: Building the Information Utility to Meet Global Challenges," The Center for Information Management Studies (CIMS) Working Paper 90-08, 1990.

Lambert, Craig, "The Electronic Tutor," *Harvard Magazine*. November-December 1990, pp. 42-51.

Morris, Charles R., *The Coming Global Boom*. New York: Bantam Books, 1990.

Morton, Michael S. Scott (edited), *The Corporation of the 1990's—Information Technology and Organizational Transformation*. New York: Oxford University Press, 1991.

Naisbitt, John, and Patricia Aburdene, *Ten New Directions for the 1990's Megatrends 2000*. New York: Morrow, 1990.

Palvia, Shailendra, *Global Information Technology Management Series*. Harrisburg, Penn.: Idea Group Publishing, 1991.

Peters, Tom, *Thriving on Chaos*. New York: Knopf, 1987, pp. 65-87.

Toffler, Alvin, *Powershift*. New York: Bantam Books, 1990.

Case Study: Three B's, Inc.

On a cool fall day, Bob Perry reported for his first day's work as staff assistant to Warren Coolidge, vice president in charge of production, at Three B's, Inc. Coolidge had hired Perry as a special staff assistant to assume general responsibility for all production and inventory control activities in the company. Perry understood that Coolidge expected him to improve the production organization's performance in meeting customer demand while maintaining a more balanced inventory position. He was also to concern himself with rising production costs. One of the first things Ferry did upon joining Three B's was to review the overall company background and organization.

COMPANY BACKGROUND

The principal products of Three B's are bicycles of all types and sizes, ranging from the basic single speed model to the Japanese and Italian-style twenty-speed racing bikes. They also manufacture motor bikes and other power-assisted bikes as well as tricycles, scooters, and kiddie cars.

This year marked the thirtieth of business operation for Three B's. The company was founded by the Barrett Brothers and is still operated as a tightly controlled family organization. Bill Barrett is president and chief executive officer; his brother Sam is chairman of the board. Several of the Barretts' sons and sons-in-law hold positions with the company. Sales in the first year were less than a million dollars and have risen substantially each year to the point where the sales volume for the latest operation year was $580 million. The Barrett brothers expect sales to continue to grow in the future. They feel that they produce the highest-quality bicycle on the market, and their reputation is second to none. Of concern to the Barretts was the fact that although sales were rising, profit margins in their opinion were not rising proportionally. Foreign competition is the principal factor.

The Three B's line is handled by company salespeople and jobbers throughout the country. All bicycles are manufactured in the main plant in Cleveland, Ohio, and are shipped directly from Cleveland. Salespeople take orders from large department stores and bicycle shops as well as from smaller outlets, and mail the orders to Cleveland where they are processed and filled. Figure A.1 presents a profit-and-loss statement for the year and a balance sheet as of year end. Cost of sales is comprised of 35 percent labor, 50 percent material, and 15 percent expense.

FIGURE A.1. Profit and loss statement and balance sheet

Profit and Loss Statement
(000 omitted)

Sales		$578,760
Variable costs	$328,100	
Administration costs	$28,920	
Costs of sales		$357,020
Fixed costs		$164,060
Net Profit before taxes		$57,680
Federal income tax		$24,216
New profit after taxes		$33,464

Balance Sheet

Assets			*Liabilities*		
Cash	$18,700		Accounts payable	$15,860	
Accounts receivable	$28,930		Accrued expenses	$6,000	
Inventory	$96,460		Short term debt	$1,250	
Other current assets	$11,690		Other current liabilities	$1,500	
Total current assets		$155,780	Total current liabilities		$24,610
Plant		$72,430	Stockholders equity		$146,860
Equipment		$54,850	Retained income		$121,860
Other fixed assest		$18,440	Other liabilities		$8,170
Total assets		$310,500	Total liabilities		$301,500

FIGURE A.2. Company organization

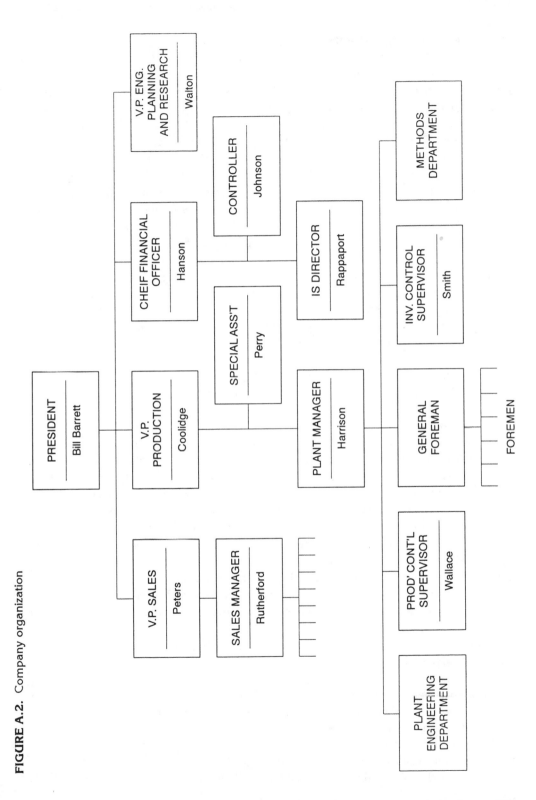

COMPANY ORGANIZATION

There were no organization charts at Three B's, as the Barretts didn't believe in them. However, Perry sketched out his own rough chart (see Figure A.2). Warren Coolidge, vice president in charge of production, and Paul Peters, vice president in charge of sales, are the senior officers of the company and have considerable influence in the decision making process within Three B's. The Chief Financial Officer (CFO), Henry Hanson, has been with Three B's since its inception and is a brother-in-law of Bill Barrett. Hanson is 62 years old, and expects to retire in a year or two. His assistant, Dexter Johnson, is a recent graduate of the Harvard Business School, and joined Three B's a year ago as the result of an accidental meeting with Bill Barrett on a flight from Cleveland to Los Angeles. Barrett considers his company's IS operations extremely backward and was most interested in Johnson's IS background. Johnson was an IS specialist for a manufacturing company and also served as a systems manager and sales representative for IBM. The plant manager, Burt Harrison, is the man who really keeps Three B's production lines running. Harrison has 25 years of varied production experience starting as a milling machine operator and working his way to night foreman, general plant supervisor, and finally plant manager. He is considered a rough customer to deal with, but he has a reputation for getting his job done. He is adamant in his feelings toward computers and so-called sophisticated systems approaches. Although he complains about the inaccurate production and inventory records, he is very skeptical about expanding IS into their operations. His idea is that the best system is the simple system. When it comes to computers, Harrison defiantly proclaims "My theme is the KISS theory — Keep it Simple, Stupid."

Perry began to gather statistical information concerning the finished products, assemblies, and piece parts manufactured and assembled by Three B's. He discovered that there are approximately 300 finished goods items, of which approximately 200 are active items that are produced on a regular basis and carried in stock. Approximately 8000 assemblies and piece parts support the 300 finished goods items. There are an average of six parts per assembly. On the sales side, Three B's receives about 4000 sales orders per day, the typical order containing eight items. Even though a good amount of Three B's business is in the southern and western part of the country, there is still a strong seasonal influence on sales. Of the 8000 piece parts, approximately two-thirds are inventoried. Purchase orders average 400 per day, with a typical purchase order containing four items. There are approximately 40 machine centers, split about evenly between fabrication and assembly operations. Since most of the products are produced on a repetitive basis, large production runs are the rule.

IS BACKGROUND

The IS department reports directly to Harry Hanson, CFO of the company. It is run by Dennis Rappaport and has an annual budget of just under $4 million. Recently, Hanson and Rappaport had a lengthy discussion with Bill Barrett, in which the latter was quite critical of their operation. Barrett had just returned from an executive session on IS run by their major hardware vendor and was impressed by the strides of that company's own use of IS. His general feelings were that with Three B's rapid growth, it was time to take another look at where the company was headed in the area of information processing, to develop a long-range plan for some type of strategic information systems, and to explore the use of newer technology. Hanson had conducted a reengineering study five years earlier aimed at initiating strategic systems for Three B's. The conclusion was that Three B's should first get its existing systems and installation running efficiently before considering a more advanced system. To Hanson's way of thinking, the systems had not lived up to the promises of their computer vendor, who in reality provided the leadership and direction to their current approach. Rappaport did the majority of the fact finding for the feasibility study.

COMPANY INTERVIEWS

During the first month of employment with Three B's, Perry spent a good deal of time with the sales manager, the inventory control supervisor, and the production control supervisor. He started with the sales manager, Bill Rutherford. In reviewing the sales picture, Perry discovered that two weeks prior to the beginning of each month, Rutherford would project the expected sales activity for the coming month. Rutherford based this primarily on previous months' sales, his own ten years' experience with Three B's, and his monthly meetings with key company salespeople. The sales manager was also responsible for a six-month forecast twice a year. Order turnaround time was approximately 30 days. In other words, a salesman mailing an order to Cleveland could expect his customer to receive the goods 30 days from the time he mailed the order. This caused a good deal of customer dissatisfaction, as certain customers needed merchandise quicker than 30 days from placing an order, particularly in areas that had a short spring selling season. The salesperson had to explain that this was the best he could do. On rush orders, salespeople were bothered by the fact that although the inventory records showed certain bicycles were in stock, when they placed the order they were informed that they actually were not in stock. The salesperson would then have to relate this back to his customer. More and more, salespeople were beginning to hear the story, "If you didn't make the best bike on the market, we'd certainly place our business elsewhere." Rutherford was seriously concerned, because two other major bicycle manufacturers were improving their bikes, and the quality edge that Three B's enjoyed was narrowing.

The inventory control supervisor, Jay Smith, was continually besieged by the production people, who claimed they had to shut down production lines due to unavailability of particular parts and assemblies. At the same time, the CFO was pointing out the increasing amount of capital that Three B's had tied up in inventory. One of his basic concerns was the lack of a systems that could take the sales manager's forecast and rapidly obtain the necessary piece parts and assemblies to produce enough bicycles to meet the forecast.

About 60 percent of piece parts and assemblies used in production were purchased. The other 40 percent were fabricated from base metal stock. Smith indicated his major problems were connected with purchased parts and assemblies. The number of parts had risen substantially with the addition of bike styles and new product lines. He could obtain certain parts with short lead time, but others came from plants with a bad reputation for meeting delivery schedules. Unfortunately, these were the only plants producing the quality of parts that Three B's demanded. Smith also knew his inventory records were unreliable.

In some cases, production lines were shut down for lack of parts when the parts were actually available in another part of the plant, but were not recorded as such. Some departments had built up their own staging areas where they maintained a day or two's supply of piece parts and assemblies in order to ensure a full day's production run.

The inventory control department kept a record of price breaks for each of the vendors. When a particular part or assembly hit a reorder point (the reorder point was a month's projected usage plus an additional half-month's buffer stock for items ordered from the "unreliable" vendors), the inventory clerk handling that item would initiate a purchase requisition. It usually took two to three days from the time a purchase requisition was prepared to the time the purchase order would be executed. The order quantity was based on the price breaks. The quantity ordered was at the price break point where the quantity ordered would not exceed eight weeks' usage. Usage figures were maintained on computer files in the inventory control office. The files were posted from the weekly inventory reports issued by the IS department. Smith knew these usage figures were historical and did not reflect changes in buying habits or seasonal factors.

J. B. Wallace, production control supervisor, indicated that his main problem was the constantly changing order requirements. He placed little faith in the sales manager's forecast and knew from experience that he must adjust it himself in order to anticipate the changes that inevitably occurred during the month. He realized that an important company asset was its highly skilled labor force which was one of the key reasons for the high-quality bicycles produced by Three B's. A prime consideration from the president on down was to maintain level production so that there would be minimal fluctuation in the labor force. "Accomplishing this, while keeping costs and inventory balanced, is all there is to do," facetiously stated the production control supervisor. Wallace felt that he was doing a good job, considering the rapid growth of operations over the last five years. He was gravely concerned over the effect further expansion would have on production operation.

Wallace continued to elaborate on the problems as he saw them.

Three B's is not the small company it was five years ago, but in many ways it still acts like it; we're literally breaking out at the seams. Our labor costs are extremely high. This relates back to the scheduling problem and the inventory problem. We've had to shut down lines and have expensive help sitting around idle while we're hunting around for parts. I've been able to adjust by rescheduling these men, but the work then is below their skill level. We not only incur high costs, but we run the risk of a morale problem if we continue to do it.

Wallace related the decision rules he used to schedule production.

My primary consideration is keeping a level work force. This puts a greater burden on the availability of piece parts and assemblies. I always shoot for long production runs to minimize set-up costs. We have outside storage facilities which I can use for temporary overstocks. If I had a forecast I could rely on, I could do a better scheduling job. Some of our unskilled help is part time, so we can call on them as needed. This gives me a way to increase or decrease production at relatively short notice; however, even in this situation, I'm beginning to hear about it from the union steward. The key to our problem is getting a more accurate long-range forecast to work from—then I can level off production while keeping costs down. For example, we've incurred major overtime last month because of several urgent rush orders from our two largest customers.

At a recent meeting attended by Warren Coolidge, Paul Peters, Henry Hanson, and Bob Perry, Bill Barrett indicated that the time had come to take some action to resolve the major problems of the company and to improve the profit picture. Barrett was convinced that the answer was enhanced and advanced use of information technology, which could start form sales forecasting and go right on to improve inventory and production control and to reduce production costs. He specifically stated that Perry should get together with Dexter Johnson and bring in whatever and whoever was needed to develop a system and a plan for utilizing more advanced IT to improve the situation. He mentioned taking a look at electronic data interchange, expert systems; and telecommunications networks.

STUDY QUESTIONS

1. How do you assess Three B's use of computers up to now? What are the main reasons for the situation?

2. What kind of business is Three B's in, what is the background, company organization, management perspective and capability, and, in general, the environment for future IS growth?

3. Give an analysis of the following executives and their receptiveness to MIS development: Bill Barrett, Warren Coolidge, Paul Peters, Bill Rutherford, Henry Hanson, and Burl Harrison.

4. Comment on the organization of IS within Three B's.

5. Do you think Three B's is spending too much or too little for IS?

6. Do you think Jay Smith and J.B. Wallace have reflected an accurate picture of Three B's inventory and production control systems?

7. Do you think Barrett was wise in pushing the hiring of Dexter Johnson? What did this say about his attitude toward IS at Three B's?

8. What role should Perry have in the design of an IS? How should he and Johnson work together?

9. Do you think Three B's should resort to outside consultants?

10. Do you think Three B's will have the proper level of management involvement and leadership? Is there a danger that they could have too much?

11. Does the profit-and-loss statement give you any indication of the priorities that you would establish for computer applications?

12. Do you think Three B's can continue on their present course, or is there danger of extinction if they don't change their strategies?

13. Assume that you are Bob Perry. Outline the steps you would take to develop an effective plan for obtaining maximum benefit from a computer at Three B's, Inc.

14. State three keys that you consider most significant to computer success at Three B's and explain why.

15. How important is the introduction of advanced information technology to Three B's?

16. Establish a schedule of events and milestones that might be established for Three B's after the meeting of Coolidge, Peters, Hanson, Perry, and Barrett.

Case Study: Citibank, Managing the Effectiveness vs. Efficiency Issue

There are competing views of company strategy in computer operations. In one view, the major emphasis should be on effectiveness or customer service—that is, on producing results and adding new applications. Proponents conjecture that efficient machine operation is strictly secondary. They argue that an inordinate amount of time devoted to saving a few minutes of machine time or avoiding the purchase of new disk drives is counterproductive to the main goal of IS, which is delivering information to management and their people. They also point out that hardware costs are dropping sharply, so that the price of redundancy or inefficiency is less each day.

Those geared to efficiency say that computer operations have gotten out of hand, that IS operations managers have no idea what is going on inside their equipment. Multimillion-dollar mainframes are being utilized the same as their transistor predecessors; applications are not taking advantage of the revolutionary new features of fourth-generation hardware. Jobs are taking two and three times what they should if they were fine-tuned to better utilize the hardware on which they run. The efficiency proponents point out that hardware is being added promiscuously, with prior inefficiencies being merely passed through to the new gear. The answer thrown at any problem is bigger and faster equipment—solve problems with capacity overkill. The efficiency folks point to a day when added capacity won't help any more and operations will reach a point of no return. Ignoring or downplaying efficiency will inevitably lead to this type of cul-de-sac; it's either pay now or pay later.

THE EXPERIENCE OF A LARGE INTERNATIONAL BANK

Citibank faced this problem directly in a classic case of the efficiency vs. effectiveness issue. It has been widely written about in the *Harvard Business Review* and other publications and extensively covered in a series of case studies used by the Harvard Business School. Though it occurred some years ago, the case remains most pertinent in describing a situation still facing IS today.

The case opens with Citibank facing a crisis in its operations group. This group was responsible for check processing, statement preparation, funds transfer, and in general all the bank's paperwork processing. This back office group consisted of 8000 people when Senior Vice President John Reed, at age 31 the youngest man in the bank's history to become a senior vice president, took it over. This is the same John Reed who rose to become chairman of CitiCorp, the huge international finance corporation that includes CitiBank. The operating group was responsible for all the computer systems that processed the huge number of daily business transactions. For example, they sent out 30,000 check accounting statements per day and processed 7.5 million checks (a stack of 7.5 million checks would be as tall as a 66-story building).

The problem was that for the past ten years, the number of employees in the back office had risen an average of 18 percent per year while transactions had grown an average of 5 percent per year. Citibank was spending $1,983,000 in overtime. Task forces of clerks, secretaries, trainees, and junior officers would spend evenings and weekends to get the back room out of repeated holes. There were some 36,000 unresolved errors in customer accounts in the backlog. This was the situation when John Reed took over.

John Reed decided that the back room was really not a computer center, it was a factory. As a result, he brought in managers who had experience in production scheduling and control in an operation that featured high-speed, continuous-process production operation—the assembly line of the Ford Motor Company. Bob White and several other Ford managers brought to Citibank the Bob McNamara philosophy that budgets, measurements, and controls were the only way to run a production operation. A new type of organization was instituted, whereby each line of transactions was viewed as a product line and managed by a single individual. Quality control measures were established under a strict umbrella of top-down budgeting and target setting. Also, many manual operations were computerized. When this program was initiated, labor represented 90 percent of the total cost of the operation. It gradually was reduced to 75 percent as more and more jobs were converted to the computer.

The results of Reed's program were impressive. Head count was reduced 30 percent in five years and this in the face of an inflationary trend; overtime was dramatically reduced as well as lost cash availability (lost interest on funds because of paperwork transfers). The following summary is taken directly from the case study:

Citicorp Bank Operating Group
Results

| Year | Headcount | | Overtime | | Lost availability | |
	Number of employees	Cumulative % decrease	$ (000)	Cumulative % decrease	$ (MMs)	% of potential
1	7,975	—	1,983	—	56.4	4.0%
2	6,610	17%	1,272	35%	32..8	2.0%
3	5,870	26%	845	57%	26.5	1.8%
4	5,528	30%	564	71%	14.2	0.5%

This program was not without its problems. First, the reaction to what old-timers called "The Ford Kids" was quite severe; turnover and morale problems were significant during this period. The following is a sample of comments from the case study recorded during the Reed/White transition era.

My frustration is I wish there were more old-time bankers in there, and fewer systems and organization types. There is a huge loss of old guys I can turn to for help in getting things done, people who know banking. Maybe they should keep just a few. Some. A few cents a share might well be worth it.

One of John Reed's magazine articles that came around *said something about people being replaceable, like machines.* That hurt. You lose solidarity.

Somebody asked me once if I liked it that we were working in what Reed called a factory. That really struck home. So, maybe it is like a factory. *Why do they* have to *say* it?

I'll tell you why people didn't protest the change, or question their instructions. We were scared—afraid of losing our jobs if we didn't seem to understand automatically.

The changes were accompanied by a great fear that people would get fired. Most lower managers and clerical workers felt management—that's AVP level and above— was highly insensitive to people.

At the end of this five-year period, Citibank launched another program aimed at customizing service by reorganizing along market segment lines. This would involve Citibank's early entry into the world of minicomputer and distributed data processing. Like the cost reduction program, the approach was bold and radical and was not without its negative as well as its positive ramifications. The basis for this new decentralized approach was noted by Richard J. Mattais, a senior vice president of Citibank, in an article in the *Harvard Business Review* entitled, "The New Back Office Focuses on Customer Service":

In taking our cue from the production management disciplines of manufacturing enterprises—a necessary first step, to be sure—we had tended to blur the difference in what a customer expects from a manufactured product as distinct from a service delivered. In gaining the control needed to achieve production efficiency, we had perforce homogenized the services that we processed. By imposing a kind of product uniformity on our processing, we had sacrificed what is the very essence of a financial transaction service: its uniqueness.

There was a second message in survey results. We were being told that another premise of service had been devalued: personal ministration to the customer. Obviously, we could not go back to the "pre-boom" era of lower volume and a slower pace. But, just as obviously, it was necessary to find a way to build in the kind of personal service that our customers were still finding in other banks— particularly, as the survey made clear, in smaller ones.

Bob White stated it this way in a document sent to management:

We believe the importance of our contribution (efficiency) has been understood by top management, but because our approach has been counter to the conventional wisdom that says "you have to spend money to provide good service," and because it has had negative impact on the security of people, and because it has stretched some of the bank's heritage and bruised its culture, it has been misunderstood or unappreciated by the rest of the bank.

We believe we have built an infrastructure of management, processes, procedures, and systems that will continue to achieve optimum operational efficiency for the next five to seven years. This is a machine-intensive operation that will keep costs flat by being on the computer learning curve rather than on the labor intensive 6-8% a year automatic cost increase curve.

We now want to change the thrust of our strategy to one of effectiveness in Institutional Service rather than efficiency in Operations. We have hired and trained the right people, developed the management disciplines and procedures to provide better support to the marketing groups. The key is to move away from our posture of planning and producing average products for an average customer.

Additionally, we would now like to provide increased employment security for our staff, to provide them with the atmosphere they need to help us positively implement the new systems and organization. Although few people have actually left the bank as a result of layoffs or firing, the continuing possibility has kept our staff tense and less receptive to change than if we had a full employment policy.

The Citibank experience is a classic case of the efficiency vs. effectiveness conflict. It is extreme in that one mode of operation was emphasized at almost the total expense of the other for a full five-year period. The message is that attention must be paid to both. No doubt effectiveness leads, because the starting point of any information system is the specification—what is to be accomplished—working on the right problem. However, efficiency, or *how* something is accomplished, becomes increasingly important, because a company obviously doesn't have unlimited resources to devote to the task.

STUDY QUESTIONS

1. What is more important, effectiveness or efficiency: in general and in the Citibank company?
2. Could Reed and The Ford Kids have avoided the negative reaction of the Citibank employees?
3. What kind of rating would you give John Reed for the job he did in automating the bank's operations?
4. Do you think Bob White is the right man to tackle the effectiveness strategy?
5. Do you think this type of background is desirable for a future senior bank officer?

Appendix **C**

"Of Course The Service Was Good, I Did It Myself!"

In the whitewashing episode in *Tom Sawyer*, Tom got his friends to do his whitewashing chore by convincing them it was a privilege. That was a classic example of creating an opportunity. Today, companies are continuing the tradition by using technology to create similar opportunities: getting customers to do their work for them.

THE EVOLUTION OF TRANSACTION PROCESSING

Not long ago, transaction processing was accomplished exclusively by large mainframe computer systems. A customer transaction is the life blood of a business, and the thinking was that this activity could not be entrusted to anyone outside the central I/S group. Therefore, anything that affected the official customer or inventory records on the central file was under the control of I/S central. This was not all bad because procedures were in place that backed up files, kept an audit trail, and had restart procedures if there was any machine malfunction during processing.

The advent of minicomputers decentralized some of the transaction processing work. Personnel within the company, but not in the central I/S department, could initiate transac-

From J. Faye Horn, Jerry Kanter, and Stephen Schiffman, "In Depth," *Computerworld.* August 27, 1990, p. 75.

tions that affected inventory and customer records. Files were decentralized to departments that had control over specific product sets or specific customer sets. This was the beginning of the I/S decentralization era.

The arrival of the personal computer and easier-to-use software meant that more people could initiate transactions. Transactions were recorded closer to the locus of the transaction, ushering in the "point-of-sale" era. A key element is that with personal computers and properly designed screen menus, you don't have to be a well trained, dedicated user of the system to operate it effectively. You can be an intermittent user. This opens up exciting new opportunities for handling customer transactions.

A simultaneous I/S development has been the use of technology to give a company a competitive advantage in the marketplace. Information systems are used to differentiate a product or a service offered to one's customers. Thus terminals are placed in the offices of customers to facilitate ordering and expedite product delivery. The terminals are connected directly to the supplier's computer systems. Such systems can materially compress the order replenishment cycle.

This is a first step in the implementation of electronic data interchange (EDI). EDI was first introduced to the distribution function, that is, a connection between the supplier and the distributor. Thus a distributor, such as an electrical contractor, can restock its warehouse by ordering via EDI from its supplier. But with the advent of bar code scanning and other point-of-sale devices, the electronic linkages have been extended outward to the retail store and more recently to the retail customer.

POINT-OF-SALE DATA CAPTURE

A major directional shift is that technology allows the capture of transactions at point of sale, integrating them electronically with a company's billing and order replenishment systems. Thus far the major benefits have not been in improving customer service. But now, another technological approach holds the promise of improving customer service while managing the growing labor cost of customer transactions. The new approach is "letting the customer do it."

Letting the customer do it may be more than just an option. A report in *The Wall Street Journal* by Peter Francese, President of American Demographics, points out that the rapid increase in the number of elderly, combined with declining numbers of young adults and a record low population growth rate will put the nation in demographic vise in the 1990s.[1] Nationally the number of people in the age group 20 to 29 is projected by the Census Bureau to drop 12 percent in the next decade. With the continued growth of our service-oriented economy, there may not be enough people to satisfy the demand for retail clerks and service attendants.

The concomitant technological developments and demographic shifts are forcing retailers, financial service providers, or any company that deals directly with consumers to take a hard look at letting the customer do it. Thinking of this kind may well become a key determinant of survival in the retail world. Examples of customer involvement in the

[1]Peter Francese, *The Wall Street Journal*, March 27, 1990.

transaction process are becoming more common. The Automatic Teller Machine (ATM) is the most widely used and accepted system. Customers make tellerless transactions on a routine basis. Additional applications are self-ticketing of air line flights and self-actuated kiosks which produce insurance policy and mortgage options. Also you can design your own home deck or price a car based on a selection of options by keying in your specific requirements. In certain areas of the country, the full automatic gas station enables you to pump your own gas and pay by credit card without a human attendant. Citicorp has developed a telephone with a built-in screen to facilitate banking at home. Home buying services like CompuServe have been in business for years, and are now joined by additional entries in the home buying market. Buying directly from the home cuts out the middleman.

The purpose of this report is to describe three examples of the do-it-yourself movement, specifically automatic teller machines (ATMs), automatic checkout machines (ACMs) for the supermarket industry, and the Prodigy home buying service. Then general observations, conclusions, and advice for companies whose products are sold directly to consumers will be reviewed.

AUTOMATIC TELLER MACHINES

In the twenty years since their introduction, money machines, or automated teller machines (ATMs) have become an accepted method of convenient access to cash. By 1988, approximately 65,000 ATMs were in use in America for nearly half a trillion transactions. Financial institutions originally intended ATMs to provide customers with convenient banking services at a lower cost than teller salaries.

Nearly half of all cash withdrawals are made from ATMs. According to Payment Systems, Inc., a Florida consulting firm, "ATM use appears to be an activity added to usual activity, rather than a substitution or replacement for existing activity." As widespread as ATM use appears, they report that only 33 percent of ATM cards are used as often as once a month or more with the prime locations becoming saturated. Secondary locations, such as supermarkets and convenience stores, are expected to increase. ATM banking is no longer a differentiator between financial institutions, but has become a commodity service. Most major banks and even the smaller ones now offer ATM service. They have become as common as telephone booths used to be.

Banks are looking at two major strategies to increase ATM profitability. One is to join network systems. The other is to increase the range of services and their attractiveness to ATM users, and to generate revenue from fees charged accordingly. This second option assumes that the 33 percent usage level can be increased. If the history of credit card usage is any guide, that assumption may be valid. Most credit cards were introduced in the mid-1960s. After five years, usage was in the 33-percent range. Now, 25 years later, an average of 90 percent of all cards are in use. ATMs have a comparable usage rate at a comparable time in their history.

The challenge for bankers is to offer profitable services which convince customers that automation is the most effective way to conduct their financial affairs. While some innovative options are within one or two years of implementation, they require rethinking the role of automation in financial institutions, and in some cases the nature of the banking business.

According to the president of the Electronic Funds Transfer Association, Dale L. Reistad, ATM cards will evolve into "supersmart cards" with keypads, readouts, and a small battery. They will be used not only for personal banking, but for stock transactions, worldwide special-interest electronic mail systems, and a variety of data bases. Because transaction volume is the basis of profitability, sponsoring institutions will probably rely heavily on frequent usage bonuses and other usage incentives. Reistad says, "In the United States, I suggest that this all will lead to one's own individual bank, custom designed to fit the available or desired components in the home, and customized to meet one's banking, investment and transactional needs as well."[2]

Other technological advances that can abet the use of ATMs include voice recognition. One systems employs a chip in the ATM card that will verify the voice of the card holder. This can be considered a "voice print" and offers voice withdrawals as opposed to the current method of using a keypad.

To recoup the investment in technology and equipment, ATM systems owners must look beyond labor savings—to innovative marketing outside traditional financial services— to provide services for which customers will happily pay to use and use often.

THE AUTOMATIC CHECKOUT MACHINES

The automated checkout machine (ACM), a product of Florida-based CheckRobot, Inc., enables shoppers to check out their own merchandise before paying a centrally located cashier. It incorporates a security systems to ensure that each item departing the store has been scanned and paid for. It combines laser scanning, local area networks, and data base management to produce a user interface with the store's central computer. CheckRobot claims that the ACM system offers the perception of improved customer service because it is easy to use, decreases shopping time, and increases customers' control over their shopping environment. It also provides a high return on investment primarily because of decreased labor costs. While the current target market is supermarkets, plans are to expand to retail organizations in general.

The ACM system consists of a central computer linked with the ACM stations and point-of-sale computer, and the ACM stations, each consisting of (1) a laser scanner which reads bar code labels, (2) a color video "touch screen" which displays a description of the items being purchased along with their prices and running subtotal for the transaction, (3) a produce key pad and produce video screen for handling produce and other variable weight bulk items, (4) a proprietary and patented merchandise security systems, and (5) a conveyer belt running through the merchandise security system to the bagging area.

A shopper activates the auto-scanning process simply by scanning the first item. As items are scanned, the ACM displays prices, identification data, and a running subtotal of the transaction on the video screen. At the same time, a printer produces a sales slip of the

[2]Dale L. Reistad, *Bankers Monthly*, April 1988, p. 54.

transaction. The approximately 3 percent of items with bar code labels that are unscannable can be processed via a video key pad.

After scanning an item a shopper places it on the conveyer belt which transports it through the ACM merchandise security systems. This systems compares height and weight of each product with a data base of product dimensions using the item's UPC code as a reference. If the characteristics do not match, the conveyer belt stops and reverses direction, returning the item to the shopper. If an item is scanned and not placed on the belt, it will automatically be voided from the receipt.

After the items pass through the security systems, a clerk or the shopper bags them at the rear of the ACM station. While one shopper's merchandise is being bagged, another shopper can begin the scanning process. The shopper then pays for the merchandise at a central cashier. In a typical ACM Systems installation, one cashier is required for every two or three ACM stations. Since each ACM cashier station can monitor all ACM stations simultaneously, shoppers may pay for their purchases at any cashier station.

BENEFITS OF AUTOMATIC CHECKOUT

CheckRobot developed the ACM system as a response to the evolving retail market. It responds to the changes in the nature of the labor pool. Retail checkout operators, typically young, entry-level, and unskilled, represent a shrinking segment of the labor pool. The ACM reduces workforce needs, thereby not only easing staffing pressures but also lowering costs and increasing profitability. CheckRobot estimates that one cashier is needed for every three to four ACM checkouts, plus one optional bagger (usually at a lower wage than checkout operators) for every one to two checkouts.

The use of autoscanning leads to a customer perception of improved service. Customer service in supermarkets is becoming an increasingly important differentiator in a competitive industry. By far the most important factor in supermarket service is efficient, speedy checkout.

Clearly the ACM's primary application to customer service is in the checkout category. Independent market research found that over half of ACM users responding felt that ACMs were "much faster" than conventional checkouts; two-thirds preferred the ACM to a conventional checkout, perceived self-scanning as an additional service offered by the store, thought overall service was better than in stores without automated checkout, and felt their overall checkout time was shorter than before ACMs were installed. And five-sixths of respondents ranked the ACMs as easy to use.

Why does this high-tech system cause a perceived improvement in a low-tech area such as customer service? In general, customers judge service quality perceptually, not quantitatively. There are four possible reasons for this perception. First, autoscanning responds to shoppers' number one complaint, waiting in line. ACM-equipped checkout lines are always open, regardless of the number of checkout operators working at the time. However, the actual time spent scanning is longer. Customers do not operate the scanning system as fast as trained employees. But the longer real time does not affect their perception of faster checkout. Second, customers perceive autoscanning as more accurate than staff-operated scanning systems. As they scan, they can see the item listed with its price on the video screen, and can verify its accuracy. Another effect of the labor shortage is that supermarkets increasingly omit price tagging of individual items. Thus, price verification becomes increasingly important to shoppers. Third, customer research indicates that ACMs are readily accepted across demographic lines of age, sex, or income. Finally, autoscanning frees available workers to provide other customer services, such as answering customer queries and keeping shelves full. This means that service efforts are more visible and more effective. Currently, available workers provide nonautomated services.

In summary, the three most significant benefits are savings on cashier labor, an increase in scanning productivity, and reduced shrinkage. Cashier labor costs are difficult to predict for until customers become more adept at autoscanning, they scan more slowly than cashiers. While ACM Systems have good security, it is not perfect. It is still possible to "beat the system" by product substitution: scan a cheaper item with the same dimensions as a more expensive item, and bag the more expensive item. No hard usage data is yet available to verify these claims. When the financial desirability of the ACM System is firmly established, autoscanning may become a familiar part of everyday life as have ATMs—and may someday encounter the same challenges of evolution that the money machines are now undergoing.

PRODIGY—HOME INFORMATION AND SHOPPING

Prodigy Services Company, a joint venture combining IBM's technological expertise and Sears retailing expertise, offers personal computer owners an "on-line electronic mall of information and shopping services."[3] Operating from telephone networks connecting 22 minicomputer centers around the country, it provides shopping, banking, news and data base access to an estimated 160,000 subscribers in 21 U.S. cities as of January 1990. Prodigy's launch in October 1988 was greeted with skepticism because of the earlier failures of similar ventures. In particular, home banking services were expected to become widely accepted when they first became available in the mid-eighties. But earlier technology was not "user-friendly" and applications were not geared to the mass markets. Those systems disappeared.

Prodigy faces stiff competition. Not only do 1.3 million computer owners subscribe to similar systems such as CompuServe, but telephone companies are starting information ventures on their own. However, according to Sears Chairman Edward Brennan, Prodigy's edge is that "many of the other services are either too narrow or too expensive—in most cases, both."[4]

Features of Prodigy

To meet the challenges of a mass market that demands ease of use, Prodigy is menu-driven and widely deemed to be friendly. Its pricing policy is also mass-market-oriented. A new subscription costs $9.95 and includes systems software, six passwords, and

---

[3]Michael Antonoff, "The Prodigy Promise," *Personal Computing,* May 1989, p. 67.

[4]Subrata N. Chakravart, and Evan McGlinn, "This Thing Has to Change People's Habits," *Forbes,* June 26, 1989, p. 122.

three months of free use. The multiple passwords increase usage and enable the system to keep track of six sets of user interests. After three months, unlimited usage is $9.95 per month. For only the cost of a local phone call, subscribers can browse—a new twist on window shopping.

Currently available services address Brennan's demand to his Prodigy staff: "Give me more things I want to buy."[5] Subscribers can order from Sears, J.C. Penney, and 45 other direct mail retailers. In some cities, local grocery stores offer shopping and delivery by helicopter. Subscribers can bank with over a dozen affiliates, including Manufacturer's Hanover. They can make a plane reservation through American Airline's Sabre system. They can access national news, world news, and business news. They can get 15-minute delayed stock quotations from Dow Jones, with a batch tracking capacity of two 15-stock portfolios. They can read columnists from Sylvia Porter to Jane Fonda and excerpts from *Consumer Reports*. An electronic mail facility enables private and public messages, including special interest forums. Nationally released films and videos are reviewed. Games include business simulations, adventure serials, jokes, contests, and an art gallery.

A writer with *Personal Computing* used the electronic bulletin board feature to conduct an informal market survey. Respondents complimented the convenience of on-line shopping and the entertainment provided by the bulletin boards. They complained about the limited information available on each screen because of the 40-character display, the *USA-Today* nature of the news coverage, the limited functions described above, and slowness in general. The deliberate mass nature of Prodigy's marketing appeal works to its advantage in another way: providing an attractive base of subscribers for potential advertisers. Almost 200 companies, including American Express and J.C. Penney, pay Prodigy every time an ad is accessed, a lead generated, or a product sold.

Using a network approach in operations as well as in technology, Prodigy signed an agreement with Nynex Corp. to operate its delivery and storage systems. This allows a concentration on expanding services and the ability to market them which is crucial if Prodigy is to recover its estimated $750 million investment in development, software and marketing. Edward Papes, Prodigy Chief Executive, doesn't expect Prodigy to break even for another few years. However, IBM and Sears consider Prodigy a long-term project. Brennan says, "In the final analysis, what this thing has to do is change people's habits."[6] If Prodigy continues to upgrade its electronic package of time-saving, entertaining features to its rapidly increasing target market, it could become a new American addiction.

CUSTOMER-ACTIVATED TRANSACTION PROCESSING SYSTEMS

The idea of letting the customer do transaction processing is not new. Since the 1920s we have been dialing telephone calls ourselves without the assistance of an operator. The Bell Systems recognized that it could not afford to hire enough operators to switch the increasing volume of calls and so shifted this labor onto the customer. Why did this scheme succeed?

[5] Ibid.
[6] Ibid.

A cynic might argue that the customer had no choice; after all, the Bell Systems was a monopoly. But automated teller machines (ATMs) and automated checkout machines (ACMs) are being implemented in highly competitive business environments. What accounts for the success or failure of these customer-activated transaction processing systems (CATPSs)? This question is examined first from the point of view of the customer and then of the business.

Customers are willing to operate a CATPS if they perceive a benefit greater than the effort incurred by doing it themselves. Michael Porter discusses the significance of a variety of buyer purchase criteria including delivery time, sales force quality, sales aids, and conformance to specifications.[7] The three CATPSs discussed in this paper provide benefits that address these criteria in different ways. In particular, a customer's perception of delivery time may be positively enhanced when he or she uses an ATM or ACM. Prodigy may not shorten delivery time, but customers may view it as a sales aid. If a CATPS does not appeal to some buyer purchase criteria in a meaningful way, it may well fail to gain acceptance.

The Importance of the User Interface

To customers, the effort required to do it themselves includes both the time taken for data entry/response as well as the mental energy expended in first learning and then actually using the systems. These are significantly effected by the bandwidth of the communications channel between the customer's input device and the rest of the transactional systems. High bandwidth allows both for rapid response time as well as for a user-friendly graphical or video interface such as found in the CheckRobot ACM. The relatively low bandwidth of an ATM interface and its data lines is not a obstacle now because the request for cash requires that only a small amount of well structured data be input and sent over the network. The Prodigy user interface is certainly of much higher bandwidth than text oriented videotex systems which have fared poorly in the past, yet Prodigy still cannot compete with the high bandwidth environment of a glitzy live display of merchandise in a store or even with television's high production values.

Ease of use is also affected by the complexity of the information that must be exchanged between the customer and the CATPS. For example, when a customer wants cash he or she determines that they want to withdraw an amount, $50.00, and makes that known to the ATM. The knowledge of how much to withdraw resides entirely with the customer. Compare this to the scenario of a novice ordering a fly rod through Prodigy. A good salesperson would know that certain rods are suitable for salt water fishing, others for river fishing, and yet others for lake fishing. If the customer is not prompted for specific requirements, they could well end up with the wrong rod. In this case the locus of information resides both with the customer as well as with the salesperson.

In Porter's terms the attractiveness of Prodigy as a sales aid could be adversely impacted by the absence of the benefit of a quality sales force. Expert systems built into CATPS could play a beneficial role here by allowing more complex information to be interchanged effectively between the customer and the CATPS. For example, the leading

[7]Michael E. Porter, *Competitive Advantage: Creating and Sustaining Superior Performance*, The Free Press, New York, 1985.

producer of elevators, the Otis Elevator Company, provides its customers with PCs and the required software to guide them in selecting, ordering, and scheduling the construction of elevators.

Using CATPS for Competitive Advantage

Business implement CATPS for different reasons. Porter has pointed out that generic business strategies of cost leadership, product differentiation, or market niche can be supported by product and process technology change.[8] For example, an ATM might be viewed as a process technology intended to allow a bank to reduce its labor costs and so provide a cost leadership position relative to the industry, or it might be conceived as a product technology aimed at differentiating a bank's services from those offered by its competitors. Sears might support Prodigy in order to exploit a new market niche, one not currently addressed through catalog or showroom sales channels.

It is now recognized that competitive advantage gained through the deployment of information technology is not necessarily sustainable. As an example, even small banks eventually responded to the ATM challenge by joining regional and national bank card networks. This forced leading banks to evolve their ATM services to stay ahead of the competition. For example, BayBanks has just introduced a service that lets the customer see which checks have cleared most recently.

New Technology for CATPS

Several new promising technologies for allowing the customer to do more of the ordering are emerging. Wide bandwidth communication between the customer and the ordering device was mentioned earlier. A whole host of multimedia devices are coming on the market which will transmit video, voice, and even 3-D pictures to potential customers. For example, a real estate office can simulate a walk through a house or an architect can superimpose a home or garden addition to an existing property. You can take a car on a test run, see how different hair styles look, or see the results of plastic surgery before it occurs.

An associate of ours just returned from Milan where he went into a bank and stacked his U.S. bills in an automatic scanning device which returned Lira, both paper and coins, and an itemized record of the transaction. The device handles sixteen different currencies. He was told that the scanner does a much better job of detecting counterfeit bills than the human eye.

Voice recognition, like optical scanning, is another option for letting the customer do it. There is no question that most of us are more comfortable speaking than keying or typing.

Akin to optical scanning are machines that can read handwritten data. This form of input allows office workers or customers to record information the same way they always have, by filling in the blanks, checking off boxes, and adding their personal comments. The potential also exists for processing handwriting in foreign languages with automatic translation. With the demographic changes in our society, this could be a real boon. Thus, information systems are emulating the way people have been communicating for centuries.

---

[8] Ibid.

It is a simple precept of making the computer change its ways to suit the human, not the other way around.

CONCLUSION

Letting the customer do transaction processing is not a fad. It is driven by such factors as population demographics and industry competition. This paper has looked in detail at three examples of customer-activated transaction processing systems (CATPSs). ATMs are well established, but continue to evolve. They represent an approach to a well known process that covers a narrow set of consumer transactions. Automated checkout machines are still in the trial stages. This class of applications covers a broader set of transactions but is limited to a single store and a single location. The third, Prodigy, is a new attempt to enter the home information and home shopping market. It covers a broad array of products and services and an assortment of vendors. It is probably the most challenging CATPS that has been attempted to date.

As with the introduction of any new technology, some will fail and some will succeed. Technological improvements in computing hardware and software and in the telecommunications infrastructure will allow for the introduction of new CATPS. The successful ones will provide a perceived benefit to customers because of the reasons described in this paper.

STUDY QUESTIONS

1. What are the ultimate advantages for the customer and for the company in "letting the customer do it?"
2. In your experience, where are other potential business areas where the customer could directly interact with the system?
3. Can this approach give a company a major competitive advantage?
4. Discuss some possible extensions to each of the three major applications described: ATM, automatic grocery checkout, and Prodigy.
5. Could legal, ethical, or criminal issues surface or result from such a close customer involvement in the system?
6. What kind of companies and in what industries are these type of applications most appropriate? Are there any industries where there appear no applications?
7. What new technologies aid the process of having greater customer involvement in systems?
8. Do you think that the appeal of this type of approach depends on the customer's cognitive style?
9. What might be a process for assessing the potential of these kinds of applications? What type of person is most likely to select potential applications?
10. What are factors, both positive and negative, for expanding applications for the home?

Appendix D

The Spectrum of Computer Technology and Services

Technology, as defined here, covers a broader spectrum of products and services than is usually connoted. Technology includes not only the hardware or physical elements, such as central processors, electronic storage units, and input/output equipment, but also the wide variety of software, application aids, and support services. Figure D.1 divides information systems technology into a triangle of three elements: hardware/communications, systems/application software, and support services. The last is viewed as tying together the other three. For purposes of definition:

The *hardware* element represents the things you can see, touch, and feel, such as a computer, a printer, a disk, or a communications processor. These devices are built from a variety of electronic and mechanical parts.

Systems software is defined as the programs written for a specific computer to aid programmers and operators of that computer, performing input/output tasks, organizing memory and moving data inside the processor.

Application software refers to the programs that the user programmers write to accomplish a specific application, such as inventory control, payroll, or production scheduling. In so doing, they utilize the systems software written for the specific computer. Hardware and software are really meaningless unless they can be utilized for the implementation of applications.

414

Support services provide the people power, consulting, and educating services and a whole array of service facilities ranging from the use of contract programmers to the subcontracting of a company's total data processing operation.

Thus the definition of computer technology covers the three elements in Figure D.1. The subelements that comprise each of the major elements will now be described. This should facilitate a better understanding of the type of products and services that comprise the IS industry.

HARDWARE/COMMUNICATIONS ELEMENTS

Figure D.2 lists the hardware elements. Included in hardware is communications even though it is recognized that there are software as well as hardware elements that fall within this category.

Computers

Computers range from small micros (the size of a note pad and the new palm-top computers) to huge supercomputers with processing speeds in the range of a billion instructions per second. Cray is a leading producer of super computers along with IBM, Hitachi (Japan), and NEC (Japan). Also playing in this arena are the parallel processing companies like Thinking Machines, INTEL, Pyramid Technology and Sequent Computer Systems. These machines derive their power from a multitude of micro-processors, as many as 65,000 working simultaneously. They are used for weather forecasting, data management, geophysical and petroleum exploration, biomedical research, and aircraft design and range from a price of $1 million to more than $20 million.

IBM continues to dominate the mainframe market accounting for over 70 percent of shipments in the area, a market which includes UNISYS, Bull, NCR and DEC along with NEC, Siemans Hitachi and Fujitsu. This market can be considered rather stagnant as companies continue to downsize, but can be considered a cash cow for IBM. Amdahl leads the plug-compatible manufacturers (PCM), which comprise another 15 percent of the

FIGURE D.1. Information Systems Elements

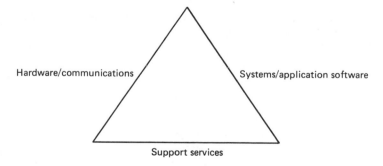

Hardware/communications

Systems/application software

Support services

FIGURE D.2. Hardware/Communications Elements

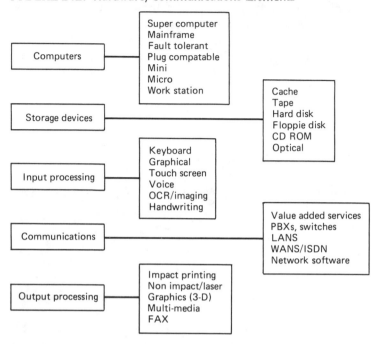

mainframe market. These machines emulate the characteristics and performance of their IBM counterparts.

A niche has developed for fault tolerant processors such as Tandem Computers and Stratus Computers. These machines come with complete system redundancy and a self diagnostic capability so they can operate around the clock without interruption. More and more companies, particularly in the finance and banking industry, find these features extremely attractive.

Much has been said about minis and micros, and they continue to be the processors of choice to a wide range of users spanning all industries. The mainframers like IBM are players in this market as well as DEC, Hewlett Packard and Apple, Compaq, and Commodore. Personal computers are shipping at a rate of about 25 million per year and this includes a growing number of laptop, notepad, and palm-top portables.

SUN, DEC, IBM, and Hewlett Packard lead the market for the *workstation,* defined as single-user, high-performance computer with advanced graphics that are used primarily for computational intensive scientific and engineering applications. However, PCs are becoming so powerful that the difference between workstation and PC is becoming blurred.

Storage Devices

Since record storage access often is the limited or gating factor in IS response time, special high-speed buffers, called *disk cache,* are used to balance the high speed of the central processor with the relatively slow speed of disk rotation.

Main memory is the only true random access device, for every piece of data can be obtained in exactly the same time—there is no minimum or maximum. However, main memory is relatively expensive and has limited capacity. It has an access time rated in nanoseconds (billionths of a second). Drum storage, used only in rare cases, offers more capacity at lower cost per character, but with much higher access time than main memory. Diskettes of the 5¼- or 3½-inch variety are found on most personal computers. They can hold up to a million or so bytes of information, have slow access time, and are used as inexpensive storage for small microcomputer systems or for limited auxiliary removable media in some larger installations. Fixed disk is the principal medium for storing the bulk of today's IS files. Although its average access time is much higher than that of either drum or main memory, it is fast enough to satisfy the majority of demands for data file access. Tape is still the workhorse of many computer systems, but its slow average access time (astronomical when compared to main memory or even disk) limits its use to batch operations and the storage of historical and backup data. Archival storage devices using magnetic cartridges are employed for files requiring capacity in the multibillion range but only moderate access time such as several seconds.

Because of the need for rapid access to data files, the on-line storage device is the crucial storage medium. Disk technology has provided the foundation for storing multi-billions of characters of information. Disk technology relies on a technique of recording magnetic spots on a disk surface. Data is represented on the surface by the presence or absence of magnetic spots on ferrous oxide surfaces running sequentially along concentric circles (tracks). Each character or group of characters has a unique address, so that the information can be transferred to the computer for processing. Each disk surface has its own recording head. The head can either read information from the disk into computer memory or write from computer memory onto the disk. The head moves mechanically across the disk surface, which is continually rotating.

Disk technology has been and continues to be improved mainly through higher-density recording techniques (laser) and increased speed of head positioning and disk rotation. This combination of increased density, accelerated head positioning, and faster disk rotation continues to give disks more capacity and lower access time. However, these are essentially mechanical techniques that have their theoretical and practical limits. Many feel that eventually the new nonmechanical techniques will drive these mechanical devices into the dinosaur age. These new techniques employ elements such as CD/ROM (compact disk/read only memory). Whether the reader understands the technology or not, the important thing is that the resultant storage devices can provide trillions of characters of information with high-speed access and eventually at much lower cost per character than today's storage devices. The ideal storage device has the speed of main memory, the capacity of archival storage devices, and the cost of tape. The disk storage devices hold the possibility of approaching this objective.

Of increasing interest is the video or optical disk. An optical disk is in reality a piece of plastic in which is embedded a strip of thin film such as aluminum foil. A laser writes the information on the disk by burning small holes in the foil. These are the same disks that are used for storing movies for home use. A major drawback in the use of video disks for business information storage is that you can only write information on the disk; you cannot erase it. They are called *worm* devices—write once, read many. However, erasable optical disks are now available.

Input Processing

Peripheral devices comprise the equipment necessary to provide the input and output to the users of IS. The keyboard/visual display of the PC has become the workhorse for feeding data to today's computer systems. The graphical user interface (GUI) has become a standard way to enter data, fueled by its ease of use in conforming to the cognitive style of many computer users. Optical and magnetic fonts can be interpreted and transferred to electronic medium without human intervention. The most relevant example of *magnetic font* is the magnetic characters found on bank checks. Examples of *optical font* are the bar codes on grocery items that are sensed by optical readers at supermarkets and the optics on a price tag that are scanned by light pens at a retail store. The interpretation of a limited voice vocabulary is used in some instances, and is growing as an input medium. Also appearing on the scene are image readers which can scan an entire page of data, including pictures, and convert it to electronic medium. Dial and embossed card input is characterized by factory data collection devices, where the worker places an ID card into a special reader and moves dial settings or depresses buttons to record the job item and quantity of work completed. The automatic teller machines (ATMs) in banks are activated in a manner similar to the factory data collection device.

Other input devices are the touch screen, allowing the user to touch an icon or a button to activate a programmed routine, and handwriting recognition whereby characters and numbers written in a person's own hand are translated into binary equivalents for subsequent processing.

Output Processing

The major output device is still the printed copy—either a serial printer, which prints a character at a time (typewriter), or a line printer, which has a drum or chain that can print an entire line at one time. Nonimpact printing, where a photoelectric process is used rather than the physical contact of a print drum or print stylus against paper, is increasing in popularity. This allows upwards of 18,000 lines of high-quality print per minute. Laser printers provide high-quality high-speed printing. Visual output screens now display high resolution graphics, some with 3-D capability. Color has been added to many graphic devices. Also in use are audio devices where a digitized message can be selected under computer control and sent back to the inquirer.

More exotic output can be obtained via multimedia wherein screens contain words, graphics, high resolution pictures as well as voice. This is very appealing for management presentations, for marketing specific products and as an impressive educational tool. Also a form of output is the fax which is in common use and has become a fixture in most offices. This completes the ever growing array of input and output devices with which we interface our computers and storage devices.

Communications

Hardware and software are embedded in communication systems so we discuss both under the communications heading. Chapter 5 has reviewed the entire communications area describing the ways companies transmit data within the company as well as to a variety of outside agencies. More than 2000 companies provide telecommunications services in the United States. Local telephone service is provided by the seven Regional Bell Companies, GTE, United Telecom, and some 1500 smaller independents. Long-distance service is provided by AT&T, MCI, US Sprint, Telecom USA, and 600 smaller carriers. Large and well-funded companies such as IBM, EDS, GE (General Electric), Boeing, MCI-Mail, Telenet, and TYMNET provide value-added services including electronic data interchange, voice mail services, credit validation, electronic funds transfer, information retrieval, and a host of other enhanced telecom services.

As for hardware and software, many companies have installed their own PBXs and switching networks and have developed themselves or acquired the software to manage the networks. Local area networks (LANs) of varying capacities are found in most companies. Electronic mail and voice mail systems are commonplace. ISDN and all-digital communications represent the mode of the future and many institutions are gearing up to the new wave of advanced telecom services. Suffice it to say, communications represents a good portion of the hardware elements we have just covered. We now turn to explore the software elements.

SYSTEM AND APPLICATION SOFTWARE ELEMENTS

Figure D.3 lists the major categories of systems software and application software. Application software is further subdivided into business and specialty. The major distinction between systems software and application software is that the former is tied directly to the

FIGURE D.3. Systems/Application Software

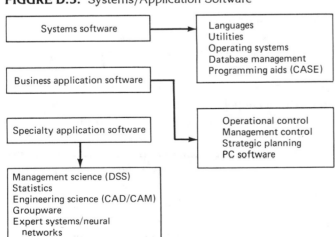

computer and consists of aids to assist the programmer in translating a particular application into machine language. This class of software also includes aids to assist the computer operation group in scheduling and running the computer efficiently. Applications, on the other hand, are the end product—a spread sheet application, an order processing or inventory control system in productive operation on a computer. These applications utilize the systems software, which in turn utilizes the computer hardware.

Systems Software

Systems software is divided into the groupings listed in Figure D.3. Languages have evolved over the decades and we currently work with fourth generation language or 4GL. The first generation were machine language where programmers actually instructed the computer in binary or binary coded decimal. Assembly languages, using mnemonic codes and data addresses were second generation while COBOL is a prime example of a third generation language. Other third generation languages through the ages have been FORTRAN, Basic, PL1, APL, Pascal, and ADA. Now 4GL, the most popular one being SQL, standing for Structured Query Language, and a language called C++ are in wide use working in concert with a host of data base management systems.

Utility programs assist the programmer or operator in performing common functions, such as sorting, collating, and various audit and checking routines that aid in program preparation and testing.

Because of the incompatibilities within a manufacturers' lines, the need exists for conversion software to aid the transfer of data and programs from one computer system to another. These conversion software aids may be required in order to interchange data files from one system to another or to replace one computer with another. The scope of the problem differs, depending on whether the former or the latter is the situation, but the nature of the job embodies similarities that can be materially aided by well-conceived conversion or interconnection aids.

Operating systems are the internal monitors that reside in computer memory and direct and manage the execution of programs, some sequentially (monoprogramming) and some simultaneously (multiprogramming). Operating systems also help in the economical scheduling and allocating of computer resources in performing a specified job mix. The industry is currently in a shift from proprietary operating systems to standard operating systems (i.e., UNIX).

Data-base management systems (DBMS) software provides the capability of managing and controlling the integrated data base so important to IS development. Included in the functions are the ability to organize, capture, update, and retrieve data from the various information files. Data-base software was treated in depth in Chapter 4.

Programming operating aids represent software techniques that enable the programmers and operators to accomplish their jobs in a more expeditious manner. Examples of this category are automatic flowcharting programs that can produce flow charts from written application descriptions and automatic logging programs that can produce summaries of machine time utilization. The former aids the programmer, the latter the operator. This area has received significant attention as application backlogs grow and skilled systems analysts become scarce. Elaborate software, termed CASE (computer-aided software engineering) has been built to expedite software development. These tools were described in Chapter 7.

Business Application Software

This is the ultimate objective of computer hardware and software, to execute the business functions of an enterprise. These applications can be either developed using the systems software described above or acquired from an application development company. Application software that run on today's PCs can be categorized somewhere along the line between systems software and application software, but for the most part it is closer to the latter. Spreadsheets are an example. They are really templates on which financial applications are built. Application software performs a business task, spreadsheets don't until one writes the formulas for the prescribed cells. Desktop publishing systems fall into a similar category.

Computer vendors and a host of third-party software and system houses as well as consultants have realized there is a dollar to be made in supplying turnkey (or close to it) software offerings for specific user application requirements. If a particular application is general enough or if the solution can be generalized, it is possible that it can be used for a broad spectrum of customers. With the rising cost of systems analysts and programmers, package application software has become a very attractive business. A prime example are the elaborate accounting packages that include general ledger, accounts receivable, accounts payable, and payroll.

The application software industry has grown dramatically over the years. The general business software business is typified by the former companies, McCormick, Dodge and MSA which have been merged under Dun & Bradstreet Software Services. D&B specializes in accounting and payroll packages for IBM and DEC mainframes and minis. Companies like Pilot Software, Comshare, and Execucom specialize in executive support systems while ASK computers focuses on the manufacturing application arena.

The PC proliferation has caused the same phenomenon in PC software companies. Microsoft specializes in spreadsheets and word processing and also produces PC operating system software. LOTUS is noted for spreadsheets (1-2-3) and other software such as Agenda & Notes, while other major players are Ashton Tate (Dbase), Wordstar International, Software Publishing (Harvard Graphics), Oracle and Borland International. Computer Associates, Inc., with its acquisition of Cullinet and its data-base software, is now a big player in the software field. Xerox and Aldus specialize in desktop publishing software.

The category of engineering science includes such functions as stress and failure analysis, coordinate geometry programs, and programs designed to aid the engineering departments of larger companies. Also, packages are available in the area of computer-aided design (CAD), where complex designs can be visually described on special screens and then drawn on graphic plotters and computer-aided manufacturing (CAM) where fabrication and assembly process are described such that a robot or numerically controlled machine can produce the part or product with no or minimal human intervention.

The fact that engineering science is better understood and more precise in its measurement facilitates the usefulness of scientific application software. Even though the scope of the application area is greater, the imprecise nature of operations in the business area accounts for the lower evolution of package application software.

Two additional specialty categories complete the list of specialty application software. The first is *groupware,* which is a generic name for software that supports the way people work together in groups. This class of software allows people to communicate both more efficiently (faster) and more effectively (improved sources and currency of information). The software includes facilities for electronic mail, bulletin boards, project scheduling, information retrieval and group interaction via tele- or video conferencing. LOTUS' Notes is an example of groupware.

The remaining category is *expert systems* and *neural networks.* Though these are separate approaches, they both allow the focus on problems that have heretofore been considered too unstructured or fuzzy for the application of computer logic. Both apply the thought logic of experts to problem solution. Neural networks model the function of a biological neuron that mimics the workings of the human brain.

SUPPORT SERVICES ELEMENTS

Support services are rapidly becoming predominant in the information processing industry. What has lagged is the people and support power for an effective merger of hardware and software in order to produce a viable information system. Figure D.4 breaks down support services into the categories of Computer Time, Professional Support, and Subscription Services.

FIGURE D.4. Support Service Elements

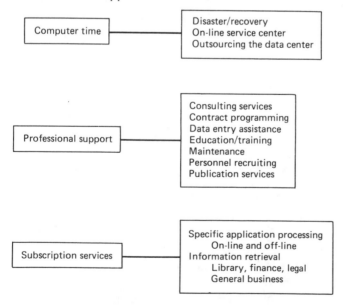

Computer Time

Computer time services (buying computer time) was initiated for the smaller companies who could not afford or did not desire their own computer. However, the service center is a source of ancillary computer power of both a generalized and specialized nature. Computer users need extra capacity to handle peak loads and also as backup facilities in case of prolonged downtime problems. One of the fastest growing computer services is disaster recovery. Sunguard Systems and ComDisco are two major providers, maintaining computing, data storage, and communications backup in case of a major computer failure.

The on-line service center is significant as a source of specialized assistance. A company may have 95 percent of its computer applications devoted to business use, with a 5 percent need for scientific use. It may prove wiser to utilize the facilities of an on-line service center for the engineering department rather than it is to add the necessary facilities and support capability to implement the engineering applications in house. Medium-size and large users are continuing to avail themselves of the specialized capability offered by on-line service centers. Typically the use is of a scientific or professional nature, where an engineer or financial planner uses the statistical routines of modeling tools provided by the service to solve a specific ad hoc problem. Geisco and McDonnell Douglas are two major players.

Another area is that of outsourcing. This is a form of buying computer time, in this case a company turns over the entire operation of its data centers to a third party. Usually the third party, companies like DEC, IBM, McDonnell Douglas, EDS, or Andersen Consulting will take over a company's current computing facilities, adding or exchanging equipment where appropriate.

Professional Support

A wide range of support functions are available to supplement or complement the user's own capabilities. They range from broad consulting help in the areas of IS organization, long-range computer plans, and top management IS orientation to specific areas, such as providing temporary programming assistance or data entry operators to reduce a backlog of customer transactions. The user can obtain assistance during every step of the application development cycle. The list of support includes broad consulting and systems/programming support that can be employed during various phases of the application development cycle. Education is a critical item, and a company may develop the need to enroll key IS and non-IS personnel in various classes and seminars offered by companies specializing in educational programs, or it may require the services of a company to tailor a training program to its own particular requirements. The cost and efficacy of outside services should always be measured against the relevant in-house capability.

Computer maintenance, which is usually provided as part of the rental price, can be secured from a third party or separately negotiated with the manufacturer of the equipment if the hardware is purchased. This is true of third-party leases.

Personnel recruiting services can be utilized to assist in the hiring of in-house system and programming capability. As mentioned earlier, data entry operators can be employed or work can be contracted out to handle peak data-preparation work loads. Finally, publication services, which include magazines, periodicals, books, special reports, surveys, competitive product information, researching services, and the like can be utilized to complement training programs and provide necessary background information for making system and product decisions.

There are a wide range of companies doing business in the professional services area. Full line consulting is available from the large auditing/consulting firms such as KPMG Peat Marwick, Andersen Consulting, Coopers Lybrand, as well as from hardware vendors like IBM and DEC. All of these firms offer systems integration services wherein they assume responsibility for entire systems design and implementation, arranging for subcontractors as appropriate—in other words, they take over the entire job.

Companies like Computer Associates and Electronic Data Systems are large multi-capability companies that provide services from single application development to systems integration to outsourcing. Automatic Data Processing (ADP) is another broad-base information services company that still does a good line of business in performing the payroll application for all sized institutions. Companies like Keane, Inc., Computer Task Group, Computer Partners, and Computer Assistance, some of whom are arms of larger service companies, provide more specific application development expertise.

Subscription Services

Subscription services refer to companies who offer to implement specific application areas for subscribers of the service. The subscription service companies have concentrated on specific areas and have built up expertise in applying computer solutions to these problems. An example of this type of service is a system designed for handling the business applications of small to medium-sized hospitals. Such a system produces customer bills and the required ancillary accounting reports from input furnished by the hospital's clerical staff. The service can either be off-line such that the input data is delivered to the subscription service company by manual means, or it can be on-line where each hospital has appropriate terminal and communication facilities. Similar arrangement exist with Automatic Data Processing for payroll and stock market brokerage services.

Information retrieval services usually center on business areas where there is a need to access data from a common set of files. An example is the National Library of Medicine, which maintains an index of medical research documents cross-referenced by several keys. PCs can interrogate the files and obtain the listing and location of reference material pertinent to a specific inquiry. This type of service can be used by public libraries, financial institutions, educational institutions, legal firms, and general business firms. In the latter case, commercial data banks such as supplied by Standard & Poor, Dialog, McGraw Hill, Dun & Bradstreet, and Dow Jones are providing useful data that is external to a company's data base. Home-based services include Compuserve, The Source, and Prodigy.

Companies may not fall neatly into one of the support service categories listed, for many are engaged in a combination of two or more activities. Also, some companies are developing unique approaches by combining these services in different ways. It is becoming very difficult to slot companies or to segment the market.

This completes the run-down of the technology required to power today's IS. This is a broad and complex subject, with new and varied products still emerging with a rapidity found in no other industry. This section has presented a classification scheme for grouping and understanding the vast array of equipment available to IS designers and implementors. While the focus of the book is on management rather than technical considerations, the latter cannot be overlooked.

Appendix E

Computer History and Application

This section will give a brief history of computer development and present a general outline of computer application and use.

A BRIEF HISTORY OF COMPUTERS

In his widely quoted book, *Future Shock*, Alvin Toffler points out that almost as much has happened since we were born as happened before we were born. This barrage of change, scientific acceleration, and technological turnover is causing a psychological shock wave throughout society. Toffler indicates that if the last 50,000 years of human existence were divided into lifetimes of approximately 62 years each, there have been about 800 lifetimes. Of these 800, fully 650 were spent in caves. Only during the last 70 lifetimes has it been possible to communicate effectively from one lifetime to another—as writing made it possible to do. Only during the last six lifetimes did masses of people ever see a printed word. Only during the last four has it been possible to measure time with any precision. Only in the last two has anyone anywhere used an electric motor. And an overwhelming majority of the material goods we use in daily life was developed within the present, the 800th, lifetime. This type of analysis holds for computers and the science of information processing. Certainly computers have been characteristic only of the 800th lifetime—in fact, the last half of the 800th lifetime, if you consider computers in the commercial scene.

You should view the progress of computers with this perspective; that a fantastic amount of technological change has occurred in a very short time. The learning curve has been rapid despite the experience of some who have borne the brunt of abortive attempts to reach out too far, too fast. The Toffler "lifetime" concept places the computer in its proper framework in time and projects a sobering view of its potential.

Although the abacus is not a computer, the history of computing really began with this device. The abacus is a manual device combining two fundamental concepts. It uses objects (small beads) to represent numbers, and it uses one object to represent several numbers. On an abacus the number nine is represented by one "five" bead and four "one" beads. In the hands of a skilled user, the abacus makes extremely rapid arithmetic calculations. The abacus is still a widely used computing device in China.

The first machine to add numbers mechanically was invented by Blaise Pascal, the French mathematician and philosopher, in 1643. Pascal used geared counter wheels that could be set to any of the positions zero to nine. The geared tooth was used for carrying one to the next position when nine was reached. Following Pascal's lead, G.W. Leibnitz, a German mathematician, invented a machine in 1671 that could control the amount of adding. This was the first multiplying machine. These early machines are the direct ancestors of the electric-powered, but hand-operated adding machines and desk calculating machines that became a familiar part of the business scene. These adding machines and calculators accomplish only one operation at a time and are key driven; that is, they are activated by depressing a key.

Charles Babbage, a professor of mathematics at Cambridge University, England, attempted in 1812 to build a difference machine—a machine that could add, subtract, multiply, divide, and perform a sequence of steps automatically. The last function is the forerunner of the stored program. Babbage called his machine a difference engine because he intended to use it to compute mathematical tables by adding differences such as the time between the high and low tides. For example, if the moon rises exactly one hour later each day, and the high and low tides are 6½ hours apart, and if on August 14, high tide is at 12:00 A.M., then low tide will be at 6:30 P.M. On August 15, high tide will be at 1:00 P.M. and low tide at 7:30 P.M., and so on. A table was to be built by adding differences. Babbage failed to get the necessary funds for his machine, and in 1833 the project was dropped. Babbage also was thinking of making an analytical engine with three parts: store (memory), mill (arithmetic), and sequence mechanisms (control). These parts are very similar to the elements of a computer. Babbage didn't gain the necessary funds and support for this project either, but his concepts were sound in every respect. It is generally stated that the technology in Babbage's time just didn't permit the development of instruments with the precision required by his analytical engine.

At this point we are introduced to one of the few romantic figures in computer history, Ada Lovelace. Ada was the only legitimate daughter of Lord Byron. Unlike other ladies of her time and background, who occupied themselves with light studies, recreation, and serving tea, Ada took to mathematics and at age 15 had covered Paisley's geometry text on her own as a diversion. She became known to Charles Babbage through a translation she did of a French work that helped the development of the difference engine. Ada, described as brilliant, charming, and feminine, became a vital assistant to Babbage. The Ada language was a government standard for a considerable time. Molly Gleiser, computer historian, writes that at her death at age 36, at her own wish, she was buried at the side of Lord George Gordon Byron (also dead at age 36), "All passion stilled, passionate and noble daughter of a passionate and noble father." Sometimes an emotion or two crops up even in a book on computers and information systems.

A major development occurred in 1886 when statistician Herman Hollerith was working on the 1880 census of the United States. After six years of constant work the census still had not been calculated. Obviously, a new way to handle large amounts of data was needed if the census was to be completed before the next one came around. For 80 years, cards with punched holes representing numbers had been used to control the weaving of cloth on Jacquard looms. Hollerith had the idea that these holes could be sensed by a machine that would then sort and manipulate the arithmetic sums represented by the holes. The punched card withstood the rapid innovations in computer technology for nearly 90 years.

The same Herman Hollerith became the chief asset of the Tabulating Machine Company (as William Rodgers wrote in his book, *Think*, a biography of the Watsons and IBM). Thomas J. Watson left NCR in 1913 and in the following year, through a holding company called the Computer-Tabulating-Recording Company (C-T-R) headed up by a noted American financier, Charles R. Flint, became a general manager of one of the component companies, the Tabulating Machine Company. In 1924 C-T-R became known as IBM, with Tom Watson its eventual president. Rodgers points out that Watson never got along with the volatile inventor Hollerith, who was to drive Watson literally out of his senses. Out of his senses or no, Watson parlayed Hollerith's concept of the punched card and the punched card machine into an empire that today employs more than a third of a million people and has sales of over $60 billion per year. Appropriately enough, the formation of C-T-R in 1914 corresponds almost exactly to the beginning of Toffler's 800th lifetime.

The first automatic digital computer that worked was constructed at the Bell Telephone Laboratories in New York in 1939 by George Stibitz. Stibitz, an engineer, faced the problem of performing arithmetic operations on complex numbers. He decided that ordinary telephone relays could be wired together to do this time-consuming job. Stibitz represented each decimal digit by a code of ones and zeros (the beginning of binary notation), such that four relays arranged in a pattern of being energized or not could represent a number. The machine was completed and successfully demonstrated in 1940. It is interesting to note that mathematicians at Dartmouth College sent problems to this machine via teletype and received answers. This was the beginning of on-line communications to the computer.

The first general-purpose, automatic digital computer was the Harvard/IBM automatic sequence-controlled calculator called the Mark I. It began operations in 1944, under wartime pressure. It was developed by Professor Howard Aiken with the help of engineers from IBM. The Mark I performed about three additions per second and had 72 internal storage registers. This is a modest capability, to say the least, when compared to the millions of additions per second and the millions of registers of internal storage available in today's computers. The slow operation was caused by the use of the relay, an electromechanical device, as the major component.

At the same time a group of engineers at the University of Pennsylvania, headed by John W. Mauchly and J. P. Eckert, was working on an automatic electronic digital computer using radio tubes, which function at higher speed than relays. The ENIAC (Electronic Numerical Integrator and Automatic Calculator) was completed in 1947. It had only 20 storage registers but it could accomplish 5000 additions per second, which made it the fastest computer in operation.

THREE CONTRIBUTORS TO THE DEVELOPMENT OF COMPUTERS

At this point, it would be inappropriate to proceed without at least the brief mention of three men, who though not necessarily associated with specific computer hardware development, were instrumental in the introduction of logic and programming elements enabling the computer to execute complex instructions and to control a wide gamut of business and scientific operations. These men are George Boole, Norbert Wiener, and John von Neumann.

George Boole lived in Babbage's time (early and mid-1880s). Though not involved in hardware development, he used his genius in mathematics to lay the groundwork for the theory behind computer logic. Modern computers operate with a binary or two-stage operating logic; each instruction or piece of data is converted to this two-stage form before entering the computer and being processed. The data is then converted back to decimal and alpha mode at output time. The binary representation and internal arithmetic manipulation are called *Boolean algebra*, after George Boole, and this indeed represents a most significant contribution to computer development.

Norbert Wiener, who received a Ph.D. in 1913 at the age of 19, reincarnated the word *cybernetics* from the Greek *kubernetes* (steersman) in the 1940s. The science of cybernetics describes how automatic machines or computers function, including the elements of input, output, processing, communications, and feedback loops. Wiener's work helps us understand the basic concept of a system is the foundation of the systems theory we use to solve today's business problems. Wiener's writings develop an analogy of the automatic feedback system to the human nervous system. Thus intension tremor and Parkinsonism are impairments of the normal feedback loops between brain and motor functions. Wiener's work assists us in comprehending the overall science or body of thought in which the computer plays a significant part.

John von Neumann (1903-1957) is a prominent name to people familiar with the early development of computers in the United States. In a book entitled *The Computer from Pascal to Von Neumann*, Herman Goldstine, who worked with von Neumann, cannot say enough about the latter's contribution to the computer field. Von Neumann, a brilliant mathematician, had a profound influence on the development of early hardware but he concentrated on the memory and software side, the latter being an area that is finally receiving the emphasis it warrants. Von Neumann showed earlier hardware developers how to store instructions and what these instructions should do. His initial concept of storage in a mercury delay line is the forerunner of core memory and today's semiconductor memory. Prior to von Neumann, paper tape was the accepted vehicle for getting instructions to the processor. John von Neumann's contributions are immense.

THE COMMERCIAL ERA

From 1946 to 1951 the computer field was dominated by the government, universities, and small companies working with government or university grants. It was five years before the world's first commercial computer was produced by Remington Rand (now UNISYS). Remington Rand had purchased control of the Eckert-Mauchly Computer Corp., developers of the ENIAC. The first commercial computer, UNIVAC I, was delivered in 1951 to the same U.S. Bureau of the Census that first spurred Dr. Hollerith to use punched cards in calculations. The first non-government installation of a UNIVAC I was at General Electric's appliance plant in Louisville, Kentucky, in 1954.

The installation of UNIVAC I at the Census Department and at General Electric opened up the commercial era of computers, and few could forecast what was to come. Several prominent prognosticators of the time proclaimed that no more than 100 of these machines would be needed to handle the computations for the entire country.

Though Remington Rand had the lead and dominated the market from 1951 to 1956, IBM made its delayed entry into the market and via a strong sales and support force, was the dominant vendor by 1957, a position they have maintained to this day.

The rest of the story is told in this book—the introduction of minicomputers, microcomputers, the wave of new software and telecommunications technology, storage devices, and the like. A major shift has been the entry of powerful foreign companies into a market place that is now global. Japanese companies, Fujitsu, NEC, and Hitachi, as well as Siemans in Germany are now in the top ten list of information technology companies. While the U.S. still leads in technical innovation, the Japanese have made huge investment in manufacturing process equipment that enables them to lead in chip and digital component production. It is something about which the U.S. manufacturers and the U.S. government are increasingly concerned.

COMPUTER APPLICATION BY INDUSTRY

The following listing (Figure E.1) shows the variety of computer applications by industry segment. A discussion of these applications, divided into the categories of basic and advanced will give us a perspective of how IS is being employed throughout the U.S. economy.

Manufacturing

The basic business applications are the same in both the discrete and the process type of manufacturing. Accounting, order processing, purchasing, and inventory applications are computerized in most manufacturing companies. Inventory status reports, sales analysis, and cost reports are commonplace documents to the management of manufacturing companies. In more advanced applications, forecasted sales volume is used as prime input into other subsystems—production scheduling, for example, to plan and control the entire

FIGURE E.1. Use of computers by industry

Industry Segment	Basic Applications	Advanced Applications
Discrete manufacturing	• Accounting • Order processing • Purchasing • Inventory control	• Forecasting • Numberical control • Production scheduling (MRP) • Design automation
Process manufacturing	• Accounting • Order processing • Purchasing • Inventory control	• Mix formulation • Process control • Simulation • Revenue models
Banking and finance	• Demand deposit accounting • Check processing • Proof and transit operations • Cost control	• Online savings • Centralized file system • Portfolio analysis • cash flow analysis
Federal government	• Accounting and administration • Tax reporting and auditing • Order processing • Census analysis	• Information retrieval • Intelligence • Command and control • Pollution control
Insurance	• Premium accounting • Customer billing • External reports • Reserve calculation	• Actuarial analysis • Investment analysis • Policy approval • Cash flow analysis
Business and personnel service	• Service bureau functions • Tax preparation • Accounting • Client records	• Econometric models • Credit checking • Engineering analysis • Data base
Education	• Attendance accounting • Grading and scoring • School administration • Alumni records	• Student scheduling • Computer-aided instructions • Library cataloging • Student counseling
Utilities	• Customer billing • Accounting • Meter reading • Inventory control	• Rate analysis • Line and generator loading • Operational simulation • Financial models
State and local government	• Utility billing • Tax recordkeeping • Payroll • School administration	• Traffic analysis • Budget preparation • Police identification (CAD) • City planning
Retail	• Customer billing • Sales analysis • Accounting • Inventory reporting	• Point of sale automation • Sales forecasting • Merchandising • JIT and EDI

FIGURE E.1. Use of computers by industry (continued)

Industry Segment	Basic Applications	Advanced Applications
Transportation	• Rate calculation • Vehicle maintenance • Cost analysis • Accounting	• Traffic pattern analysis • Automatic rating • Tariff analysis • Reservation systems
Health care	• Patient billing • Inventory accounting • Health care statistics • Patient history	• Lab/operation scheduling • Nurses' station automation • Intensive care • Preliminary diagnosis
Distribution	• Order processing • Inventory control • Purchasing • Warehouse control	• Vehicle scheduling • Merchandising • Forecasting • EDI
Printing and publishing	• Circulation • Classified ads • Accounting • Payroll	• Automatic typesetting • Home finder • Media analysis • Page layout

production process. An increasing use is made of numerical control applications of CAM (computer-aided manufacturing) to control, for example, the drilling or milling of a machine part. In design automation, an engineer designs a part or product with the aid of a computer that tells how the part will react under stress and other conditions. This is called CAD (computer-aided design).

MRP and MRPII systems are prevalent in manufacturing companies. Material requirements planning (MRP) looks to the future in forecasting future product needs and from their projects flow production schedules and future material needs, quantities by item and the dates they will be required. It's a proactive rather than a reactive approach. Manufacturing resource planning (MRPII) ties the production process into all the interconnecting subsystems, i.e. order entry, billing, accounts receivable, purchasing, accounts payable— eventually tieing everything into the general ledger. The just in time (JIT) approach, copied from the Japanese, reverse the large lot concept of previous manufacturing and attempts to reduce inventory costs by scheduling materials and parts form vendors just in time to manufacture and meet customer orders. A higher level of integration that views the manufacturing process as a single system is Computer Integrated Manufacturing (CIM) tying in automated physical production and engineering facilities (CAM and CAD).

In the process or continuous-flow type of manufacturing, process control computers are used to control the flow of the product automatically. Mix formulation is used to aid petroleum refining, food processing, or other areas where an optimum blend of raw material is needed to produce the finished product while meeting cost and other constraints. For example, percentages of different octanes are constraints in petroleum, and nutritional and vitamin content are constraints in food processing. This complex process is materially aided by the computer. Simulation and revenue models are other examples of advanced manufacturing applications.

Business and Personnel Services

The business and personnel services category covers a broad range of companies. It includes computer service centers, consulting firms, certified public accountants, credit agencies, personnel companies, and the like. The applications in this industry segment cover a wide spectrum, ranging from basic service bureau applications such as payroll and order processing to the preparation of tax returns, accounting, and the maintenance of client records (in the case of service companies). The advanced applications include complex econometric input-output models, credit checking, computer-aided engineering design performed by architects, and various data base applications such as legal and medical information retrieval.

Banking and Finance

Banks and financial institutions are major users of computers. Much of their work centers around paper, an area where data processing finds its greatest utility. Checks with magnetic ink characters are sorted by individual and bank before demand deposit or savings account records are updated. Proof and transit and other accounting and cost control operations are common computer applications in banks.

On-line teller systems are in place in most banks. Centralized file systems combine savings, checking, personal loan, and mortgage files for an individual into a single integrated file. Banks and financial institutions also use computer-aided techniques such as portfolio analysis and cash flow analysis to invest and control the funds essential for efficient operation. Automatic cash dispensers are everywhere, while bank-at-home services are being extended. Electronic funds transfer applications are increasing and services extended to where individuals can debit or credit their accounts instantaneously via a money card over a communication line.

Federal Government

The use of computers in the federal government is a microcosm of their use in the rest of the business community. The federal government operates manufacturing plants, financial institutions, service operations, hospitals, education facilities, transportation, distribution outlets, and the like. Basic applications include accounting and administration, processing and auditing tax returns, maintaining and analyzing census data, and order processing and billing for the services the government performs for individuals and businesses.

The government uses advanced applications such as information retrieval for various functions of intelligence work, for command and control systems for the armed services, as well as for analyzing a variety of data—for example, demographic and ecological data to help curb the spread of pollution.

Education

Educational use of computer applications has expanded. Machines handle the attendance, grading, and scoring of students, as well as other administrative functions of a school. Other computer applications include student scheduling, a serious problem in large schools with a varied curriculum. Communication networks allow access to computing power by students and faculty throughout the university. Electronic mail and voice mail connect departments. Computers maintain indexes and cross-indexes to enable students and teachers to make better use of school library facilities. Connections to other libraries and research data can be made from a student's room or a faculty home to optical disks storing gigabytes of data within campus libraries. Computer-aided instruction also is a growing field. In addition, computers are being used to combine student records and personal data in order to correlate interests and suggest courses of study and career paths that the student might not have considered. Microcomputers are commonplace in elementary schools.

Insurance

The insurance industry was an early user of computer equipment to simplify the handling of administrative paperwork. The volume and repetition of activities such as the calculation of customer premiums or the billing of policyholders make them ideal computer applications. In addition, computers produce a variety of external reports and handle statistical jobs such as calculating insurance reserves. The advanced applications move the computer into calculating actuarial statistics, approving policies, analyzing historical patterns, and predicting future actions on projected probabilities. Wouldbe insurees can activate policies by answering questions at a computer kiosk powered by an expert system. In addition, the computer is being used in investment and cash flow analysis—two areas vital to insurance company operations.

Utilities

The utilities industry includes the gas and electric companies as well as communications services, the teletype, and telephone companies. With the volume of customers and variety of available services, the computer made early inroads into the basic applications of customer billing and accounting, as well as meter reading and inventory control for the variety of products and supplies handled by the utility companies. Advanced applications center around analysis of rate structures and facility scheduling and loading. In addition, simulation and financial models are used to determine the impact of population growth and other ecological factors on power and service demands.

State and Local Government

The applications in state and local governments range from the basics of utility billing, city and state payrolls, tax records, and school administration, to the advanced applications of analyzing traffic patterns and assigning traffic lights accordingly, budget preparation and administration, and as an aid in city planning. In addition, some cities and states have police systems that maintain data banks on criminals, suspected criminals, stolen cars, and the like, to improve law enforcement. Police officers are assigned by computer-aided dispatching.

Distribution

The major function of a distributor is to maintain the flow of merchandise from manufacturer to retailer, and computers have aided materially in this process. Computers are used extensively for order processing, inventory control, purchasing, and warehouse control. Computers also aid in vehicle and load scheduling and in forecasting and merchandising, where the computer aids in spotting fast- and slow-moving items and in projecting the probable success of new items. Advanced systems can facilitate the development of ethnic and cultural models, which when combined with traffic patterns and competitive factors can aid in the selection of successful store and sales outlet sites. Electronic data interchange (EDI) links customer to retailer to distributor via a computer network.

Transportation

Transportation includes motor carriers (truck and auto leasing) as well as the airlines, ship lines, and railroads. Basic applications center on cost analysis and accounting, calculating tariff rates from rather complex formulas and regulations, and handling vehicle maintenance by projecting repair schedules based on historical patterns. Advanced applications include the complex reservation systems developed by the airlines and sophisticated analysis of traffic patterns to optimize routing and scheduling. In addition, computers are being used to analyze, update, and maintain tariff tables, and to automatically calculate bills on the basis of individual loads, routes, and local conditions. Computers are tracing overnight delivery of letters and packages.

Health Care

Computers are becoming commonplace in the administrative functions of a hospital, performing jobs such as patient billing and inventory control of medical instruments and facilities, and also producing health care statistics and maintaining patient histories. Computers are beginning to cater to the more exciting advanced applications. Computers are scheduling lab tests and operations and scanning patient symptoms for preliminary diagnosis. Gradually the computer is being used to reduce the administrative load on nurses, giving them more time for other important nursing functions. In addition, the hospitals are using computers to monitor patients in intensive care wards, employing the principle of process control more familiar in process manufacturing. The CAT scanner that x-rays patients for tumors is an advanced use of computer-aided diagnosis. The computer has helped health insurance companies manage and control the growing cost of health care, linking doctors and insurees directly to the health care data base where historical records are maintained.

Retail

Retailing, a slow industry to computerize, is now moving more rapidly. Computers handle the basic paperwork procedures of customer billing, sales analysis, inventory reporting, and the other accounting functions within a retailing environment. Some retailers have moved into the more advanced applications of sales forecasting and merchandising, where a computer can be used to spot trends in item movement and discern the impact of advertising and special promotions. Retailers are turning to source data automation—the point-of-sale device that records the movement of goods from the store on machine-readable media can then be used directly as basis for reordering, inventory control, sales analysis, and profitability accounting, and linking to their own warehouses and their suppliers for JIT delivery thus optimizing material and cash flow. Today these applications fall under the umbrella of electronic data interchange (EDI).

Printing and Publishing

In the printing and publishing industry, computers are used to automate newspaper and magazine circulation as well as to bill for advertising and other services. In addition, accounting functions and payroll are commonplace computer applications. At most installations, computers directly feed typesetting machines to produce hyphenated and justified copy. The computer with color graphic software composes an entire page layout. Telecommunications enable newspapers like the *Wall Street Journal* and *USA Today* to be printed simultaneously in multiple locations with instant delivery of news. Computers also can be used to determine the optimum advertising space for maximizing revenue without reducing reader acceptance. Another application is maintaining a history of classified ads. For example, a subscriber could receive a listing of houses for sale in a particular price range, location, and size.

Applications are what information systems are all about. More and more, IS is providing the data upon which company departments and functional areas depend. This has been stressed throughout the book. This section catalogues applications by industry segment. It is only the tip of the iceberg; experienced practitioners can add to the list, allowing us to see the broad expanse of business processes that can be aided by IS. And yet there will always be an application that the ingenious or imaginative systems/business analyst can uncover that has never been tried before. This is when we begin seeing how IS can provide strategic advantage to an organization.

Index

437